Prof. Werner Breitschwerdt, Chairman, Board of Management, Daimler-Benz AG

THE STAR
AND
THE LAUREL

THE CENTENNIAL HISTORY OF DAIMLER, MERCEDES AND BENZ

1886  1986

BY BEVERLY RAE KIMES

PRODUCED BY HARRIS LEWINE

MERCEDES-BENZ OF NORTH AMERICA
MONTVALE, NEW JERSEY
1986

TO EVERYONE WHO EVER
WISHED UPON A STAR

An original publication of Mercedes-Benz of North America, Inc.
THE STAR AND THE LAUREL

MERCEDES-BENZ OF NORTH AMERICA, INC.
ONE MERCEDES DRIVE
MONTVALE, NEW JERSEY 07645

Library of Congress Cataloging-in-Publication Data
Kimes, Beverly Rae, 1939-
    The Star and the Laurel.
       1. Mercedes-Benz of North America — History.
    2. Automobile industry and trade — North America —
History. I. Mercedes-Benz of North America.
II. Title
HD9710.N57K55   1986   338.7'6292222'097   85-28512

ISBN 0-936573-01-5
Printed and bound in the United States of America

A NOTE ON THE TYPE

The text of this book was set in a digitized version of Cheltenham, designed by the architect Bertram Grosvenor Goodhue in collaboration with Ingalls Kimball of The Cheltenham Press of New York. Cheltenham was introduced in the early twentieth century, a period of remarkable achievement in type design. The idea of creating a "family" of types by making variations on the basic type design was originated by Goodhue and Kimball in the design of the Cheltenham series.

This book was composed by Centre Typographers, Inc., Freeport, New York. It was printed by Halliday Lithograph, West Hanover, Massachusetts. The color separations, color printing, jacket and endpapers were handled by The Chaucer Press, Duryea, Pennsylvania. Binding was by A. Horowitz & Sons, Fairfield, New Jersey. Harris Lewine produced and art directed. Design was by Paul Gamarello/Eyetooth Design, New York. Anne Murphy was the copy editor.

CONTENTS

AUTHOR'S NOTE

This chronicle and celebration of Daimler-Benz's first century has evolved with the contributions of many. Our gratitude is manifold . . .

To Béla Barényi, Eugen Böhringer, Briggs Cunningham, John Fitch, Heinz Hoppe, Karl Kling, Hermann Lang, Günther Molter, Rudolf Uhlenhaut and the late Manfred Lorscheidt, for sharing their personal reminiscences.

To Max von Pein, curator of the Daimler-Benz Museum and Archives, for opening the door to one of the world's finest company historical collections and for offering the assistance of Rainer Karnowski, Michael Rau and Stanislav Peschel of his staff. To Hans-Peter Kassai for supplying answers to numerous questions, and to Gerhard Haerle and Elisabeth Kolb for providing voluminous detail on the company's competition record. To auto motor und sport, for access to the Weitmann Archives, and to Walter Gotschke for courtesies extended in Stuttgart.

In the United States, to Henry Austin Clark, Jr., William L. Bailey and Fred W. Crismon for their generous cooperation throughout the project; to Ron Grantz, Gloria Francis and Margaret Butzu Peters of the Detroit Public Library's National Automotive History Collection, James A. Wren of the Motor Vehicle Manufacturers Association of the United States and the many assisting librarians at the New York Public Library and the New York Society Library for access and guidance in researching those collections; to John Burgess of the Briggs Cunningham Automotive Museum, Jack Martin of the Indianapolis Motor Speedway Museum, and Charles L. Betts, Jr., James H. Cox, Ralph Dunwoodie, David L. Lewis, William J. Lewis, Keith Marvin, John B. Montville and John M. Peckham of the Society of Automotive Historians for counsel in historical research. And to Peter Helck, for many kindnesses.

In England, to Keith Fletcher of H.M. Fletcher Books, London, for allowing photographs to be taken of Roy Nockolds' paintings; to David Moncur of Quadrant Picture Library, Surrey, for permission to reproduce paintings and illustrations by F. Gordon Crosby; to Kathy Agar of Motor Sport and LAT for access to that magazine's photographic archive; and to photographers Geoffrey Goddard, Louis Klemantaski and George Monkhouse.

To Barrett Clark in the United States, Norman Halsey and Mac Hanna in England, and Hervé Poulain and Francis Paudras in Paris for research, advice and counsel about illustrative material.

Memories shared in years of personal friendship with Alice "Baby" Caracciola were continually evoked as this book was being written, and were enriched by the recollections of René Dreyfus, who cheerfully answered queries about the ambiance of motor sport's golden years at any time of day or night. Published reminiscences and private correspondence of those who drove for, or against, the three-pointed star were essential sources, as were the recorded memories of those who were there when Daimler-Benz corporate history was being made, and of those who made it. The Daimler-Benz Archives have carefully preserved all this lore. We gratefully acknowledge the guidelines provided by the works of such scholars of the marque as Karl Ludvigsen, David Scott-Moncrieff, St. John Nixon, Friedrich Schildberger, Paul Siebertz and Alec E. Ulmann.

Finally, to Leo Levine, our mentor throughout, and his staff at Mercedes-Benz of North America, particularly Pat Gunther through whose typewriter all words passed; to Christa Ficken, who translated at least twenty pounds of research and as many hours of tape from German to English; to Jacques Vaucher of L'Art and L'Automobile, whose help extended beyond the call; and to Paul Gamarello of Eyetooth Design, Inc. for his book design — more thanks than words can express.

Beverly Rae Kimes
Harris Lewine

FOREWORD

I am one of those fortunate enough to be employed by Daimler-Benz as the company and the industry it created are about to celebrate their 100th anniversary—on January 29, 1986, just a few months after this is written. Whether you read these words before that date, or on it, or at some time afterward, consider them as written on the birthday itself, as a reflection on being a part of something that is celebrating a century of existence. Reaching a hundred does not bring with it any great degree of exclusivity; people reach that age every day (there is even a community in the Caucasus where one hundred is considered little more than middle age). Any number of public companies have long since gone past the century milestone; countless family-owned proprietorships have been in existence for *several* centuries. But in this case one hundred years are special for several reasons. First, this is not, with all due respect, the centennial of some butcher, baker, or candlestick maker, but of an industry that has changed the way man lives. Further, we can say with pride that Daimler-Benz at the age of one hundred stands at the highest level of the industry we founded, with a reputation for quality unmatched anywhere in the world.

Reaching this point has been an adventure. In the United States alone more than 5,000 different carmakers have existed, in one form or another, for shorter (mostly) or longer periods. The 5,000 have boiled down to four, if we consider only the native-born. The numbers of people and companies who have tried to make cars in other parts of the world, most notably in Europe, can only be guessed at, but they can certainly be counted in the thousands. The fact that the union of Daimler and Benz has survived this almost Darwinian selection process, and also two world wars during which the company was in the defeated country, and dozens of other social and economic upheavals, yet has reached its present status, is indeed noteworthy.

To organize a century of activity into a narrative of reasonable length that would be of general interest— more a popular history than one concerned with the business dealings of the company—is a formidable task. I know this from personal experience, since I wrote a much more limited history some years ago; the main problem was constantly deciding what *not* to include. But when Mercedes-Benz of North America decided to publish a centennial history, the choice of Beverly Kimes, with her considerable reputation as an automotive historian, to write it was an obvious one, and our confidence in her was not misplaced. She has our thanks for a job well done.

Equal thanks go to Harris Lewine, who produced this volume. The title "producer" is usually associated with films or television; in publishing it is comparatively new. What it means in this case is that Lewine, one of the preeminent art directors in contemporary publishing, took our idea and made it tangible. He decided how this volume would look and feel and what the graphic presentation would be, and he also oversaw all the mechanical steps that led to the finished book. The results of his dedication, which included a massive task of graphic and pictorial research, are now in your hands.

Particular thanks should also go to Anne Murphy, one of those increasingly rare people who know how to manage the English language, and who functioned as copy editor for this volume. Beverly Kimes has included the rest of the acknowledgements in her author's note, and to hers I can only add the thanks of Mercedes-Benz of North America to all who have made a contribution in one way or another.

Contribution to what? one may ask. Why is an auto manufacturer, or the North American subsidiary of an auto manufacturer, expending so much effort on publishing a book? The reason is simple. When we began to discuss the centennial celebrations, we made two decisions. The first, obviously, was to celebrate the anniversary at the proper time. The other was to insure that, after the celebrations were over, we would have a permanent record of our first century. This book, along with two films, is the centerpiece of our attempt to present some of our history in accessible, popular form. The first printing has been set at 50,000 copies, which is probably a record for a company-sponsored book. And we intend to make it available to as many of our customers as possible, to libraries, which are receiving a copy as our birthday present, to the nation's press—and to have some copies left for Mercedes fans who are also book collectors.

Some of us in this business still view the automobile as something more than just transportation from A to B. We look upon it as a personal statement, as something that demands creative talent from its designers and builders, a quality above and beyond the utilitarian and mundane. We know the automobile has a multitude of problems, but we also know that the same creativity that produced and developed it in the first place will eventually find solutions, and that this medium of individual transport will serve us and our children in the future. In the meantime, as we reach one hundred, it is our hope that you enjoy the results of Beverly Kimes' and Harris Lewine's labor.

Leo Levine
Montvale, N.J.
November, 1985

INTRODUCTION

Vulcan produced twenty tricycles in a single day, Homer tells us in the *Iliad*. Vulcan had the advantage of divine power; man alone would need centuries to accomplish the same thing. The idea of the automobile is at least as old as recorded time. How to make one was the stumbling block.

Self-propelled vehicles were forecast by Roger Bacon in the thirteenth century, sketched by Leonardo da Vinci in the fifteenth, discussed by Isaac Newton in the seventeenth. Who tried to build the first one will never be known. Two-masted carriages fitted with sails are known to have plied the roads of the Netherlands by 1600, and a clockwork carriage unwound its way through Paris streets around 1750. Neither idea made much headway. Steam seemed more promising.

Since ancient Alexandria, when Heron used its power to open temple doors, harnessing the energy of steam had engaged inventive minds. Again, we do not know who first tried to build a steam vehicle. The earliest inventor known to have succeeded, however fitfully, is Nicolas Joseph Cugnot, the French military officer whose three-wheeled tractor, with a huge pot-shaped black boiler suspended in front, managed approximately three miles an hour during a short trial run in the summer of 1771. Towing artillery was the Cugnot's intended purpose and when it could not effectively manage that, it was abandoned in a corner of the Paris Arsenal.

Steam was not enough to make the Cugnot work, but it was the source that provided the power for the Industrial Revolution, the single greatest agent for material change that the world has ever known. It is impossible to say just when the Industrial Revolution started, but it could have been the day in 1775 when, after improving the Newcomen steam concept and patenting the result, the Scottish instrument maker James Watt allied himself with the English engineer Matthew Boulton and began making steam engines at Soho, near Birmingham. They were visited shortly afterwards by George III, who was curious to know what was going on. "Power, Your Majesty," Boulton answered, "I possess what all the world desires." The King's reply is not recorded. Presumably he had other things on his mind, not least the treason being perpetrated in his colonies across the Atlantic.

But Boulton was right. Steam, previously used only to pump water from mines, now replaced workers or water wheels to power machines; machines replaced handwork; manufacturing moved out of piecework shops and into great factories. By the early nineteenth century, steam had taken to the water, augmenting sail for the first time in a transatlantic crossing in 1819. George Stephenson built his first steam locomotive in England in 1814. In 1830 Peter Cooper's *Tom Thumb* replaced the horses that had previously pulled the cars of the Baltimore and Ohio Railroad in America.

What of a vehicle for the road? The idea had not been forgotten. Soon after patenting his steam engine, Watt declared his resolve "to try if God will work a miracle with these carriages . . . but I have small hopes of their ever becoming useful." He gave up quickly; his low-pressure steam engine was unsuitable for vehicular use. A steam carriage was included in his 1784 patent not because he intended to build one but to dissuade others from doing so, a strategy that worked in at least one case. Watt's foreman, William Murdock, built a single steam carriage model and then went on to invent coal-gas lighting.

Experimentation in high-pressure steam engines for vehicular use followed both on the Continent and in America. In England, beginning about 1830, a coterie of inventors and entrepreneurs built elaborate steam coaches to carry passengers through the countryside. Gloucester to Cheltenham was Sir Goldsworthy Gurney's route, nine miles in 45 minutes, four scheduled round trips a day. With a driver up front, an engineer in the engine room, and a boy at the rear to feed the fire with coal, these steamers were a colorful sight, and not a welcome one. The public was not enthralled, nor was Parliament. Stones and trees were often laid in the steamers' path. The tolls charged them were exorbitant: 5 pounds for passing the same tollgate at which a coach and horses was charged just threepence. But still the inventors struggled for success and acceptance, arguing before the House of Commons that hooves wore down British roads three times faster than wheels, and enjoying some support from the Scottish roadbuilder John Loudon McAdam. To no avail. The horsemen were joined in their anti-steamer cause by the railroad interests, the carriage owners, who objected to having their horses terrified, and the thoroughly frightened pedestrian populace.

Meanwhile, the Industrial Revolution was stimulating progress in other fields. The printed word was spread faster after Friedrich Koenig's development of the power-driven flatbed press in 1811, and faster still with Robert Hoe's rotary press of 1846. The Italian Alessandro Volta, the Frenchman André Ampère, the German Georg Simon Ohm, the Englishman Michael Faraday, and the American Samuel F. B. Morse made enormous strides in the science of electricity. By 1862, 150,000 miles of telegraph wires stretched all over the world. The transatlantic cable was laid in 1866.

Cheaper and better steel was revolutionizing bridge building. Sophisticated machinery was advancing road and tunnel construction. Refrigeration and pasteurization were realities, and so were packages for foodstuffs and the soon-to-be-ubiquitous tin can. Clothing could be bought ready made. There were machines for sewing and washing and mowing the lawn. Elisha Otis invented his elevator in 1852. Alexander Graham Bell talked on a telephone in 1876.

But the ultimate machine of the machine age had not yet arrived. At this point the story of the automobile remained one of abandoned dreams and unfulfilled hopes, with as many forces impeding its progress as were propelling it into being. But the spread of industrialization made the automobile inevitable. As the nineteenth century wore on, the technology needed to create it was rapidly being developed.

Now the concept needed someone to make it work.

CHAPTER ONE

THE DREAMERS
ARE DOERS

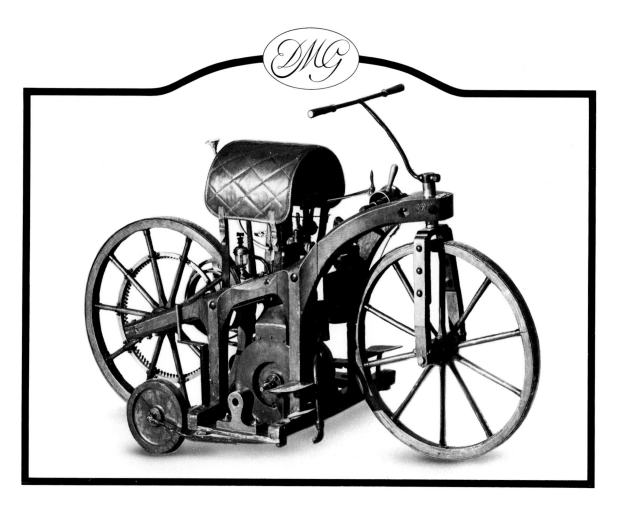

1 8 5 1 — 1 8 8 6

A journey of a thousand miles
must begin with a single step.
—LÂO TZU,
TÂO TEH CHING

I came back quite dead beat," the Queen wrote in her journal, "my head really bewildered by the myriads . . . of wonderful things." Among them were machines . . . more of them than had ever before been gathered in one place. It was the summer of 1851, and Victoria had just returned from a visit to the Crystal Palace, site of the Great Exhibition—the first world's fair.

There were foreign inventions at the Crystal Palace, of course: from Germany, Alfried Krupp's cast steel field gun and Siemens and Halske's electric telegraph; from America, Cyrus McCormick's reaper, Elias Howe's sewing machine and a pair of Robbins and Lawrence rifles built with interchangeable parts. But Britain was the home of the Industrial Revolution and the Great Exhibition was Britain's show. The Crystal Palace itself boasted of British progress, its skeletal cage of 5,000 slender iron beams supporting 300,000 panes of glass, an architectural display that would be imitated in America and on the Continent. If any single year marked Britain's peak as an industrial and technological power, it was 1851. Within a few decades, Germany would be the leading industrial nation in Europe; after a few more, America would be the foremost in the world.

But at mid-century much of the United States was a vast landmass waiting to be conquered. The railroad extended west only to Chicago, and travel be-

Leonardo da Vinci (1452-1519), Italian painter, sculptor, musician, architect, engineer and scientist.

yond by wagon train was made difficult by mountains, deserts and the danger of Indian attack. Indeed, interchangeable parts had been developed early in America simply because they had to be, making a land that was essentially a frontier society the country that developed the basic principle of mass production. Whether scout or soldier or settler, any American venturing to the frontier was dependent upon his firearm; without recourse to a gunsmith, repairs with spare parts or by cannibalizing another

Workable principles of transmission and gearing were first propounded by Leonardo, as this model of a spring-driven car constructed from his sketches indicates.

German intellectual leaders of the early 19th century. From the left: Johann Wolfgang von Goethe (1749-1832), novelist, dramatist, poet and scientist; Heinrich Heine (1797-1856), revolutionary and lyric poet; Johann Christoph Friedrich von Schiller (1759-1805), dramatist, poet and historian.

weapon were a necessity for survival. Following his invention of the cotton gin, Eli Whitney was the first to standardize gun parts when he began to manufacture muskets for the government in 1798. By 1815 interchangeability was a prerequisite for commercial success: the government would accept nothing else.

As for Germany, in the early nineteenth century it was essentially geography, a patchwork of sovereign principalities, each with its own system of laws, currencies, weights and measures, each levying its own tariffs and tolls, the whole conglomeration linked only by cultural tradition. Medieval walls circled many small towns, artisan industry remained dominated by guilds, the marketing of goods was largely confined to the neighboring countryside. But change was at hand. In 1828 Goethe had recognized that "good roads and future railways" would one day break down feudalism and promote national unity. And in 1832 the Swabian engineer and economist Friedrich List, who had directed the building of a railroad line in the Pacific Northwest, returned from America to champion the railroad and the *Zollverein*, a reciprocal tariff agreement which would allow the free flow of goods among the various German principalities. On January 1, 1834, a parade of carts and barges began ceremonially to travel roads throughout Germany, grandly sweeping by the old customs and toll barriers. In December 1835, in Bavaria, the first railway opened from Nürnberg to Fürth. By 1845, no fewer than 240 locomotives were operating in Germany.

In 1848 the end of the Mexican War, when Mexico

Model of the steam tractor invented by Nicolas Joseph Cugnot (1725-1804). Its design was inspired by Cugnot's reading of *Theatrum machinarum,* a technical science handbook published by Jacob Leupold of Leipzig in 1723. The Cugnot was tested in 1770-1771 and ran, but neither far nor fast.

After winning a British trial in 1829, the "Rocket" of George Stephenson (1781-1848) was put into service between Liverpool and Manchester, and influenced future locomotive development.

gave up its claim to Texas and all lands north of the Rio Grande, and the discovery of gold at Sutter's Mill in California were the great attractions that moved the American nation westward. In Germany, the revolutionary disturbances of that same year would bring the first concerted attempts toward unification. In both nations, the force of industrialization was about to change the way people lived.

Gottlieb Daimler and Carl Benz were born 60 miles apart in southern Germany, Daimler in the Kingdom of Württemberg, Benz in the Grand Duchy of Baden. These two adjoining states were bounded on the west by the Rhine and France, on the east by Bavaria, on the north by the Kingdom of Hesse, on the south by Lake Constance and Switzerland. In their midst stretched the dark pines of the Black Forest. In the mountains rising out of the Neckar Valley the Hohenstaufens and the Catholic arm of the Hohenzollerns had built their splendid castles. It was a gentle landscape of vineyards, orchards and wooded hills, a region of unspoiled love-

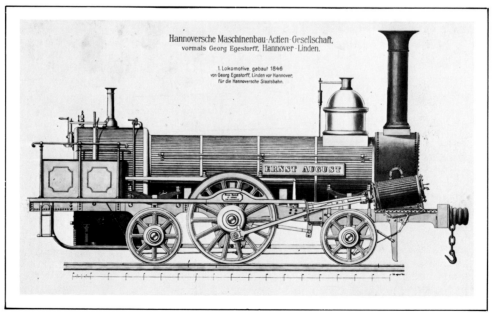

Locomotive designed by Georg Egestorff of Hanover, 1846. Railway building in the 1840's, wrote German historian Heinrich von Treitschke (1834-1896), "affected all walks and habits of life so deeply that Germany presented a completely new face."

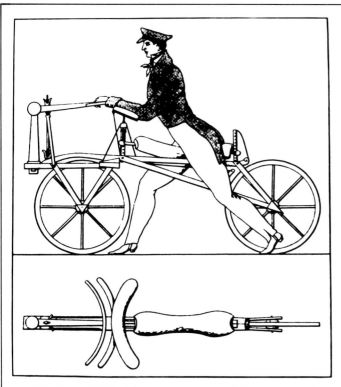

Origins of the bicycle. The first practical dandy horse (top, right) was developed by Baron Karl Drais von Sauerbronn in 1816 for his inspection tours as chief forester of the Kingdom of Baden. His concept was improved upon by French photography pioneer Nicéphore Niepce in 1818 (center, right) and English coachbuilder Dennis Johnson in 1819 (top, left). By the mid-1860's the "swift walker" had developed into the pedal-driven velocipede, perfected by Pierre Lallement. To increase speed, a velocipede's front wheel reached a diameter of up to 64 inches (above, left) by the 1880's. In America, Colonel Albert Pope (above, right) was the biggest bicycle builder.

liness and an unlikely setting for revolutionary inventions by two native sons with the same idea.

Other than a fascination with machines, the native sons had little in common. All his life Carl Benz remained a provincial, figuratively bound by the borders of his principality. Gottlieb Daimler was a man of the frontier, stretching in every sense beyond boundaries. This difference between them was partly the result of circumstance, partly of temperament.

The village of Schorndorf, nestled in the Rems Valley just east of Stuttgart, had been home to the Daimlers for nearly two centuries before Gottlieb Daimler's birth on March 17, 1834. For four generations the family had been prosperous bakers. Gottlieb's father, Johannes, owned a bakery and wine shop, a traditional business combination in Württemberg; his uncle Heinrich was Schorndorf's chief builder, and subsequently chief architect. The boy's childhood was pleasant and uneventful. In school he showed an aptitude for mathematics, and a civil service career was planned for him until the Revolutions of 1848, when Johannes decided apprenticeship to a local carbine manufacturer might pave the way to a more profitable career. Gottlieb completed the apprenticeship, but making guns did not interest him.

At 18 Daimler moved to Stuttgart and met Ferdinand Steinbeis, a Württemberg civil official who provided a grant-in-aid which sent Daimler to Grafenstaden near Strasbourg in French Alsace. There, at a firm managed by Friedrich Messmer, a former teacher at the Karlsruhe Polytechnikum, Daimler worked at building railway cars, bridge components and machinery. Evenings he studied mechanics and began learning French, which Steinbeis had suggested might be useful later.

In 1856, with locomotive building next on the factory's agenda, Daimler was offered the position of foreman, a flattering invitation for one just turned 22. But Daimler believed he lacked the necessary theoretical training. Messmer finally agreed to grant him a leave of absence to study at the Stuttgart Polytechnikum, with the promise that upon completing his studies he would return to Grafenstaden and get on with the job of building locomotives. Daimler agreed.

Gottlieb Daimler was lucky. He was acquiring a solid engineering background—unusual during this period, and most unusual for a German from a family that today would be termed middle class. Without Steinbeis and the government-sponsored programs he arranged for his protégé, Daimler would never have

The Crystal Palace, home of the Great Exhibition in Hyde Park in 1851, rebuilt in Sydenham in 1852, destroyed by fire in 1936. Celebrated internationally for his pioneering in iron and glass buildings, English architect Joseph Paxton was honored with knighthood for this design.

On a run from London to Bath in 1829, Goldsworthy Gurney's steam carriage (center, left) was attacked by a mob and Gurney was forced to add horses. Although their steamer was exhibited at London's International Exhibition in 1862, Alfred Yarrow and James Hilditch (above) had nowhere to go. (Top) Dudgeon steam wagon, 1866. New York City machinist Richard Dudgeon had been persuaded to build his first steam car in 1857 (it was destroyed by fire) "to end the fearful horse murder and numerous other ills inseparable from their use." (Center, right) English steam traction engine built by the Boydell Endless Railway Company in 1857. James Boydell's concept ultimately developed into the crawler or caterpillar tractor.

received the education he very much desired. And although Daimler did not yet know precisely what brand of engineering he wanted to specialize in, he was preparing for the future with every step he took.

Meanwhile, Carl Benz was growing up.* His childhood had been neither pleasant nor uneventful. He was born a decade after Daimler on November 25, 1844, in the village of Pfaffenrot in the Black Forest. His father, a blacksmith as the Pfaffenrot Benzes had been for generations, went to work for the railroad first as a stoker, then as an engineer, as soon as the line between Karlsruhe and Heidelberg opened in 1842. One day in the summer of 1846 a switchman's mistake resulted in a locomotive being derailed. Johann-Georg Benz and a handful of others saw to the herculean task of getting it back on the rails. Benz then climbed back into his own locomotive and proceeded on his way, dripping with sweat and shivering in the rush of air that enveloped his open cab. A few days later he died of pneumonia.

Josephine Benz's world was shattered. Her son was not quite two years old. Her widow's pension was meager but her determination was great, and young Carl's schooling became her first priority. Since Pfaffenrot offered no opportunity to supplement her income, Frau Benz moved to Karlsruhe where her cooking skills found ready customers and her son

*His birth certificate spelled his name Karl, but he preferred the spelling Carl.

could study at the Karlsruhe Lyzeum. At school he excelled in physics and chemistry. He was also fascinated by the invention of Louis Daguerre and displayed a lively interest in timepieces, avocations which helped financially as he tramped the Black Forest taking pictures of any peasant who was willing to pay for the result and offering to fix any Black Forest clocks in need of repair. Because of the tragedy that had befallen her husband, the last thing Frau Benz wanted for her son was a career with locomotives, but he was continually sketching them. When he graduated from the Lyzeum in 1860, he told his mother he wanted to continue his studies at the Karlsruhe Polytechnikum. To help with his tuition, Frau Benz began taking in boarders and spending more time at the stove.

By 1860 Gottlieb Daimler had completed his courses in Stuttgart and had returned, unenthusiastically, to his job in Grafenstaden. His studies had convinced him of the basic weakness of steam. For any given power output a small steam engine consumed up to six times as much coal as a large one, any steam engine required a long time to generate any power at all, and no steam engine was complete without a boiler and chimney. Steam power was too limiting, Daimler concluded. Having read of experimentation in alternative engines, he wanted to build one and asked Messmer to change his job from steam locomotive foreman to experimental engineer. Mess-

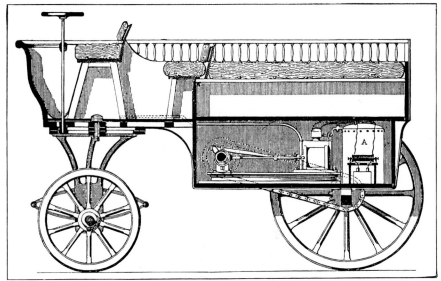

Artist's sketch from 1860 of the car of Jean-Joseph Etienne Lenoir (1822-1900), which could not have operated as drawn. Lenoir later said he built his car in 1863, and he admitted it was not successful. The engine developed 1½ hp at 100 rpm.

Gottlieb Daimler (1834-1900). The family name evolved from Teimbler or Teumler to Däumler and finally Daimler. Daimler was about 30, a bachelor and the new manager of the engineering works of the Bruderhaus Reutlingen when this portrait was taken.

mer refused. Although his relationship with management remained cordial, by the summer of 1861 Daimler had decided to leave. He was unsure where to head next until his former mentor Steinbeis suggested Paris and provided him with enough money to get there and to stay long enough to investigate an internal combustion engine that was creating a sensation.

The concept of internal combustion was not new. It could be traced back at least as far as the late seventeenth century, when the Dutch mathematician Christian Huygens experimented with an engine that burned gunpowder, a rather risky proposition. Subsequently, in Paris, Isaac de Rivaz patented a gas engine with electric ignition. By the early 1800s he had mounted his creation in a wagon bed for test purposes, but he soon gave it up to devote himself to a political career in his native Switzerland.

But of all the many early inventors of internal combustion engines, the most successful was a Belgian who had moved to France in 1838 and initially earned his living in Paris by waiting on tables: Jean-Joseph Etienne Lenoir. Earlier efforts at internal combustion had been designed to use turpentine or alcohol, fuels so expensive as to render them less attractive than even the clumsiest steam engine. Lenoir's unit, patented in January 1860, was differ-

ent. It used the illuminating coal gas which William Murdock had invented for James Watt after being

Carl Benz (1844-1929). Ten years Daimler's junior, Benz was a student at Karlsruhe Polytechnikum at the time of this portrait. He completed his four-year course in 1864.

19

discouraged from his attempts to invent a steam carriage, and which now coursed through underground pipes to light most of the major cities on the Continent. It was a good idea, as the gas was readily available, and it was cheap.

"The age of steam is ended," pronounced *Scientific American* when the Lenoir engine was introduced. "Watt and Fulton will soon be forgotten." Within a few years over 130 Lenoir engines had been sold in Paris alone, and several hundred more were powering factories elsewhere in Europe, among them a machine tool works in Stuttgart. When that Lenoir engine arrived, Carl Benz was given leave from his studies to assist in its installation. In less than a year at the Karlsruhe Polytechnikum, young Benz had become the star pupil of Ferdinand Redtenbacher, a teacher well known for his theoretical and practical exploration into internal combustion principles. In 1863, when Professor Redtenbacher died, Carl Benz was among the student pallbearers.

By then the Lenoir engine had lost some of its appeal, its purchasers having discovered that economy was not well served by the prodigious quantities of gas (80 cubic feet per horsepower/hour) it devoured, in addition to copious amounts of grease and oil and four times more water than a steam engine. Though his work would point the way for others, Lenoir did not succeed in making the world forget Watt and Fulton.

While in Paris, Gottlieb Daimler had come to two conclusions about the Lenoir engine. First, it was so protected by patents that any further development could be done only within the Lenoir organization. Second, he wasn't very impressed with it anyway. He is supposed to have told Lenoir just that. Tact was never one of Daimler's long suits.

With his investigation of the Lenoir engine, Daimler's Paris sojourn was over. He was offered a job in a small saw-making factory but turned it down. England, the heart of the Industrial Revolution, was where he wanted to travel next, and with another grant-in-aid from his friend Steinbeis he went there. England made a formidable impression.

In his foundry in Manchester James Nasmyth, who

had invented the steam hammer in 1839, was breaking new ground in drop forging and die sampling. In Coventry Joseph Whitworth, who had developed the standard screw gauge in 1830, was operating machines capable of measuring one-millionth of an inch. At Enfield, near London, rifles were being made with interchangeable parts at the Royal Small Arms Works, which had been established by the government following a visit to American gun makers after the Great Exhibition of 1851. In Sheffield the Bessemer Steel Works was in full cry. Henry Bessemer's process for making steel from pig iron, patented in 1856, was one of the keystones of industrialization, as it made cheap steel possible and paved the way for, among other things, mass-produced automobiles at reasonable prices. But that was still a long way off.

The only thing Daimler didn't see in England were engines other than steam, nor any steam coaches chuffing along country roads. His arrival during the summer of 1861 coincided with the passage of legislation inhibiting their use, to be further restricted in 1865 by what became known colloquially as the Red Flag Act, which limited road vehicle speeds to four miles an hour in the country and two miles an hour in cities and required a man carrying a red flag (a red lantern at night) to walk in front. The horse-coach interests and the railroads had won the first round in their war against the automobile.*

But what Daimler did see in England was progress, and he was mesmerized. He traveled everywhere, picking up the language and a knowledge of English patent law. Whenever his money ran low, he took on a factory job, most notably with Whitworth in Coventry. And in August 1862 he visited the International Exhibition in London.

---

*This is not to suggest that steam vehicle development ended. English inventors continued to build carriages for their own personal use, though they could not take them very far or very fast without incurring the wrath of the constabulary. Steam vehicles continued to be built in America and on the Continent as well, though most inventors were quickly discouraged, went broke trying or went on to something else. In New York City, for example, Richard Dudgeon built two steam wagons at mid-century and then chose to devote his time to another invention, the hydraulic jack, which he supplied in vast numbers to the builders of the Brooklyn Bridge.

Because Queen Victoria was in mourning for Prince Albert, this world's fair was considerably subdued from the extravaganza of the decade before; there was a complete "absence of court ceremonials." But the International Exhibition was grand nonetheless, with more than 28,000 exhibitors clustered in one gargantuan building. Hogarths, Gainsboroughs and Reynolds were hung in the Fine Arts section; the industrial sections roared with machinery. All the major nations of the world were represented except America, which was embroiled in its Civil War. Walking among the displays of German manufacturers and craftsmen, Gottlieb Daimler realized he was homesick.

Returning to Württemberg in the spring of 1863, he went to work as a hardware designer for the father of a school friend. The job quickly bored him. By late summer, his letters reveal, he was thinking of setting up a factory of his own "to build machine tools and small woodworking machines such as I saw in England." His parents were not inclined to finance him, however, and negotiations with a friend from his Grafenstaden days fell through. So, not surprisingly, Daimler turned to Ferdinand Steinbeis for advice. Steinbeis provided it, and in December 1863 Daimler took over the management of Bruderhaus Reutlingen, near Stuttgart.

Part orphanage, part vocational school, part engineering complex, the Bruderhaus was the idea of the Lutheran theologian Gustav Werner and an ingenuous religious answer to Marxism. It was Daimler's job to reorganize the machine works, which included a paper mill, a saw mill and a lumber yard. The gentle and generous principles on which the Bruderhaus was founded could not be faulted, but it was questionable whether a work force composed of abandoned youngsters and unskilled laborers could ever be commercially viable. Yet Daimler proved an able administrator and by 1867 had managed to turn a profit. Profit-making not being high among Bruderhaus priorities, however, his achievement was not applauded.

But 1867 was also the year of the Paris Exhibition, which gave Daimler a good excuse to get away from his frustrations in Reutlingen. Inside the eleven-acre oval building in the Champ de Mars was a large-scale model, complete with ships passing through, of the engineering triumph of the age, Ferdinand de Lesseps' Suez Canal. The great hall was alive with inventions. Emperor Napoleon III had added something new to this world's fair—a sequential clustering of exhibits which allowed a visitor interested in a single product to follow it through all the nations that produced it. The peripheral ring of the building was devoted to machinery, and there, next to the Lenoir exhibit, under a sign reading "Otto und Langen," was a newly patented internal combustion engine. Undeniably awkward and incredibly noisy, the engine consumed only a third as much gas as the thirsty Lenoir. Initially, the Lenoir people suspected subterfuge and searched the new engine for a hidden conduit they were convinced was there somewhere supplying the machine with additional fuel. Unable to find one, they watched as Emperor Napoleon awarded the gold medal to their competitor. Daimler was impressed with the engine, but had time to examine it only briefly before returning to Reutlingen. He had already decided to remain with the Bruderhaus only until something better came along. In 1870 something did.

The 1860s were not rewarding years for Carl Benz, either. During the summer of 1864, having completed his studies at the Karlsruhe Polytechnikum, he began his career at the town locomotive works. He was working with engines, but his 12-hour days were spent boring and filing in the semi-darkness of the damp workshops, and though he was subsequently promoted to draftsman and a more congenial environment, he decided the job was a dead end. By the spring of 1867 Benz was in Mannheim designing scales for Karl Schenck, work that was neither emotionally fulfilling nor financially remunerative—but he was out of work within months in any case when a new partner bought into the company on condition that he get Benz's job. In December 1869 Benz moved on to Pforzheim, to build bridges for Benckiser Brothers.

Six months later, in June 1870, Gottlieb Daimler left Reutlingen. His destination was Maschinenbau

In November 1867, Gottlieb Daimler married
Emma Kurz of Maulbronn. He was 33, she 24.

Gesellschaft Karlsruhe, the company that Carl Benz had quit three years earlier. But Benz had been in the drafting office, and Daimler would be in the executive suite. He had been hired as managing director of all the factories: the locomotive works, the engine works, the bridge works . . . the whole works. Joining him was an orphan he had met at the Bruderhaus.

In later years Gottlieb Daimler would reflect upon his Reutlingen period as a disappointment in all ways but two. One was meeting, and marrying, Emma Pauline Kurz, the comely daughter of a Maulbronn druggist. The other was meeting Wilhelm Maybach. Orphaned at 10, Maybach had been taken in by the Bruderhaus and entered apprenticeship in the drafting room of the engineering works. "I began inventing things during my last year of study," he wrote in his memoirs. "Among other things I fitted the gold leaf stamping press book-bindery with oil heat." Gottlieb Daimler recognized Maybach's talent immediately, and found a job for him at Karlsruhe soon after he himself arrived there.

Life became markedly more satisfactory for Daimler now. Emma presented him with their first child, Paul, in 1869; a second son, Adolf, followed two years later. And managing the Karlsruhe factories was a challenge.

Carl Benz was still building bridges in Pforzheim.

In addition to professional frustrations, he had been devastated by the death of his mother in March 1870. But some months later he met Bertha Ringer, the spunky 20-year-old daughter of a Pforzheim building contractor. Carl Benz was smitten. With marriage on his mind, little money in the bank and no professional future in Pforzheim, he went to Vienna to look into bridge-building there, believing that the prospect of life in the glamorous Austrian capital might convince Bertha to say yes. But employment opportunities in Vienna were even less inviting than in Germany, so Benz returned home and asked Bertha if Mannheim would do; a local mechanic named August Ritter had, after all, suggested that he and Benz go into partnership. Bertha was amenable.

So in August 1871 Benz and Ritter purchased a bit of land with a small wooden shed in the middle of town, and set themselves up in business as machinists. Within months there were problems, most of them having to do with Ritter's cold feet. His enthusiasm had not extended much beyond the initial purchase of the lot, and when Benz pointed out that more money was needed for tools, Ritter balked. Bertha came to the rescue, arranging with her father for an early transfer of her dowry so that her fiancé could buy out Ritter's interest. And then on July 20, 1872, Carl Benz and Bertha Ringer were married.

By this time Gottlieb Daimler had also negotiated

a new alliance. He was on his way to Deutz, near Cologne, to take over as technical director of the company that manufactured the Otto und Langen atmospheric gas engine.

In the year following the debut of their machine at the Paris Exhibition, Nicholas Otto and Eugen Langen had sold a grand total of 46 engines. The engine itself was Otto's doing, but Langen's money had put it into production. There were teething problems, with complaints about reliability from early users who were almost as noisy as the engines themselves, but the partners seemed to be on to a good thing. The Paris gold medal had given them enormous publicity. As soon as purchasers could be schooled in the proper use of the engines and a proper factory set up to build them, the future would be assured. But in the wake of the Franco-Prussian War money flowed freely in victorious Germany, now a unified country at last, and the death of Langen's father had brought him a tidy inheritance. So the hurdle of financing a new factory was quickly surmounted.

But by January 1872 the newly designated Gas-motoren-Fabrik Deutz was still struggling, with more than 500 orders on the books, inquiries from more than 2,000 prospective purchasers, and no real idea of how to cope with all this potential. Obviously Deutz needed a technical director experienced in factory management. A friend of Langen said he knew the right man.

When Eugen Langen interviewed Gottlieb Daimler in Karlsruhe and saw his operation there, he was so impressed he offered Daimler the position on the spot. Daimler demurred, agreeing only to visit the Deutz factory, which he did in early March, meeting Otto, talking terms, but signing nothing. "You can readily realize with what impatience I am looking forward to your next letter," Langen wrote Daimler on March 11, mentioning that he would begin looking for suitable accommodations in town just as soon "as I have news from you." Daimler waited a week before replying.

The agreement he eventually signed gave him complete managerial authority over workshops, drawing offices, plants, personnel and materials. In addition to a handsome salary, Langen had offered a bonus of three percent of the net profit; Daimler said he would take five. As for suitable accommodations, Langen initially would move the Daimler family into an apartment in the building he lived in, awaiting completion of a fine double house in the Mülheimerstrasse for both families. Gottlieb Daimler had pulled off quite a coup. At last he would be working with the type of power plant which had fascinated him since his Grafenstaden days. Here was a job he wanted more

Carl Benz in 1870, shortly after his mother's death. In Pforzheim, Benz joined the fraternal organization *Eintracht*, where he met Bertha Ringer, the daughter of a prominent local builder. They were married in 1872.

than any other, a fact he undoubtedly did not mention during the negotiations which preceded his accepting it.

Left out of all this, and upset by his exclusion, was Nicholas Otto. That he had neither the expertise nor the temperament for factory management was evident perhaps even to himself, but Daimler's negotiations, which had been calculated to guarantee that his position in the organization would not be secondary to Otto's, meant friction between the two was inevitable. And it was not long in coming. Though Daimler's contract in Karlsruhe had stipulated his giving six months' notice, his superiors agreed to his departure at the end of July. Even before that, however, he began exerting his authority. "The plans submitted are entirely unsuitable," he wrote after receiving drawings of a new foundry. He would draw up new plans and procedures himself, he announced, and would see to personnel matters as well. Machinery and workshop equipment were dispatched from Karlsruhe, with Wilhelm Maybach sent along to help set things up at Deutz; Daimler had already decided to make Maybach the company's chief designer. When Daimler himself arrived, he brought with him a contingent of skilled workers.

Transforming Deutz from a pell-mell operation into an orderly one was Daimler's first task. Incessantly he stressed that for the engines to enjoy commercial success they must be manufactured by the precision methods he had learned in England and with the most painstaking care, since their abuse by purchasers who had never before encountered such machines had to be taken into account and compensated for. Daimler made this point in no uncertain terms. Tact remained his short suit. And Nicholas Otto was not the phlegmatic sort.

Still, Daimler's results spoke for themselves. Within months he had increased production to 25 engines a month. By the beginning of 1874 he had doubled that, and complaints about unreliability virtually ceased. The work force of 20 which had greeted him upon his arrival was expanded to 240, there were branch factories in Paris and Milan, and in England Crossley Brothers of Manchester began building the engine under license. Though there was a temporary threat from a hot-air engine, and smaller steam engines came on the market, none could approach the popularity of the Cologne product. To factory owners all over the Continent, having an engine from Deutz was the mark of a progressive entrepreneur.

As the 634 Deutz-built engines sold in 1875 were generating their total of 735 horsepower (they were sold in half- and two-horsepower models), back in Cologne an exciting new engine was in the wings.

The Deutz two-stroke worked just fine, if cacophonously, so long as minimal power was required and the workshop ceiling was high enough—10 to 13 feet—to allow for the vertical free piston. But if the gas charge could be squeezed beforehand, the result would be more muscle in less space, and considerably greater sales appeal to owners of small workshops or factories needing additional power. The four-stroke cycle—induction, compression, ignition, exhaust—had been described and patented by the French engineer Alphonse Beau de Rochas during the 1860s, and Nicholas Otto had begun wrestling with the idea and how to make it workable about the same time. By now he was positively obsessed with the project—which had the side benefit of isolating him from Daimler.

When in the spring of 1876 Otto finally emerged from his laboratory with a four-stroke engine that worked, Langen described it as a "joy for the angels." Daimler set his people to adapting the engine for production. Always at his best when the pace was feverish and the schedule herculean, Daimler became a demon. Wilhelm Maybach was in the thick of things. An intellectual bond existed between Maybach and Daimler that needed few words. No one else ever would be able to translate Daimler's ideas into reality as Maybach could, and adapting the four-stroke engine for production was their first important collaboration. By late summer prototypes were completed and tested in horsepower increments from one-half to eight, and Daimler began to set priorities for vastly increased production to meet the anticipated demand. Maybach was exhausted, and even his hard-driving mentor recognized a reward was due.

On September 9, Wilhelm Maybach set sail for America, arriving in New York on the twenty-second.

There was a reason other than reward for Daimler allowing Maybach an extended leave. He was convinced that America would be a lucrative market for gas engines, so Maybach's sabbatical was, in part, a reconnaissance mission. For four long years American industrial growth had been subordinated to the waging of the Civil War, but after 1865 the country had leaped forward, with new factories sprouting throughout the East and across the Appalachians as far west as Michigan and Illinois. On May 10, 1869, at Promontory Point, Utah, the Union Pacific met the Central Pacific, a golden spike was driven, and the transcontinental railway was a reality. In

1876 the nation was 100 years old, an event that cried out for celebration, and what better way to celebrate than a world's fair? Thirty-eight nations agreed to exhibit; the individual exhibitors numbered more than 30,000. Deutz was among them.

On May 10, President Ulysses S. Grant opened the Centennial Exposition at Philadelphia to the strains of a march that Richard Wagner had written for the occasion. The march was not very well received and even Wagner didn't like it, commenting later that "the best thing about the composition was the money I got for it" ($5,000). But the great exhibition was the talk of the nation; and even the news in late June of Sitting Bull's victory over George Armstrong Custer and the Seventh Cavalry at Little Bighorn in Montana did not take the headlines away

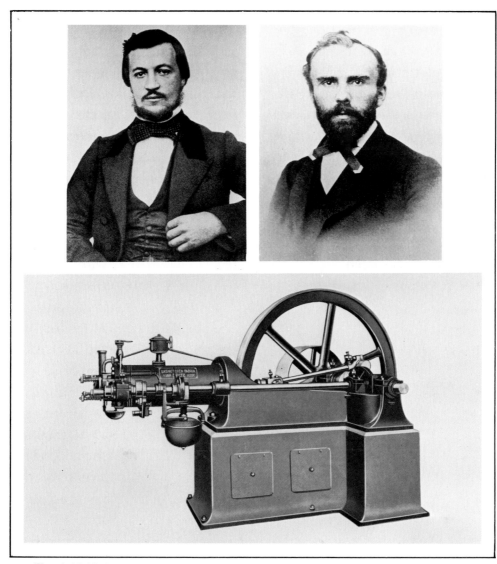

(Top, left) Nicholas August Otto (1832-1891). (Top, right) Eugen Langen (1833-1895). (Above) The 1876 four-stroke Otto gas engine. In 10 years more than 30,000 were built worldwide. Licensed manufacture in the United States was begun in 1882 by Schlier, Schumm & Company of Philadelphia.

from the centennial celebrations for long.

Wilhelm Maybach arrived in late September and spent most of his time in Machinery Hall, where a mammoth Corliss steam engine rose 40 feet and supplied power for all the exhibits that required it. Britain had a steam-operated road roller on display. Of internal combustion engines, there were two types: a two-stroke developed by George B. Brayton, an Englishman living in Boston, which was used to pump air for the aquarium, and six two-stroke Deutz engines, five on exhibit in Machinery Hall and one operating a printing press for the London *Graphic* in the main building.

After making careful notes and concluding that America was indeed an excellent prospect for a branch factory, Maybach returned to New York, where he visited his brother and met his brother's employer, one William Steinway, who manufactured pianos on Long Island. In the two decades since the Steinways had arrived in America (the name had been Steinweg in Germany), the family had prospered in a variety of other businesses, among them a gasworks, an ink company and a horse-drawn street railway in Manhattan. Maybach told Steinway of the new engine that had been developed at Deutz, and Steinway was fascinated. Before leaving New York on November 11, Maybach promised to keep him informed of developments.

In early December Maybach arrived back at Deutz. Now that the wheels had been set in motion for the manufacture of the new engine, the problem was what to call it. Otto insisted on his own name. Daimler said it should be called the Deutz because its refinement had been, and its exploitation would be, a company effort. Langen was in the middle. "Are you two still leading a cat-and-dog life?" he wearily asked Otto. "And can you never work together in peace, although you both have the same objects in view?" Apparently not. Otto and Daimler remained adamant. To Langen's entreaties that "your name will be famous enough . . . depend upon me for that," Otto turned a deaf ear. On August 4, 1877, the four-stroke engine was patented . . . in Otto's name. To this day, even though Otto's contribution to the automobile was a fleeting one, his name remains alive in engineering circles: in many countries, "Otto-cycle" is the name by which the four-stroke engine is known.

America's first world's fair was opened in Philadelphia's Fairmount Park in May 1876 with a lavish program of events, including a concert series conducted by French composer Jacques Offenbach. (John Philip Sousa was a member of the orchestra.) Less melodious was the noise made in Machinery Hall by the Corliss bevel-gear-cutting machine.

(Top, right) France's only condition for giving *Liberty Enlightening the World* to America was that Americans pay for building the base. The torch of Frédéric Auguste Barthold's colossal statue was exhibited at the Philadelphia Centennial Exhibition to encourage contributions. (Above) The steam engine designed by George W. Corliss of Providence, Rhode Island powered all the machines in Machinery Hall. Its cylinders measured 44 inches in bore, 8 feet in stroke; the 56-ton flywheel had a diameter of 30 feet. The engine was completed on April 10, 1876 — the day promised by its inventor — and the $200,000 spent in its construction was borne entirely by Corliss.

At the same time, in Mannheim, Carl Benz was about to be taken to court. Thus far his machine shop had produced bending and metal-forming devices, and other products not requiring a heavy capital outlay. "Unless otherwise expressly specified," his invoices read, "all deliveries are C.O.D." Most likely "otherwise" was never "expressly specified." Benz was going nowhere. And after the Vienna financial panic of 1872, his circumstances became precarious. A colleague from his Benckiser bridge-building days lent him enough money to develop a hydraulic press for baling tobacco, but when this proved not to be a best-seller the friend had to resort to a court order to compel Benz to repay the loan. Now the precarious threatened to become even worse. Even in her nineties, Bertha Benz remembered those awful days. Only its real estate value prevented the machine shop from going on the auction block; by pledging the inventory to the bank holding the mortgage, Benz was able to repay the loan.

But the one thing his business needed was business—a product that would sell. Since thinking small had done him little good, Carl Benz decided to think big. He had always been fascinated by engines. The internal combustion engine was the future, he told Bertha, and that's what he was going to build. Bertha, who knew nothing about mechanics, said fine. She had just given birth to their third child.

Because the Otto patent dictated the payment of royalties by anyone constructing a four-stroke, that avenue was obviously closed, and Benz began experimenting with two strokes less. Induction-compression-ignition-exhaust occurred in a two-stroke engine as well, the first two steps simultaneously, then the final two, theoretically providing the advantage of a power stroke for every crankshaft revolution, though the practical result of a two-stroke cycle was a noisier and rougher product. On New Year's Eve of 1879, after a year of trying, Carl Benz's engine still had not run. It was Bertha who suggested they go over to the shop that night—and that was the night when the contraption finally came to life, sounding, as Carl Benz would fondly remember, "as no magic flute in the world ever had." The Benzes stood and listened to it until they heard the town bells ringing in the new year.

Now Benz had something to manufacture, but no money to do it. The few odd jobs he had taken on during his months of experimentation had put food on the table, but no more. The Benzes were effectively penniless. But one day the local court photographer, Emil Bühler, happened by the shop to order a polished steel plate. Desperation being Benz's principal motivation at the time, the new engine inventor quickly made the customer what he wanted. Bühler was impressed, not only with the plate but also with the engine in the corner of Benz's shop, and offered to subsidize him so that manufacture might begin. Life, it seemed, might become sweet for the Benzes at last.

At Deutz, meanwhile, matters had soured for Gottlieb Daimler. His financial rewards were great—about 5,000 two-stroke engines had been sold, the company was on its way to producing 30,000 of the four-strokes, and five percent of those profits represented a tidy fortune. But Daimler had not experienced such frustrations since the Bruderhaus. Not only did Otto take as a personal insult any of Daimler's suggestions for product improvement within the overall manufacturing program—contractually Daimler's territory—but his anger was really roused whenever Daimler set foot into research territory, which Otto considered strictly his own.

As developed to this point, the Otto engine was limited to the city machine shop, and there it would remain until freed from the umbilical cord of the gasworks' pipeline. Once it was cut loose the possibilities seemed endless; the engine could go anywhere, out into the countryside, even onto the road. But what would move it there? Possibly, Daimler thought, a fuel as old as the earth itself.

Petroleum is known to have been used by the ancient Egyptians for embalming their dead; it is spoken of in the Bible—Noah's ark was pitched "within and without"; "slime had they for mortar" in the construction of the Tower of Babel. In fifteenth-century Bavaria, petroleum was scooped out of streams or holes in the ground and sold by monks as the "oil of St. Quirinius" for healing purposes. In America, Indians used it for making paints, and hucksters enjoyed a brisk trade selling it as a patent medicine. But it was not until 1858, when Colonel Edwin L. Drake drilled for oil at Titusville, Pennsylvania, that the petroleum industry was born.

Because the idea of using petroleum was Daimler's, Otto was not particularly enthusiastic. And because its properties were still largely unknown, working with it was not without peril. As Maybach later described one experiment: "Otto and Daimler were standing beside me and I was crouched down at floor level to watch closely a single flame ignition when suddenly the [carburetor] apparatus, which was made of tin, exploded and sent the cover over the heads of Otto and Daimler to hit one of our workmen on the head." Happily, the workman was not badly hurt. "Those first experiments of ours were fairly hazardous," Maybach concluded matter-of-factly. But even more incendiary were the words that flew whenever Otto and Daimler shared the same room. Their mutual antagonism had reached the point where agreeing on even the most minor matter represented a defeat neither was willing to accept. Langen finally decided that not only should Otto and Daimler not share the same room, but, for a while, the same country. So Daimler was sent to Russia in September 1881 to look into the prospects for gas engine sales in the land of the czars.

Certainly Langen did not expect absence to make the two men any fonder of each other, only that a cooling-off period might make tolerance easier. What he got instead on November 22 was a memo from Otto declaring that he found it "impossible to work any longer with Daimler," but if Daimler resigned he was willing to stay on the job. This ultimatum left Langen no choice; if he lost Otto, he also lost the Otto patent.

Daimler returned from his trip the following month, and presented his facts. "Here everything is crying to be brought to life by technical progress," he wrote about Russia, and advised that a plant in St. Petersburg was as viable as a plant in Vienna or Philadelphia, where new branches were about to be opened. On December 28 Daimler received a letter from Langen noting that his Russian report had been so comprehensive and convincing that a branch fac-

tory in St. Petersburg would be established, and perhaps Daimler might like to be in charge. As for Daimler's further employment in Cologne, Langen reminded him that their contractual arrangement stipulated termination by either party with six months' notice, "and we have to allow this clause to operate."

Gottlieb Daimler had been fired. Ten years of seven-day weeks and 14-hour days to build up an organization, and now he was being summarily booted out of it. Daimler was enraged, but Emma Daimler was not. Doctors had begun warning her about Daimler's weak heart and, having just given birth to their fifth child, she longed for the life of serenity and peaceful retirement that their savings and Deutz dividends would allow them—if she could just talk her husband into it.

What she did talk him into was moving back to Württemberg where, in the Stuttgart suburb of Cannstatt, they found a fine big house in an idyllic park setting. Daimler promised her to make regular visits to the therapeutic mineral springs nearby. As for retirement, Emma lost that one: Daimler had invited Wilhelm Maybach to join him.

Whether Daimler had glanced more than briefly at the house when he and Emma went to inspect it is doubtful. But there were other structures on the grounds that he had certainly looked over. He would turn the tool shed into his office, he would enlarge the greenhouse into a workshop, he would lay in gas and waterlines, he would install a large tank to hold fuel, he would broaden and reinforce the driveway surrounding the house. There was no question about what Daimler was planning.

Meanwhile, in Mannheim, matters had run amok, partly because Carl Benz was thinking along the same lines as Gottlieb Daimler. Ever since his student days, Benz had dreamed of building a vehicle which, in his words, "runs under its own power like a locomotive but not on tracks, but like a wagon simply on any street . . ." The velocipede, a contrivance popularized in the 1860s, gave him inspiration now. With a huge wheel in front, a small one in back and a single seat perched high in the air, it deserved its nickname of "bone-shaker," as Benz decided no doubt after fre-

29

quently falling off the one he had bought from a friend in Mannheim. But the velocipede had taught him a few lessons about the application of power, and these came back to him now that he had built his engine.

Unfortunately, he also happened to pass his thoughts on to his new partners. Early on Emil Bühler had invited a local businessman, Otto Schmuck, to handle the sales agency for the Benz engine. Schmuck emptied the venture's modest treasury, with the result that the Mannheim bank which had previously lent Benz money suggested incorporation before extending the additional loans the partners now needed to proceed. In October 1882, Gasmotorenfabrik Mannheim was officially born with nine stockholders. Reluctantly, Benz moved out of his workshop and into premises in the Schwetzinger Garten chosen by the company board, one member of which was Bühler's brother, a cheese merchant who considered himself something of an expert in technical matters. Changes were suggested to the basic Benz design.

Carl Benz was irate and said so. When Benz told the board he wanted to experiment with adapting his engine as a road vehicle, the board was aghast and also said so. A few unpleasant words about the state of Benz's mental health were exchanged and, in January 1883, just three months after incorporation, Benz asked to be allowed to resign, a request the board

cheerfully accepted.

On the face of it, Benz's decision was ill-advised. All his tools were in the Schwetzinger Garten building, which belonged to the company, and he had rented his old workshop to an iron foundry. So he had nothing to work with, no place to go, and not enough cash to do anything about either. Bertha remained staunchly behind him, though with four children in the family now, she had to be worried.

Fortunately, Benz's cycling adventures had brought him into contact with Max Kaspar Rose and Friedrich Wilhelm Esslinger, successful businessmen and velocipede enthusiasts both. Not only did they like Benz, they also believed he was of sound mind and his engine was a sound business proposition. Very soon Carl Benz had a new company, organized on October 1, 1883, and registered December 1 in the district court of Mannheim: Benz & Cie., Rheinische Gasmotorenfabrik. Favorable terms were concluded with the iron foundry people at Benz's old workshop: they moved out and Benz moved back in. Gas engines were to be his product, but his new partners promised him that he could experiment with the road vehicle idea "once the business is making enough money."

By now, in Cannstatt, with the greenhouse turned into a workshop and an iron stove installed to brew

Edouard Delamare-Deboutteville (1856-1901) and a sketch of his 1883 gas car. Though he abandoned vehicle-building efforts, Delamare-Deboutteville moved successfully into stationary engine manufacture. His 100 hp 1889 Paris Exhibition engine was the largest industrial unit in Europe.

KAISERLICHES PATENTAMT.

PATENTSCHRIFT
№ 28022.

CLASSE 46: Luft- und Gaskraftmaschinen.

G. DAIMLER in CANNSTATT.
GASMOTOR

Patentirt im Deutschen Reich vom 16. Dezember 1883 ab.

Die Neuerungen in Gas- und Oelmotoren bestehen in dem Verfahren, in einem geschlossenen, wärmegeschützten oder nicht gekühlten Raum am Ende eines Cylinders Luft mit brennbaren Stoffen (Gasen, Dämpfen, Oel etc.) gemischt durch einen Kolben so zusammen- oder gegen die heissen Wände des Raumes zu pressen, dass am Ende des Kolbenhubes durch die Wirkung der Compression eine Selbstzündung, sozusagen pneumatische Zündung, und rasche Verbrennung durch die ganze Masse des Gemisches eintritt, und die dadurch entstandene erhöhte Spannung als Triebkraft zu verwenden.

In Fig. 1 der Zeichnung ist A ein Cylinder, in dem sich der Kolben B luftdicht bewegt. Das eine Ende des Cylinders ist durch einen Hut C geschlossen, der mit schlechten Wärmeleitern (Lehm, Schlackenwolle etc.) umhüllt ist, und von dem Cylinder möglichst wärmeisolirt ist.

Der Kolbenboden ist ebenfalls nach aussen mit schlechten Wärmeleitern belegt.

Beim Anhub des Kolbens B wird durch das Ventil d Luft mit Gas oder Oel gemischt, eingesaugt oder eingepresst.

Durch den Rückgang des Kolbens wird das Gemisch in den Raum C gepresst und entzündet sich am Ende des Kolbenhubes.

Durch Verbrennung und Ausdehnung des Gemisches wird der Kolben mit bedeutender Kraft zurückgetrieben und kann dann seine Kraft, sei es durch Kurbel oder andere Mechanik, übertragen.

Beim zweiten Rückgang des Kolbens werden die Verbrennungsprodukte ganz oder theilweise durch das Auslassventil g ausgetrieben; nachher beginnt ein neues Spiel u. s. f.

Nach einigen Wiederholungen dieses Spieles nehmen die Wände des Raumes C und der Kolbenboden eine normale erhöhte Temperatur an, bei welcher sich das Gemisch regelmässig in oder um den todten Punkt des Kolbenweges in innerster Kolbenstellung infolge der Compression entzündet, nach dem Erfahrungssatz, dass brennbare Gemische, die unter Atmosphärendruck nicht oder nur langsam verbrennen würden, bei rascher Compression wieder rasch verbrennen und sogar explodiren. Damit am Anfang der Arbeit, wo die Wände des Verbrennungsraumes noch kalt sind, das Gemisch doch explodirt, wird ein metallener Zündhut f, dessen Inneres in fortwährend offener Verbindung mit dem Verbrennungsraum ist, mittelst Flammen von aussen so erwärmt, dass die Zündung erst am Ende des Compressionshubes eintritt, so lange, bis die Selbstzündungen ohnedies stattfinden.

Patent-Ansprüche:

1) Bei Gas- oder Oelmotoren das Verfahren, eine Ladung brennbaren Gemisches (Luft mit Gas oder Oel etc. gemischt) in einem geschlossenen heissen Raum rasch zu comprimiren, damit es sich erst im Augenblick der höchsten Spannung von selbst entzündet und Explosion oder rasche Verbrennung durch die ganze Masse erfolgt, und die durch die Verbrennung erhöhte Spannung auf dem Rückwege des Kolbens als Triebkraft zu verwenden.

2) Der mit dem brennbaren Gemisch in fortwährender offener Verbindung stehende Zündhut f, welcher so erwärmt wird, dass die Zündung erst am Ende des Compressionshubes eintritt. —

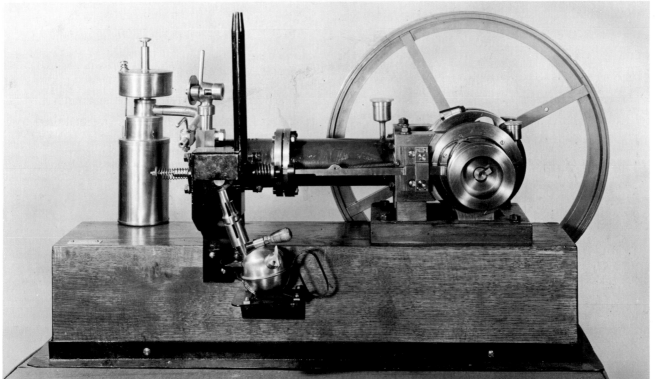

(Top, left) Patent No. 28022, dated December 16, 1883 for the first high-speed, lightweight engine in the world. (Above) The engine itself. Of the development of its hot-tube ignition, Daimler wrote: "I could only continue working and experimenting; it was not possible to enter the combustion chamber ... and no theory existed, so the most learned professor could not have assisted." (Top, right) The vertical engine, patented in 1885. Interestingly, Daimler offered his new engine to his old adversaries at Deutz. Uninterested then, they later sued Daimler unsuccessfully. Daimler was careful to protect his ideas, and by 1889 he had been granted 68 patents in 16 countries.

coffee on, Daimler and Maybach were engrossed in their engine experiments. Maybach's leaving his seemingly secure job at Deutz to "throw in my lot with Gottlieb Daimler" was a decision he had made after weighing a number of factors. Daimler's successor at Deutz was Hermann Shumm, Langen's brother-in-law, who had recently returned from America after establishing a plant for the manufacture of Otto engines in Philadelphia, and Maybach quickly recognized that Shumm was not about to allow him the creative freedom he had previously enjoyed. On the other hand, as Maybach said, "I knew Daimler's nature very well . . . certain qualities he had led to more than one disagreement." Further, there was a personal consideration: Maybach was a family man now, having married Bertha Habermass in 1878. Their son Karl Wilhelm was born a year later.

But pivotal in Maybach's decision was his interest in Daimler's engine ideas. They were exciting in the extreme. The financial terms Daimler offered, moreover reflected his respect for Maybach's abilities: a salary of 3,600 marks a year, plus the four percent annual interest on a fund of 30,000 marks set aside for Maybach in a local bank. As for family considerations, Maybach probably had little difficulty convincing his wife of the wisdom of the move; Frau Maybach and Frau Daimler had been close friends before either one had met her husband. And so the die was cast. In October 1882 Wilhelm Maybach left the huge Deutz factory near Cologne for the greenhouse-cum-workshop in Cannstatt, fully expecting that in the months to come work days would always be long and tempers frequently short. Actually, as it turned out, only the former condition prevailed. Away from the tumult at Deutz and with only his own objectives to worry about, Daimler began to enjoy himself. The two-man team got to work.

The engine Daimler wanted to build posed a set of problems it had not been necessary to confront in industrial units where size and weight were secondary to power produced. With a smaller and lighter unit the aim now, Daimler believed similar performance might be possible if the engine could be made to run faster. Fuel was part of the key. Since the oil strike at Titusville, wells had been dug throughout the area

and the entrepreneurs had moved in, John Davison Rockefeller giving up the produce business in Ohio to build an oil refinery in 1863; he followed this up by establishing the Standard Oil Company in 1870. A few years later drilling had begun near Baku in the Russian Caucasus. Thus far distillation had resulted in three distinct products. The heaviest and least volatile, "heavy oil," was used as a lubricant. The mediumweight kerosene had by now replaced candles and whale oil for all home lighting not supplied by fixtures tied into the local gasworks. The lightest and most volatile was considered a waste product, too dangerous for most commercial use. *Benzin* was the German word for it; the French said *essence de pétrole*. English-speaking countries used three designations: petroleum spirit, petrol, or gasoline.

Daimler had already decided to use this "waste product" for his new engine, to turn to advantage its ostensible disadvantage of volatility. To do this, something other than the "flamethrower" type of ignition heretofore used in gas engines was required. The hot-tube type Daimler and Maybach devised did not come easy. "It was a long road," Daimler remembered later. "Premature firing of the mixture occurred again and again when the engine was being started and during compression, before reaching dead center, when the flywheel was suddenly and unexpectedly thrown backwards instead of forwards and the crank would be ripped out of the . . . hand like a bolt of lightning."

As the months of experimentation continued, with curious noises coming from behind the doors of a workshop that was always locked, the Daimler gardener became suspicious. Something illegal had to be going on in there, he concluded—probably counterfeiting. He alerted the Cannstatt police. Since the Daimlers seemed so outwardly respectable, a certain discretion was called for, and the gardener was advised to surreptitiously make an impression of the workshop key. The impression in hand, a key was made, and early one morning, the gardener having been told beforehand to tie up the Daimler dog, the authorities moved in on the workshop. After satisfying themselves that whatever was going on there was not criminal, they retired as gracefully as possible.

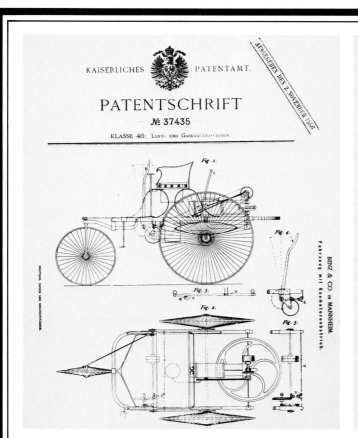

(Top, right) Early catalog for the Benz engine. The world's first successful two-stroke had been patented by Scotsman Dugald Clerk in 1878. Benz improved upon it in his fuel and air pump design, which eliminated the hazard of the fuel mixture igniting inside the pump, and in his use of a governor to regulate air and gas flow into the engine. (Top, left and above) The first Benz car and its January 1886 patent. The Otto litigation easing Benz's fears, his car's powerplant was a four-stroke. Although Daimler's high-revving engine was more sophisticated, Benz's was more prophetic in one particular: his use of electric ignition by coil and battery. Because spark plugs were unknown, Benz designed his own. His car's tubular frame and wire spoke wheels were borrowed from bicycle practice.

Daimler seems not to have been informed of the incident until some time later. There is no evidence he was unduly distressed about it—perhaps it even amused him. By this time his spirits were high because his engine worked.

Like a rifle to a blunderbuss was the way Daimler compared his engine to Otto's. An Otto weighed as much as 750 pounds, Daimler's less than 100. About 180 rpm was the best an Otto could do; Daimler's was capable of 900. No engine had ever revved that high. But there was a potential problem. Daimler's new engine was a four-stroke — and there was the matter of the Otto patent.

For the people at Deutz, however, that patent was a source of even more concern. By now it was being attacked from all sides, and even blithely ignored. In Munich, a watchmaker named Christian Reithmann had a four-stroke engine in his shop that had not been made by Deutz. In Montgrimont, France, a textile manufacturer named Edouard Delamare-Debouteville was preparing to manufacture the four-stroke engine which he had previously built to drive his factory's spinning machines.* The Otto people sued the watchmaker, and demanded royalties from the textile man. Both cases landed in court. Reithmann was able to prove that his engine was running in 1873, four years before the Otto had been patented. Delamare-Debouteville resurrected the work of Beau de Rochas, which represented an even earlier state of the art. The Otto patent was ultimately declared void. Four-stroke engine operation might continue to be popularly known as the Otto cycle, but now anyone was free to use it without fear of a lawsuit.

*In 1883 Delamare-Debouteville, in collaboration with his master mechanic Charles Malandin, built a three-wheeled vehicle using city gas as fuel. His was not the first, however. Lenoir had installed one of his engines in an experimental vehicle in Paris in 1863. In Vienna in 1870 Siegfried Marcus had outfitted a handcart with an Otto-inspired atmospheric engine. Undoubtedly there were others as yet unknown. From a practical standpoint, dependence upon a convenient gas main or gasworks was a major disadvantage, and the Delamare-Debouteville experience demonstrated another. During testing later that year, the vehicle's tank of city gas exploded. The idea behind this experiment was to try a four-wheeler and liquid fuel next. That vehicle was unsuccessful, its chassis "shaken to pieces," in Malandin's words, during a preliminary test. This dissuaded Delamare-Debouteville from further vehicle experimentation, though he did proceed, and most successfully, into stationary engine manufacture.

The definitive conclusion of the Otto case arrived on January 30, 1886 with a decision handed down by the German Supreme Court, but since mid-1883, when the Reithmann litigation began, newspapers and technical journals had speculated on its outcome. In Cannstatt, Daimler gambled on the decision early, patenting his new engine on December 16, 1883. In Mannheim, Carl Benz was more cautious, though during the fall of 1884 he decided to chance it too. Benz began development of a four-stroke engine, but to be safe he kept quiet about it.

Benz's stationary two-stroke engines were selling well, which delighted his partners Rose and Esslinger, and testimonial letters from satisfied users began arriving at the shop, which delighted him. His ego bolstered, and putting food on the family table no longer a crying concern, Benz returned to his vehicle idea. Rose and Esslinger were not enthusiastic, regarding the money he was spending on the project as lost, but since his engines were turning a profit, humoring him seemed the best course.

Though he had used coal gas for his early two-strokes, a freak fire in Mannheim following the explosion of a bowl of *benzin* a local housewife had bought to clean gloves had convinced Benz, as it had Daimler earlier, that the fluid's volatility could be channeled to advantage and would, moreover, lead to less carbonization than coal gas. His new four-stroke engine would use *benzin* too.

As it had for Daimler, ignition proved to be the "problem of problems" for Benz: "If the spark does not work," he wrote, "then all is in vain." His solution was a battery and trembler coil system with spark plug. Finally, the engine was finished. It was smaller and faster-revving than his stationary units, naturally, developing about two-thirds of a horsepower at about 250 rpm. This "seemed to be enough" to propel a vehicle, "actually a lot," in Benz's words. Of all the engines then known, Benz's was the fastest. Daimler's was faster, of course, but Carl Benz didn't know about that one.

From the time his engine was finished, Benz was breaking new ground. He was attempting to build something he had never seen, and therefore spent a good deal of time answering questions he asked himself. For a while he dreamed of nothing but wheels. Should the vehicle have three or four, should the power be transmitted to a single one or to all, how should the power be taken to the wheels in the first place? Finally, some of the questions answered themselves. The first Benz, for example, had three wheels because Carl Benz couldn't figure out how to steer a four-wheeler. To avoid turning the three-wheeler over at corners, he placed the engine on its side at the rear, with the flywheel running horizontally. Precisely when the vehicle ran for the first time cannot be determined. The likelihood, based on latter-day reminiscences of Benz himself and workers then in his employ, would be that sometime during the fall of 1885 the little 580-pound car was rolled out of its shop in Mannheim into the courtyard and tried. It ran long enough for Bertha to clap her hands with joy, but not long enough for her to climb aboard. Suddenly the engine died: an ignition wire had broken. That fixed, the car was started again; then the chain driving to the rear wheels snapped. Weeks of repair and revision followed, and Benz was ready again. This time Bertha sat next to him, and this time Benz drove into the brick wall of the courtyard. He decided he had better work on the car some more before taking it out in public.

By early 1885 the Daimler engine had been refined from air cooling to water cooling and from horizontal configuration to vertical, the entire unit enveloped in a dust-free, oil-tight housing including the flywheel. This version was patented in April 1885.*

An air-cooled unit powered the first vehicle Daimler and Maybach built. It was the world's first motorcycle. Interestingly, Benz had not even considered two wheels, probably because of his numerous falls from the bone-shaker. But the two-wheeler Daimler and Maybach built during the summer of 1885 was no velocipede; its wheels, front and rear, were the same size, just as on the "safety bicycle" which had just been put into manufacture by James Starley in Coventry, England. But only after 1888, when John Dunlop's pneumatic tire was fitted, would the bicycle as we know it begin to supplant the high-wheeled velocipede in popularity. In 1885, in the absence of anything better, Daimler and Maybach shod their motorized bicycle with heavy iron bands shrunk onto wooden wheels and provided two small side wheels for balance, since no one in either the Daimler or Maybach family was a cyclist.

Gottlieb Daimler chose not to try the thing himself; indeed it is not known for certain how often, if ever, Maybach did. There was a test driver available, however; the Daimlers' eldest son, Paul, had just

*Shortly before this Daimler had offered his engine patents to Deutz, probably because of his written promise to the Otto people not to compete with them for five years after his departure. Deutz was not interested in the patents when Daimler offered them, though a few years later the company sued the engine inventor, unsuccessfully, over this very point.

The greenhouse workshop in Cannstatt, 1882. Gottlieb Daimler was amenable to leaving Deutz for more than professional reasons. He had always preferred his native Swabia to the Rhineland and regarded his return to Württemberg as "coming back home."

turned 16 and, as most teenagers would, jumped at the chance. That fall he drove the vehicle to Unter-türkheim (about three kilometers away) and back—and prepared a short report for his father. Young Adolf Daimler tried the vehicle too; he is known to have complained that, with the exhaust located precipitously close to the saddle, the ride became quite warm.

As winter set in, Daimler attempted to fashion the motorcycle into a motorsled by adding teeth to the rear wheel and a runner in front. Tests over the frozen surface of a lake, however, were not very successful. Daimler also had the notion of making a motorized wheelchair, but ultimately was persuaded by Maybach to return to the idea they had in the first place.

Shortly after that Daimler called on the coach-building house of W. Wimpf and Sons in Stuttgart and ordered a carriage as a birthday present for his wife, asking that it be "handsome but very solidly built." Emma's birthday—April 29—came and went, Herr Wimpf probably apologizing profusely that delivery was taking longer than expected because of the detailed specifications he had been given, Daimler perhaps accepting the apologies with grace because the carriage wasn't for Emma anyway. Still the delays were irksome, and Gottlieb Daimler was not a man known for patience.

On January 29, 1886, the day before the Otto patent was declared void, Carl Benz received his patent and began taking his vehicle out on the roads near his workshop, his son Eugen trotting alongside with a can of gasoline since Benz, fearing fire, put in only one and a half liters at a time. These trips were made at night, both to avoid the attention the vehicle would bring and also the embarrassment when it broke down. And it broke down frequently. Though he might have given his kingdom for a horse at times, Carl Benz was persistent. Each evening the trip became a little longer before father and son had to push the auto back to the shop. Finally, one glorious night, they made it all the way home... nonstop. Now Benz's goal was a trip around the perimeter of Mannheim, from his workshop to the Waldhofstrasse to Waldhof and Sandhofen, and back via Käfertal. He made that one too. On July 3, 1886, there was a small notice in the *Neue Badische Landeszeitung* that a three-wheeled motor vehicle "was tested this morning early on the Ringstrasse, during which it operated satisfactorily." The local press, it would seem, had taken five months to notice that a device which would change the world was operating almost literally under its nose.

The following month, in Cannstatt, while waiting

Daimler family portrait, taken on the terrace of the Cannstatt home, 1885. From the left, Gottlieb, his sister-in-law Maria Kurz, sons Paul (16) and Adolf (14), his father-in-law, wife Emma with Wilhelm (4), and daughters Ema (12) and Martha (7).

Testing on the Neckar, 1886: Daimler and Maybach behind the engine compartment of their first motorboat. They camouflaged what its "special propelling mechanism" was.

with mounting impatience for delivery of the Wimpf carriage, Daimler and Maybach built a motorboat which they tested on the Neckar. "It appears to be propelled by some unseen power up and downstream with great speed, causing astonishment on the part of the bystanders," a newspaper reporter wrote. "The man at the tiller needs only to press in one direction or another to have the boat go anywhere he wants, either fast or slow."

The reporter's bafflement was exactly what Daimler and Maybach had hoped for. Unwilling to go public with their experiments, they had installed porcelain knobs with wires strung between them on the boat's engine housing, believing that people who saw the wires might draw the conclusion that the power was electrical. They also removed the engine every night. When pressed for details about the boat

by journalists or bystanders, Gottlieb Daimler had a stock answer: *"Es läuft Öllektrisch,"* a complicated German pun that served his purpose nicely, allowing him neither to lie nor tell the truth. He did have an engine that "licked oil," but saying the phrase quickly made it sound like "electric."*

The Wimpf carriage was finally delivered on

---

*Alexander Graham Bell had already demonstrated the effectiveness of electric impulses in conveying voice messages by telephone, and Thomas Alva Edison's incandescent lamp was on its way to replacing gas and kerosene to light the world. With Werner von Siemens' development of an efficient generator in the late 1870s, the battery-powered electric motor had become a practical proposition. By the early 1880s, some experimental electric vehicles had been built, N. J. Raffard's three-wheeler and Charles Jeantaud's four-wheeler not causing undue alarm on the streets of Paris. The general consensus during this period was that electric power was comparatively safe. A gasoline-driven vehicle was unknown, of course, but the potential hazards of benzine were — which explains Gottlieb Daimler's caution.

The world's first motorcycle, and Daimler's last, 1885. "The engine . . . is well situated under the saddle and between the driver's legs," reported *Die Gartenlaube.* It made for a warm ride.

August 28, and its conversion to motor carriage was quickly accomplished at a machine works near the Daimler home, the workshop being too small for the task. The first test runs were made there, the machine shop workers being sworn to secrecy; further road testing on the driveway surrounding the Daimler home followed. "The carriage ran well and reached a speed up to 18 km/h," Paul Daimler remembered. "We had a good firm seat to sit on and were able to make short trips, slowly but surely; 'slowly' by reason of the fact that we never ran risks by going too fast." The risks included problems with the local authorities. Indeed, when Daimler first requested approval from the Cannstatt police to operate his car on the road, he was refused.

Whether either Daimler or Benz was yet cognizant of what the other was doing was doubtful. Their approaches were certainly dissimilar. Carl Benz had a single thought: the automobile. "The difficult task of inventing it may now be considered over and done with," the *Mannheim Generalanzeiger* reported on September 15, "and Benz intends to proceed with the manufacture of these vehicles for practical use."

At this point Gottlieb Daimler was choosing not to reveal his plans, but they were ambitious. "Indescribably wonderful" were the words he used for the automotive age he saw approaching. Of the practicality of his engine, he had no doubt: as Baudry de Saunier would write, "Its first necessity is air, which costs nothing, spirit which is purchasable anywhere, a little oil and some water for cooling purposes." Its universality was what gripped Daimler. His engine could be adapted to vehicles for the road, vehicles for rails, vehicles for water, vehicles for all purposes — possibly even vehicles for the air.

At the end of 1886 Carl Benz stood ready to put the world on wheels. Gottlieb Daimler was ready to motorize the world. The question was . . . was the world ready for them?

Adolf Daimler takes his father for a drive, 1886. Unlike Carl Benz's first car, which was built from the ground up, Gottlieb Daimler's was literally a "horseless carriage." The carriage was by Wimpf. Daimler's engine made a horse unnecessary.

CHAPTER TWO

THE SPREADING OF THE GOSPEL

Benz & Cie.

1 8 8 7 – 1 9 0 0

Nothing else in all the world . . . not all
the armies . . . is so powerful as an idea
whose time has come.
—VICTOR HUGO,
THE FUTURE OF MAN

In 1886 President Grover Cleveland married Frances Folsom in the White House, Theodore Roosevelt gave up ranching in the Dakota territory to enter politics in New York, and Geronimo surrendered near the Mexican border, ending the last major Indian resistance. In Britain, William Gladstone was prime minister, Home Rule for Ireland was an issue in Parliament, and preparations were under way for the celebration of Queen Victoria's Golden Jubilee. In Germany, Otto von Bismarck was forcing massive social reforms as part of a policy of economic nationalism that would rapidly expand German commerce and industry.

Steam had replaced sail in more than half of Britain's merchant ships, and the railroads ruled the vast expanse of America. But the political power wielded by the railroad barons was about to be curtailed by a Supreme Court decision that would lead to the establishment of the Interstate Commerce Commission in 1887.

Locomotives steamed along the rails of the Third Avenue El, but below on New York City streets the horse ruled the road. A stagecoach was operating on the Boulevard (renamed Broadway in 1899), and on Eighth Avenue the horsecar line carried Wall Street workers in swaying discomfort to their homes on the Upper West Side. The Vanderbilts, the Goulds, the Fisks, and the Fricks traveled to their Fifth Avenue mansions by carriage.

The vehicles built by Carl Benz and Gottlieb Daimler went unnoticed in America in 1886 and, except for the few lines in Benz's local newspaper, were ignored in Germany. This neglect admirably suited Daimler's purposes; he viewed his invention as merely the beginning of experimentation. Where *his* invention was concerned, Benz thought otherwise. Though he had told the Mannheim reporter that his "difficult task of inventing" was over, he was by now aware that his car needed further work. Still he was sure that with just a few more changes he would be ready for manufacture. But he did not tell that to his partners.

By 1886 Benz & Cie. was bursting at the seams. Demand for stationary engines had increased so steadily that new quarters were needed. That year, Rose and Esslinger purchased a vacant lot in the Waldhofstrasse and construction began on a new 40,000-square-foot factory. The work force was increased from 25 to 40 men. With expansion plans occupying his partners' attention, Carl Benz thought they might not notice that all of his attention was being devoted to his car. Although a few of his workers were involved, vehicle development remained largely a family affair. In the evenings, after the children were in bed, Bertha Benz was in the workshop helping out or in the living room pedaling furiously on her sewing machine to charge the accumulator for the car's ignition. Twelve-year-old Richard helped out.

From Daimler's Cannstatt workshop (above, a museum today) and Benz's in Mannheim, the world moved into the horseless age. Neither man was yet aware of the other. It is possible they met once, years later.

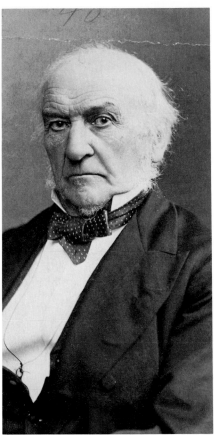

In 1886 . . . Teddy Roosevelt left his ranch to run unsuccessfully for mayor of New York City. Apache chief Geronimo surrendered to General Nelson Miles of the U.S. Cavalry at Camp Bowie, Arizona. Advocacy of Irish Home Rule defeated British prime minister William Gladstone. German chancellor Otto von Bismarck formulated accident and old-age insurance laws despite Reichstag opposition. Queen Victoria celebrated her sixty-seventh birthday.

Carl Benz testing his Patent Motorwagen, c. 1887, with friend
Josef Brecht, who succeeded Julius Ganss as company business manager in 1904.

The Benzes were already a two-car family. Carl
Benz continued his test drives, taking the newer vehicle for short trips, then returning to his tinkering.
Bertha was becoming impatient. Surely there must be
something she could do to convince her husband his
car was already good enough. In a few weeks she and
her oldest boys were planning to travel by train to
Pforzheim to visit her mother. Eugen, now 15, suggested they take the car instead. Why not, Bertha
thought. Pforzheim was a good 50 miles away; if the
Benz could make it there, her husband would have the
evidence he needed.

The first long-distance trip by car began before
dawn. Leaving a note on the table, Bertha and her
sons stole out of the house as quietly as possible,
pushing the vehicle far enough away before starting it
so the noise would not awaken Carl. They got to
Heidelberg easily, stopping there for a snack. At
Wiesloch they filled the radiator and went to a phar-
macy to purchase ligroin (a petroleum distillate used
as a solvent) for the fuel tank. In Bretten they encountered their first big hill and their first problem: the
Benz could not make the climb. Richard, being the
lightest, remained at the tiller; Bertha and Eugen got

The woodcut which accompanied the January 1889 story and subsequent Benz ad in
Scientific American. Benz was in a quandary about pricing a product no one else in
the world was selling. By now he was charging 2700 marks and had sold one car.

out and pushed. All subsequent hills were climbed the same way.

Other problems had other remedies. Bertha removed an obstruction in the fuel line with her hatpin, and made an insulator out of one of her garters when an ignition wire short-circuited. In Bauschlott a shoemaker nailed new leather onto the brake block. Finally Pforzheim hove into view. Night was falling, the Benz had no lights, and the travelers did not relish the thought of pushing the car uphill after dark. Fortunately, the last few kilometers into town were downhill, and Bertha could soon telegraph her husband that they had arrived.

Relieved but proud of both Bertha and his Benz, Carl telegraphed back asking her to ship the car's driving chains to him right away because he needed them for a *third* version he was putting together for exhibition in Munich. So the first woman driver and her sons remained in Pforzheim until Benz made a spare set of chains. When they got back, they suggested to their husband and father that something really needed to be done about hills. Benz added a low gear to his third car's transmission. Now he was positive he had a product to sell.

The Munich Engineering Exposition of September 1888 provided Benz with his first big opportunity for publicity. Not only did he have his car on exhibition, he offered test drives to anyone who asked. Munich was dazzled. "Seldom, if ever, have passers-by in the streets of our city seen a more startling sight," said one newspaper. Another reported, "Without any sign of steam or other visible means of propulsion, human or otherwise, the vehicle proceeded on its way without difficulty. . . . It was followed by a great crowd of breathless pedestrians." Even better publicity would follow a lengthy story with a woodcut illustration in the influential *Leipziger Illustrierte Zeitung* in December; *Scientific American* reprinted it a month later.

Carl Benz won a gold medal at the Munich Exposition, but what he wanted were sales, and those he did not get. Now that he was ready to manufacture, no one was ready to buy. In later years he liked to reminisce that his only prospective customer in Munich was carted off to a lunatic asylum before the sale could be consummated; at the time, friends thought that was infinitely more humorous than did either of the Benzes. After the Munich Exposition they clipped all the favorable reviews the car had received, incorporating many of them into a sales catalogue. *"Neuer Patent-Motorwagen"* was its title, with the product described as "an agreeable vehicle, as well as a mountain-climbing apparatus" fully capable of replacing a horse and carriage. The price was 2,000 marks, and Benz had calculated the car could be operated at a cost of 30 pfennigs (about seven and a half cents) an hour. At the end of the year *Naturwissenschaften 1888*, a German yearbook of science and nature, was less optimistic. Though they conceded that the Benz had "caused some stir at the Munich Exposition," the editors concluded "this employment of the gasoline engine will probably be no more promising for the future than the use of the steam engine was for road travel."

But Carl Benz did manage to sell one car—to Emile Roger, the Benz & Cie. representative for France, who thought the vehicle might be a worthy addition to his engine line. During the spring of 1888, before the Exposition, when Carl Benz went to Paris on stationary engine matters, he had paid a call on the saw-manufacturing firm of Panhard & Levassor and was surprised to find his car there. Roger was already trying to drum up business. To no avail. Although Benz took Emile Levassor on test runs around the Porte d'Ivry factory, Levassor remained less impressed with the commercial potential of the Benz car than with its engine. But no deal was concluded for that either.

If Carl Benz wondered why, there was a ready answer. Gottlieb Daimler had been there first.

Actually, Daimler had first been in contact with Panhard & Levassor years before, in 1861, when he turned down a job there to make his way to England. At that time the business was owned by two men named Perin and Pauwels; upon Pauwel's death, Perin had taken in René Panhard as partner. When Perin died, Panhard brought in Emile Levassor. Panhard and Levassor continued the firm's traditional business. It was an attorney who got them interested in engines.

During Daimler's days at Deutz, Edouard Sarazin was the French representative for the Otto engine. The two became close friends; Sarazin handled Daimler's legal matters in Paris and was one of the first visitors to Daimler's greenhouse-workshop in Cannstatt. In October 1886, after taking out the first French patent on Daimler's new high-speed engine, Sarazin began considering where it might be manufactured. He thought of Levassor; Sarazin had known him since both began their careers in Belgium, and now Levassor was a partner in a prosperous factory in France with facilities adaptable to engine building. Intrigued by the Daimler engine, Levassor agreed to produce the few examples necessary to protect the French patent. Then the unexpected happened.

On Christmas night, 1887, Edouard Sarazin died. Levassor was at his bedside. In almost his last words Sarazin pleaded with his wife, for her own and their three children's sake, to continue to work with Daimler. "No living person today has any idea of the enormous possibilities of these engines," he told her.

On January 4, upon learning of Sarazin's death, Gottlieb Daimler wrote his widow a long and poignant letter in which he expressed his shock ("the only indication I had that something was amiss was a change I had noticed in his handwriting"), his anger at

Bertha Ringer Benz in 1888, age 39 and the mother of four. That August, impatient with her husband's tinkering, she made history as the world's first woman driver.

himself ("I shall always deplore . . . that I was not able to pay my promised visit to Paris and see him once again before he passed away"), and his grief at the loss of his friend. As for the French rights to the patents, Daimler promised Mme. Sarazin to do nothing without first consulting her. "I trust you will continue to participate in the Daimler business in France," he wrote. He also mentioned that because he was "too occupied with design work," he would be unable to come to Paris to see her for the present.

That left matters too unsettled for Louise Sarazin —and for Emile Levassor, who was uncertain about his own position. At his urging, Madame Sarazin was soon on her way to see Daimler. The sequence of events indicates that Benz's visit to Panhard and Levassor occurred during her trip to Cannstatt. Perhaps Levassor, who was obviously interested in engine building now, was hedging his bets in those tentative negotiations with Carl Benz. But Louise

Early Benz ads stressed the critical success the car enjoyed in Munich. Popular success remained elusive.

Sarazin, a formidable lady, returned from Cannstatt not only with the French rights to the Daimler engine, but with one of the newest versions in her luggage. Back in Paris, she immediately told Emile Levassor she needed his help. That settled *that* question.

His French connection secured, Gottlieb Daimler turned next to the New World—where he already had a contact, made more than a decade earlier by Wilhelm Maybach. When he returned from the Philadelphia Exposition of 1876, Maybach had told Daimler of his conversations with William Steinway and of Steinway's interest in engine development. Steinway and Daimler had something else in common. Singing in the New York *Liederkranz* was a favorite pastime of Steinway's; the only relaxation Gottlieb Daimler allowed himself, besides reading Schiller, was bursting into song occasionally, and he too belonged to a choral group. Steinway regularly returned to his homeland to visit relatives or to participate, as a member of the *Liederkranz*, in the German *Sängerfests;* and it was on one of the latter occasions a few years later that Maybach introduced him to Daimler. Correspondence among the three men followed, becoming more frequent after Daimler and Maybach left Deutz to begin their independent experiments.

By the summer of 1888 Daimler and Maybach had motorized three trolley cars for Baden-Baden, Stuttgart and Cannstatt, installed another engine in a horse-drawn wagon to pump water at a fire-fighting

exhibition in Hanover, and fitted an engine to a dirigible balloon, which took to the air for a short distance on August 12. On August 17 William Steinway, in Germany for a *Sängerfest*, arrived in Cannstatt at Daimler's invitation. He got rides in the Daimler-powered carriage and the Daimler-powered trolley and an excursion on the Neckar in a Daimler-powered boat. Then it was on to the Daimler workshop, which by now had moved out of the greenhouse and into a former nickel-plating factory at 67 Ludwigstrasse, only a few minutes from the Daimler home. Steinway saw further demonstrations of the Daimler engine. "If you are convinced of its usefulness," Daimler wrote Steinway several days later, "and are willing to do so, we may work together in my business for America." After giving the man a ride in every mode of transport thus far Daimlerized except the balloon, which was probably deemed too risky, Daimler had to be confident Steinway was convinced. A few weeks and some legal work later, Gottlieb Daimler of Cannstatt, State of Württemberg, Empire of Germany, empowered William Steinway of New York to create the Daimler Motor Company in the United States.

Unlike Benz, who was almost endearingly unworldly, both Daimler and Steinway knew that the public would not necessarily accept a new idea just because it had been introduced. Steam as a motor

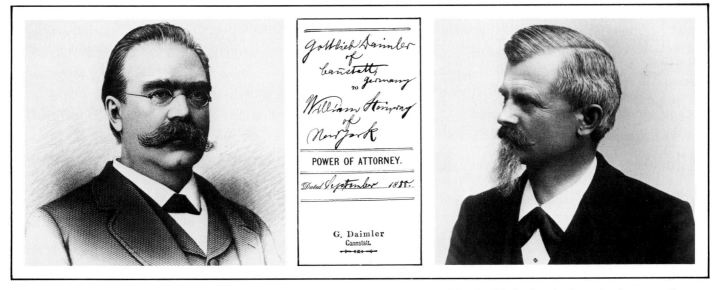

(From the left) William Steinway, his 1888 agreement with Gottlieb Daimler and Wilhelm Maybach, who brought them together. Engines and motorboats were the mainstay of U.S. production, though Steinway also produced Daimler-engined fire apparatus, tree sprayers and railway inspection cars.

On October 15, 1887, the first experimental Daimler-engined railway inspection car was demonstrated on the siding at Baden-Baden. In the right front passenger seat is Daimler; at the controls is Maybach.

force by now was well established, and electric power had made great strides since the late 1870s. The world's first commercial electric railway had begun operation in Berlin in 1881. In 1887 Frank J. Sprague, a former colleague of Thomas Edison, inaugurated America's first successful electric street railway in Richmond, Virginia. Almost immediately the horsecar lines in major American cities began to be electrified partly to remove a source of environmental pollution: sanitation experts estimated the average horse deposited 22 pounds of manure per day on city streets. Daimler's and Benz's idea that internal combustion engines could replace the horse as well was logical, but so new it was considered bizarre or dangerous in many quarters.

Americans were also skeptical that powered vehicles of any kind could operate on anything other than rails. Europe, with a road-building tradition dating from the Romans and reinvigorated during the Napoleonic era, had a splendid system of highways. But the United States had no such heritage. The North American Indians had used waterways for travel, resorting to narrow footpaths when they had to go overland. In colonial times these paths had been widened into wagon trails, and the westward movement had brought about some rudimentary turnpike building. But then came the railway. The rapid growth of railroads after the Civil War made highway construction less urgent: if people wanted to travel somewhere quickly, they took the train. In rural America, where two-thirds of the nation's population lived, the livery stable, the blacksmith shop and the

watering trough were reminders that everyday life was still bound to the pace of the horse.

American inventors had tried their hand at building steam cars. Sylvester Hayward Roper's vehicles were exhibited at county fairs throughout the East and Midwest after the Civil War. Possibly it was the demonstration of a Roper at a circus in Grand Rapids that inspired the Michigan machinist Ransom Eli Olds to build his first steam car in 1887. The following year the success of the electric railway spurred inventors, most notably William Morrison of Des Moines, Iowa, to experiment with the electric car. Of road vehicles with gasoline engines, there were none. And there had been no attempt at commercial production of *any* road vehicle.

William Steinway saw little hope for the automobile in America's foreseeable future, but he believed the Daimler engine had exciting possibilities for immediate application in boats and possibly in streetcars. Daimler agreed. Even though German roads were better than those in America, Daimler believed acceptance of the gasoline-powered automobile would follow, not precede, acceptance of the gasoline engine in other modes of transport. Daimler's pride was involved, too; he was loath to subject himself to ridicule, so he favored the comparative anonymity of waterways over roadways for much of his engine testing. Passersby onshore might conclude the boat was the invention of Edison, a notion Daimler encouraged, and neither real nor verbal brickbats were tossed at him whenever he plied the river Neckar. In addition, he remained firmly convinced that the

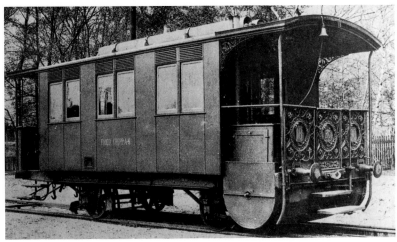

Daimler-engined streetcars were built for Stuttgart in 1888 (center, left) and for Bremen in 1889 (top). "One can only see one man operating the vehicle," reported *Die Gartenlaube*. "Next to him is a box which makes a rattling tick-tick noise." Rail cars were ordered by a Blaubeuren cement works in 1887 (center, right) and by Krupp in 1890 for its artillery range (above, left). A narrow-gauge locomotive was built in 1890 (above, right).

47

motorboat would play a major role in overcoming public prejudice against engines using gasoline as fuel.

Similarly in America Steinway focused on engine and motorboat production. At Daimler's suggestion he did not manufacture the engines himself, contracting that work to an established machine shop in Hartford, Connecticut. The hulls were built in the Steinway plant in Long Island City, with final assembly there following delivery of the engines from Connecticut. Today a plaque marks the site in Hartford where the first "automobile type gasoline engines" were produced in the United States.

By the end of 1888, with the Daimler Motor Company a reality in New York, Gottlieb Daimler's energies were channeled to Paris, where the following year France was to celebrate the centennial of its revolution with the biggest and brightest world's fair yet. Already Alexandre Gustave Eiffel was directing the construction of the tower in the Champ de Mars that was to be the centerpiece of the exposition and a bold symbol of technological progress. Daimler and Maybach were determined to be there with every possible example of their own progress, including a new car.

Unlike their first effort, this one was a vehicle conceived from the ground up. Initially Daimler's concern had been only his engine, which he believed could be sold by itself, with the task of making a horse-drawn carriage horseless left to the purchaser. It was Maybach who—like Carl Benz—envisioned the automobile as a homogeneous whole, and perhaps news of Benz's activities had been sufficient to persuade Daimler, too. The first drawings of the new Daimler were dated December 1888, after the Benz had won the gold medal in Munich and been favorably reported on in the *Leipziger Illustrierte Zeitung*. Benz's piquant little three-wheeler probably convinced Daimler that he and Maybach could do better — and certainly they could. The wire-wheeled car, with two-cylinder engine and four-speed transmission, was a clear step forward.

Daimler and Maybach mounted an impressive exhibit in Paris. In addition to the new car, there was a scale model of the trolley and an example of every engine they had built thus far; one of these turned a small dynamo which kept 30 incandescent bulbs aglow. No fewer than 30 different makes of engines, Ottos and Benzes among them, were displayed in Paris, and a post-Exposition report judged one of Daimler's the most innovative. Gottlieb Daimler needed this kind of tonic: his beloved Emma had died just a few months before. Several of his children went to Paris with him, as a sort of holiday from the sadness at home, and Adolf, who had just turned 18, is known to have driven René Panhard up and down the banks of the Seine in the new Daimler car. And on the Seine, Daimler and Emile Levassor got to know each other better as they cruised with Louise Sarazin as far as St. Cloud and Suresnes in one of the Daimler boats. But the Daimler car was viewed as a curiosity, or ignored altogether, among the tens of thousands of exhibits that vied for spectator interest in the great Exposition halls. Twenty-five million people visited the 1889 Paris Exposition, and few seemed aware that, as Pierre Giffard of *Le Petit Journal* commented a short while later, "off in this hidden corner . . . was germinating the seed of a modern technological revolution."

Though Carl Benz himself is not known to have attended the Exposition, his three-wheeler was on hand. His French representative, Emile Roger, entered it under his own name, a tactic which annoyed Benz but which he tolerated since Roger was almost the only person (besides Bertha) who really believed in his automobile. Also on display were three three-wheeled steamers, one built by Count Albert de Dion, another by Henry Charles Brasier, and the third by Léon Serpollet in association with the Peugeot Company.

Les Fils de Peugeot Frères was big business in France: manufacturers of steel products since 1810, umbrella ribs during the reign of Louis Philippe, crinoline frames when Louis Napoleon was on the throne, coffee mills, pepper grinders, hair clippers and pitchforks thereafter. It was Armand Peugeot, freshly graduated from the University of Leeds in England, who added bicycles to the company's product line in 1885, and Armand who was behind the building of the experimental steamer for the Paris

Exposition. "A diabolical invention," a Paris reporter called it, and Armand had to agree. During the Exposition he told his chief engineer, Louis Rigoulet, to try to wangle a ride on the Daimler. Maybach was pleased to oblige and took Rigoulet for a drive to Argenteuil, a distance of fourteen kilometers.

When Daimler and Maybach packed up after the Paris Exposition, they left their car behind in the shops of Panhard & Levassor. A formal agreement had been signed cementing the partnership between Madame Sarazin and Daimler. And another partnership was in the offing. Emile Levassor had asked for Louise Sarazin's hand in marriage.

Back in Cannstatt, Daimler and Maybach set to work designing a four-cylinder engine which, typically, they installed first in a boat. By now some Daimler engines had been sold for marine use, and Daimler stepped up his promotional efforts in this field—discreetly following the imperial tug, for example, when the Kaiser toured the Hamburg harbor. More forthright was the gift of another Daimler motorboat to Bismarck in 1888, when the chancellor's power was at its height. Two years later Daimler may have regretted that he had not made the presentation to the Kaiser himself, for Bismarck was dismissed because of some differences of opinion with his emperor (among them who should rule the empire). But if Daimler had miscalculated there, he was right about the advantages the small and maneuverable motorboat would have over larger steam launches in congested harbor traffic.

Nor were his trips into the air flights of fancy, though they had their amusing side. Daimler had read of the successful ascent of a dirigible balloon developed by Georg Baumgarten, a Saxonian forester, and Karl Wölfert, a Leipzig bookseller, and he promptly invited both Wölfert and his balloon to Cannstatt. A single-cylinder two-horsepower engine with a transmission for both vertical and horizontal propellers was fitted to the balloon's gondola, and in August 1888 a successful test flight was made from the hill adjacent to the Daimler shop. Daimler was not aboard, nor for that matter was Wölfert; with him in it the dirigible remained steadfastly on the ground, so a

less corpulent colleague went up instead, and Daimler concluded that he had to reduce even further the power-to-weight ratio of his engine. News of his aerial experiments soon reached a Bavarian aristocrat by the name of Ferdinand von Zeppelin.

Meanwhile Carl Benz was keeping his feet on the ground and his car on the road, doggedly pursuing his single idea. His partners, Rose and Esslinger, were at their wit's end. It was not so much that Benz was tinkering with his car, but he was devoting none of his time to the gas engine business in which, as they rightly pointed out, they had made "a nice pile of money." Heaving great sighs, Max Rose would lament, "My God, my God, where is all this going to end?" And Benz would invariably reply that some sacrifices were necessary if his automobile was to be a commercial success. But his partners were fearful of losing everything, and in May 1890, they retired amicably from Benz & Cie., to be replaced by Friedrich von Fischer and Julius Ganss, well-to-do local merchants who promised to handle the gas engine business and provide Benz with ample funds and a free hand in developing and promoting his automobile. This was a fortunate turn of events, for Benz now had another mouth to feed: Bertha had recently given birth to their fifth child.

That Benz was trying to drum up business for his car is indicated by a letter he at this time received from the postmaster of nearby Speyer. Benz had written him regarding the possibility of motorized mail delivery, mentioning that he was now considering a four-wheeled version of his car. The postmaster must have seen Benz's three-wheeler in action because he offered a few criticisms, among them "Why are there no controls for going backwards? The fact that you cannot go backwards is really something to puzzle at." But most of the letter was a panegyric to Benz's efforts. A century later it is delightful to read: "There is another thing about your vehicle: it comes to a stop and turns off and that's it. It doesn't need any feed, or any groom, no blacksmith, no danger of having a horse shy; it just moves along as if a ghostly hand were pushing it, and one stroke of the brakes and it stops. That is what makes it so inexpensive to operate. Even

Paris Exposition, 1889. The Machinery Palace was the most extensive building on the grounds, covering over 11 acres, with locomotives and printing presses dwarfing other exhibits inside. The Daimler and Benz automobiles on display were but two of the 55,000 individual exhibits at the Exposition and were largely ignored by both visitors and the press. "In the matter of attractions," a reporter wrote afterwards, "there is not much doubt but that the Eiffel tower attracted the most attention and proved the greatest card possessed by the entire exhibition."

the stupidest blockhead must be able to see such an immense advantage as this.

"The vehicle in motion does have something comical in appearance from the aesthetic point of view," the letter went on, "and someone who did not know what it was might think it was a runaway chaise he was looking at. That is because we have not yet grown used to it. But here also, in my opinion, a lot of minor changes and adjustments can be artfully made to improve its appearance without in any way losing sight of the characteristics that serve its purpose. If this were done, the lack of an animal in front to pull it would not be so striking to the beholder."

At last, someone in the neighborhood besides Bertha had faith in what Benz was trying to do.

On May 17, 1890, Louise Sarazin and Emile Levassor were married in Paris.. Whether Daimler attended the wedding is not known, but he might well have, for the bonds of friendship and respect among these three people had grown strong. After the ceremony the bride gave her husband the Daimler patent rights to do with as he wished. The newlyweds probably enjoyed a short honeymoon, for there was much work to be done. Word that Panhard & Levassor was tooling up for full production of the Daimler engine had reached Armand Peugeot, who was both a business and personal friend of Levassor's. He wanted to meet Daimler and a visit was quickly arranged, Levassor and Daimler arriving at Peugeot's Valentigny factory in the Daimler wire-wheeled car. Just as quickly, a deal was negotiated. Building automobiles was Armand Peugeot's goal, and he wanted Daimler's engine. The Peugeot arrangement was a boon for Levassor; he could use the money it brought in his own development work. He too was anxious to build a car. Daimler returned to Cannstatt and continued his work with Maybach. These experiments were expensive. Royalties from France and America were promising for the future but a pittance for the present, and Daimler's personal funds were by now running low. For all these good reasons, in 1890 Gottlieb Daimler made a bad mistake.

The establishment of Daimler-Motoren-Gesellschaft mbH was not in itself an error. Certainly Daimler's venture needed to be put on a solid business footing. Since the move to Ludwigstrasse, when an administrative manager and two apprentices were hired, the venture had grown to 22 employees. Motorboat sales in particular were healthy, with orders arriving from as far away as Africa and South America.

By now Daimler's work had caught the eye of Kilian Steiner of the Württembergischen Bank (now part of the Deutsche Bank). He dispatched Max Duttenhofer, a successful gunpowder manufacturer

The Daimler motor gondola which powered Karl Wölfert's dirigible balloon. On August 12, 1888 a test flight of 2½ miles was made near the Daimler workshop.

from Rottweil, and Wilhelm Lorenz, equally successful in the munitions business in Karlsruhe, to suggest the formation of a corporation. Well aware that he needed money to expand, Daimler was receptive, and the Daimler-Motoren-Gesellschaft was incorporated with a capitalization of 600,000 marks on November 28, 1890. Yet "imprudent" was the word Gottlieb Daimler later used in telling William Steinway about the signing of the contract. Daimler provided the patents to date, the engine orders on hand, and the Ludwigstrasse workshop. In exchange he received a third of the stock in the new company. Duttenhofer and Lorenz were in control.

Within a year the business had indeed expanded, from 22 employees to 163. But the disagreements were many. Daimler argued that development of his high-speed engine for vehicle use should have priority. Duttenhofer and Lorenz countered that the company's most profitable course was exploitation of low-speed stationary engines for which a demand already existed, and that pouring money into "utopian inventions" did not make sense. Daimler was further distressed that experimental work was being conducted by people without the necessary expertise, and that much time was being wasted experimenting in areas that he had long since gone beyond. Moreover, rapid expansion had brought unskilled workers into the business, engine quality was affected, and

engines were now being returned by dissatisfied customers. In March 1892, Daimler wrote his partners that he felt "tied to an elephant."

In August he received a letter from Paris convincing him that, in one particular, he was right and they were wrong. By now Emile Levassor and Daimler were corresponding weekly, lengthy letters exchanging ideas and reporting the latest developments. Peugeot's Daimler-engined test car was completed, Levassor wrote on this occasion, and he himself had several such experimental cars on the road. "I wish to inform you that Benz cars are being sold in France," Levassor concluded, "therefore I should say that we must act quickly."

But Daimler's hands were tied, as he told Levassor. Taking matters into her own hands, Louise Sarazin Levassor went to Cannstatt to urge Daimler to join them in France to continue his development work. But Daimler, unwilling to leave his home or his homeland, decided to leave his company instead. That fall the garden hall of the defunct Hotel Hermann in Cannstatt was rented and outfitted with machinery, and early the next year Daimler and Maybach moved in.

A decade had passed since the two of them began their engine work in the greenhouse-workshop, and it now seemed as if they were back where they had started. Yet much had happened during those ten

Daimler 4 hp belt-drive car, 1891. Facing Daimler and Maybach are two friends from the Esslingen machine works, where the first Daimler car had been built. Maybach's hand on the tiller is typical. Legend has it Gottlieb Daimler never learned to drive; it is certain he preferred being chauffeured.

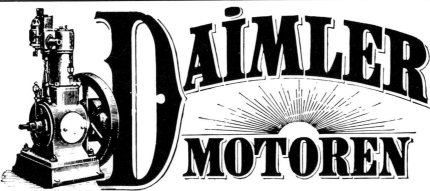

Early ad for a new company. The transformation of the Daimler-Maybach laboratory workshop into Daimler-Motoren-Gesellschaft in 1890 was the work of Max Duttenhofer (center, right) and Wilhelm Lorenz (center, left). The Daimler work force was increased from 22 to 163 that year. Experimentation from 1891 bore fruit in 1896 when the world's first motor truck was put into series production. The model shown above was one of four producing from 4 to 10 bhp.

years. They had proven that their engines could move vehicles on land, in the air and on water. Their French and American alliances had been firmly established. They had even managed to sell one car, to the Sultan of Morocco—but more important, each car they built was an improvement over the last. In 1891 they had begun development of a truck, knowing that once the automobile caught on, commercial vehicles were sure to follow. Now they would continue their work in the Hotel Hermann.

That March Daimler was informed that henceforth he was merely a stockholder and a member of the board of Daimler-Motoren-Gesellschaft. He was stripped of all authority as technical director.

In Mannheim, meanwhile, Carl Benz's persistence had finally paid off, though the old prophet-without-honor dictum held sway. There were few Benz sales in Germany, but at 52 rue des Dames in Paris Emile Roger's business was brisk—partly because Roger's brochures promised more than any car could possibly deliver for years, and partly because Paris was alive with enthusiasm for the automobile. "Germany was its birthplace," the British historian T. R. Nicholson wrote, but "France became its nursery." By the end of 1892 Emile Roger had sold about two dozen Benz three-wheelers in Paris and was crying for more. The cars delivered to him now would have four wheels, for

Carl Benz had solved his steering problem, had patented the result and called his new car the Victoria. As far as he was concerned, his automobile was perfected. By the end of 1893 he had built 45 Victorias, and again, Emile Roger sold most of them. But Benz was getting fewer orders at home, because in November that year he had received a document from the Ministry of the Interior of the State of Baden setting down the conditions under which his vehicles could be operated on public roads: "Speed . . . shall not exceed 12 kilometers per hour outside the towns and within town limits and around sharp corners it shall not exceed six kilometers per hour." This was ridiculous, Benz thought. His *first* car had been capable of 12 kilometers, and he had spent much time and effort working the engine in his Victoria up to 20. And now this. And the document went on to say that this "probationary permission" to drive motor vehicles on public roads could be withdrawn at any time "in the interest of public order and safety, or further restrictive conditions may be added." How could he sell cars in Baden if no one could use them?

In later years, Benz enjoyed relating how he got around this problem. When he learned the Minister of the Interior was to visit Mannheim, he invited him for a drive. He then began planning how to change the minister's mind about the regulations. A local milkman was hired and a dress rehearsal staged. On

Emile Levassor and Louise Sarazin. In October of 1888 Levassor accompanied the widowed Sarazin on her second trip to Cannstatt to discuss business with Gottlieb Daimler. Levassor was impressed with the Daimler-engined vehicles (car, boat, streetcar) which he saw for the first time — and with Madame Sarazin. They were married in 1890.

Panhard & Levassor began production of Daimler engines shortly after the Paris Exposition and, with partner René Panhard's concurrence, Levassor built an experimental car. After months of frustrating test trips, during which the firm's name was lampooned into "Pannard" (from *panne* or "breakdown"), Levassor's car was successful. His production prototype placed the engine in front, for the first time in a gasoline automobile. The Daimler-engined Panhards here are mid-1890's vintage.

the appointed day, one of Benz's workers met the minister at the railroad station and off they motored with the Benz at its funereal legal pace until the milkcart and its horse trotted past them, the milkman shouting a few carefully prepared insults on the "get-a-horse" theme. The milkman must have played his part well, because the minister was so infuriated by the fellow's insolence that he practically begged the Benz driver to go faster. But that would be breaking the law, the driver pointed out. Perhaps never again in history were new traffic regulations so quickly enacted. As the Benz overtook the cart, the minister shouted triumphantly at the milkman—and when the car arrived at his factory, Benz had his triumph, too. Baden officialdom was on his side.

In 1893 Gottlieb Daimler visited the United States, arriving on July 21 and remaining till November 2. There were two reasons for his visit. On July 8 he had married Lina Hartmann, the widow of a hotel proprietor and 20 years Daimler's junior; a trip to America was her wedding present. But the principal reason for the couple's voyage across the Atlantic was that William Steinway had written

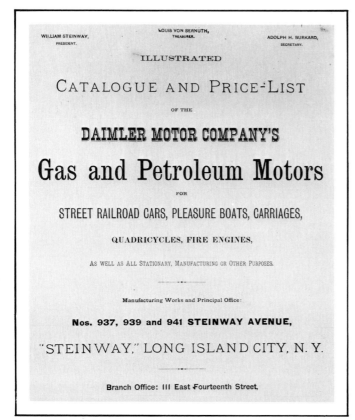

First page of Steinway catalogue. Daimler engines were displayed at the 14th Street showroom in Manhattan.

Daimler in June urging him to come; the Daimler exhibit at the Chicago world's fair was attracting considerable attention, and it would be helpful if Daimler could be there to explain and promote his inventions. Perhaps even more quickly than Emma, Lina Daimler understood precisely the sort of man she had married: a man who would take a working honeymoon.

Since their agreement in 1888, Steinway had actively promoted the Daimler engine in the United States, although not until early 1891 did Steinway's diary note that "at last a demand seems to arise." That year an elaborate catalogue was published illustrating all the Daimler products. Engines for industrial and marine use were priced from $300 to $725. Two Daimler cars were included and their advantages described: "Daimler motor vehicles do away with the heavy expense and unpleasantness connected with horses, such as stable smells, harness and feed bills, clouds of dust from horse hoofs, to smother you while out riding, and they present novelties as attractive as they are useful." But because of American road conditions Steinway remained unconvinced that the automobile was practical. His was the only company in America offering cars for sale at this time—and he had not sold a single one. By contrast, Daimler boat sales were admirable. By 1893 there were models ranging in price from $815 for a 16-footer to $7,000 for a 50-foot cabin launch. Testimonial letters from 69 satisfied Daimler boat owners would be published by the company a few years later.

In New York City Steinway maintained a permanent showroom for Daimler products, but a world's fair promised an audience of millions. From the moment the city of Chicago outbid New York, St. Louis and Washington, D.C. for the privilege of holding the Columbian Exposition to commemorate the four-hundredth anniversary of the discovery of America, Steinway and Daimler began making plans for the Daimler Motor Company exhibit.

"Great and grand indeed was the exhibition at Paris in 1889," a journalist wrote, "but infinitely greater, infinitely grander must be that at Chicago in 1893 when several times more the amount of money will be spent, with all other preparations on a simi-

Daimler motorboats, c. 1890. Worldwide marine sales represented a major source of income for Daimler during the early years. Pleasure boats were offered with 2 or 4 hp engines, capable of 10 and 15 mph respectively. Onboard propellers for faster speeds were tried experimentally. The patented Daimler reverse gear ("U" in the illustration above) was advertised as "somewhat expensive (but) far superior to all others; instantaneous in action, the boat can be stopped and turned within its own length, thus being a great safeguard against accidents by collision."

larly increased scale." Granting a certain chauvinism, the reporter was essentially right. The World's Columbian Exposition was bigger — nearly four times bigger. Chicago was in the mood to celebrate. After the disastrous fire of 1871, the city had been rebuilt in brick and steel, and the first section of elevated track that would encircle the "Loop" had just been opened. Taking a cue from the Eiffel Tower, which had been the centerpiece in Paris, the Chicago fair managers hired George W. G. Ferris, an engineer from Galesburg, Illinois, to design a gigantic wheel with 36 cars to carry 40 visitors 250 feet into the air for a bird's-eye view of an exposition that sprawled over 150 buildings and 633 acres in Jackson Park. Steam power for the Ferris wheel and all the other exhibits that required it was raised by oil piped from Whiting, Indiana, to a 600-foot bank of furnaces. Rock drills, bandsaws, printing presses, machines of all kinds bellowed in the great halls. Edison's incandescent bulbs burned everywhere. And on the Midway Little Egypt hootchie-kootchied the "genuine native muscle dance" that many found scandalous. Never had so colossal a show been staged in America and, after its ceremonial opening on May 1 by President Cleveland, over 25 million Americans, more than a third of the nation's population, flocked to see it.

Shortly after arriving in New York on July 21, Daimler and his wife boarded a train for Chicago, where they remained for six weeks. Lina enjoyed the show, her husband worked the Daimler Motor Company exhibit in the Transportation Building, designed by Louis Sullivan. There mighty locomotives loomed, dominated by the New York Central's "999," which had been clocked at a phenomenal 112.5 mph pulling the Empire State Express over one short stretch on its regular run to Chicago. Abraham Lincoln's state coach was displayed among the exhibits of nearly 300 American carriage builders, including the Studebaker brothers from South Bend, Indiana. The redoubtable Colonel Albert Pope had the largest display among the 43 bicycle builders promoting their wares.

But the Daimler Motor Company had the automotive section all to itself. Daimler's was the sole car in the Transportation Building. "The only missing feature in the vehicle exhibit was that of steam and electric carriages for use on common roads," a reporter wrote after attending the Exposition. "In the German section there was a road carriage driven by the Daimler petroleum motor which made occasional trips about the grounds." The absence of any American steam vehicles was curious, although the reporter had missed the one other car at the Exposition, the electric completed by William Morrison in Des Moines two years before and exhibited by Harold Sturges, a battery manufacturer, in the Electrical Building. William Steinway's pessimism about the automobile in America was well founded.

Gottlieb and Lina Daimler, photographed shortly after their marriage in July 1893.
He was 59, she 38. Lina bore Daimler two children: Gottlieb in 1894 (he was killed
at Ypres during World War I) and Emilie in 1897.

In addition to the latest version of the wire-wheeled car, the Daimler exhibit included two smaller wagon-ettes, two Daimler engines, a fire engine pumper on a two-wheeled hand cart, and a miniature streetcar on its own set of tracks. How many of the Exposition's millions of visitors passed by the Daimler stand is not known, though one of them was an employee of the Edison Illuminating Company of Detroit named Henry Ford. * Most of the excitement connected with the Daimler enterprise occurred out of doors, where the marine exhibit was moored. On September 3, in a storm, a sailboat capsized on Lake Michigan, tossing its six occupants into the water. The husky lifesaving crew of the USS *Illinois* rowed furiously to save them and the official launch of the Exposition steamed out as well—but Gottlieb Daimler got to them first with his motorboat. The incident provided the Daimler Motor Company with its best press in Chicago.

In October the Daimlers returned to New York, traveling back from Chicago with Frederick Kübler, the Cannstatt-trained engineer William Steinway had hired as the United States Daimler company's super-intendent. Daimler spent the next several weeks at the Long Island City factory, experimenting with Kübler and the Daimler wagonette and exasperating Stein-way. As Wilhelm Maybach well knew, when Daimler was being creative there was no stopping him. His mind worked as fast as his engines, ideas poured out, and he talked incessantly. William Steinway was now given the full Daimler treatment. "Nearly drives me to despair," Steinway told his diary after a session with

---

*There were a number of stationary and marine gasoline engines at the Exposition, Otto of Philadelphia and Sintz of Detroit among them, but the unit Ford remembered best was the one pumping water at the Daimler stand. It was similar to the engine Ford himself was then attempting to build, and he examined it closely, returning to Detroit encouraged to continue experimental work. On Christmas Eve that year Henry Ford tested his first engine in the kitchen sink of the Ford home, with his wife, Clara, dribbling gasoline into its intake valve. Like Bertha Benz a half decade before, Clara Ford was her husband's staunchest supporter and assistant during his earliest devel-opment work. It is tantalizing to speculate about whether Henry Ford met Gottlieb Daimler in Chicago. Years afterward, when Ford was the world's largest automobile manufacturer, the only engine he remembered specifically from the Exposition was the one on the Daimler stand. Certainly he must have spent some time there — perhaps when Daimler was on hand. Another exhibit that impressed Ford was the New York Central locomotive; nine years later he named his race car "999."

Daimler on October 25. "A long exciting scene with Gottlieb Daimler, who claims the most Godforsaken things," he wrote on the twenty-seventh. Daimler was now nearly 60; Steinway was a couple of years younger, a man of enormous energy and vision too, but Daimler and his ideas were running him ragged. "Gottlieb Daimler and wife sail by steamer Colum-bia!!" was Steinway's entry for November 2. The exclamation points were eloquent.

"A Marvelous Motor," a headline in the *New York Sun* had proclaimed six days earlier. "The New Propelling Power That Has Come Out of Poetic Germany." Another New York paper prophesied, "Soon you will have your own petroleum-wagon; Paris has eagerly taken up the fad." Since Gottlieb Daimler was in New York at the time, he probably saw one of those stories. Unfortunately, they were not about his car. They were about the Benz.

In the Astor Building at 10 Wall Street, the Benz Motor-Wagon Company had opened its offices. Em-ile Roger and Fred Haas, one of Benz's mechanics, had just arrived in New York with a Benz car. Apparently the plan had been to demonstrate the vehicle at the Columbian Exposition, but that did not happen. Not that it mattered: the publicity in New York was far more extensive than Daimler had re-ceived in Chicago.

The *Sun* story was full of hyperbole ("perfect lines of construction . . . no noise, steam or odor . . . noth-ing in the handling to injure the finest clothing"), dropped names ("in it, on September 9th, the Em-peror William rode from Maxau to Lauterburg"), and bent the truth a bit ("during the past two years over 300 of these carriages have been turned out"). Roger had a vivid imagination. But if Benz had not yet made 300 cars he was about to. He had just introduced two new models, the Vis-a-Vis and the Velo, and he was rearranging his factory in order to increase output. Between 1894 and 1895, annual production doubled from 69 to 135, and it would double again in two years. But something new was now being added to the automobiles: competition among the people building them. Carl Benz didn't like that at all.

On December 19, 1893, came news from Paris

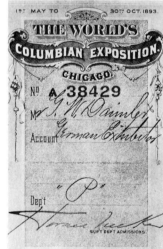

World's Columbian Exposition, Chicago, 1893. Two of the most popular attractions were George W.G. Ferris's gigantic wheel and Little Egypt's scandalous belly dancing. The scale of the Exposition was grand throughout, as indicated by the Administration and Electrical buildings (center, left) and the Court of Honor (center, right). The Daimler car exhibited in the Transportation Building is seen above, flanked by Gottlieb Daimler's exhibitor's pass.

that *Le Petit Journal* was sponsoring a road trial for *voitures sans chevaux*, to be held the following summer. The idea was the brainchild of Pierre Giffard, the reporter who had been so impressed with the Daimler wire-wheeled car at the Paris Exposition of 1889, and since the *Journal's* sponsorship of bicycle contests had proven to be a good circulation booster in recent years, he had been given the go-ahead. For the newspaper's circulation manager, the contest was a promotional dream; for Pierre Giffard, it almost became a nightmare.

The "*sans chevaux*" stipulation permitted the entry of any vehicle that could move under its own power. By the April 30 deadline Giffard had received no fewer than 102 entries with an alleged motor force. They ran the gamut from gravity to compressed air to mineral oil to pendulums; there were even four entries insisting the "weight of the passengers" would provide sufficient power. Had only a quarter of these *voitures* made it to the starting line, the 78.5-mile road to Rouen which was to be the course would have been bedlam. The vast number of entries was a good index of Parisian automobile mania, but fortunately all the bizarre notions of what a car could be remained in the backyards, or the imaginations, of their inventors. Only 21 vehicles—eight steamers, 13 gasoline-powered—succeeded in passing the preliminary test to prove they could indeed run.

The contest was postponed twice, first because the publisher of the *Journal*, who wanted to hand out the prizes, could not be there on the date selected, and second because the competitors asked for more time to get ready. Finally on Sunday, July 22, at 7 A.M., they assembled at the Porte Maillot in Paris. At eight, they were off. Among the spectators were Gottlieb Daimler and his son Paul.

The Daimlers watched the start and then followed behind in their own car, marveling at the wonder of it all: more horseless vehicles than had ever before been assembled in one place. "Heavy, massive, steam-driven cars with trailers and powerful engines competed with . . . steam tricycles, and these in turn competed with the gasoline-driven automobiles," Paul Daimler would remember. "The variety of types made an odd impression. In the heavy steamers, we saw the fireman, his face running with sweat and covered with soot, working like mad to get fuel on the fire. We saw the driver of the little steam tricycle constantly looking at the water level and pressure gauges on the small, cleverly built tubular boiler and reaching in to regulate the oil flame. In sharp contrast, the drivers of the benzine and petroleum burning cars were leaning back relaxed in their seats, adjusting this or that lever occasionally, and driving as if they were just doing it for fun."

A certain bias may have crept into Paul Daimler's recollection of the event, but certainly there was no doubt the gasoline car carried the day. True, Count de Dion had arrived first in Rouen, but the *Journal* jury decided his entry, a powerful steam tractor pulling a carriage, had not precisely met the spirit of the contest, so he was awarded second prize. The 5,000-franc first prize was presented jointly to Peugeot and to Panhard & Levassor, "both employing the petrol motor invented by Herr Daimler of Württemberg." Of the 13 gasoline cars in the contest, five were Peugeots (one of them arriving in Rouen two and a half minutes after de Dion, for an 11.5 mph average, compared to the Count's 11.6), and four were Panhards (one driven by René Panhard, another by Emile Levassor).

Trailing them at the finish line was Emile Roger in the little Benz. Carl Benz was annoyed that his Paris concessionaire had entered the contest; when newspapers referred to the car as a Roger, it made him no happier. Though the Paris-Rouen Trial had been designated as just that, not as a race, it was clear a new sport had been born. Carl Benz wanted none of such nonsense, partly because his little car was not as powerful as the Daimler-engined Peugeots and Panhards, partly because his only thought of speed now was building his automobiles fast enough for a rapidly growing clientele. In July, 1894, the Austrian industrialist Theodor von Liebieg had driven one of the first Benz Victorias from Reichenberg in Bohemia by way of Mannheim and Gondorf on the Moselle all the way to Rheims and back. This was the first three-country motoring tour in history and totaled over 1,000 miles, which Benz maintained was far better proof of a car's performance than the 78-

mile romp to Rouen.

But the following year the enterprising Count de Dion decided France should hold an automobile event of 732 miles, the distance from Paris to Bordeaux and back. The straight, tree-lined Route Nationale linking the two cities was a splendid road. So far as de Dion was concerned, the jury system of the previous year, with prizes for safety, reliability, handling and economy, should be dispensed with entirely: Paris-Bordeaux-Paris should be a speed event pure and simple. Pierre Giffard was agreeable; his newspaper was not. Paris-Rouen had demonstrated that these new automobiles were capable of as much as 20 mph and the thought of a couple of dozen of them careening toward Bordeaux at such speeds was too much. If an accident occurred, if anyone was killed, competing newspapers would have a field day. *Le Petit Journal* declined participation.

The Count, of course, was not without his own resources, and many wealthy friends wanted to be involved, too. Contributions totaling nearly 70,000 francs arrived, largely courtesy of the French sporting aristocracy but with a smattering from other sources, including two Americans who spent a good deal of time in Paris: William K. Vanderbilt and James Gordon Bennett. To stage the event, an organization was needed. The committee assembled for that purpose included the Baron de Zuylen de Nyevelt (who had seconded de Dion's idea the moment he heard it), the Marquis de Chasseloup-Laubat, Armand Peugeot, Emile Levassor, Léon Serpollet, Emile Roger, Pierre Giffard and Paul Meyan, a reporter for the daily *Le Figaro*. From this committee was born the Automobile Club de France, which became the model for all other auto clubs around the world.

At nine in the morning of June 11, at the Place de l'Etoile in the shadow of the Arc de Triomphe, 22 cars assembled; six steamers, a six-seater electric from Charles Jeanteaud of Limoges, and 15 gasoline-driven vehicles. Of these, four were Peugeots and four were Panhards, all with the latest Daimler engine, and two were Benzes entered by Roger. For one of these Carl Benz had selected the co-drivers: Fritz Held, the Benz distributor in Mannheim, and Hans Thum, who had driven the Baden Minister of the Interior during the rules-of-the-road contretemps. Benz himself remained opposed to competition, but thought that if his own people from Mannheim were on hand the press would be reminded whose car the Benz was.

At the start Count de Dion, this time driving a proper steamer, went into the lead, but a shaft broke at Vouvray, and he had to drop out. As did the majority of competitors in this grueling event: only nine of the 22 starters got back to Paris. The last to

Carl Benz and his daughter Clara in the first Benz four-wheeler, the Victoria of 1893. This was Benz's favorite car, and he continued driving it well into the new century.

The Benz factory, Mannheim, 1894. Company workers numbered nearly 250. Business was booming. By now more than 1000 stationary engines had been produced, and future output was scheduled at 200 units annually. The 69 Benz cars built in 1894 were well in excess of the entire automobile population of the United States. Production of motorboats (based on Carl Benz's 1888 patent) had begun, and commercial vehicles were next on the agenda.

(Top) The Benzes and friends on an outing to Worms, 1895. Flanking Carl and Bertha in the Victoria are two Benz Velos, the world's first quantity-produced car. (Center) An outing in 1894 with Victorias, Carl Benz standing hand on hip, his customer and friend Theodor von Liebieg in the car at right. (Above, left) Benz in the courtyard of his factory that year with the Velo and children Richard, Thilde, Ellen, Clara and Eugen. (Above, right) Benz workers and friends enjoying beer and a game of cards after a Sunday test drive in 1895. Fritz Held is third from the left. Richard Benz and Fritz Erle are on the far right.

arrive, after 90 hours, was Amédée Bollée's omnibus *La Nouvelle*, the only steam-powered vehicle to finish. Both Benzes made it, the Held-Thum car placing fifth. All the other finishers were Panhards and Peugeots, the winner among them being the car driven by Levassor, which arrived in 48 hours, 48 minutes, nearly six hours ahead of the second-place Peugeot.

Levassor had driven the entire distance himself. That had not been his plan, but his pace from the start was so quick, even after night fell and the only light was from his flickering oil lamps, that he arrived in Ruffec at 3:30 A.M., hours ahead of schedule, to find his relief driver fast asleep. Rather than lose time waking him, Levassor drove ahead to Bordeaux and turned around for the return trip, resolutely refusing to turn over the wheel to his relief lest the man be unable to maintain the lead he had built up. Levassor's effort remains one of the epic drives in the history of the sport, yet though he won, he did not get first prize. The only stipulation for winning the race, in addition to finishing first, was that the car seat more than two persons. The organizing committee was wary about public reaction to a vehicle built only for racing purposes, and apparently concluded that if a car had more than two seats no one would think it was a race car. Since Levassor had known this beforehand, it probably bothered him little. He received 12,600 francs, and the four-seater Peugeot that finished third got the 31,500-franc first prize.

There were three winners in the automobile contest held in Chicago in November 1895. One was a Benz. One was a Duryea. The third was the cause of American automobilism.

In 1893 Congress had granted the Department of Agriculture an appropriation of $10,000 to collect data proving how abysmal American roads were—perhaps a superfluous effort, but at least a step in the right direction.* Herman H. Kohlsaat, the publisher of the *Chicago Times-Herald*, took a bigger one in July 1895, when his newspaper announced its sponsorship of a motor vehicle contest offering $5,000 in prizes. The idea came from science reporter Frederick U. ("Grizzly") Adams, who had read accounts of Paris-Rouen and was aware of the plans for Paris-Bordeaux-Paris. It was endorsed by Kohlsaat, who thought the contest would be good for circulation so long as it didn't turn into a race. "That the horseless carriage has 'arrived' is beyond question but its availability to American roads is looked upon with scepticism," the newspaper editorialized on July 14. ". . . The horseless carriage will confer an incalculable benefit upon mankind if it shall hasten their construction . . ." This represented an interesting reversal. In Europe good roads, particularly in France, accelerated the acceptance of the automobile;

*The first road census a decade later revealed that only seven percent of the nation's highways were "improved," which meant surfaced at all—with stones, gravel, sand, shells, or planking.

Emile Roger and the Benz Vis-a-Vis prior to the start of the Paris-Rouen in 1894. Roger finished the 78.75-mile trial in 10 hours 1 minute for a 7.9 mph average.

in America the automobile would advance the cause of good roads.

Word of the *Times-Herald* event spread, and entries poured in, nearly 100 of them. On August 2 William Steinway, who just the year before had been negotiating with William McKinley, the Governor of Ohio, about buying Daimler streetcars to provide motor transport for the city of Cleveland, wrote excitedly in his diary, "Daimler Motor Company overrun with applicants for horseless carriages."* Probably most of these applicants were American sportsmen who wanted a car to enter the contest. Since his base of operation was now the garden hall of the Hotel Hermann, Gottlieb Daimler could not possibly deliver. The *Times-Herald* had announced the event in July, and it was to take place in November. Kohlsaat received letters from many would-be inventors saying that it wasn't easy to build a motor vehicle in four months, and also a number from people asking for money to do it.

The contest announcement found Emile Roger in London tending to Benz sales. Believing the event open to American-made entries only, he was unhurriedly making plans for a trip to the New York office when he learned foreign cars would be accepted. That spurred him to move quickly. The number of Benzes he had thus far sold in the United States is uncertain, but his sales did include cars to the De La Vergne Refrigerating Company of New York City and the Hieronymus Mueller Company, which manufactured brass goods in Decatur, Illinois. Roger brought three Benzes with him this time, one each for Macy's, Gimbel's and Hilton, Hughes & Company (the predecessor of Wanamaker's)—the department stores having ordered them to test motorized delivery service.

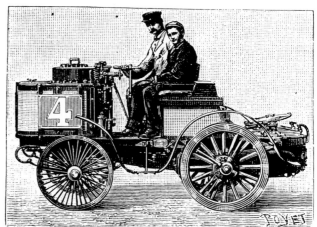

*Steinway's diary entry indicates another conundrum facing the automobile before the turn of the century: what to call it. "Horseless carriage," which it literally was, was unwieldy. So was "motor vehicle." The *Times-Herald*, soon after revealing its forthcoming road competition, announced another contest: a $500 prize for the best single world to describe a carriage which did not require a horse. The winning entry, submitted by G. F. Shaver of the Public Telephone Company of New York, was "motorcycle." Its vogue was short-lived. So were such other coinages as autobain, petrocar, viamote — and, fortunately, motorig, mocle and mobe. By the turn of the century the French word "automobile" had come into general use, with "car" soon following as a more familiar designation.

Contemporary French line engravings of 1894 Paris–Rouen competitors. Fastest of the steamers was Count de Dion's No. 4; he drove with partner Georges Bouton and pulled behind him a carriage (not shown) carrying three of his aristocratic friends. Fastest of the gasoline cars were the Daimler-engined Peugeots and Panhards. Among the former were Georges Lemaître's No. 65 and Peugeot engineer Michaud's No. 30. Panhard engineer Mayade drove No. 64, one of four company entries; Levassor himself was on No. 15. Smallest of the cars was Emile Roger's No. 85 Benz, which trailed all the Daimler-engined entries but was faster than seven of the steamers — a performance which earned Roger fifth prize and 500 francs. M.J. Scotte on the No. 10 steamer of his own design was awarded a consolation prize of 500 francs for "the most deserving car of those which failed to reach Rouen." The first prize of 5000 francs was shared by Peugeot and Panhard & Levassor. Second prize and 2000 francs went to Count de Dion.

Roger was a showman. He had a sense of the theatrical and a promoter's awareness of what made news that the dignified Steinway lacked. No sooner had Roger set foot in New York than he arranged to have two local lady reporters taken for a Benz ride. Grace Spencer of the *New York Recorder* betrayed a winsome mechanical naiveté when she commented that apparently all one had to do "was to look at the lever and the thing started . . . all as smooth as velvet. . . . We had reached [Washington Arch] . . . and I directed him to turn into Fifth Avenue. We met people in carriages, bicycles and pedestrians who all strained to look at us. Women seized each other, regardless of puffed sleeves for once, exclaiming, 'Good gracious Mary, do look!' We were decidedly the centre of attention."

As the contest date approached only a half-dozen vehicles were on hand in Chicago, and most of them were not ready. Reluctantly, because he worried about winter setting in, Kohlsaat advanced the contest date to Thanksgiving Day, November 28. But to avoid the jeers of competing newspapers, a consolation event was arranged for November 2: $500 for the best run from Chicago to Waukegan and back. Only two accepted the challenge: the Duryea brothers of Massachusetts, with a gasoline automobile they had built after reading about Benz's car in *Scientific American*, and Oscar B. Mueller in his father Hieronymus' Benz, which had been prepared in their factory in Decatur. Frank Duryea drove into a ditch to avoid a horsecart. The Mueller Benz won. This was, therefore, the first motor sports contest in America, a year before Henry Ford built his quadricycle—which is still, according to American popular misconception, the world's first car.

As Thanksgiving approached, more contest entries arrived in Chicago. De La Vergne shipped in its Benz. Roger talked R. H. Macy and Company into entering the contest, too, though he overdid it by suggesting to Macy's bicycle department manager, Frank McPherson, that the car be driven to Chicago. McPherson, whose motoring background thus far consisted of a few runs in the Benz to learn about its operation, agreed, thinking what good publicity it would be for the store. More than a thousand people

In early June of 1895, colorful posters were tacked up all over Paris to advertise two events: the Paris-Bordeaux-Paris race and the world's first automobile show. Though exhibition of the cars before and after the speed contest was the idea of the race organizers, the car builders found it superb promotion and cheerfully submitted to picture-taking and ceremonial parading. Two Benzes were on hand; Hans Thum and Fritz Held represented the factory. French distributor Emile Roger drove Benz No. 13 and finished seventh to Thum-Held's fifth.

gathered in front of Macy's at noon on November 15 to cheer McPherson and Jeremiah O'Connor, another Macy's employee, on their journey. Given the fact that the drivers were inexperienced, they did rather well, getting as far as Schenectady before a snowstorm obliterated the roads and indicated the wisdom of taking the train the rest of the way.

On November 25 another snowstorm, 12 heavy, wet inches, had fallen in Chicago. The promoters said the show must go on. The participants agreed: the three Benz entrants, the Duryea brothers, and Henry Morris and Pedro Salom of Philadelphia and Harold Sturges of Chicago, who were to drive electric cars. Because of the conditions, the time limit for the 55-mile route from Jackson Park to Evanston and back was waived; simply getting back would be considered sufficient evidence of the car's performance.

The contest began at 8:55 A.M. Neither of the electrics was expected to last the distance and they did not, both giving up by Lincoln Park, their batteries and their drivers exhausted. Fred Haas, in the De La Vergne Benz, fought a snowdrift in Washington Park and lost. Early on, the Macy entry had slid on the icy streetcar tracks in the city and crashed into the back of an Adams Street horsecar, fortunately with no discernible damage to the Benz. McPherson and O'Connor carried on, picking up a passenger, one Everett E. Ettinger, who jumped off at his home to fetch some Thanksgiving turkey for the crew. At the turnaround point in Evanston, the car slid into a sled but continued on to Douglas Park before something needed fixing. Neither McPherson nor O'Connor could figure out what that was, so Ettinger rode a streetcar and the elevated back to the starting line to get Roger, who could not be found. Two hours and another streetcar-and-elevated ride later, Ettinger was back in Douglas Park suggesting to the shivering Benz drivers that they come home with him — an invitation they readily accepted. This left only the Mueller Benz and the Duryea struggling on, now 10 hours into the event. At this point, there were two people in the Benz, Oscar Mueller and Charles King; a third passenger, felled by exposure, had been taken by sled to the hospital near Riverview Park. Mueller and King overcame the icy road conditions

somewhat by wrapping the Benz's tires in twine and throwing sand on the belt drive, but there was little they could do to protect themselves from the cold. And they were hungry, having had nothing to eat since breakfast. About eight that evening, Mueller fainted at the wheel. King managed to stop the car and, aware that the rules stipulated the starting driver must be in the car at the finish, moved Mueller to the passenger seat, grabbed the tiller and drove on, steering with one arm, holding on to the unconscious Mueller with the other, and arriving one hour later at Jackson Park only to find Duryea had got there first. A handful of spectators stood in the bitter night to witness his arrival.*

Neither Gottlieb Daimler nor Carl Benz had been present in Chicago for the *Times-Herald* event. Benz was in Mannheim making his cars; Daimler and Maybach were in Cannstatt making up with Duttenhofer and Lorenz and returning to the fold of the Daimler-Motoren-Gesellschaft. That was inevitable. In the half decade since Daimler and Maybach had departed for the Hotel Hermann their shop had become, as Baudry de Saunier said then, "the true Mecca of all the most progressive *chauffeurs.*" From all over the Continent they came, many in motor wagons of their own construction, to seek the advice of the now celebrated German engineers—a parade of automobilists that helped convince Duttenhofer and Lorenz that Daimler's ideas were not so utopian after all. As for Daimler and Maybach, although experiment and development had been their passion before, they were now eager to get into production. Panhard and Peugeot were building cars with Daimler engines; Carl Benz was building his own cars as fast as he could. It was time they did the same.

Both Daimler and the company that bore his name sought a reconciliation, though ill feelings remained. Duttenhofer and Lorenz had been hard in their dealings with Daimler—but Daimler was often difficult to deal with. He had not been forced to sign the contract

---

*The Duryeas' visit to a blacksmith shop to repair its steering gear was a rules violation which could have resulted in disqualification. National pride was among the reasons it did not. And by the time the *Times-Herald* race was over, everybody involved was probably too exhausted to think of anything other than getting out of the cold. The Duryea won $2,000, the Mueller Benz $1,500.

Chicago Times-Herald, 1895. Posing before the start were Oscar Mueller with black-hatted contest officials in the Mueller Benz (top, left) and Jerry O'Connor at the tiller of the Macy Benz (top, right). Shown at the start (above) are the No. 25 Sturges Electric, No. 5 Duryea and No. 7 De La Vergne Benz. At the Rush Street Bridge (center), helping hands assisted the Sturges. Strictly speaking being pushed was a rules violation, though since most cars had to be extricated from snowbanks occasionally, it was overlooked. The Duryea's winning speed was 5.05 mph.

and, given his earlier negotiations over employment with Deutz, it was curious that he would have put his signature to a deal that was plainly not in his favor. Duttenhofer and Lorenz, better businessmen, were able to draw up the document in terms that favored them. But without Daimler they had problems. The company's losses after his withdrawal to the Hotel Hermann were higher than the gains during the first two years Daimler-Motoren-Gesellschaft had been in business. Each side had underestimated the other.

A catalyst was needed to bring them together, and Frederick R. Simms provided it. A mechancial engineer from a respected Warwickshire family, Simms had met Daimler in 1890 at an engineering exhibition in Bremen and purchased the Daimler patent rights for the British Empire the following year. Though the Red Flag Act proved a hindrance at first, Simms joined like-minded British motoring enthusiasts in lobbying for new legislation, and in 1893 started a small private company to promote Daimler products as soon as the laws were changed.

From his correspondence with Daimler, Simms realized that for the patents to be of maximum value, Gottlieb Daimler himself was needed, since so many

technical advances had been made at the Hotel Hermann. On November 1, 1895, with Simms mediating, the Daimler-Maybach and Daimler-Motoren-Gesellschaft reconciliation was effected. "We are in A-1 condition," reported the DMG business manager, Gustav Vischer. Simms became a member of the board of directors of Daimler-Motoren-Gesellschaft and Gottlieb Daimler became a board member of the Daimler Motor Company Ltd. of Coventry, Warwickshire.

In the late spring of 1896, the Imperial Institute of London staged an automobile show, inviting members of Parliament and influential Londoners to stop by and ride in a motorcar to observe how safe it was. Among those accepting the Institute's offer was the Prince of Wales, the future King Edward VII, who on May 14 rode in a Daimler with Simms and declared himself highly pleased with the "novel experience"—though, since he was a horse lover, he hoped the motor vehicle would not entirely supersede equine travel. In November, following the enactment of legislation favorable to automobiles, a triumphant procession of cars motored from London to Brighton in the "Emancipation Run" that is reenacted annually to this

Stationary engines were what DMG emphasized in 1893, as this factory photo indicates. In March that year, after quarreling with partners Duttenhofer and Lorenz, Gottlieb Daimler left for the Hotel Hermann to continue vehicle development with Maybach.

Daimler taxi, 1896 (center, left); omnibuses, 1898 (above); 2-ton truck, 1899 (center, right); first bus exported to England, 1899 (top). climbing hills and a sedentary pace were early problems, though the English bus proved capable of a 12 per cent grade and 10 mph. Otto Salzer raced a Daimler truck against steamers in England in 1899. "It was difficult because of the iron tires," he recalled. "When the roads were wet I . . . had to hammer screws into the tires to get traction." He won the event. His prize: an engraved silver cigarette case.

Benz preceded Daimler with a bus in 1895, though it balked at hills and the bus service was soon discontinued. But the Benz car, with 1200 built by January 1898, was the world's best seller. Advertising stressed export and competition success. South Africa's first car, an 1896 Velo, is seen center, right; above, Fritz Held and Hans Thum are shown after winning a Frankfurt to Cologne race for Benz in 1899.

Founder of the Daimler Motor Syndicate in 1893, Frederick R. Simms (top, left) invited London newspaper reporters to lunch at the Crystal Palace and a demonstration of the first Daimler imported into England in December 1895 (center, right). At the Imperial Institute in May 1896, the Prince of Wales (top, right, with Simms' associate, the Hon. Evelyn Ellis, behind the tiller) was given his first ride in an automobile. In November more than a dozen cars — most of them Benzes, Daimlers or Daimler-engined Panhards — participated in the Emancipation Run (above).

day. Frederick Simms and Gottlieb Daimler drove together in a Daimler.

Once back within the DMG fold, Daimler and Maybach pushed production with vigor. Two dozen Daimler cars were built by the end of 1895, truck production began the following year, and DMG put itself into the taxi business . . . with mixed results. In Munich police authorities limited the number of cars allowed on the streets to 25, believing more would create excessive noise and traffic jams. The taxi stand that Adolf Daimler set up in Stuttgart, where he was a student at the technical college, was more successful. His drivers, sporting uniforms complete with top hats, enjoyed a lively trade in what might best be described as a nineteenth-century equivalent of a pub crawl, their passengers inviting them into every *gasthaus* they visited just to prove they had been driven to the place. Adolf Daimler made a tidy profit with his Stuttgart taxi service, and his drivers enjoyed a good many free beers.

Proving the automobile's superiority over the horse for other than an evening of fun was the reason behind DMG's dispatch of a mechanic, Otto Salzer, to Austria to drive a Daimler taxi against horse-drawn carriages in an eight-day tour from Vienna. By the fourth day, all the horses had gone lame and Salzer was the easy winner. But it had not been a easy run. "The worst part of this trip was the gas situation," Salzer later remembered. "Gas was sold in drugstores and pharmacies and you had to be glad if they would sell you five liters at a time. Of course we had to be our own repairmen. We brought many spare parts and tools with us. We could never count on any help from strangers because especially the farm population considered the automobile to be the devil itself. You could only pass somebody in those days with the help of your fists, and a big mouth."

At home, Gottlieb Daimler's heart condition had worsened. Since 1896 his doctors had confined him to bed for extended periods, warning that any exertion might be fatal. In August that year Steinway joined the Cologne Men's Singing Society to honor Daimler (who had been a member during his Deutz days) with a serenade early one morning. Daimler was asleep at the time, but quickly donned a suit jacket over his nightshirt, put on his silk hat, and thanked the serenaders from his window. That was the last time Daimler saw Steinway, who died the following November in New York City. And in Paris the following April Levassor collapsed over his drawing board. On the day that Levassor died, Lina Daimler gave birth to a daughter, whom Gottlieb

British Daimler, 1900. Although Gottlieb Daimler's patents were the reason it was founded, the English Daimler company pursued an independent course early on. After importing the German cars, the company began building its own.

named Emilie. Two friends who had encouraged his efforts from the beginning were gone.

The "indescribably wonderful" automotive age that Gottlieb Daimler had forecast 10 years earlier was about to become a reality. Though the motor vehicle was still an oddity, automobile fever was catching on everywhere. In 1896 *Harper's Weekly* called the *Chicago Times-Herald* contest the "signal event in the interest of our automobilism." That summer William Jennings Bryan barnstormed Decatur, Illinois, in the Mueller Benz during his presidential campaign against William McKinley. About the same time, in Michigan, *Times-Herald* hero Charles King finished *his* first automobile; bicycling behind him during his test run in Detroit was Henry Ford. In Massachusetts, the Duryeas had begun manufacture.

In England, with favorable legislation at last enacted, British automobile builders redoubled their efforts. Though Daimler in Coventry imported the Cannstatt cars for several years, the company began producing its own automobiles in 1898. By the turn of the century, Peugeot and Panhard & Levassor ended their Daimler licensing agreement and commenced building their own engines. The automobile industry was on its way to becoming international—and on the top rung of the international ladder was the man in Mannheim.

By the end of 1899, Carl Benz had built 2,000 cars and was the world's largest automobile maker. The death of Emile Roger in Paris in 1897 had put a temporary crimp in the export sales, but Julius Ganss had quickly taken over the program. Of the 603 Benzes built in 1900, 341 were sold outside Ger-

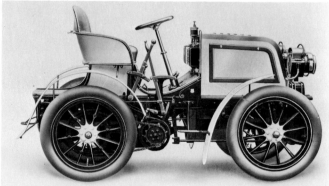

The first front-engined Daimler was the 4 hp two-cylinder Phoenix produced in 1897 (above, left). In 1899 a 6 hp Phoenix was delivered to Kaiser Wilhelm's War Ministry in Berlin (top). A four-cylinder racing version of the Phoenix (above, right) was Daimler's most powerful car.

many. Benz cars were in use all over the world. A Benz was the first automobile in South Africa; in Australia it was the first to climb the mountains of New South Wales; there were three Benzes in India, two in Singapore, one in Java. In Germany, William Esswein had two of the Mannheim cars—one fair-weather without a top, one foul-weather with—which he had been using daily since 1894 to commute to his job as director of the Bavarian railroads. How much of the abuse endemic to automobile ownership Esswein endured has not been recorded, but another Benz owner offered some proposals to counteract the work-of-the-devil reputation the automobile suffered in many quarters. "Much can . . . be done by taking friends out for rides, and explaining the working of the car to them, and the entire absence of danger," this owner wrote. "I also find it a good plan to give policemen when they are making their rounds a lift now and then. They seem to take great interest in the vehicle, and it gives them an opportunity of seeing how much faster a car appears to be going to what it actually is."

By now Carl Benz was in the commercial field as well—after a false start. In 1895, having built his first truck, Benz decided that the best way to demonstrate it was to transport something. He had a friend who owned a store. Without a word to this merchant, Benz sent his truck to pick up a consignment at the railway station. But his friend refused to accept delivery; the shipment was sacks of oats, and he feared coachmen would no longer buy from him if they knew their horse feed was delivered by motor vehicle. Such resistance was gradually broken down. Within a few years a large London department store, W. Whiteley, had a fleet of delivery trucks from Mannheim. The store had previously stabled 350 horses, and discovered that one Benz could replace three of them.

Not all Benz commercial ventures were successful. A bus line between Siegen, Netphen and Deuz did not work out principally because the large vehicles could not climb hills. But the general prospect in Mannheim was rosy. Completion of the company's 1000th stationary engine had been celebrated in 1893; sales were about 200 units annually thereafter. Production of motorboats had begun; and a pool had even been installed in the factory to test them. Ganss was the real marketing leader of Benz & Cie. by now. Truck production had been his idea, and his untiring efforts saw to it that Benz was represented throughout Europe and that inroads were made in Argentina, Mexico, South Africa and Singapore. Ganss liked big sales, and in 1899 managed to sell 200 cars in both Great Britain and France. August Horch, who was working for the company at the time, recalled that such mass orders alarmed Carl Benz because he feared quality might suffer. But Benz & Cie. was big business now. By 1899 its capitalization was 3.25 million marks.

In Cannstatt, even though their company was in full production, Daimler and Maybach had hardly changed their own routine, although Daimler's poor health prevented him from spending as much time as he used to in the experimental department. He had mellowed a great deal in his later years: Papa Daimler, he was called now. Drives into the countryside were not considered stressful for him, and he took many of those. They were "working" tours, of course; one cannot imagine Gottlieb Daimler taking anything else. DMG had already commenced bus production—which during this period was not much more successful than Benz's similar venture—and Daimler would occasionally invite a bus-load of workers to join him on Sunday jaunts to his birthplace in Schorndorf. Mid-week trips were usually taken to test a new device—to drive it until it broke and then find out why. Daimler would meet the team for the day's expedition early in the morning. "His first question was always, 'Have you had breakfast?' If this was not the case, you had to go to the kitchen and eat. Only then could one leave," Otto Salzer remembered. "We usually drove for half a day, and these tours were always extremely eventful. . . . A lot of time was spent with repairs, but we also always had plenty of time to eat." A longer tour through the Tyrol was undertaken during the summer of 1898 to test the new Bosch ignition. Otto Salzer again: "Clean the ignition, set the timing, make sure the brakes were okay. We were never bored in the evenings. Gottlieb Daimler would come and watch me work for awhile, he always made sure that we didn't work too late, and we would sit and discuss the day's events and plans for the next day while sipping a few wines."

Daimler made his last excursion in 1899, when he collapsed and fell from the car. His motoring days were nearly over, but his confrontations with Duttenhofer and Lorenz were not. In 1897 they had founded Motorfahrzeug-und Motorenfabrik Berlin AG in the Marienfelde quarter of the capital city. By now it was building Daimler engines and cars in direct competition with Cannstatt—yet another attempt to lessen Daimler's influence in the company which bore his name. But he was too ill to fight back. The letter objecting to the Berlin manufacture was signed by Vischer and Maybach.

During the late fall of 1899, Kaiser Wilhelm II asked to see examples of all Daimler-Motoren-Gesellschaft vehicles. At the factory Adolf Daimler, just graduated from college, was in charge of mounting the expedition, an enterprise that required several months. His father was gravely ill now, confined to bed. Adolf gathered 12 different models—cars, trucks, buses—and before sending them on the road to Potsdam, routed them past the Daimler home on Taubenstrasse. Gottlieb Daimler was propped up in a chair in front of his bedroom window, and watched his life's work pass by. Two weeks later, on March 6, 1900, he died.

There were many tributes. Wreaths arrived from the reigning monarchs of Europe and from the Czar of Russia. René Panhard and Mme. Levassor journeyed from France for the funeral. Gottlieb Daimler's pallbearers were his oldest employees, followed by his family and every worker in his factory.

Otto Salzer wept over the loss of "our honored and much loved Gottlieb Daimler."

In England, Frederick Simms paid respects to the friend he called "unquestionably the father of modern automobilism." And that he was.

---

*Conspicuous by his absence was Max Duttenhofer, who sent a telegram saying he had an important business engagement he could not break and asking Lorenz to lay a wreath in his name. The enmity between the Daimlers and Duttenhofer did not end with Gottlieb's death. Apparently Mme. Levassor had personally given Daimler monies derived from his French patents, probably during his Hotel Hermann days. According to the terms of the company contract, this was clearly illegal, and Duttenhofer threatened in a letter to his widow to "soil the name Daimler" by announcing that fact. The following year an agreement was reached: the Daimlers were allowed to keep the French patent money in exchange for not making further demands on the company, and their status in DMG henceforth was that of a minor stockholder. Although Duttenhofer's tactics frequently offended propriety, there is no doubt that he was largely responsible for transforming Gottlieb Daimler's work into a modern business enterprise—and that was a considerable achievement.

The four-cylinder Daimler was built because a client in Nice, Emil Jellinek, requested it. In 1899 Jellinek sold two such cars to the Baron Arthur de Rothschild. Baron Henri de Rothschild (above) bought his Phoenix direct from the factory.

CHAPTER THREE

THE ERA
OF MERCEDES

1 9 0 0 — 1 9 0 7

Thus the Mercedes
Comes, O she comes,
This astonishing device,
This amazing Mercedes
With Speed.
—WILLIAM ERNEST HENLEY,
A SONG OF SPEED

The first time he appeared at the factory in Cannstatt, he must have created a stir. Especially if he wore his pith helmet. He was an excitable little man with flowing muttonchops and a large moustache he was fond of twirling. He wore a pince-nez, as much affectation as for utility; it perched precariously on his short nose and, when he gesticulated or talked rapidly, it would fall down and bob on his chest. His name was Emil Jellinek. His effect on the fortunes of the Daimler-Motoren-Gesellschaft was monumental.

Jellinek was born in Leipzig in 1853, the son of a Bohemian rabbi. He was a problem child. Not knowing what to do with him when he came of age, his parents packed him off to the Austro-Hungarian embassy in Tetuan, the capital of Spanish Morocco. There he settled down somewhat, marrying into one of the city's prominent families. In Oran, Emil went into the tobacco trade and, when a position with a large French banking house became available, the Jellineks moved to Algiers, and eventually back to Austria. A variety of entrepreneurial pursuits followed, Jellinek becoming something of a merchant prince in Vienna and prospering sufficiently to be able to move to Nice, which he had wanted to do for

some time since he hated cold weather and loved high society. On the Côte d'Azur he continued to wear the helmet that was a nostalgic reminder of his North Africa days, and looked around for something interesting to do. The automotive age, he concluded, was interesting.

Jellinek's first cars were a de Dion tricycle and a little Benz four-wheeler, neither of which moved fast enough to muss his muttonchops. In 1896 he noticed a Daimler-Motoren-Gesellschaft ad in a German magazine and promptly went off to Cannstatt to order a car. When it arrived, he found it reliable but hardly exciting, as it was capable of little more than 15 mph. Since all the big races thus far had been won by cars powered by Daimler engines, Jellinek knew DMG could build a faster automobile. He wrote Cannstatt ordering four cars, provided they could do 25 mph. Speed was his first priority; if he ordered four he assumed the factory would have to pay attention. The factory did. Maybach and Gottlieb Daimler were reluctant, questioning the wisdom of installing high-horsepower engines in chassis not designed for them, which was often the way races were won in that era (and in many others). But the order was too good to turn down.

Of Nice the German poet Heinrich Heine wrote that he wished "to make a diadem for thine anointed brow...a court mantle for thy royal shoulders." It was in this most cosmopolitan of European resorts that Emil Jellinek introduced the new Mercedes. The view shown here is of the Quai Masséna at the turn of the century.

Jellinek and his pre-Mercedes transportation. The French Acatène bicycle, an 1895 purchase, was *le dernier cri* with shaft drive, free-wheeling, back-pedal brake and convenient foot rests on the front forks. Had his sons not pooh-poohed the bicycle as too unsporting for their cycling Arabesque Club, Jellinek would have acquired its distributorship. In 1897 Jellinek purchased his first Daimler, a 6 hp two-cylinder Double Phaeton, which he found reliable but too slow. Though his next Daimler was faster, Jellinek remained unsatisfied and in 1899 ordered a four-cylinder 28 hp model, which he delighted in showing off to friends in Semmering, Austria. Daimler mechanic Hermann Braun is seated beside him.

In 1899 more than 100 cars gathered in the Boulevard Gambetta for Nice Week. A 128-mile race to Castellane and back was planned, but some competitors tried the course beforehand and complained that the road from Levens to Vésubie was abominable and too narrow for passing. The organizers neutralized that stretch and, to dissuade the overzealous, required a minimum time of three hours to complete those 51 miles. Fernand Charron is shown at the starting line on the Promenade des Anglais with his Daimler-engined Panhard. He finished seventh at 20.9 mph. A Daimler-engined Peugeot won at 26 mph. Another Panhard finished second, two more Peugeots third and sixth.

When the quartet of 25-mph speedsters arrived, Jellinek tested one and wrote Cannstatt that it had not fallen to pieces and that he was still in one piece, too. Now his only problem was what to do with the three other cars, and that question answered itself: he would sell them. Enter the Rothschild factor.

Baron Arthur de Rothschild, who spent his winters on the Riviera, as did virtually everyone in Europe who was fashionable and could afford it, took pleasure in racing his Panhard up La Turbie hill every morning to "thrill the populace," in the words of Fred Moskovics.* One morning another automobile appeared as the Rothschild car was ascending the hill, the stranger sailing by without so much as a glance in the Panhard's direction. "This was unheard of and piqued the baron," Moskovics related. It also intrigued him. Rothschild found out that the car was a Daimler, and that the driver was "Herr Mercedes." Baron de Rothschild bought Herr Mercedes' car on the spot.

Two weeks later, having returned to Nice from Cannstatt, where he had gone for some tuning,

Jellinek waited for the Baron to appear with his new Daimler. When he did, Jellinek raced up the hill with his newer version and overtook Rothschild again. The Baron also bought that car on the spot. "The thought that anyone could drive up La Turbie faster than he could was unbearable to my uncle," Henri de Rothschild said later. Now the Baron had two Daimlers. He was about to get a third. On the top of the hill, after stashing the Baron's check in his pocket, Jellinek told Rothschild that an even faster car was being developed back at the factory, and did the Baron want one of those, too? Of course he did.

With Daimlers proving so easy to sell, Jellinek wrote Cannstatt again with an order for six, provided they had four-cylinder engines (the previous four had two-cylinder engines) mounted up front, as in the Daimler-engine Panhards. "The engine should be in front, because that was where the horse used to be,"

* Just graduated from college in the United States, Moskovics was working as a draftsman in Maybach's drawing office during this period. He was soon to return home to continue his automotive career and become famous as the man behind the Stutz of the mid-twenties.

Daimler factory foreman Wilhelm Bauer and mechanic Braun with the 28 hp Daimler-Phoenix before the start of La Turbie hill climb in 1900. At the first corner, Bauer swung wide and lost control. Braun jumped to safety, but Bauer crashed into the rocks and died the next day. The tragedy was the impetus which led to the building of the first Mercedes.

he wrote. "The engine replaces the horse, therefore it should be in front." Not a great deal of engineering acumen was revealed by that pronouncement, though Jellinek had fired an early salvo in a battle that went on for decades. In most Daimlers, the engine had been installed amidships; the front-engine car built a few years earlier had been a twin, and Daimler and Maybach worried now about the nose-heavy condition that would result if a four-cylinder engine was put in front. Still, Panhard had mounted a four up front, Jellinek was a good customer—so the cars were built.

When the first of them was delivered, Jellinek, as Herr Mercedes, entered it in Nice Automobile Week. In this period, the use of a pseudonym was not uncommon in auto racing. Some members of the nobility considered racing under one's own name *infra dig;* others preferred anonymity to avoid unpleasant scenes with parents who did not cotton to the idea of their heirs engaging in competition. Henri de Rothschild, for example, raced as Dr. Pascal, the same name he used for practicing as an oculist. Jellinek placed his Daimler well in the week's touristic events, though he won neither the race nor the hill climb. Fortunately, Baron de Rothschild's interest remained. "The earlier the car is delivered, the more bottles of brandy you will get," he wrote Jellinek. "I am sending you today two hares and two pheasants; I hope you like them."

What Emil Jellinek did not like was not winning. He wanted a car built specifically to win, so the factory built him one for that purpose. It was huge and unwieldy, and its debut during Nice Week in March 1900 was calamitous. At La Turbie, factory foreman Wilhelm Bauer lost control at the first corner and hit the outer wall. He died the next day.

Blame was passed around. Jellinek said the car was at fault; DMG said building it was his idea in the first place. Morale at the factory was low. Just a few days before, Gottlieb Daimler, the company's beloved Papa, had died, and now the factory had suffered its first racing fatality. Daimler-Motoren-Gesellschaft wanted no more of competition.

But Jellinek was relentless. "If you do not enter, the conclusion will be drawn that you are unable to enter," he contended. "It would be commercial suicide to abandon racing." What Daimler-Motoren-Gesellschaft needed, he was convinced, was a completely new car—a car that was lighter, lower, wider and longer, with an engine of 35 horsepower, seven more than the engine in the vehicle in which Bauer was killed. Such an automobile, Jellinek said, would not only win races, it would sell itself. In April, a month after Daimler's funeral, Jellinek said he would order 36 such cars in return for the exclusive sales agency for Austro-Hungary, France, Belgium and America. One further thing: the company might market the

Le Carnaval de Nice, c. 1901. The "Battle of Flowers" festival held annually in the resort city originated with the floral games of ancient Greece. Jellinek's float celebrated himself and the Mercedes.

vehicle as the New Daimler, but he wanted to use the name of his 11-year-old daughter, the same one he had adopted as a racing pseudonym. He wanted to call the cars Mercedes.

It was an offer Daimler-Motoren-Gesellschaft could not refuse. Thirty-six cars represented 550,000 marks, or about $130,000 in 1900 dollars. Max Duttenhofer was captivated by that fact. Wilhelm Maybach was challenged by the idea of the car. So was Paul Daimler. In 1899, when the Austrian Daimler company was founded in Vienna, Gottlieb Daimler's 30-year-old son had been scheduled to go there as chief engineer, but he was designing a small car at the time, and that kept him at DMG. Now the Jellinek proposal did the same. Maybach recognized in Paul Daimler's small car some elements of the automobile Jellinek proposed. Paul Daimler stayed on to assist him, but the new car was really Maybach's baby. It did not have an easy birth.

Jellinek had asked for delivery of the first example by October 15, 1900, just six months from the date of his order. That would have been possible if the car were merely a revision of an existing model, but the new Mercedes was a total redesign. Jellinek bombarded Cannstatt with letters and telegrams, alternately asking where the car was and offering further suggestions. Incredibly, Maybach did not crumble under the assault; somehow he was able to take every notion Jellinek had about an automotive beau ideal and make it workable. In the process, he probably designed the car five times over.

During this development period rumors were spread, most likely by Jellinek. In July a journalist from *Le Figaro*, Paul Meyan, who was also general secretary of the Automobile Club de France, visited the Cannstatt factory. "Every previous production is far surpassed by this new car," Meyan wrote. "These pretty rumors are not pretty rumors any longer but established facts. The French factories would do well to get busy extremely quickly in order that Daimler shall not set the fashion in Paris." The British *Autocar* picked up Meyan's warning: "The entire workmanship, design and performance of this car have struck terror in the heart of a capable critic like Paul Meyan."

On November 22 the car was finished and driven in Cannstatt. Modifications followed, as Jellinek fidgeted. On December 22 the car was shipped to Nice. Jellinek took it for a short drive and then shipped it to Paris. During testing there, it had transmission trouble and its engine seized. Sent to Toulouse by rail to compete in the Grand Prix at nearby Pau in February, the car was withdrawn soon after the start of the race; the clutch was slipping, and there was transmission trouble again.

But all the necessary adjustments had been com-

The first Mercedes, as raced at Nice in March 1901. Export planning began immediately, and by June the first sample car had arrived in New York City. *The Horseless Age* was astounded at the Mercedes' lowness and predicted that "for the average American roads the limit in this direction has been reached with this vehicle."

Mercédès Adrienne Manuela Ramona Jellinek, a happy child at age 11 in 1901. Illness and tragedy marked her adult life. Two marriages to barons were failures. In February 1929 she died in a small Vienna apartment.

rounding the city rose villas of breathtaking opulence. Each March Nice was host to a week of motor sports events: a long-distance race, this year of 244 miles; a one-mile sprint and a climb up La Turbie. Virtually everyone in residence for the season attended. Emil Jellinek was well aware of the importance of Nice Week, and so was Daimler. The factory sent Wilhelm Werner to drive the new car and Hermann Braun as mechanic; they were both skilled technicians, and Werner had also worked as chauffeur to Baron Alfred Springer of Vienna.

What happened at Nice Week was phenomenal, surpassing perhaps even Jellinek's brash expectations. The new car simply dominated the week's events, winning the distance race, the sprint and the hill climb. No other car was even close. By the end of the week, Mercedes was the talk of the town. And Jellinek did two things. First, he telegraphed the factory asking for 1,000 marks each for Werner and Braun in appreciation for their splendid performance, a request Max Duttenhofer was quick to accommodate. And then he replaced the racer's two seats with a gleaming white four-seater body and spent the next few days parading along the Promenade des Anglais so everyone could see that this race-winning car was really a *boulevardier* in disguise. And, of course, that

pleted in time for Nice Week in March. Nowhere was a good showing more significant for any new automobile. Nice was the *ville de saison* of the Continent, the favorite resort of the wealthy and the titled on both sides of the Atlantic. Grand hotels lined the Promenade des Anglais and in the gentle hills sur-

La Turbie, a village on the mountain above Nice and Monte Carlo, was famous only for its Roman ruins until 1897, when the annual hill climb began. At the summit Baron de Rothschild joined Wilhelm Werner on the winning Mercedes in March 1901. Werner's 18-minute-6.8-second climb was 43 seconds faster than the second-place car.

it could be bought . . . from Jellinek.

What made the new Mercedes so startling was that everything about it was innovative, from its pressed-steel frame to its gate-type four-speed transmission to its honeycomb radiator. This last remains a symbolic feature on Mercedes cars and is perhaps the only non-functional component of a contemporary Mercedes.

The car was built for performance, but instead of attaining it with a larger engine, which had been standard practice, Maybach had traveled the opposite route: the new T-head four-cylinder unit was lighter and smaller. The comparison was extraordinary. Whereas the previous Daimler had 28 hp and weighed nearly 4,400 pounds, the new Mercedes had 35 hp and weighed 2,200 pounds. The previous Daimler had a top speed of 37 mph, the new Mercedes 55. The previous Daimler had averaged 19.5 mph up La Turbie, the new Mercedes 31.9. And the new car did all this without, relatively speaking, a great deal of racket. Technical reporters on both sides of the Atlantic commented on the Mercedes' "noiseless running," its "wonderfully quiet running." *The Autocar* of Britain said, "We can compare it to nothing else but the ticking of a somewhat robust eight-day clock."

All this represented a completely new idea of what an automobile should be. The Mercedes was the first real car in history, and it was a masterpiece. In concept, automobiles have not changed since. That December, in his annual summary of the year's automotive happenings, Paul Meyan wrote, "We have entered the era of Mercedes."

The new Mercedes was not good news in Mannheim. By the end of 1901 Benz sales dropped to 385, from more than 600 in 1900. "The single-cylinder horizontal motor has been beaten in its greatest stronghold," a technical journalist wrote, "though whether it has entirely lost its position in the automobile industry can only be ascertained by future developments." This was true. The stronghold spoken of was Germany, of course, but in Michigan in 1901 Ransom Eli Olds began building his little curved-dash Oldsmobile, which soon became the best-selling car in the United States. As in Europe, America entered the horseless age largely by courtesy of a simple little car. The problem in Mannheim was that Carl Benz continued to believe *his* simple little car would sell indefinitely. His sons, Eugen and Richard, did not agree. Now in their twenties, they were

Fritz Held and his Benz after winning the 102-mile Mannheim-Pforzheim-Mannheim race in 1900. A personal friend of the Benz family, Held had been competing in motor sport since 1895 and was among the first gentleman race drivers on the Continent.

The 1903 Parsifal was Benz's answer to the Mercedes. Among its modern specifications was a two-cylinder vertical engine—the first for Benz—mounted in a shaft-drive chassis. Top speed was 37 mph. Because the company was so identified with outmoded belt-drive motor carriages, the new model was promoted in Europe with emphasis on the name Parsifal, not Benz. In America, where the curved-dash Oldsmobile remained the best-selling automobile, the Mead Cycle Company stressed the Benz name and the German company's position as the world's oldest automobile manufacturer. Marius Barbarou is shown above in the Benz race car he designed in 1903.

WET WEATHER EQUIPMENT

Automobiling and fashion. Ladies' hats featured heavy "goggled" veils, full-length dusters were standard garb for both sexes, rain aprons covered oneself and one's car, and driving gloves were worn regardless of the weather. For winter motoring, fur was *de rigueur*; Henri de Toulouse-Lautrec spoofed it in his 1898 lithograph *L'Automobiliste*.

anxious to travel faster than their father's cars could take them. In the Paris-Marseilles-Paris race of 1896, Eugen and his friend Fritz Erle (then a journeyman locksmith at Benz & Cie.) had followed behind the competing cars in a Benz. In 1899 Carl Benz allowed Richard to accompany Fritz Held in the Berlin-Leipzig, won by the 12-hp Benz at a 35.2-kph average. Carl Benz continued to believe that "a car which can attain a speed of more than 60 kph will soon rattle itself to pieces."

Now with the introduction of the Mercedes, the Benz sales director, Julius Ganss, began begging for a modern product. When Benz did not deliver, Ganss took matters into his own hands and asked Georg Diehl to design a car. A graduate of the technical college at Karlsruhe, Diehl had worked under Maybach at Daimler-Motoren-Gesellschaft before joining Benz, where he had been head of the drawing office since 1899. Carl Benz was now going on 60; Diehl

was 25 years his junior. Diehl designed a car with a vertical engine (Benz's were all horizontal) mounted in front (Benz's were under the seat) and employing cardan universal joint transmission (Benz's had belt drive). The car, completed in September 1902, was not a success. Carl Benz breathed a sigh of relief. Now he could return to building his cars just as before.

But Ganss did not give up easily. He called in Marius Barbarou, a French engineer about the same age as Diehl who had worked for Clément in Levallois-Perret and who arrived in Mannheim with a team of French designers. Although production cars were part of his assignment, Barbarou's principal task was the design of a 60-hp four-cylinder race car. The Mercedes was producing 60 horsepower by now, and Ganss believed in the promotional advantage of competition. At the same time he directed Diehl to continue his development work. So Benz &

"Herr Direktor Emil [sic] Mercedes" was the caption for this caricature of Jellinek which appeared in *Fliegende Blätter* (a German humor magazine like the English *Punch*). Jellinek attached the name "Mercedes" to many possessions, including his villa, yachts and boats — and, ultimately, to his own surname.

(Top, left) The fifth annual Salon de l'Automobile, 1902. The Paris show remained the social climax of the motoring season, though some complained that the growth in the automobile industry had overcrowded even the spacious Grand Palais. Both the German company and French distributor C.L. Charley were represented on the Mercedes stand. A 40 hp chassis dominated the exhibit and the several touring cars on display indicated, as one reporter said, that "no skill or expense had been spared to attain the height of luxurious comfort for the passengers." (Top, right) Daimler factory manager Balz driving Adolf Daimler and his wife in an 8/11 hp Mercedes, 1903. Balz's candor made him a journalists' favorite. When a *Car Illustrated* reporter visiting the plant suggested the Daimler company had "a smart lot of men," Balz replied, "Oh no, a smart lot are hard to find . . . but we try at least to get smart overseers." (Above) At the factory in 1903, with Wilhelm Maybach in the front passenger seat of the 18/22 hp Mercedes-Simplex.

Cie. had two separate design offices, each working frantically to produce new cars, with intense rivalry between them. Carl Benz, left out of all the competitive excitement, resigned from his company's board of directors on April 21, 1903.

Three weeks earlier at La Turbie, Mercedes took the first three places, while Barbarou's Benz failed to finish. In May, in the Paris-Madrid race, his Benz was almost the lightest car in the heavy car class and was well back in the field when the event was halted at Bordeaux. That Barbarou had held little hope for his entry was indicated by the fact that he had not even removed the car's headlight brackets. But then he squeezed his 60-hp engine into a Light Car Class racer and did much better. At Huy, Belgium, in June 1903, he achieved 74.0 mph over the flying kilometer, faster than the 72.1 of Baron de Caters, who was running in the Heavy Car Class. In European sprints Barbarou also finished well.

But in the competition in the Benz design offices, Diehl was victorious too. Whereas Barbarou had come out on top in chassis design, Diehl's new two- and four-cylinder engines were superior. A pooling of Diehl and Barbarou ideas resulted in the Parsifal production car, introduced late in 1903. Like the early Benzes, it enjoyed healthy overseas sales, being imported into the United States by the Mead Cycle Company, the sole agency in America for Benz during this period.

Despite the success of the Parsifal, the dual design office concept was not working, and something had to give: Barbarou. He left in May 1904, and returned to France to work for Delaunay-Belleville, a marine engine manufacturer about to enter the automotive field. Diehl was now in charge of all engineering and design. Fritz Erle, who had just received his degree in mechanical engineering, became head of the experimental department. But Ganss left and, with his exit, the prodigal returned: Carl Benz rejoined his company, though his work now was largely of a consulting nature, and the evidence suggests he was not consulted very often.

With the introduction of the Parsifal, the single-cylinder car was discontinued. That it was outmoded was obvious to all but the company's founder and a small band of his followers. Despite the new Benzes on the market, Carl Benz continued to motor around Mannheim in his little belt-drive car, and there were others equally as loyal elsewhere. When the British writer R. W. Buttemer suggested in 1904 that discussion of the belt-drive Benz was "somewhat an excursion in palaeontology," he was practically assaulted by the Benz fraternity. "You are very hard on the poor old Benz," one owner wrote, mentioning his 3½- and 4½-hp models, both of which "have a habit of doing their worth without trouble" and wondering how many cars would do as well after several years in service. In 1902 the Benz importer in England had driven a 4½-hp model 5,000 miles in 50 consecutive days save for Sundays: "Never once, from end to end of the route, did she falter or slacken, responding to every motion of her driver with perfect promptitude," reported Sir J. H. A. MacDonald, who had joined the ride for a while. As late as 1910 another 4½-hp Benz owner was still driving the car he had purchased in 1901 and pointed out the "multitude of sorrow" he had escaped by being true to his first love.

Others who graduated to more sophisticated automobiles rued the day they disposed of their Benz. Winthrop E. Scarritt, president of the Automobile Club of America, wrote in 1904: "Since I parted with [it], I have had 22 different automobiles, but I state a simple fact that all the 22 combined never furnished me the . . . mental excitement afforded by my Benz." One's first car is usually remembered fondly; Carl Benz's little one-lunger provided several thousand people with their first experience of driving on a road with something other than reins in their hands. Benz made his car work, and that was enough for him; it took people from one place to another, which was as much, he thought, as should be asked of any automobile.* "I like motoring because I have suffered for its sake," Rudyard Kipling wrote in 1904, referring to his own early driving adventures. Any fool might enjoy an invention when it was thoroughly perfected, Kipling noted, but "the men to reverence, to admire, to write odes and erect statues

---

*During the 1920s Henry Ford displayed the same obduracy when Ford Motor Company associates suggested America might be ready for a more modern car than the Model T.

to, are those Prometheuses and Ixions (maniacs, you used to call us) who chase the inchoate idea to fixity up and down the King's Highway with their red right shoulders to the wheel." Carl Benz had been the first man to do that. His place in history is secure.

But Benz's time was past. This was unquestionably the era of the Mercedes. By 1902 the name had been adopted and officially registered as a trademark by Daimler-Motoren-Gesellschaft, and in 1903 Emil Jellinek secured legal permission to add it to his surname. Now he was Emil Jellinek-Mercedes; his home in Nice was Villa Mercedes; one of his yachts was called *Mercedes-Mercedes*, another *Mercedes II*. Overkill was typical of the man.

As competing manufacturers sent their engineers to the drawing boards, Maybach refined the 1901 Mercedes into the 1902 Mercedes Simplex, even longer and lower, its engine putting out 40 horsepower with a deep, slow beat. In October 1902, Paul Meyan visited the Cannstatt works and gave his readers a preview of "the many ingenious devices" that would be offered on the new Mercedes to be introduced at the Salon de l'Automobile in the Grand Palais that December. The Paris Salon was the glittering highlight of the automobile year, and this year it was brighter than ever. Thousands of electric lamps were turned on at dusk to flood the exhibition area with light and produce a spectacle that many likened to a fairy-tale setting. Walking the glass-domed elegance of the Grand Palais were the wealthy and titled of several continents: Prince Arthur of Connaught, Lord Ashburton, Lady Sarah Wilson, the Baron de Zuylen, the Marquis de Chasseloup-Laubat, Baron Bleichroeder, the Baron and Baroness de Langdale, Baron de la Grange, the American millionaires Clarence Gray Dinsmore, Richard Croker and William K. Vanderbilt. And most of the Barons de Rothschild.

At the Mercedes stand, Wilhelm Maybach chatted with King Leopold of Belgium. The King already had a 40-horsepower Mercedes but wanted something faster. "Unless I can touch 130 kilometers an hour (about 80 mph), it is no use to me," he said. Maybach said his company could do it. Back at the factory another car was being built for Charles N. Schwab, who having convinced Andrew Carnegie and J. P. Morgan to consolidate as the United States Steel Corporation (of which he, Schwab, was now president), felt the need for something faster than the Mercedes he already owned. The order he placed with DMG was for a car capable of attaining 87 mph

Count Elliott Zborowski was an ardent fan of the Cannstatt cars. In January 1900 he purchased a 28 hp Daimler which he raced in numerous Continental events, here during Nice Week in March 1902. A few months later his first Mercedes was delivered, just in time for the road race from Paris to Vienna.

(Charlie Schwab was always precise); he would pay $6,000 for the vehicle itself and an extra $2,500 "if the car really will travel at the stipulated speed" (Charlie Schwab was also generous)

"This year . . . the cars on every side are palpably different," *The Car Illustrated* of Britain reported after visiting the Paris Salon, "for the simple reason that the French trade has plunged into wholesale imitations of the Mercedes car." An editorial in the American trade publication *The Automobile* cautioned: "To look upon the . . . Mercedes cult as a new vagary of fashion would be a blunder . . . it seems obvious that those French manufacturers who enjoyed celebrity would not have abdicated and renounced the forms, designs and construction details of their own famous machines unless confronted with something whose vital strength in the automobile market was superior to theirs." Commenting that the French cars remained the "masters among speed merchants," the magazine nonetheless concluded that "Mr. Maybach, of Cannstatt, across the Rhine, has led the way to a new epoch in automobile construction and has compelled the world to follow."

French cars continued to win the big races, which included Paris-Vienna, at least officially. But the success of the first Mercedes had dictated that the company's priorities be devoted to production. Fifteen cars a month was the output at first, and the factory was trying to raise it to 40. Property had been acquired in nearby Untertürkheim, a vineyard village along the Neckar, for construction of a new plant.

Early in the summer of 1902, Daimler-Motoren-Gesellschaft announced it would not compete in the Paris-Vienna race in late July. Emil Jellinek followed suit; he had already sold his allotted cars for 1903, so there was no reason to incur the expense. Because all the Mercedes produced since the beginning of 1902 had been exported to either England or America, *The Autocar* predicted no Mercedes at all would be in the event, Americans not wishing to travel to Europe

Though E.T. Stead insisted on a discount before buying a 40 hp Mercedes, Jellinek was happy to give the Englishman a good price because he invariably raced his cars and frequently won. Here Stead is seen in the paddock at Nice, following victory at La Turbie in 1902 with a 16-minute-37-second climb, a minute and a half faster than Werner's winning time in 1901.

for a single race and the English not likely to either, since King Edward's coronation was scheduled for the same time.

But there was at least one resident of England who would be competing with a Mercedes in the Paris-Vienna: Count Elliott Zborowski, owner of two magnificent estates at Melton Mowbray, whose midnight cross-country steeplechases had made him known throughout the countryside. He was not English, which meant foregoing the coronation would not be too distressing. And whether he was even noble is questionable, though apparently his family tree somehow included John Sobieski, the seventeenth-century King of Poland. Zborowski's immediate ancestors were American. By the time Elliott arrived the family was wealthy, with a Manhattan town house and a summer cottage in Newport. When Elliott Zborowski and his wife, John Jacob Astor's great-granddaughter, moved to England to settle at Melton Mowbray, he also bought a chateau in Nice and a suite in a Paris hotel. He was obviously Mercedes material.

He was also the fun-loving sort and thought it would be amusing to race his new Mercedes, purchased through Jellinek, in the Paris-Vienna. The new international scope of racing meant that it was becoming more complicated to organize. Switzerland, for example, was adamant that there would be no racing on its roads. So the first leg of the 615-mile event, from Paris to Belfort in eastern France, was to be a race. After that the cars would drive carefully through Switzerland and then begin racing again at Bregenz, Austria, for the run to Salzburg; the last leg would be Salzburg to Vienna. Zborowski would have won Paris-Vienna except that he drove a car the way he steeplechased: full bore for the distance. At the conclusion he was penalized a half-hour for exceeding the speed limit in Switzerland, and first place went to Henri Farman's Panhard—which rather upset the usually imperturbable Count; when they placed a laurel wreath around his neck he took it off, stuck it around his waist and stalked off. His frustration was shared by the Daimler factory, but they had some satisfaction too: Zborowski's Mercedes was the 40-hp model, the

winning Panhard was a 70-hp.

Across the Atlantic the Mercedes interests were being championed by William Kissam Vanderbilt, Jr., whose allegiance to the marque dated back to the days when it was called Daimler. Of all the rich young American automobilists of the period, none was more dedicated to the cause of the automobile than the Vanderbilt everyone called Willie K.

The Daimler Vanderbilt bought from Cannstatt in the late 1890s, nicknamed the "White Ghost," caused law enforcement officials no end of grief. Willie K. was a demon behind the wheel—a fact of which he was apparently very proud, considering all the clippings in his personal scrapbooks describing his various brushes with the police for speeding. The record does not indicate that he ever hit a pedestrian, but his Daimler did encounter a good many animals, for a reason: Willie K. usually handed the owner of the stricken beast his card and said he would pay the damages. "The Long Island farmer has been taught by his parents to 'do' a New Yorker whenever possible," a newspaper reported, "and the Vanderbilt automobile has offered a fine chance. The farmers have discovered that a horse that isn't worth over $6 for glue and fertilizer will bring from $65 to $100 when killed by the Vanderbilt auto." Whenever Vanderbilt and his Daimler approached the Manhattan end of the 34th Street ferry bound for his Long Island home, the news spread quickly. Animals were routinely shoved in the way of his car. Fights would break out over who should have the privilege of having his horse hit first, and several farmers who did not own animals found it profitable to buy disabled streetcar horses just to join in the venture. Newspapers estimated that it cost Willie K. $47.23 a mile to take pleasure trips on the island. The carnage ended when a couple of nearsighted speculators had their beasts struck by non-Vanderbilt vehicles; Willie K. grew suspicious and announced plans to "employ a claims agent to adjust losses."

By then, the Daimler "White Ghost" had become a legend on the East Coast. As soon as the new Mercedes was introduced, Willie K. bought one; he called it the "Red Devil." "The report that W. K.

Vanderbilt, Jr. has ordered a new and faster machine than the one with which he has terrorized Long Island and Eastern Massachusetts the past season raises the question where this venturesome young multi-millionaire intends to use so powerful a machine," wondered the conservative *Horseless Age* in February 1901. The answer was the same places and a few more.

Road conditions negated any city-to-city racing during this period. Competition was largely confined to climbs up Mount Washington in New Hampshire, runs along Ormond-Daytona Beach in Florida, and sprints on dirt tracks usually used for horse racing, like Aquidneck Park near Newport, Rhode Island, where on September 14, 1901, W. K. Vanderbilt and his wife entertained 100 of their closest friends for lunch and a day of fun on the track. There were events for trikes and two-wheelers, steamers and little electrics, in addition to gasoline cars. Willie K. won every race he entered with the "Red Devil," including the championship, the cup for which was presented by Mrs. Oliver Hazard Perry Belmont.

Then, doubtless to the vast relief of *The Horseless Age*, Willie K. and his Mercedes embarked for Europe. During Nice Week, 1902, he challenged his friend Baron Henri de Rothschild to a match race on the road near Albi. Both had 40-hp models, and Willie K. won. Then he did Monte Carlo to Paris in 14 hours, and after that Paris to Nice, in a romp that was interrupted by the police at Luc-en-Diois. Ironically, Willie K. for once was innocent of the speeding charges. The guilty car had preceded him, but it was Vanderbilt and his companions who were put up for the night to await trial, in accommodations not in the manner to which Willie K. was accustomed. About three in the morning, "finding it impossible to stand our suffering any longer," as he said later, Vanderbilt sneaked out to the barn and got his car. At a prearranged signal his companions dashed past the policemen on guard outside the house where they had been held and vaulted into the seats beside him. The getaway was easy because, in Willie K.'s words, "these 40 Mercedes were absolutely noiseless." But he didn't turn on the headlights until he was five kilometers down the road.

Like the bicycle, the automobile began as a rich man's toy. Before the turn of the century owning an automobile marked one as an eccentric; after 1900 it became a necessity for keeping up with the Astors (which wasn't easy, since Colonel Astor's garage housed 17 cars). Speed was the new elixir. To dash

Otto Hieronimus aboard the 60 hp Mercedes after he won La Turbie in a record-breaking 14 minutes 26 seconds in 1903. Hieronimus had worked in the Benz factory before becoming a Mercedes race driver. Standing next to his car's rear wheel is budding automobile engineer Ferdinand Porsche.

The race from Paris to Madrid in 1903, organized by the Automobile Club de France in cooperation with Alfonso XIII of Spain, was the tenth and last of the classic city-to-city races. As the crowds and cars gathered behind the gilded gates at Versailles on Saturday night, May 23rd, preparations were being completed for the special grandstands and magnificent reception which awaited participants at the finish line in the Spanish capital city. The start at Versailles began at 3:45 Sunday morning, with Mark Mayhew's Napier the 138th car to be dispatched.

Paris-Madrid was Camille Jenatzy's first Mercedes race. He started eighty-sixth, passed 16 cars in the first 17 minutes, and was third by Angoulême. Then engine trouble — diagnosed as a fly in the carburetor — dropped him back to eleventh.

around the countryside on one's motorcar was a new and heady experience. No one better expressed the general acceptance of the automobile than the English poet William Ernest Henley, author of *Invictus* ("I am the master of my fate, I am the captain of my soul") and, in the late Victorian era, an acceptable literary alternative to the decadence of Oscar Wilde. Henley's last poem, *A Song of Speed,* written in 1903, was about the automobile. It was not very good; the ailing poet called it "an effusion" before he died. But the very fact that he wrote it put society's stamp of approval on the automobile, and the further fact that it

was inspired by the Mercedes, which it specifically mentions, was telling. But a whole new culture was developing around the automobile. It was generally acknowledged, for example, that automobiling was good for you. "The easy jolting which occurs when a motorcar is driven at a fair speed over the highway conduces to a healthy agitation," said Sir Henry Thompson, "it 'acts on the liver,' to use a popular phrase, which means only that it aids the peristaltic movements of the bowels and promotes the good performance of their functions; thus accomplishing the good in this respect which arises from riding on horse-

Representing the Benz factory in the Paris-Madrid was Barbarou on the 40 hp race car he designed. He had averaged 39.8 mph and was officially classified forty-sixth when accidents halted the race at the halfway point in Bordeaux.

Three of the dozen Mercedes in the Paris-Madrid. Driving his own 60 hp car (No. 114) was famous American polo player Foxhall Keene. He was not among the finishers at Bordeaux. Baron de Caters (No. 27) was competing in one of the new 90 hp models. While chasing Charles Jarrott's De Dietrich and Marcel Renault's Renault, which were running abreast ahead of him, de Caters left the road and hit a tree, luckily with injuries only to his car and his dignity. Fixing the Mercedes required an hour and a half; de Caters was twenty-seventh at Bordeaux. The best Mercedes finish was by American amateur John B. Warden on his 60 hp car (No. 99), which averaged 57.7 mph and was accorded sixth place.

back." And motoring had its own etiquette: "Remember that if you whoop through a village at 30 miles an hour some Sunday morning in the summer time and meet a crowd of decent villagers going to church, the clouds of dust that you raise may spoil their Sunday clothes, fill their mouths with grit and their hearts with bitterness," warned the Honourable Filson Young.

Since virtually all cars were open, driving apparel was a matter of prime concern. "When driving at 20 miles an hour, the wind will actually pass through tweed overcoats and cloth garments; the air will be felt whistling round the ribs, and coats become distended behind like balloons," wrote Baron de Zuylen. "On the Continent [an overcoat] made of rough fur is worn, with the fur outside. . . . In addition to the heat-retaining qualities of the fur, such coats have the advantage of readily shooting off rain and of drying very quickly after a shower. They are provided with very high collars, which in cold weather are turned up, and almost surround the head." Another convenience for open motoring was marketed by Tiffany & Company in New York: a small device for protecting the ends of cigars and preventing the ashes from blowing in the smoker's eyes.

Plainly automobiling was here to stay. Lady Jeune mourned that at some future date "we shall sigh for the smooth glossy skin, the tender eye, the soft neigh that greeted us in the days when we fed our monsters with carrots and sugar." Lady Jeune was in the minority.

But automobiling in the early days did not mean getting into one's car and driving off. It demanded preparation; and the preparation demanded depended upon the car one drove. If it was a steamer, patience was a prerequisite. Firing up entailed heating a U-shaped steel pipe until it was red hot, inserting it in the burner and connecting it to a fuel valve. Raising steam took a good half hour. If one owned an electric, starting was easy, but getting there was slow: at the turn of the century, electrics could not travel much faster than a good horse and buggy, their cruising range between charges was only about 25 miles and charging stations were only in urban areas. There were home charging machines, but the nightly directive to "put the cat out and the car on charge" was seldom heard in the hinterlands; the electric was almost exclusively a city car, and a lady's one. Gasoline automobiles, though faster to start than steamers and faster on the road than electrics, had their foibles and problems. The filling station was not yet ubiquitous, the cars were more odiferous, and hand cranking to start them (the practical self-starter did not arrive until 1912) required muscle and, if there was a backfire, could break an arm.

James Gordon Bennett, Jr., among the most colorful American expatriates on the Continent. Said his managing editor Eric Hawkins, "For . . . years he enchanted Europe as publisher and playboy." The 1905 Gordon Bennett Cup is pictured.

U 94018

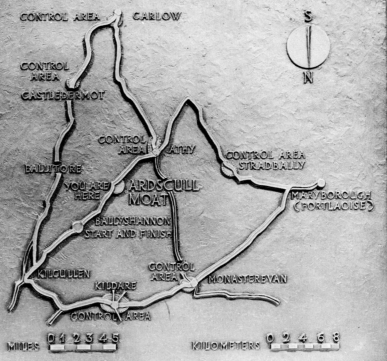

GORDON BENNETT COURSE

THE 1903 RACE WAS RUN OVER THE CIRCUIT SHOWN, WITH START AND FINISH AT BALLYSHANNON. THE TWO LOOPS WERE DRIVEN ALTERNATELY FOR SEVEN LAPS, BEGINNING WITH THE SHORTER AND ENDING WITH TWO LAPS OVER THE LONGER, FOR A TOTAL DISTANCE OF 327.5 MILES.

CONTROL AREA — CARLOW

CONTROL AREA
CASTLEDERMOT

CONTROL AREA — ATHY

CONTROL AREA
STRADBALLY

BALLITORE

YOU ARE HERE

ARDSCULL MOAT

BALLYSHANNON
START AND FINISH

MARYBOROUGH
(PORTLAOISE)

KILCULLEN

KILDARE

CONTROL AREA

MONASTEREVAN

CONTROL AREA

MILES 0 1 2 3 4 5

KILOMETERS 0 2 4 6 8

(Top, left) A prominent race driver since 1898, Camille Jenatzy was lured out of semi-retirement in 1903 after Jellinek offered Baron de Caters a Paris-Madrid factory drive on one of the new 90 hp Mercedes in return for de Caters' lending Jenatzy his personal 60 hp car to race in the same event. (Top, right) Wilhelm Werner and a 40 hp Mercedes with the car's owner, Clarence Gray Dinsmore, beside him. This photo was taken in 1902 following Semmering, which Werner won at 35 mph. Though Dinsmore occasionally competed in minor events himself, chauffeur Werner took the wheel for important races. He dominated Nice Week that year and won the international track race at Frankfurt as well. (Above) Daimler-Benz plaque commemorating the 1903 Gordon Bennett Cup race won by Jenatzy.

The gasoline-engine car was dominant in Europe simply because Daimler and Benz were there. In America at the turn of the century 40 percent of the 2,000-odd native-built cars were powered by steam—New England was a hotbed of steam-car enthusiasm—38 percent by electricity, and 22 percent by gasoline. Though the Stanleys built their steamers into the 1920s and a few electrics were produced for even longer than that, the American shift to the gasoline car began in 1901, when Ransom Olds started producing his curved dash Oldsmobile in Michigan. By 1903 Henry Ford, who earlier had focused his efforts on motor sport ("My company will kick about me following racing but they will get the advertising and I expect to make $ where I can't make ¢ at manufacturing"), was finally into production in Detroit. So was David Dunbar Buick, whose previous inventive efforts had been in bathtubs. Henry Martyn Leland had begun building his Cadillac, the Packard Motor Car Company had moved to town from its birthplace in Warren, Ohio, and the concentration of automobile activity began its slow but inexorable move to the area around Detroit.

At the turn of the century, New York City had recorded only one reckless driving fatality: a man struck down on Central Park West as he was getting off a trolley. Mrs. Hamilton Fish hit a pedestrian with her electric on Fifth Avenue, but he picked himself up and walked away—three times, as a matter of fact; in her excitement Mrs. Fish couldn't remember how to stop the car and ran into her victim twice more before she finally came to a halt. But there were still not enough cars on the road, either sedate non-threatening electrics or powerful gasoline runabouts, for the automobile to be a significant public peril.

It was in motor sport that speed was proving to be dangerous. At La Turbie in April 1903, the new 60-hp Mercedes made its debut and the result was a resounding victory, Mercedes cars finishing one-two-three. The fourth car, carrying Count Zborowski, didn't make it. Shortly after starting up the hill Zborowski, anxious to better the record of the three Mercedes drivers who had preceded him, failed to slow for a curve, crashed into the rocks and was killed instantly. Apparently the impeccably tailored Count had caught the stiff cuff of his sleeve in the hand throttle during the turn and was traveling too fast to correct.

Worse was to come. The following month the big country-to-country race was from Paris to Madrid.

Jenatzy is wished good luck by Baron de Caters before the 1903 Gordon Bennett. Fourth of the twelve entrants to be dispatched, Jenatzy executed what the press described as "the most clean and perfect start of the day." Several other entrants stalled their engines; another tried to get away with his hand brake on.

The Gordon Bennett, 1903. "The cars came scudding in towards Dublin, running evenly like pellets in the groove of the Naas Road," James Joyce wrote in his story "After the Race" (in *Dubliners*). This was not the case for all the entries, however. Foxhall Keene, who reportedly held the world's record for the number of joints dislocated in a sportsman's career, was fast but brutal and retired his No. 12 Mercedes early with a broken rear axle. Baron de Caters was a more circumspect driver; ten miles from the finish, when his No. 8 Mercedes retired, the Baron completed the circuit on a touring car "placidly smoking his pipe and looking the picture of contentment." Winner Jenatzy, in the No. 4 Mercedes, hit an unofficial 90 mph on one downhill stretch and commented afterwards that "I had never been so near heaven."

Like most monarchs, Alfonso XIII of Spain was a racing enthusiast and signed a decree allowing racing on Spanish roads. The event was planned in three stages: Versailles to Bordeaux, Bordeaux to Vitoria, Vitoria to Madrid. A total of 275 cars were entered.

Daimler-Motoren-Gesellschaft entered a full dozen cars. DMG and Jellinek were anxious to publicize the recently introduced 60 Mercedes and to try out the new 90-hp car, which was as powerful as any other entrant in the event except the 110-hp Gobron-Brillie, which Maybach considered an exercise in the excessive. Excessive, too, were the crowds. A reporter on the scene commented that not since the beginning of the French Revolution had there been such "a stream of human beings directed toward Versailles." More than 20,000 people gathered behind the gilded gates which opened onto the Route Nationale to Bordeaux; estimates of the numbers lining the 342-mile course ran as high as 3 million.

A gala air prevailed. Spectators had been gathering since dusk the evening before—cyclists and pedestrians carrying lamps and lanterns, two- and four-horse char-à-bancs filled with revelers, picnic baskets and bottles of wine. All along the route entrepreneurs had set up stalls with more food and drink. There were campfires, songs and the music of thousands of concertinas and mouth organs. Most of these people had never been in an automobile, and once the race started they wandered close to the road for a good look as the cars surged by.

Since the beginning of open-road racing it was inevitable that a catastrophe would occur. But at Paris-Rouen in 1894 just 21 cars competed, and the winner averaged less than 12 mph. Now, less than a decade later, nearly 300 cars were racing at speeds more than five times faster. The dust they raised was treacherous, blinding the drivers, who had to guess just where the car ahead of them was, and creating a curtain that spectators blithely walked through to get closer to the action. And accidents happened. The Mercedes team was not involved in the tragedies, but one of the dead drivers was the popular Marcel Renault. An estimated 11 other spectators and drivers died that day. The French government halted the race at Bordeaux. The cars were horse-drawn to the railroad station and returned to Paris.

Paris-Madrid marked the end of city-to-city races on the European continent. Henceforth racing would

John Jacob Astor and his Mercedes about to leave New York City for Philadelphia in 1903. Such long-distance treks were often crowd gatherers then.

104

be removed from courses that were hundreds of miles of dusty, unprotected highways and relocated to circuits of about 50 miles per lap, with the roads tarred to keep down the dust, barriers constructed at spectator vantage points and scores of soldiers to cope with the crowds. Such a race was next on the agenda: the Gordon Bennett Cup, sponsored by James Gordon Bennett, Jr., the proprietor of the *New York Herald* and a Francophile who had come to Paris in the late 1880s to launch a European edition of his paper. Bennett's personal ardor for motoring did not extend much beyond specifying that a big white Mercedes leave his printing plant at three each morning to deliver copies of the *Paris Herald* in time for breakfast in fashionable Deauville. But he did have a sense of the spectacular and of what made news. Sending Stanley to find Livingston in darkest Africa was Bennett's idea, and he enjoyed involving himself in whatever was considered *au courant*. He was among the founding members of the Automobile Club de France. In drawing up the regulations for his motor race he took his cue from the America's Cup yachting events: each country could enter a maximum of three cars, the cars had to be built entirely in the country they represented, and their drivers had to be chosen by their country's national automobile club.

For the past three years the Gordon Bennett had been simply a segment within a city-to-city race. Only five cars participated in 1900, three in 1901, four in 1902. Nine of these cars had been French; there had been no German entry except in 1900, when a "Herr Eugen" was set to participate in a Benz tourer until Carl Benz found out about his son's plans and the entry was scratched. In 1902 Selwyn Francis Edge, in a Napier, was England's sole representative, and he won. This victory transferred the site of the 1903 cup from the Continent, as Gordon Bennett rules specified that the race be held in the country of the last winner.

Daimler-Motoren-Gesellschaft was now very much interested. Britain was a good market for Mercedes cars, and this race could provide valuable publicity. But there were problems from the beginning. The Deutsche Automobile Club was delighted to have DMG represent Germany but disagreed about who should drive. Since the better the showing the better the publicity, Emil Jellinek wanted the most experienced drivers available, and he nominated DMG factory personnel, including Nice Week hero Wilhelm Werner, who was now serving as personal

After establishing eight speed records in 1903 — the longest 50 miles in 40 minutes 49.6 seconds, the fastest the flying mile in 39 seconds flat — Vanderbilt arrived at Ormond in 1904 with a new and faster 90 hp Mercedes. He is seen here lining up for a match race with A. E. MacDonald's 90 hp Napier. After the Napier won, Willie K. lamented that his car had been "geared too high."

Ormond Garage, January 1905. Here the race cars gathered for the 35-event speed week. Louis Ross used two steam engines in the special Stanley racer that resembled a capsized canoe and was nicknamed the "Teakettle." H.L. Bowden's No. 2 "Flying Dutchman" used two Mercedes 60 engines in a lengthened Mercedes chassis. Engine vibration was so fierce that after each run on the beach all nuts and bolts on the car had to be checked and tightened, but Bowden did a mile in 34.2 seconds, bettering the "Teakettle" by four seconds, and faster than any car had traveled before. E.R. Thomas, Buffalo, New York, automobile manufacturer (top), raced a less thunderous Mercedes.

chauffeur to the American millionaire Clarence Gray Dinsmore.* By automobile club standards, however, Werner was not a proper gentleman and therefore ineligible.

A considerable fracas followed. Jellinek fumed, Max Duttenhofer struggled to keep the peace, and Maybach busied himself at the factory getting the new 90-hp cars ready. Finally Jellinek and the Deutsche Automobile Club agreed on three drivers who qualified as gentlemen.

Two of them had raced Mercedes in the Paris-Madrid; the third had wanted to. Baron Pierre de Caters was a well-known Belgian sportsman and driver of French cars, particularly the Mors, before he switched his allegiance to Mercedes for the Paris-Madrid. Camille Jenatzy, also a Belgian, was described as an "engineer by graduation and a gentleman by choice." In 1899 he drove his electric, *Jamais Contente*, to a land speed record; after that he had raced French cars in the big city-to-city races and was about to give up racing for a desk in his family rubber business when DMG tempted him back with the Paris-Madrid ride.

The last member of the trio was the Honourable Charles Stewart Rolls, third son of Lord Llangattock, a London importer of French cars who had acquitted himself admirably racing Panhards and Mors in major events on the Continent. Rolls had written to Cannstatt offering his services for Paris-Madrid, but no car was available. Now DMG took him up on his offer.

That problem solved, another arrived, and it was a catastrophe: on June 10, the Cannstatt factory burned. The fire began early in the morning and consumed the machine and assembly shops and the entire drawing office. The damage, estimated at

$500,000, was covered by insurance — but the three race cars were inside. With the race just three weeks away, Mercedes' Gordon Bennett hopes had seemingly gone up in smoke.

Jellinek searched for replacement cars, knowing that the only Mercedes available were the previous year's models, but showing up for the Gordon Bennett with those would be better than not showing up at all. Dinsmore lent Jenatzy his personal car; another Mercedes 60 was secured from the Paris dealership for Baron de Caters. A third was offered by the American Foxhall Keene, though he insisted on driving it himself—so Rolls lost his Mercedes ride. He remained automotively inclined, of course; he met Frederick Henry Royce the following year and became something of an automobile manufacturer himself. As for Rolls' replacement, Daimler-Motoren-Gesellschaft was not keen on Keene. Although he was an experienced driver, he tended to be, as one reporter said, "the biggest sinner in recklessness." But his credentials as a gentleman were impeccable. Having made a fortune in the stock market, the Keenes were now agreeably engaged in dominating thoroughbred racing in the United States and England; Foxhall was also one of the world's best polo players and a good golfer as well.

And so the stage was set for the Gordon Bennett. Because racing was not allowed on English roads, a pretzel-like circuit was selected in Ireland, passing through Counties Kildare, Queens, and Carlow, seven laps to be run for a total distance of 327.5 miles. This was the first truly international Gordon Bennett, so colors were selected to identify the competing nations: the English cars were green, the French blue, the Americans red, the Germans white. Two Panhards and a Mors comprised the French entries, three Napiers the English; America sent over two Wintons and a Peerless. They were all at the circuit practicing while Jellinek was casting about for Mercedes replacements — and becoming exercised about another snag.

The Gordon Bennett regulations stipulating that each car be made entirely in the country it represented meant exactly that. DMG had assumed the use of Michelin racing tires would be allowed since they

---

* Although Dinsmore had been in Newport for Willie K. Vanderbilt's races in 1901, he spent most of his time in Europe and was especially fond of Germany. Tall and thin, with water-blue eyes, he appeared to Germans like the quintessential "Uncle Sam." Among the Germans he counted as friends was Kaiser Wilhelm II. An avid Mercedes enthusiast, Dinsmore suffered from severe asthma, for which his doctors had prescribed fast drives in open cars, which Werner regularly provided him. When Dinsmore died in 1905, Kaiser Wilhelm acquired one of his Mercedes, in addition to the services of his chauffeur. Wilhelm Werner remained the imperial driver until the Kaiser abdicated in 1918.

were manufactured in a German factory. But the tire valves were imported from France, so the racing Michelins were out; DMG had to use standard Continentals that were entirely German-produced. The cars were hastily prepared at the factory, or what remained of it; then, since there was no time to arrange for freight transport, they were driven from Cannstatt to Le Havre to get the Channel ferry to England, driven through Wales to the Irish Sea, put on another ferry and finally driven to the course.

Three tired touring cars, all last year's models, and riding on touring tires: Mercedes was not considered a threat in the race. But the factory fire and the monumental effort to get the cars there at all had resulted in a good press and given the cars solid underdog status. If any of them finished among the leaders, a moral victory could be justifiably claimed. There was really no way Mercedes could lose.

And a Mercedes won outright. Early on, Foxhall Keene lived up to his "biggest sinner" reputation and retired. Baron de Caters was second until near the end, when he was stopped by a broken axle. But Camille Jenatzy, who had driven a masterful race from the starting flag, was the easy winner at an average of 49.25 mph. When asked afterwards what the victory meant to him, he replied, "Just about $25,000 to $30,000." Jenatzy was a practical man.

Emil Jellinek, ecstatic, sent a telegram to Cannstatt. "Today's victory message heals all wounds of the June 10 catastrophe," Maybach and Vischer, the sales director, cabled back. "We are overjoyed." And the Grand Duke of Mecklenburg-Schwerin immediately offered his duchy for the following year's Gordon Bennett.

The race in Ireland provided a tremendous boost to Mercedes sales in Great Britain: 119 cars were sold there in 1904, quadruple the previous year's total. J. E. Hutton was the local Mercedes dealer (his cable address was "Horselaugh, London"). Hutton raced Mercedes as well as selling them, winning at Phoenix Park in Dublin in 1903 and capturing the first Montagu Cup Race at the Brooklands track in Weybridge when it opened in 1907. But the most irrepressible Mercedes dealer of this period was the man Jellinek selected to represent the marque in Paris:

the former German racing cyclist Charles Lehmann, who changed his name to C. L. Charley when he opened shop at 71 Avenue des Champs-Elysées. Monsieur Charley was as flamboyant and as fond of personal publicity as Emile Roger, the early Benz dealer. In his full-page ads in the *Paris Herald*, he put his picture above Maybach's. When he traveled to New York on Mercedes business he tried, not too successfully, to speak English with a French accent.

The Cannstatt fire delayed deliveries to several Vanderbilts—Alfred, Reginald and Willie K.—and to Bernard Baruch. They all had ordered Mercedes 90s. Six months after the fire, Monsieur Charley arrived in New York. It was January 1904, auto show time at the Grand Central Palace, and the perfect occasion to inform his waiting customers that the Cannstatt factory was back in operation and the cars were on the way. At the Mercedes booth Charley smiled genially and told reporters that "I have ze grand plan": a private club for Mercedes owners in the United States. He seems not to have followed through on that idea, though such a club would have been an estimable gathering: American Mercedes owners now included Henry Clay Frick, Howard Gould and his brother George J., Isaac Guggenheim, Harlan W. Whipple, James L. Breese, Harry Payne Whitney, H. O. Havemeyer, the publisher Frank A. Munsey, Commodore Frederick G. Bourne and Colonel John Jacob Astor. Their cars would be well cared for, however, club or not. William M. Luttgen, a longtime DMG mechanic who had also served as Foxhall Keene's mechanic abroad, emigrated to the United States in 1903 and established the Mercedes Repair Company as a private garage in New York City. He remained its head until his retirement in 1926, when he sold the company back to the factory.*

---

* At the turn of the century on both sides of the Atlantic the only really skilled mechanics worked for automobile factories. Both Daimler and Benz routinely dispatched one of their workers with a new car so that the owner could be taught the fundamentals of driving, and many of these factory-trained men (like Wilhelm Werner) were subsequently surrendered to good clients as full-time chauffeurs. The Cleveland manufacturer Alexander Winton is known to have sent a mechanic as far as California to repair a Winton; the mechanic, Watt Moreland, never returned, going into the automobile business himself instead, most successfully with the Moreland truck that was produced in Burbank until the Second World War.

The 1904 Gordon Bennett began in Saalburg, site of an ancient fort which marked the border between the Roman and Germanic empires. There were four laps of the 87-mile course. Baron de Caters' 90 hp Mercedes is shown at the start.

Alfred Gwynne Vanderbilt had ordered a Mercedes 90 to put one over on his cousin—who perhaps had neglected to mention that he had ordered one, too. Unlike Willie K., Alfred G. did not drive the car himself, securing instead the services of Paul Sartori, who had an admirable record in runs at Narragansett Park, Rhode Island, and the Empire City track in Yonkers, New York. But Alfred's Mercedes did not become the star his cousin's did. When Willie K.'s Mercedes 90 arrived in New York, he immediately left for Florida and the speed week at Ormond-Daytona that was the American equivalent

of the annual event in Nice. Here the cream of motoring society gathered in late January to escape the winter cold and have some fun on the sand. The Ormond Hotel had persuaded the railway company and the East Coast hotel interests controlled by the Florida developer Henry M. Flagler to share the expenses of making its elite clientele comfortable, including the construction of a garage for the competing cars.

There were about two dozen different events during speed week of 1904. The highlight was Willie K.'s drive on the sands between Ormond and

A misfiring engine delayed de Caters 14½ minutes at the start, though he made up the time and finished fourth. Warden's No. 16 Mercedes had a clean start but retired on the third lap. Jenatzy's second place was the best Mercedes finish in the race.

MERCEDES

PRICES OF CHASSES IN NEW YORK

35 H. P.	$8,400
45 H. P.	10,150
70 H. P.	14,500

PRICES OF CHASSES IN PARIS

With license plates for importation into the United States

35 H. P.	$5,500
45 H. P.	6,500
70 H. P.	9,500

TOURING BODY PRICES IN NEW YORK

Including cape top, slip covers, two extra seats, tool boxes, tire holders, trunk rack

Widerkehr	$1,500
Vedrine	1,500
Quinby	1,730
Demarest	2,075

$150 extra for canopy top with glass front and back, making demi-limousine, in place of cape top

LIMOUSINES

Including two extra seats, glass front, toilet case, speaking tube, etc.

Kellner	$2,000
Vedrine	2,000
Quinby	2,000
Demarest	2,350
Rothschild	2,350

Specifications and prices on bodies from other builders furnished on request

The Mercedes Import Co.

Times Building, :: :: :: New York

Price list, c. 1902; Times Square showroom, 1906. The New York A.S.P.C.A. used a Daimler delivery wagon (like that pictured on the facing page); Stern Brothers and Abraham & Straus, department stores, had similar vans in their fleets, and a New Jersey baker carried 2000 loaves of bread daily in his Long Island-built Daimler. "These vehicles are able to go to distant points such as Far Rockaway, Long Island, and return the same day," *The Horseless Age* reported, "when previously, the horse vehicles had to be sent one day, put up overnight, and return the next day." In 1903 a Daimler bus was built for the San Francisco trolley shuttle and tested on the steepest gradient near the factory — Lexington Avenue between 103rd and 104th streets in Manhattan. "Twenty-two street urchins and six grown persons . . . were carried up the hill," a reporter noted, "the engine never dropping below its normal speed." The speed was about 10 mph. Though a prototype of a Daimler touring car using one of the truck engines was built in the Steinway factory in 1902, automobile manufacture did not begin until 1905. Most of the material and workmen were imported from Germany. The American Mercedes was aggressively promoted.

110

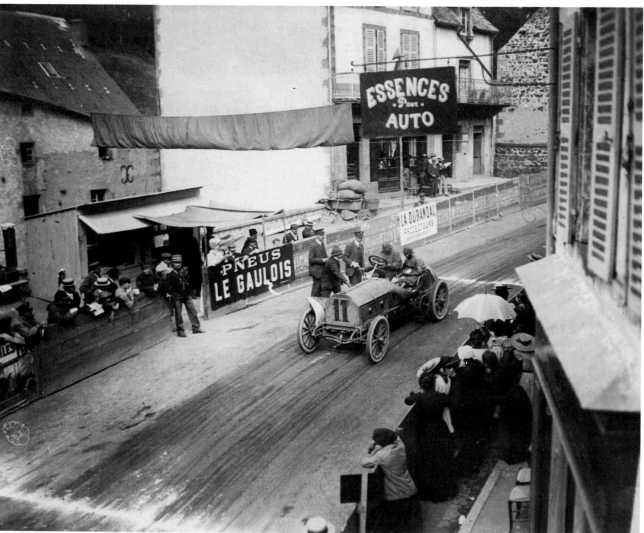

The Auvergne circuit for the 1905 Gordon Bennett was unusual. Previously race organizers had sought out roads with a maximum of long straights and a minimum of hard corners. This year the French did precisely the opposite. The 85-mile circuit lay in the volcanic district of Puy-de-Dôme, and swept from 1413 feet to more than 3500 feet above sea level at Col de la Moreno. Sudden rises and fast descents were common, numerous small villages were passed, and the course was said to have 145 corners, "all more or less awkward." The Mercedes entered in the race boasted 120 hp, but did not fare well. Werner (top, left) finished fifth, de Caters (top, right) seventh, Hieronimus (above) retired on the second of the four laps. Bickering between Jellinek and the Daimler factory followed the poor showing.

Daytona, as he and his Mercedes 90 did a kilometer in 39 seconds flat for 92.3 mph, the fastest anyone in the world had thus far traveled in an automobile. "Really, I did surprise myself," Vanderbilt said afterwards. But in May, in Belgium, Baron de Caters surprised *him*, taking his Mercedes 90 along a road near Ostend for a 97.25-mph average.

At the end of 1904, Daimler-Motoren-Gesellschaft celebrated its best annual production yet: a total of 803 Mercedes were built that year in Cannstatt and at the new plant in Untertürkheim, two or three miles away. One hundred cars, most of them already sold, were consumed in the 1903 fire, and makeshift quarters had hurriedly been set up alongside the ruined factory with double shifts working to get the company back in business. By the time the modern Untertürkheim plant—"the ultimate in automobile factories," DMG boasted—was ready for production in November 1904, DMG was thriving. The 2,200 employees worked a 54-hour week, the norm in Germany at that time. They were well paid, 40 to 50 pfennigs an hour, which could buy three pounds of bread or six eggs. Amusingly, DMG established a small factory on the grounds to produce 4,000 bottles of lemonade daily, which the company hoped would persuade workers to reduce their beer consumption. Whether or not it accomplished this aim is not known.

Of those 803 Mercedes built in 1904, twenty-five percent crossed the Atlantic. The Mercedes was America's best-selling imported car. And now it was also being manufactured in the United States.

The production of Daimler commercial vehicles began in New York shortly after William Steinway's death. The new sponsoring organization, the Daimler Manufacturing Company, had headquarters at 961 Steinway Avenue in Astoria, Queens, and was headed by Fred Kübler, Steinway's former superintendent. General Electric was a large stockholder. A prototype of a Daimler car had been built in America at the turn of the century, but at that time manufacture did not follow; the new Mercedes was on its way in Cannstatt, and the Daimler Manufacturing Company preferred to import it through arrangements with C. L. Charley. In Astoria the front and rear axles of the German cars were strengthened to withstand the abuse of the still abominable American roads.

In late 1904, however, Daimler Manufacturing, with the help of the Cannstatt factory, began production of a duplicate of the German car, with the stated object "of permitting Mercedes to be sold the American purchasers without paying the high duty of 45 percent." The cars were called American Mercedes; the first ads depicted an eagle with the flags of the United States and the German Empire in its talons. Then, in mid-February, 1907, fire ravaged the Astoria plant, destroying eight completed cars and 40 in the process of construction. Production was never resumed.

But the American Mercedes might have been doomed without the fire. For Mercedes clients price was really no object, and saving the import duty was not particularly inviting. Many American owners preferred to pick up their Mercedes in Europe. Among them was Herbert L. Bowden, a wealthy fiber processor from Boston. But the car he showed up with at Ormond Beach in January 1905 was a German-American hybrid and distinctly one of a kind: an eight-cylinder, 120-horsepower Mercedes produced by the simple expedient of shoehorning two 60-horsepower Mercedes engines into one Mercedes 60 chassis which had been lengthened to accommodate them. Both engines and chassis had come from Germany; the body was fitted in the States. The result gave new meaning to the phrase "long of hood." On January 26, resplendent in a tailor-made driving suit, Bowden drove down the smooth, hard beach at 109.756 mph, a phenomenal record. "It was a great ride," said Bowden at the end. But the run had been one-way only. The car was 400 pounds overweight according to the rules, and the American Automobile Association would not accept the mark. The disappointed Florida crowd thought this ridiculous and disagreed vocally.

The Cannstatt factory was disappointed, too, when the Gordon Bennett was run in Germany in mid-July of 1904. The previous year's winner,

Jenatzy, had driven a hard bargain to participate in 1904, as his correspondence with Jellinek revealed: simply for starting he wanted half a 90-hp car (literally, *"une demi voiture"*), though he later revised that to mean a 50 percent discount; if he won, he wanted a complete Mercedes of his choice, if he was second, a 40-hp car, if third, a 28-hp; if fourth, an 18-hp model. Jellinek agreed.

The course in the Taunus Mountains was a good one, and six nations were represented: England, Germany, France, Austria-Hungary, Belgium and Italy. A German victory in the first major international race on German soil would have been gratifying, but that was not to be. The event saw a tremendous struggle between Jenatzy and Léon Théry in a Richard-Brasier. The Frenchman's driving was unspectacular but steady and reliable (whence his nickname, "The Chronometer"; the crimson-bearded Jenatzy was known as "The Red Devil"). This day the Chronometer beat the Devil, and Théry was congratulated by the Kaiser. Jenatzy had to settle for the 40-hp Mercedes.

There were other victories, among them Semmering, Kesselberg and Gaillon, all hill climbs, which Mercedes dominated. They were good wins, though

with all the bickering going on back at the factory, they were scarcely noticed. Jellinek was part of the problem. When *Allgemeine Automobil-Zeitung* published a review of the 1906 Mercedes line without mentioning his name, Jellinek wrote them claiming that "not only the whole business, but also the whole construction of the Mercedes car, was and still is entirely built on my plans, and . . . all the faults that do creep in are caused by the unwillingness of the Daimler-Motoren-Gesellschaft to listen to me in the first place." The journal wrote back, "Once upon a time, when you pretended to have money, you were a charming person. Now that you are really rich, you are becoming a bore." When Mercedes cars failed to win the last Gordon Bennett in 1905 or the first French Grand Prix in 1906, Jellinek said that was the factory's fault, too. When the DMG people said that perhaps better drivers might help, he petulantly suggested they open a driver's school next door to the factory.

Finally in January 1907, Daimler-Motoren-Gesellschaft informed Jellinek that he would no longer be supplied with free spare parts. He elected to retire from the business later that year. But he did not retire from the social scene. With the help of Archduke

Mercedes in the Vanderbilt. (Top, left) Foxhall Keene, 1905. (Top, right) William Luttgen, 1904. (Above) John B. Warden, 1905. Warden finished eighth, Luttgen retired — as did daredevil Keene, against a telegraph pole.

OFFICIAL
PROGRAM, SCORE=CARD AND GUIDE
OF THE
THIRD INTERNATIONAL RACE
FOR THE
WILLIAM K. VANDERBILT, JR.
CUP

LONG ISLAND
October 6.
1906

PRICE
25 CENTS

SOLE OFFICIAL AND AUTHORIZED PROGRAM PUBLISHED BY
The Automobile

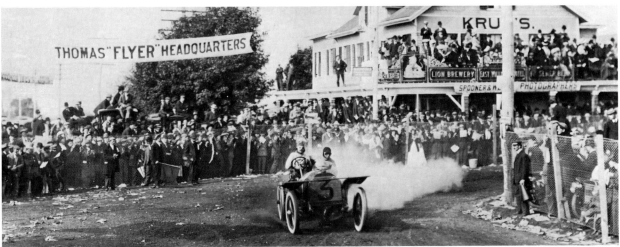

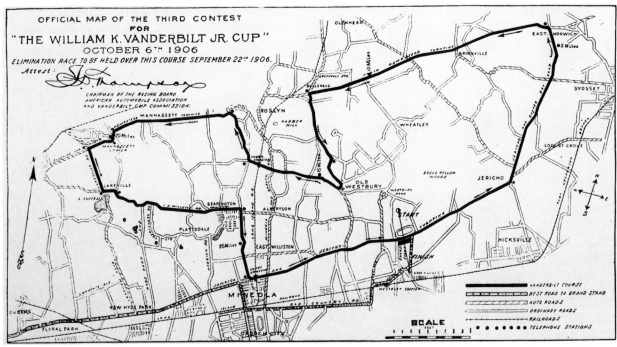

OFFICIAL MAP OF THE THIRD CONTEST
FOR
"THE WILLIAM K. VANDERBILT JR. CUP"
OCTOBER 6TH 1906
ELIMINATION RACE TO BE HELD OVER THIS COURSE SEPTEMBER 22ND 1906.

Inaugurated in 1904 on Long Island, the Vanderbilt Cup was America's first international road race. Interestingly, although sponsor Willie K. Vanderbilt (seen top, right patrolling the course with race chairman Thompson) was an ardent Mercedes man, Mercedes cars did not do well in the New York events. Al Campbell's fourth (in S.B. Stevens' car) and Warden's eighth were the best Mercedes finishes in 1904 and 1905 respectively. Seen rounding Krug's Corner en route to a fifth-place finish in 1906 is Camille Jenatzy (center). No race was held in 1907; a fourth was Mercedes' best in both 1908 and 1909. After 1910 the Vanderbilt moved — first to Savannah, then to Milwaukee and Santa Monica. In 1912 and 1914 Ralph De Palma gave Mercedes two spectacular victories

Franz Ferdinand, heir to the Austrian throne, he secured the post of honorary vice-consul in Monaco, a position that allowed him to replace his pith helmet with an ostrich-plumed hat, to wear a chestful of medals and even to carry a sword. Emil Jellinek-Mercedes was now a diplomat, of all things.

Shortly before Jellinek's leavetaking, Wilhelm Maybach also left DMG. His departure was foreshadowed in 1903, when the death of Max Duttenhofer had moved Wilhelm Lorenz into the chairmanship. Maybach had not enjoyed good relations wth Lorenz since the founding of Daimler-Motoren-Gesellschaft. He was, moreover, a sick man, requiring extended leaves to recover from a variety of ailments, and he had become extremely nervous. Design work had to proceed during his absences, of course, and he would return to find things not done his way, which hardly helped his nerves. Lorenz offered him a management position that presumably would not have been too stressful, nor too disruptive to the design staff. Maybach re-fused it and, having just passed his sixtieth birthday, left the company on April 1, 1907.

By now Paul Daimler was back from Austro-Daimler, where he had been serving as chief engineer since leaving Cannstatt shortly after the debut of the Mercedes. His departure did not leave the Austrian firm bereft, however. An engineer named Ferdinand Porsche, hired the previous year, was now promoted to Daimler's job. One of his first assignments was to design a car for Emil Jellinek, who had stuck his fingers into the Viennese company as well. The new car was called the Maja and was advertised in the United States as "The Sister of Mercedes," which was at least half-true: Maja was Jellinek's younger daughter. Few of the cars were sold, and production was discontinued by the end of 1908. With Maybach gone, Paul Daimler took over as chief engineer of Daimler-Motoren-Gesellschaft, and Adolf Daimler became factory manager. A new era was about to begin. Mercedes was facing stiff competition. Much of it was coming from Benz.

Jellinek as diplomat. The Maja, named for another daughter and built by the Austrian Daimler company in 1908. During World War I Jellinek was accused of espionage and fled from Nice. He died in exile in Switzerland in January 1918. His villa, yachts and cars were confiscated by the French, and for a while his daughter Mercédès had to beg from neighbors.

CHAPTER FOUR

WIN ON SUNDAY, SELL ON MONDAY

1 9 0 8 – 1 9 1 4

Now there is nothing gives a man such spirit,
Leaving his blood as cayenne doth a curry,
As going at full speed...
—GEORGE NOEL GORDON, LORD BYRON,
DON JUAN

By 1908 Benzes were being sold in posh showrooms on both sides of the Atlantic, from the Place de l'Opéra in Paris to the Philadelphia establishment of the Main Line Bergdoll family, several rungs up the social ladder from the Mead Cycle Company of Chicago, which just a few years before had been the sole United States importer for the marque. The Parsifal led Benz into the *beau monde*. Many of the company's full-page advertisements did not even picture the car, but simply presented a list of the prominent people who had bought one. That roster kept growing: the Czar of Russia, the King of Sweden, more than thirty dukes and princes across the European continent. Among the most devoted Benz enthusiasts was Prince Heinrich of Prussia, the Kaiser's brother. Though Wilhelm had purchased a Benz for his Imperial garage, he tended to favor Mercedes. Heinrich's preference was for Benz. So loyal was he that two decades later, when the companies merged, Heinrich refused to put a three-pointed star on his Benz's hood.

Benz's success was earned partly through competition. The Herkomer Trophy was inaugurated in 1905 by Hubert von Herkomer, a Bavarian who grew up in England, where he became famous as a portrait painter and was knighted in 1899. Returning to his homeland, Herkomer designed and donated a trophy for a 1,000-mile-plus reliability tour for production automobiles. Benz & Cie. did well in the Herkomer from the beginning and performed sensationally in 1907, when the competitors numbered 161 and Benzes won six of the thirteen prizes offered, including the Herkomer Trophy itself.

In 1908 the Prince Heinrich Tour superseded the Herkomer. Benz won that one, too. The week-long, 1,373-mile rally began in Berlin and ended in Frankfurt. On day five Willy Pöge's Mercedes was the leader, and the journalists' favorite, but Fritz Erle and his Benz passed Pöge on the mountain test and went on to a convincing victory.

Benz & Cie. had come a long way since the discontinuation of Carl Benz's little belt-drive car. By now its business outside Germany was firmly in hand. In 1906, at the suggestion of the Mannheimer Bank, the Rheinische Automobil-Gesellschaft was organized as a Jellinek-type organization to handle export sales. But only two Benz people were on its board and the company soon discovered that it did not like the arrangement any more than DMG had liked its association with Jellinek. By 1908 Benz began establishing its own wholly-owned branches in France, Belgium, England, Italy, Austria and Hungary. In

Hubert von Herkomer (1849-1914). Son of a Bavarian wood carver, Herkomer became renowned as a painter of the British aristocracy. In 1904 he designed and donated a trophy for an automobile reliability tour to be held in his native land.

The Herkomer Trophy was the forerunner of the modern-day rally. Prince Heinrich of Prussia is seen (above) driving his Benz in the 1906 event. Heinrich was encouraged by his brother, Kaiser Wilhelm II, to sponsor the Prince Heinrich Tour to demonstrate the progress of automobilism in Germany. The tour superseded the Herkomer and became the largest automobile contest on the Continent. The Benz company was an ardent participant. Fritz Erle, who won the last Herkomer in 1907, is seen (center) en route to victory in the first Prince Heinrich in 1908. In eight years Erle won 28 long-distance races and tours for Benz. Hans Nibel, who began his thirty-year company career as a Benz engineer in 1904 (he became Daimler-Benz technical director in 1929) is seen (top, right) before winning the Princess of Saxony Prize in the 1909 Prince Heinrich.

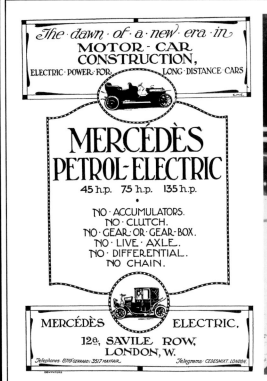

(Top, left) In 1906 DMG contracted with the Viennese coachbuilding firm of Jacob Lohner for manufacturing rights to the hybrid gasoline-electric car designed by Ferdinand Porsche. Production of the Mercedes version, sometimes called the "Mixte," took place in the Austrian Daimler factory, and was short-lived. This British advertisement for the car is from the summer of 1907. (Top, right) Kaiser Wilhelm II, in a Mercedes-Knight, is greeted by Herzog von Ratibor during an automobile club tour, 1913. (Above) The Kaiser's brother, Prince Heinrich of Prussia, at his summer home with his 70 hp Benz, c. 1908.

the United States Benz was the majority stockholder in the Benz Auto Import Company as well.

In Mannheim, with the infighting of the competing design departments now a memory, Georg Diehl settled comfortably into the overall management of design. His right-hand man was a talented engineer named Hans Nibel, just turned 27. Erle took over the competition department; joining him there was Victor Hémery, a former French seaman who had been active in motor sport on the Continent since shortly after the turn of the century. The new direction of Benz & Cie. was apparent. Though Carl Benz might wince at the thought, * his company was going racing.

The repercussions of the intramural squabbling at Daimler-Motoren-Gesellschaft during this period were apparent only in the racing arena. The cars in

---

*As was noted in Chapter Three, Carl Benz's role in the firm he had founded was now largely as board member and advisor. In 1906, in association with his son Eugen, he founded another company, C. Benz Söhne, near his home in Ladenburg. Richard Benz became the third partner in 1908. Carl Benz, approaching his mid-sixties, played a passive role in this new venture. C. Benz Söhne built automobiles into the early twenties, though probably not more than 100 in all, and remains in existence today producing parts for Daimler-Benz. Its small factory, not much changed since 1907, stands on the original site, and is still under the management of the Benz family.

the marketplace continued to bask in the renown that Mercedes had enjoyed for the past half decade. "Standing at the very top of the tree so far as general excellence of design, workmanship and material are concerned" was the phrase *The Car Illustrated* used to describe the 1907 line.

In Malaysia the Sultan of Johore owned three Mercedes, one for decorous touring and two for dashing about (depending upon how quickly he wanted to dash about, the Sultan used either the 90-hp roadster or the specially built 120-hp racer). The Countess of Warwick had a custom-made Mercedes 40, with a raised platform in the rear quarter from which she could champion the cause of labor during her campaign for Parliament. The garages of Buckingham Palace housed the several Mercedes of King Edward VII. In Germany, though his Empress preferred a sedate gas-electric Mercedes Mixte, Kaiser Wilhelm enjoyed fast touring cars. All of his Mercedes were upholstered in creamy chamois and blue, trimmed with gold and fitted with a three-chimed signal that announced the Imperial car's approach.

And DMG itself continued to enjoy the flattery of imitation. Since the introduction of the Mercedes many of its innovative features had found their way to other marques, by one means or another. There was

Franz Joseph, Emperor of Austria since 1848 and King of Hungary since 1867, alighting from his Mercedes, c. 1911. His long reign ended in the middle of World War I, which had been precipitated by the assassination of his grandnephew and heir apparent Franz Ferdinand.

the strictly aboveboard approach taken by Alfred Harmsworth (later Lord Northcliffe), publisher of the *London Daily Mail*. When he took delivery of his Mercedes 60 in Nice, he immediately dispatched it home so that, as his own newspaper quoted him, "details [of it] should be made as widely known as possible to the English automobile constructors." There was the sub rosa tactic. The Rothschild interests in Paris informed DMG that a mechanic who had visited the factory ostensibly to pick up a Mercedes for a client was in reality the foreman of Hotchkiss, the ordnance manufacturing firm at Saint Denis on the Seine, which was about to enter the automotive field and wanted to procure information on "manufacturing methods, installations . . . and other interesting items." And there was the merely amusing approach adopted by the former Daimler Manufacturing Company engineer on Long Island who decided to build his own automobile and call it the Merciless, on the assumption that that was as close as he dared get to "Mercedes" without risking a lawsuit.

Still, despite the Mercedes celebrity, the company had problems. The financial panic of 1907, which began in America with the fall of the stock market and bank failures throughout the country, spread to Europe. In Germany, among the thirty companies now manufacturing automobiles, the luxury producers were the hardest hit (to make matters worse, a luxury tax had been imposed on motor vehicles). DMG reduced its workforce by 1,200 men and cut its automobile production by more than two-thirds. Benz, on the other hand, rode out the recession easily. Indeed, the economic downturn could not have occurred at a more opportune time for the company; stationary and marine engine sales were not so hard hit, and Benz had already cut its car production by half in order to focus efforts on the construction of new facilities for a factory that was bursting at the seams. For Benz, racing was a fine new idea to enhance its image. For Mercedes, racing had become a cause of anxiety; the car's lackluster performance in major events since the spectacular win in the Gordon Bennett was the source of much concern at the factory.

By 1906 the Gordon Bennett was no more. The French had never liked the race; the rule limiting each

nation's entries to three cars was a vexation to a country that could field many more competitive vehicles. Because the 1904 race in Germany had been won by a French car, the race returned to France for 1905. But even before its running the Automobile Club de France announced that regardless of the outcome it would abstain from future cup competition. As it happened, a French car did win in 1905, which effectively killed the Gordon Bennett.

In its place the French Grand Prix was born in 1906 as a manufacturers' race.* That year Renault won; Mercedes finished tenth and eleventh. 1907 was no better; the winner was a Fiat, followed by eight French cars and in tenth place a Mercedes driven by former Darracq driver Victor Hémery, who we have seen was about to switch his allegiance to Benz. All this happened during the Jellinek-Maybach-DMG infighting. When the dust settled and Paul Daimler emerged as head of engineering, he began making plans for a concerted return to racing in 1908, with new cars and new drivers.

The Mercedes race car Daimler designed developed 140 hp. The drivers he chose to race it were Willy Pöge, Otto Salzer and Christian Lautenschlager, factory-affiliated men all. Pöge was a company director and had been a Mercedes race driver for the past half decade. Salzer was a DMG mechanic and test driver in the days of Papa Daimler and had been a race driver ever since. Though Lautenschlager was about to make his debut as a

---

*Only France held a grand prix before World War I. The event was correctly called the Grand Prix of the Automobile Club de France. After the war other European nations began organizing their own grand prix competition, first Italy in 1922, then Britain and Germany in 1926. Overseeing these events was the *Association Internationale des Automobile Clubs Reconnus (AIACR)*, the forerunner of the *Fédération Internationale de l'Automobile (FIA)*. In 1934 the European championship, an annual competition for the best driver of the year, was born. The world drivers' championship and the world manufacturers' championship followed after the Second World War, as did grand prix racing in the United States. With the rapid expansion of postwar motor sport the *Commission Sportive Internationale*, a subcommittee of the FIA, divided racing into groups or formulas, with different regulations for participation in each category. Today's Formula One is the heir of the *grandes epreuves* which began in France in 1906. A maximum weight of 1,007 kg for competing cars was the "formula" under which the 1906 event was run. Current regulations for Formula One competition require a 30-page book. Paris remains the international headquarters of motor sport and, out of respect to the originators of racing, its international rules are still written in French.

(Center, left) Camille Jenatzy before the start of the French Grand Prix at Le Mans, June 26, 1906. Mercedes had ceased being a threat in big-time competition by now, and the three-car team's best was Jenatzy's tenth. The Circuit des Ardennes on August 13 proved no better. Jenatzy finished tenth again; Otto Salzer (center, right) and J.T. Alexander Burton (above) were ninth and fifteenth respectively. Benz was more successful in European competition. Victor Hémery (top) won the punishing 438-mile race from St. Petersburg to Moscow in 1908 at an average of over 50 mph.

Official "thanks and congratulations" awarded by the German Automobile Industry Association to DMG in 1908.

competition driver, his factory experience dated to the turn of the century, when he was hired as a mechanic; in 1905 he had been promoted to chief test driver and had competed in a few races as riding mechanic.

By 1908 the French Grand Prix was solidly established as the most important race in Europe. It was to be run on the same circuit as in 1907, 47.74 miles of winding roadways beginning just outside Dieppe on a long straight, undulating for about nine miles into Envermeu, then to the S-bend at Londinières, north to Fresnoy and Sept-Meules, through a stretch of woodland country to Eu, southwest to Criel, and then a final fifteen miles parallel to the sea on the way back to the starting point.

The competitors and journalists gathered in Dieppe in early July, and the correspondents began making their predictions. Several noted that Mercedes would not "suffer from the usual complaints of unreadiness"—the previous month Daimler had sent a practice car to test the circuit—but eight to one represented the most favorable odds made on the DMG team. More optimistically regarded were the entries of what reporters called the three B's: Bayard-

Clément and Brasier, both French cars, and Benz.

Once Mannheim made the decision to compete its commitment was total. Though Benz was new to the racing game, the marque was well regarded. Benz cars had performed strongly in the Herkomer and Prince Heinrich rallies, and in May the new 120-hp grand prix car had been given its first public test over 438 miles of cart tracks and deplorable roads in a race from St. Petersburg to Moscow. Only a third of the cars in the grueling event had finished; only one car had been entered by Benz. With Hémery driving, it won.

Joining Hémery on the three-car Benz team for the Grand Prix were two race veterans: Benz's own Fritz Erle and René Hanriot, a former Darracq colleague of Hémery. All three wore khaki suits with matching helmets.

Forty-eight cars started in the race. Half were French; the remainder were divided among Italian, English and German entries. The start was at six A.M. because the organizers wanted to be sure that the slower cars would complete the distance before sundown (the last car to finish the previous year's grand prix was on the course for nearly eleven hours and finished over four hours behind the winner).

The trophy provided by the city of Dieppe for the winner of the French Grand Prix in 1908.

Meister Christian Lautenschlager dem überlegenen und glänzenden Sieger Grand Prix — Dieppe 1908

R. Weisweiller.

Failure in competition had taught a few lessons. As *Allgemeine Automobil-Zeitung* reported, Mercedes drivers seldom had the opportunity to test drive the circuit before a big race because the cars were "never finished until the very eve." By the spring of 1908 the new Mercedes (Lautenschlager's at the top) for the French Grand Prix in July were nearing completion. (Center) Mercedes team members Willy Pöge (No. 2), Christian Lautenschlager (35), Otto Salzer (19). (Above) Benz team members Victor Hémery (No. 6), René Hanriot (23), Fritz Erle (39).

(Left) Born in Magstadt, near Stuttgart, in 1877, Christian Lautenschlager had been Salzer's riding mechanic since 1906. (Center) French-born 32-year-old Victor Hémery was a famous Darracq driver before joining Benz. (Right) Born in Möglingen, Württemberg, in 1874, Otto Salzer had been driving and managing races for DMG since 1903.

Races in those days were sometimes called because of darkness as a few cars were still circling the course, grimly determined to cross the finish line.

The starting order was determined by lot. The starting signal was a pistol shot; shooting the cars off, rather than flagging them, added to the spectacle of the proceedings. Massed or rolling starts were unusual in this era principally for safety reasons; the cars were dispatched at intervals instead. In this grand prix there was one minute between cars, though half-minute intervals had been considered; the organizers feared that with the short circuit and the large number of entries, minute guns would result in the "squadron treading on its own tail." Which indeed happened;

the last six cars were sent off in the midst of a stream of competitors completing the first of the ten laps in the race. To complicate things even further for spectators, there were two races to watch: the one on the road and the one on the scoreboard. Because of the interval start, the car that was leading was not necessarily the car that was winning. Lap times were posted as each car completed the circuit, and the standings were announced as soon as the scorers could figure them out.

The first car to complete the first lap of the 1908 Grand Prix, in 38 minutes 28 seconds, was Willy Pöge's Mercedes. But Pöge had started second, and when all the cars had made their rounds and the

Willy Pöge coming out of the S-bend at Londinières. Pöge's 63.6 mph average in the French GP was good for fifth place. Winner Lautenschlager averaged 69 mph.

(Above) Hefty Frenchman René Hanriot averaged 67.4 mph to finish third in the 1908 French Grand Prix, just a tenth of a second behind Benz teammate Hémery. (Top) Lautenschlager's mechanic secures a spare tire on their Mercedes mid-race. (Center) The trench built in front of the grandstand provided the first "pits" in motor sport. Though quick-lift jacks helped speed up routine pit stops, changing tires on wooden-spoked wheels was a chore that required better than a minute. Here the Hémery Benz is being reshod as Hémery himself approaches with the refueling can.

figures were totted up, the race leader, with a time of 36 minutes 31 seconds, was revealed to be the Mercedes that had started nineteenth, Otto Salzer's. If Salzer appeared to display more dash than discretion on that first round, that was the DMG plan: he had been told to step on it hard. Salzer was the hare, and he played his role well; his nearly 80-mph first lap, the fastest of the race, was a circuit record.

The rabbit retired on lap three. Then Hémery took over the lead, with his Benz partner, Hanriot, third. Between them was Lautenschlager, who moved into first on the fifth lap. The crowd was astonished. Here were two German teams, one in its first grand prix, the other coming off dismal failures in the last two, and they were leading the pack. Equally as astonishing was the performance of the man who had never driven a race before; though the two Benzes behind him remained within striking distance, they could not get past Lautenschlager.

The contest was a debacle for tires. So great were the speeds that most cars had to be reshod every lap, and carried a spare set aboard to be used en route. "Nobody could change tires as fast as Lautenschlager and his mechanic," *Allgemeine Automobil-Zeitung* reported. "They performed veritable acrobatic acts . . . three new tires in four minutes." Tar was another problem. Though it kept the dust down, it congealed as the event wore on and chunks of it were thrown up by the speeding cars, pelting the drivers. Any driver using his hands to protect himself from this sticky onslaught found by the closing laps that he was literally glued to his wheel.

After five hours of racing, on lap seven, Hémery was less than a minute behind Lautenschlager when a stone smashed his goggles. He stopped in the pits long enough to have the pieces of glass removed from his left eye and drove on, with only his right eye open. Lautenschlager, unaware of Hémery's handicap, was worried about one of his own: as he began the last lap, his car was wearing the last tires in the Mercedes pits. Neither Lautenschlager nor his mechanic uttered a word, each waiting for the awful noise of a blowout that would mean they had lost. The blowout never came.

The 1908 French Grand Prix was like a Cin-

derella story, except that Cinderella had a moustache and a voice like a bullhorn. When Christian Lautenschlager crossed the finish line, he went from racing obscurity to the fame of a world-class driver. For Paul Daimler, the victory was especially sweet; it meant he had stepped into the formidable shoes Maybach had worn for so long at DMG.

The Benz interests must have been pleased, too. Though Mercedes had won, Hémery's one-eyed drive in the closing laps was a moral victory; close behind him, in third place, was Hanriot's Benz. Erle brought his car in seventh. Benz, a brand-new contender for grand prix honors, had entered three cars and three cars had finished—a performance rewarded with the "dependability" team prize.

The French were understandably chagrined by the outcome. They had made the rules for the race, but only one of their cars had placed in the top seven, Rigal's Clément-Bayard, which was fourth (followed by Pöge's Mercedes). Consequently, though the Automobile Club de France was willing to stage a grand prix in 1909, French automobile manufacturers were not. Publicity was the only tangible reward of competition in that era, racing was expensive, Europe was in the midst of a recession, and losing races did not sell cars. So the French manufacturers led a boycott against further grand prix competition, publicly announcing the reasons as financial and circulating a petition among all European factories; both Daimler-Motoren-Gesellschaft and Benz & Cie. signed it. France, after all, was a major export market, and irritating the French was not good for business. Moreover, without the French competing, victories on the Continent would not be nearly as impressive. So major auto racing in Europe was finished for the time being.

1908 was an eventful year for reasons other than the economy. In October Austria annexed Bosnia and Herzogovina, and the intricate network of European diplomatic alliances began stirring. In the Middle East, petroleum production began after William Knox D'Arcy's drillers struck oil at Masjid-i-Salaman in Persia. In Texas Howard Hughes' father began to manufacture rock drilling bits; his company eventually had a monopoly on the production of this essential equipment for the petroleum industry. In September, William Crapo Durant organized General Motors. In October, Henry Ford introduced his Model T.

America presented an interesting dichotomy: although it was relatively late to adopt the automobile, it was the first country to fall in love with it. Soon after horseless carriages began chugging along the roads, almost everybody wanted one. Thousands of would-be entrepreneurs rushed to fill the demand: a florist in Chicago, an artificial limb manufacturer in Topeka, a birdcage maker in Buffalo, a sewing machine producer in Cleveland, a doctor in New Jersey, a dentist in Michigan, and carriage makers, bicycle builders and machinists everywhere. More than three thousand American companies tried to build automobiles. Many produced high wheelers, a vehicle as American as the Fourth of July (the type was unknown in Europe) and nearly as primeval as the nineteenth-century Benz (Holsman of Chicago, who originated the type, initially used manila rope for its final drive). The high wheeler had two advantages. First, it was essentially a buggy without a horse ("radical simplicity" was the phrase used by many makers), mounted on wheels as large as forty-eight inches in diameter which allowed the cars to ride over rather than into the huge chuckholes of American dirt roads. Second, it didn't cost much more than a horse and buggy; the Success from St. Louis sold for as little as

$250. More than 100,000 high wheelers were produced by firms scattered throughout the Middle West, International Harvester and Sears among them. They fell from favor only after Henry Ford provided the American driving public with something better—the Model T, a real automobile at a low price. Although there remained a market for the handcrafted, high-priced motor car which was met by domestic producers as well as by the European imports, the car that put America on wheels and made the automobile industry a mainstay of the American economy was Henry Ford's Model T.

The Tin Lizzie caused a revolution—but it was a revolution that had been waiting to happen. Since 1903, when he told a friend that "the way to make automobiles is to make one automobile like another, to make them all alike, to make them come through the factory just alike," Henry Ford had been preparing for it.* From one car for every 9,500 persons in the

---

*Ford was shrewd. Already well known through his racing exploits at the turn of the century, he reaped more publicity from another sort of competition: he fought the Selden patent. George B. Selden was a Rochester, New York, attorney who, after seeing the Brayton stationary internal combustion engine at the Philadelphia Exposition in 1876, was inspired to return home and "invent" an automobile. This he did not do, though in 1879, he did apply for a patent, the issuance of which he managed to delay through various legal tactics until 1895. In 1899 Selden sold his patent rights to the Electric Vehicle Company, a consortium of Wall Street financiers who planned to make a fortune building electric taxis for major American cities. When the "Lead Cab Trust," as newspapers derisively called it, failed, the consortium turned to the gasoline car industry and, waving the Selden

The German success in the French Grand Prix was the talk of the Continent in 1908. In America William Crapo Durant incorporated General Motors that September, and Henry Ford introduced his Model T (pictured above) in October.

The world's longest-lived automobile symbol, registered in June 1909. Rolls-Royce's "Flying Lady" first appeared in 1911 and was officially adopted in 1921.

United States at the turn of the century, there was one for every 200 by 1910, three times the per-capita ownership in England, four times that in France, five times that in Germany. And then, in 1913, Henry Ford's chassis assembly line moved experimentally for the first time, and the mass production of automobiles was born. Within six months, Ford had cut his chassis-building time from more than 12 hours to under two. Soon he would be building more cars than all other American producers put together, and many more than all of Europe could manage. In Europe, the automobile remained an aristocrat. Cars were built by hand, and a single Mercedes took the equivalent of two workers one year to complete.

In Mannheim and Untertürkheim, in 1909, Benz

& Cie. and Daimler-Motoren-Gesellschaft produced 781 and 671 cars, respectively. More significantly, the three-pointed star was officially born. Alfred von Kaulla of the Württembergische Bank had succeeded Lorenz, who had retired, as chairman of the DMG board, and von Kaulla decided the Mercedes needed a trademark. As various ideas were discussed, Paul Daimler showed von Kaulla a photograph of the family home in the Deutz days; over the picture his father had drawn a guiding star and written to his wife the words, "A star shall arise from here, and I hope that it will bring blessings to us and to our children." That seemed a perfect and poignant trademark. Daimler-Motoren-Gesellschaft registered both a four- and a three-pointed star, though only the latter would be adopted—as a visual eulogy to Gottlieb Daimler and as a representation of his pioneering of motorization on land, on sea and in the air.

In 1910, for the first time, both DMG and Benz produced more than a thousand automobiles. By 1912 DMG approached two thousand, and Benz surpassed three thousand. In Prussia, Prince Heinrich ordered yet another Benz, and new orders for the Mannheim car arrived from Her Majesty, the Dowager Queen of Sweden, His Serenity, Prince Charles Anton of Hohenzollern, and His Grand Ducal Highness, Maximilian of Baden. DMG order books included requests for new Mercedes from the King of England, the Kaiser, and the Crown Prince of Japan. "The Car Which Set the Fashion to the

---

patent, demanded royalties on all such automobiles built. Most major gasoline car makers were either intimidated or lacked the financial resources to argue the point, and complied. The Association of Licensed Automobile Manufacturers was organized in 1903: "Don't buy a lawsuit with your car" warned its advertising. Hundreds of machine shops from coast to coast continued to produce gasoline automobiles, ignoring the Selden patent as Gottlieb Daimler and others had ignored the Otto patent over two decades earlier; these shops were too small for the A.L.A.M. to bother about.

Alone among the larger American manufacturers, Henry Ford fought the patent. Offering to indemnify every purchaser against litigation, he took his case to court and to the public—David versus Goliath, Henry versus Wall Street. The case raged through the courts for years, guaranteeing Ford frequent headlines, until in January 1911, the U.S. Court of Appeals ruled in Ford's favor. The Court declared the Selden patent valid, but only as it applied to engines on the Brayton principle, which had been outmoded long before gasoline automobiles began to be built in America. No manufacturer in the United States would ever again pay royalties simply for producing a gasoline car. Henry Ford emerged from his Selden patent fight as an American folk hero.

World. The Car of Emperors and Kings," Mercedes ads proclaimed. The Benz ads countered, "The Car of Emperors, the Emperor of Cars."

But cars were only part of the two firms' production. Both were now committed to substantial commercial vehicle programs. By 1907 Benz, with more truck orders than Mannheim could possibly fill, had begun an affiliation with Süddeutsche Automobilfabrik Gaggenau; merger of the two firms as Benzwerke Gaggenau Ltd. followed in 1910. Daimler's earlier venture into the commercial field had also been allied with another producer, the company that Duttenhofer and Lorenz had established in Marienfelde near Berlin to compete with the Cannstatt factory before the turn of the century. In 1902 this independent venture became a branch factory of Daimler-Motoren-Gesellschaft, producing only commercial vehicles. By 1905 buses built in Marienfelde were in use in Berlin and London. And the German post office—which in those days carried passengers in addition to the mail—had a fleet of them. By 1910 there were fifty Benz trucks in Spanish Morocco—and Daimler buses, half of which were exported, were in use as far away as Australia and

Sumatra. Together, Daimler-Marienfelde and Benz-Gaggenau were the world's leading manufacturers of motorized fire-fighting vehicles.

New types of engines were being built as well, Charles Yale Knight's among them. Indiana born, Knight was the publisher of a Chicago farm journal called *Daily Produce* when he came up with the idea of using sleeve valves in an engine instead of the usual poppet variety. Unable to tempt United States manufacturers with this concept, Knight went to Europe and interested the Daimler company in England, Panhard & Levassor in France, Minerva in Belgium and DMG in Germany. Mercedes-Knight cars were on the market by 1910.

The sleeve valve's advantage over reciprocating valves was that it was much quieter. Théodor Pilette, a Belgian DMG distributor and a protégé of Camille Jenatzy, sought to demonstrate the Knight engine's reliability through competition. Pilette entered specially prepared Mercedes-Knight cars in the Czar Nicholas Tour of 1910 and in Spa Week of 1912; both events brought victories. But the Knight's greatest day came the following year at Indianapolis, where, with the financial assistance of Chicago pub-

Gerhart Hauptmann with his 1913 Mercedes 20/50. Dramatist, novelist and poet, Hauptmann inaugurated the naturalistic movement in the German theater and received the Nobel Prize for Literature in 1912.

Other factories, other vehicles. Benz concentrated its commercial vehicle building at Gaggenau near Baden-Baden, Daimler at Marienfelde near Berlin. The Benz fire engine ad is from 1911, the Daimler fire engine from 1909. Though Benz outproduced Daimler in the commercial field, Daimler trucks were more varied and sophisticated. Daimler was among the first truck manufacturers anywhere to adopt shaft drive for quantity production. Many of its trucks were ordered for the Czar's army in Russia. The 28 hp 4½-ton DMG truck (above) is from 1907. The Daimler combination truck (center) is from 1912. The cab in front of the trailer was for the driver's partner, who took care of aft braking.

lisher E. C. Patterson, Pilette entered a car in the Indianapolis 500. The Mercedes-Knight had the smallest engine in the field—250 cubic inches, 100 cubic inches less than most of the other competitors. But Pilette stayed the 500-mile distance without relief, his car averaging 20 mpg of gasoline and 60 mpg of oil, remarkable for that day. He finished fifth to the astonishment of everyone present, including the Toledo manufacturer John North Willys, who soon negotiated to begin production of Knight-engine cars.

Another engine which interested both Daimler and Benz had been patented by Rudolf Diesel in 1892. Diesel's was a sad story. The years of experimentation before his idea worked at all took their toll: he suffered from severe gout, excruciating headaches and bouts of depression. But by the turn of the century the diesel engine was firmly established in industrial use, and Diesel was a millionaire. Bad investments cost him his fortune, however, and, as he tried to adapt his engine for railroad and automotive use, his ailments returned. In September 1913, on his way to preside at ground-breaking ceremonies for a new engine factory in England, Diesel was discovered missing from the Channel steamer he was traveling on. His overcoat, neatly folded with his hat on top, was found at the ship's rail. His body was sighted two weeks later by a Dutch vessel. Rudolf Diesel never saw a diesel locomotive or automobile. But decades later the engine that bears his name had replaced steam on the rails

and become the indomitable workhorse of Mercedes taxis that were routinely driven hundreds of thousands of miles. And his engine was the power plant that made Daimler-Benz the world's largest maker of heavy trucks in the 1970s.

Diesel engine development at Benz began in 1908 after the expiration of Rudolf Diesel's patent and the arrival of Prosper L'Orange, a German of French Huguenot ancestry who had previously been a test engineer at Deutz. L'Orange's pre-combustion chamber patent followed in 1909. This was a step forward in the idea of the diesel-engined automobile, though much further work remained to be done. Production of a diesel engine for marine use began under license from AB Diesel Motorer, Stockholm; one of these Benz-Hesselmann engines powered the ship which carried Roald Amundsen to the South Pole in 1911. The following year DMG's Marienfelde factory began producing diesel engines for marine and stationary applications.

Both Daimler and Benz were also experimenting with aircraft engines. Gottlieb Daimler had started that back in the 1880s with Karl Wölfert and in the 1890s Ferdinand von Zeppelin suggested that Daimler enter the airship business. "People already take me for an idiot for making automobiles," Daimler replied, "if I were to tell them I am going to fly in the air they would consider me an uncertified lunatic." But Daimler remained fascinated with the idea, and

Théodor Pilette and the Mercedes-Knight at the Indianapolis 500, 1913. Though his engine was grossly undersized by race car standards, Pilette finished fifth after stopping just once for a carburetor adjustment. Daimler produced approximately 5,600 Knight-engined cars in the next decade.

133

he and Maybach continued working to reduce an engine's power-to-weight ratio after the engine in the early Wölfert balloon proved too heavy. The first Graf Zeppelin airship made its maiden test flight on July 2, 1900, a few months after Daimler's death. For a decade thereafter every dirigible was Daimler-powered. When Wilhelm Maybach left DMG in 1907, he joined Count von Zeppelin in his airship ventures.

Carl Benz's introduction to the concept of motorized air travel had come after the turn of the century, when Karl Jatho of Hanover asked him for a test engine. This Benz provided, and in August 1903, Jatho made it into the air for a few minutes. That December the Wright brothers, who had built their own engine, took off near Kitty Hawk, North Carolina, and another era was born.

Aircraft development on the Continent was largely confined to France—principally to the peripatetic Gabriel Voisin, whose biplane was flown from Bouy to Rheims by Henri Farman in 1908, the world's first city-to-city flight. The next year Benz & Cie., under the direction of Fritz Hammesfahr, began experiments with aircraft engines. Shortly after that, Daimler-Motoren-Gesellschaft weighed the possibility of building not only aero engines but also airplanes. The idea was abandoned, however, after hoped-for financial backing from the Rothschilds fell through, DMG realized there would be few private aircraft orders, and the German Army seemed to be an unlikely customer (the Kaiser remained an avid motoring enthusiast, but was skeptical when it came to airplanes).

The racing department of Benz & Cie. had been unenthusiastic about the petition that led to the boycott of grand prix competition on the Continent. So after the company's good showing in the 1908 French Grand Prix, Fritz Erle sent Hémery and Hanriot to America for the Grand Prize in Savannah, Georgia, that November; they finished second and fourth. But that was the end of the racing season for the Benz drivers; when they returned to Germany, there was no place in Europe they could compete.

The cars they had driven in Savannah were sold by Jesse Froelich, managing director of the Benz Auto Import Company at 54th Street and Broadway, on Automobile Row in New York City. They could not have gone to two more dissimilar people.

Hémery's car was bought for $4,000 by a driver who unretired himself for the occasion: Berna Eli Oldfield, better known as Barney. Oldfield was a national celebrity: stocky, picturesque, fearless and profane, he was a drinker and brawler, a consummate driver and showman. His trademarks were his checkered cap and his cigar, though the latter also had a

The inventor of the diesel engine and the engineer who made it practical for vehicle use. (Left) Rudolf Diesel (1858-1913). (Right) Prosper L'Orange (1876-1939). L'Orange began development at Benz in 1908 after stationary diesel work at Deutz.

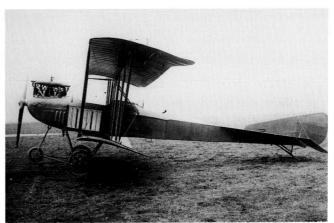

Count Ferdinand von Zeppelin (above, left) had a checkered career. Although by the mid-1880s he had reached the rank of lieutenant general in the Kaiser's army, in 1887 he was forced to retire, purportedly for criticizing the Kaiser's friends. How he happened to become interested in flight is not known. The first Daimler-engined Graf Zeppelin had its maiden flight in July 1900 (above, right), with Zeppelin at the controls. The two cars underneath the dirigible were for vertical control, achieved by moving a 550-pound weight between them. Though primitive, the airship flew for 75 minutes but attracted little public attention, just like Orville Wright's first flight three and a half years later. Heavier-than-air craft interested Benz. On July 13, 1913, Hellmuth Hirth flew his Benz-engined Albatross from Berlin to Mannheim, landing in front of the Benz factory (top, right). The 150 hp Benz-engined biplane (center) is from 1914, the DMG ad from c. 1915.

practical use, as his personal shock absorber: when Oldfield raced, he clenched his teeth so hard they hurt afterward. Oldfield disliked organized competition and sneered at racing organizations, which frequently snarled back; he had numerous suspensions from the American Automobile Association. He was much more at home on the fair circuit, where match races were his specialty. He was a hero to every kid in America when he decided to retire in mid-1908. But by the end of the year his manager, Ernie Moross, had told him about the 120-hp grand prix Benz that was up for sale, and Barney decided his retirement was premature.

In August 1909, a new dirt-track speedway opened in Indianapolis. Barney and the Benz were there for the inaugural race and did a mile in 43.2 seconds—83.5 mph, an American track record. There would be no further racing on that dirt track however; the inaugural had seen too many accidents. The management decided to pave it with bricks, three million of them, thus starting a sociological phenomenon that has flourished to this day: the Indi-anapolis Motor Speedway and the 500-mile race.

The second Benz, Hanriot's car, went to David Bruce-Brown, a handsome, serious-looking college boy whose Social Register family lived on the fashionable East Side of New York. After acquiring the car, Bruce-Brown won the Shingle Hill Climb sponsored by the Yale University Automobile Club; more significantly, he took the Benz to Florida for the Ormond-Daytona speed week in March 1909, and established a record of 5:14:2 in the ten-mile event. Bruce-Brown then sought to find out what the car could really do in a series of straight-line mile runs. His unofficial speeds were as high as 115 mph; officially, he lowered the world amateur mile record to 33 seconds, for over 109 mph and the Sir Thomas Dewar Trophy.

In Mannheim, it was Bruce-Brown's mile run, not Oldfield's, which impressed Victor Hémery. The speeds reached at Ormond-Daytona indicated the potential of the Benz grand prix car. Since the manufacturers' boycott meant developing race cars was an exercise in futility, Hémery suggested they build a

The Benz team at the Grand Prize in Savannah, 1908. Hémery (8) and Hanriot (15) finished second and fourth. Stunned mid-race when the tread from a rear tire hit him in the head, team manager Erle (19) crashed, but was only slightly injured.

record car instead. In December 1905, Hémery, driving a Darracq, had captured the land speed record in southern France at 109.65 mph. In January 1906, Fred Marriott, in a Stanley Steamer, had clocked an official 121.57 mph for the kilometer and an unofficial 127.66 for the mile on the Ormond-Daytona sands. Hémery wanted the record back.

Permission to build a record car was given, and the Benz design staff got to work. To travel faster in those days one generally built bigger, and the new Benz was big: four cylinders, 185 by 200 mm bore and stroke, 21.5 liters (1,312 cubic inches), 200 horsepower at 1,600 rpm. In November 1909, Hémery took the 200-hp Benz to Brooklands in England and was clocked at 125.947 mph for the flying kilometer, which broke the Stanley kilometer record. But in trying for the mile, Hémery found the car did not take the Brooklands banking easily; 115.923 mph was the best he could do. From which two conclusions were drawn: a more streamlined body would improve the car's speed, and a straightaway, rather than a banked track, was preferable for further runs. The sands of Ormond-Daytona beckoned.

After test runs in Mannheim, the rebodied car was shipped across the Atlantic in January 1910, and Jesse Froelich put it on display in the Benz showroom at 54th and Broadway. Now the question was who would drive it. Froelich hinted that Ralph De Palma or George Robertson might. Barney Oldfield said *he* would.

Oldfield wanted to break Marriott's Stanley record as much as Hémery did. Aware of the Benz performance at Brooklands, he knew it was the car for the job. He and his manager, Ernie Moross, quickly made the decision: Moross traded in the 120-hp grand prix car plus $6,000 in cash and bought the 200-hp Benz, which was immediately dubbed Lightning. Then Barney went to Florida.

On March 16, after several trial runs, Oldfield put cotton plugs in his ears, stuck a cigar in his mouth, pulled down his goggles and barked to the timers, "Me and the Benz here, we're gonna warm up the sand a little." A few minutes later, after a flying start, he had traveled a mile in 27.33 seconds for an average speed of 131.724 mph; his time for the flying kilometer was 17.04 seconds, or 131.275 mph. The press was agog. The *Florida Times Union* reported, "The speed attained was the fastest ever traveled by a human being, no greater speed having been recorded except that made by a bullet." And Barney pontificated, "A speed of 131 miles an hour is as near to the absolute limit of speed as humanity will ever travel." Shortly before Barney's run, the governing body in Paris which oversaw international motoring matters

CHAMPION "BARNEY" OLDFIELD'S- -RACING FACE AND CIGAR BUTT

"You know me." His trademark line was almost as famous as his trademark cigar. Barney Oldfield was irrepressible to the end. "I've been going some," he wrote in April 1946, "and I'm going to go some more so-o-o..." He died that October at 68.

had decreed that only two-way averages would be considered for records, so Oldfield's marks were unofficial. Whether he had been aware of the ruling before the run is not known, but given his contempt for establishment organizations he would not have cared. Not that it mattered. The press, and Barney himself, called Oldfield the World Speed King. Royalty, indeed, joined in the international acclaim. "I congratulate a daring Yankee on so remarkable a performance in a German car," read the cable from Wilhelm II.

Three weeks later Barney and the Benz were in California. A new race course had been built at Playa del Rey near Los Angeles. It was officially designated a motordrome; it would become known as a toothpick saucer.

By now road racing had really come to America. There was racing on Long Island and in Philadelphia, Savannah, and Elgin, Illinois. But most track events had been held on dirt ovals laid out for horse racing. Though the Brooklands track in England had been paved with cement and the Indiana Speedway people had settled on bricks, some United States entrepreneurs decided on wood. A steeply banked board oval offered phenomenal speeds, thrills a minute—and revenue. Unfortunately, the grandstands built around these ovals usually lasted longer than the tracks, which also proved dangerous: shrapnel-like flying splinters punctured tires and hit drivers in the face. Youngsters frequently went to the races not through the gates but under the track, sticking their heads up through holes in the boards to watch the action and ducking down when a race car roared by . . . which led to some awful accidents. Ultimately, the board tracks which did not fall down were torn down, or met a different fate. The fire that destroyed the Los Angeles track in 1914 prompted Damon Runyon to write, "Playa del Rey burned last night with a great saving of lives."

But in 1910 Playa del Rey was America's wooden wonder, the country's first board speedway. Its promoters invited Oldfield to drive the Benz in a one-mile trial. Oldfield finished the mile in 36.22 seconds for 99 mph, an American track record; the Playa del Rey promoters paid him $4,000 for his performance. Then he and Moross went barnstorming to the county fairs. His fee for showing up anywhere with the Benz was $2,000; the car was paid for in no time. Sometime that summer its name was changed from Lightning to Blitzen and a small reproduction of the German Imperial crest appeared on its hood. This was the idea of Oldfield's longtime lackey in county fair match races, Ben Kerscher, a good driver who was contractually permitted to come in no better than

Ormond-Daytona, March 1910. "The front wheels were shooting up and down in a weird dance," said Oldfield after the run, "and I knew that if a tire burst I would be beyond mortal help." Instead Barney had the land speed record at over 131 mph.

Following the Ormond-Daytona run, Barney barnstormed his Benz throughout the country. Its name was changed from Lightning to Blitzen that summer, but the Oldfield scenario remained the same. In Act I the great engine was cranked. An ear-shattering exhaust backfire followed, as Barney cocked his head and listened, then reached down and reconnected a loose wire. Act II was the announcement that Barney would go for a new record "at the very risk of his life." In Act III he got it. The crowd would go wild. Oldfield's circus antics should not obscure the phenomenal driver he was, however, nor the thrills he provided a generation of Americans. "If I go, I want it to be in the Blitzen Benz," said Barney. "I want the grandstand to be crowded and the band playing the latest rag."

second in any event with his boss (not that he could have won anyway once Barney had the Blitzen). The Blitzen had its own railway car, specially painted, which would arrive in town a few days ahead of Barney and be parked on a siding. Barney's advance man would arrive next to stir up the populace, ask what the track record was, and say that the Blitzen would go for it. Kids would run out to the siding to stare at the railway car, a banner would be hung in the hotel reading "Oldfield Sleeps Here," and the town would talk of nothing but the big event. A brass band and the mayor would greet Barney at the railroad station on the appointed day. And, of course, the Blitzen would set a track record.

Oldfield and the Blitzen had a good summer. But in the fall Barney went too far. A match race against the heavyweight boxing champion, Jack Johnson, was a fiasco: Johnson was not an accredited race driver, and the American Automobile Association suspended Oldfield. "So who needs the stinking AAA?" Barney inquired. He barnstormed in Mexico for a while; then, "tired of the strife and turmoil," as he said, he retired again. Moross took over the Benz, and Barney opened a saloon in Los Angeles.

The driver Moross hired to campaign the Blitzen in 1911 was Bob Burman, previously one of the stars, with Louis Chevrolet, of the Buick racing team. "Wild Bob" was his nickname, though he was not a flamboyant showman. But he was easily as fearless as Oldfield, as he proved on his twenty-seventh birthday, April 23, 1911, when he drove the Blitzen for the first time on the sands at Ormond-Daytona.

Several times during the trial runs the winds tore the lenses out of Burman's goggles, a problem solved by riveting them to the frames. Finally, with the timers set and a huge crowd on hand, Burman set off for a record. "One mountainous bump . . . threw me clear out of the seat, and my foot slipped off the throttle instantly," he said afterward, "but I was back on again quicker than I could realize what I had done, and old Blitzen and I were chasing up the beach again." When the chase was over, Burman and the Blitzen had done 140.865 mph for the kilometer,

141.732 mph for the mile—a full ten miles an hour faster than Oldfield.

That speed was considered incredible. It was twice as fast as an airplane had flown; it was quicker than the fastest train; it was faster than any automobile would attain until after the First World War. The Benz publicity department revived the *Florida Times Union* line, advertising, "Only a bullet has traveled faster." Bob Burman was the new Speed King. The following month, in a ceremony before the inaugural running of the Indianapolis 500, Harvey Firestone placed a $10,000 jeweled crown on Burman's head attesting to that fact. Though too big for the 500 itself, the Blitzen treated the crowd to a demonstration run: Burman did a mile in 35.5 seconds, the fastest ever at Indianapolis and a record that would stand for five years.

Oldfield was livid at this turn of events. "I should have never let Ernie take over the Benz," he fumed. "He knows I didn't have the Blitzen wide open last year." Of course not; Oldfield had always held back—for the next record attempt, for the next county fair. He was so furious he unretired again. But the Blitzen belonged to Burman. The Imperial Eagle on its hood was even bigger now, and there was gilt striping all over the body. The car went on the fair circuit, and the crowds were bigger than ever. The Blitzen was a legend; no one who heard it roar around a dirt track was ever likely to forget it.

For 1912 Moross and Burman reasoned that if one Blitzen was super, two would be colossal. They approached Jesse Froelich in New York to ask if he could coax a 300-hp Benz out of the Mannheim factory. With a car like that, Burman said, he could do better than 150 mph. Froelich was dubious about Mannheim's reaction, but the Blitzen was boosting Benz sales in the United States. So he suggested to Burman and Moross that *they* go to the factory to present their request, and he sent along his secretary Walter Maas to help.

As Froelich suspected, Benz & Cie. did not go for the 300-hp Benz idea. Mannheim was preoccupied at the moment, pleasantly to be sure, trying to meet the demand for Benz cars. Since the spring the factory had been working double shifts. Between 1911

Robert "Wild Bob" Burman (1884-1916). Michigan farm boy Burman began racing in 1901. Ten years later he smashed Oldfield's Blitzen record at Ormond-Daytona (top) to become the new World Speed King, complete with crown bestowed at the Indianapolis 500 (center and below). Like Oldfield, Burman had momentarily lost his sight during the record run. Said he matter-of-factly later, "I now believe the limit of speed is the point where it is no longer possible to see."

Advertising the Blitzen on the Continent, 1913-1914. The Benz exhibit at the Paris Automobile Salon, and a new runabout model, 1911. Friedrich Nallinger (1863-1937). Stuttgart-born, Nallinger worked for the Wurttemberg State Railway before joining DMG in 1904. In 1910 he left Daimler; in 1912 he became technical manager at Benz. Nallinger streamlined Benz car production, encouraged diesel and aviation engine development and reorganized the Gaggenau factory. In the twenties he would be among the principal champions of the merger of Daimler and Benz.

and 1912 car production increased from 2,265 to 3,095 and 2,000 new workers were hired, bringing the work force to 6,000. The profit for the fiscal year was 4.4 million marks, which went up to 6.3 million the following year. There were more than a dozen different Benz cars on the market, ranging in price from 7,000 to 40,000 marks. Friedrich Nallinger, born in Stuttgart and formerly of DMG but now a Benz man and board member, argued that the company should focus on fewer models, but he was overruled. Business, after all, was booming.

The French Grand Prix was to be revived the next year, the Benz people told Burman and Moross, but they didn't have the time to be interested either in the Grand Prix or in building a Benz record car one-third bigger than the giant they already had. But the company *had* built another 200-hp car, and they agreed to send that one to the States.

On September 12, 1912, it arrived, and was dubbed the Jumbo Benz. Advertising to the contrary,

David Bruce-Brown (1890-1912). International fame followed his Grand Prize victory in a Benz in 1910.

it was not more powerful than the Blitzen, but it was marginally faster, as it demonstrated in track events that year. Both cars set a blazing pace at fairs throughout the country, once literally: Burman put up a 28-second mile on a San Diego beach the first day and caught fire on the second, a situation he remedied by driving into the surf.

This was Burman's last year of record breaking. He returned to competition in sanctioned events and was killed racing a Peugeot at Corona, California, in 1916. Moross now had both 200-hp Benzes. He kept one and signed up another driver, Theodore Tetzlaff (better known as Terrible Teddy) for further barnstorming. The other car was purchased by Harry Harkness, a millionaire sportsman from New York.

The Blitzen was not the only Benz doing the company proud in America. The energetic Froelich had orchestrated a comprehensive road racing campaign that had the outward appearance of a full factory effort. He was able to put it together on a shoestring budget since most of the racing Benzes were cars he had sold—like the grand prix Benz taken in trade from Oldfield that was bought off his

THE GOLD GRAND PRIZE CUP
WON BY BENZ

Following the 1910 Grand Prize in Savannah, Jesse Froelich promoted the one–two Benz finish extensively. This illustration is from a brochure cover.

Grand Prize, Savannah, 1910. "If I can keep my cool for the first few laps I'm all right," said Victor Hémery. "My big fight is with myself." Hémery, shown before the start (top), was cool but his pace was hot. He finished the first 17.3-mile lap in 14 minutes 18 seconds, about 73 mph, and his Benz remained comfortably in the lead until Lap 8 when a long pit stop to change tires dropped him back. The pace became even hotter thereafter with challenges from the Fiats of Louis Wagner and Ralph De Palma, as well as from teammate David Bruce-Brown; the lead changed repeatedly. When it was over, Bruce-Brown (above) had won, by little more than a second and in a finish so spectacular that his mother, who disapproved of his racing, sprinted to the track to congratulate him.

showroom floor early in 1910 by young Eddie Hearne. Hearne took it to Illinois a couple of months later to win the Fox River Trophy at the Elgin road races.

Two months later, in October, as Orville Harrold was singing "Ah, Sweet Mystery of Life" in Victor Herbert's newest operetta, *Naughty Marietta*, and Fanny Brice was becoming a star in Florenz Ziegfeld's *Follies*, the word was out on Long Island: "Chain your dogs and lock up your fowl." The Vanderbilt Cup was being run again.

The contest that Willie K. Vanderbilt had inaugurated in 1904 for full-bore race cars had by now become a stock chassis event, limited to engines not exceeding 600 cubic inches. This meant the 920-cubic-inch grand prix Benz could not compete, so three 471.2-cubic-inch modified production cars were entered. Two of these would be driven by David Bruce-Brown and Eddie Hearne, and Froelich asked George Robertson to drive the third. Though amateurs and new to racing, the young sportsmen had shown themselves to be able competitors, and Robertson was a seasoned professional who had reached stardom by winning the 1908 Vanderbilt Cup with a Locomobile, the first victory of an American car in a major road race. With Robertson heading the Benz team Froelich was confident of a good showing, and became even more convinced when Robertson set the fastest practice times.

But Froelich's plans came to naught. When practice was over, a New York reporter asked Robertson for a drive around the course. With visions of a story in his head, Froelich agreed. The reporter told Robertson to step on it because he wanted to give his readers a first-hand idea of what racing was all about. Robertson complied—and the man panicked. At the first turn he grabbed Robertson's arm, the Benz ran off the road and flipped over. "As I got to my feet, about to pass out," Robertson recalled afterward, "I saw my adorable passenger. His derby was not even dented." But Robertson's back, ribs and elbow were broken.

With Robertson hospitalized, Froelich hurriedly installed one of his mechanics, Franz Heim, in the car. But the episode with the reporter had so unnerved everyone on the Benz team that the best showing in the race was Hearne's eighth place. Froelich made a mental note to think twice in the future before leaping for page-one stories.

The next month came the second running of the Grand Prize in Savannah. Here there were no stock chassis restrictions; here the 920-cubic-inch grand prix cars could be run. And both of them would be, Bruce-Brown driving his and Hearne lending his Benz to Victor Hémery, who had finished second in that same car in the inaugural Grand Prize of 1908 and who had arrived from Mannheim with victory in mind. To round out his team, Froelich prepared a

Ralph De Palma (1883-1956), the former Franklin mechanic from Brooklyn, at speed during the 1912 Grand Prize with the Mercedes that became legendary as the Grey Ghost.

Both the Vanderbilt and the Grand Prize were run in Savannah in 1911, on November 27 and 30 respectively. De Palma raced his new Mercedes wearing No. 10 in the Vanderbilt (finishing second) and No. 55 in the Grand Prize (finishing third). The Benz team contested only the Grand Prize. Posing beforehand are drivers Eddie Hearne (seated on the rear wheel), Hémery (behind the steering wheel) and Erwin Bergdoll (standing in front). The Bergdoll Benz (No. 52) suffered a cracked cylinder, Hémery broke an exhaust valve, but Hearne finished second — behind David Bruce-Brown, who had switched to a Fiat this year. The race was a close one, with Hearne leading for 240 of the 411 miles and Bruce-Brown coming from behind to snatch victory at a 74.45 mph average to Hearne's even 74 mph.

third, smaller car for Willie Haupt of Pottstown, Pennsylvania, the hill-climbing ace.

All of Savannah seemed to be on hand, as well as thousands of motoring enthusiasts from the North who arrived either on the *Wall Street Special*, a private train of stateroom and observation cars organized by the Motor Racing Association, or on one of the steamships chartered by the Automobile Club of America. Southern hospitality greeted the guests. "Welcome to everybody, without reference to Bradstreet rating," said the *Savannah Press*. The race circuit consisted of 17.3 miles of well-oiled roadway, with long straights and firmly banked curves lined by magnificent oaks laden with Spanish moss. Fifteen cars faced the starting flag on the morning of November 12. France, which regarded its boycott as international, did not compete, but Italy sent three Fiats; the favorite among the nine American cars was the Vanderbilt-winning Alco. The favorite in the Benz contingent was Victor Hémery.

Hémery lived up to his promise at the start, taking the lead and holding it until the eighth of the 24 laps. At that point a long pit stop to replace both rear tires dropped him to fifth, and two Fiats led. Frantic signals from the Benz pit urged Bruce-Brown and Haupt to step up their pace, which both did. Haupt overdid. Leading on the twelfth lap, he drove broadside into a tree, which fortunately harmed only his car.

The race continued as a competition between the Benzes and the Fiats, but in the final laps the Fiats dropped out; the last lap was a contest between Hémery and Bruce-Brown, and Bruce-Brown won it. Over 415 racing miles he had averaged 70.55 mph, an American road race record. Even more incredibly, after nearly six hours of driving, his winning margin over Hémery was just 1.42 seconds—by far the closest finish in international competition to date.

Hémery, who was well known for fits of temper when a race did not go his way, took the loss well. "I wouldn't have minded one minute," he remarked, "but one second *is* hard luck." And then he good-naturedly poured a bottle of champagne over Bruce-Brown's head. For the amateur, the victory was many-splendored; David Bruce-Brown had not only won the race, he had won over his family to the idea of racing itself. His mother had traveled to Savannah to urge him not to compete, threatening to disinherit him if he did. She decided otherwise after that last lap.

With a one-two Benz finish in America's premier road race, and the Blitzen the fastest car in the world, Froelich called his new Benz catalogue "Champion of Champions."

The news of Benz's American success was not lost

Indianapolis Motor Speedway, 1912. His Grey Ghost Mercedes shorn of its vee radiator for the 500, De Palma was reeling off laps at better than 80 mph, a full five laps ahead of Joe Dawson's National. Victory seemed assured, but then...

Joe Dawson, Winner 1912

Just three miles from the finish, the cry went up from one end of the grandstand to the other: "Where's De Palma?" His Mercedes had thrown a connecting rod on the back stretch. De Palma got out of the car and, with mechanic Rupert Jeffkins, began to push. Signaled by the National crew, Dawson "cut loose" and, after taking the checkered flag from Fred Wagner, circled the track at full speed for two more laps just to make sure fortune had indeed been so kind. To the deafening cheers of 80,000 spectators, De Palma continued to push the Grey Ghost toward the finish line. Dawson's victory won him $20,000. De Palma's eleventh place brought $1,100 — and a hero's honor. (Facing page) Illustrations from a 1913 DMG catalog showing just two of more than a dozen Mercedes models available.

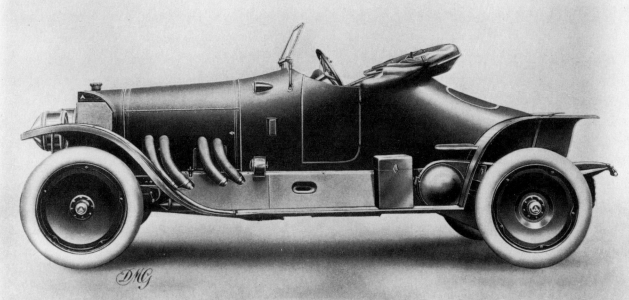

Daimler-Motoren-Gesellschaft, Stuttgart-Untertürkheim.

Nr. 13|61   *Mercedes-Daimler-Karosserie*

Daimler-Motoren-Gesellschaft, Stuttgart-Untertürkheim.

Nr. 13|58   *Mercedes-Daimler-Karosserie*

on Daimler-Motoren-Gesellschaft. Though because of the manufacturers' boycott no substantial sums were being expended on racing machines, Paul Daimler did have a few cars built especially for the United States using production engines modified and tuned for 140 hp, fitted into chassis which had been built for the 1908 French Grand Prix, and rebodied with distinctive V radiators. These cars were shipped over in 1911.

The first car was destined for young Spencer Wishart, the son of a successful Wall Street speculator from Greenwich, Connecticut. For his eighteenth birthday in 1908 Spence's father had given him a Mercedes 90 (in which he placed fourth in the 1909 Vanderbilt); the new Mercedes 140 was a gift for his twenty-first birthday (in it he placed fourth in the 1911 Indianapolis 500). Wishart was a fine driver, though his youthful exuberance sometimes got the best of him. At the Fairmount Park road race in Philadelphia later that year he won his class—until it was discovered that in the final laps his riding mechanic had fallen out of the car and rather than waste time going back to get him, Wishart had driven to the pits and picked up a substitute. This was against the rules, and Wishart was disqualified. Father and son took the matter to court, but lost there, too. (Fairmount Park was won that year by Erwin Bergdoll in a Benz.)

The second Mercedes 140 was purchased by a New Jersey lamp manufacturer, E. J. Schroeder, for a rising young professional, Ralph De Palma. He was perhaps the most heroic of all the drivers of what has been called the heroic age of American motor sport. Certainly he was the most gallant. The verve and finesse with which he drove raised the level of American racing to an art. His career was a long one—over a quarter of a century, during which he won more than twenty-five hundred of the nearly three thousand events he entered.* But his greatest years were those he raced for Mercedes with the car that became legendary as the Grey Ghost.

---

*The actual figures, by De Palma's count, were 2,557 wins in 2,889 races entered. But these figures reflected all individual events, including the short sprints (five, ten, fifteen, twenty-five, fifty miles) which on many race programs preceded the main contest. On a good day, De Palma sometimes won as many as six races.

De Palma's first drives with the Mercedes were the Vanderbilt and the Grand Prize in Savannah in late 1911, shortly after the car arrived in New York. He finished second in the Vanderbilt, third in the Grand Prize. These were very good maiden efforts, and he got to know the car.

The following Memorial Day weekend in Indianapolis, in one of the most memorable races ever run at the Brickyard, De Palma nearly won the 500. Although the always impetuous Teddy Tetzlaff and his Fiat had stormed into the lead with the starting flag, by lap three De Palma's grey Mercedes had overtaken him. From then on, De Palma began building a commanding lead. By lap 198 he was a full five laps ahead of Joe Dawson and the National, an Indianapolis-built car. Then, one and a half laps from the finish, the Grey Ghost threw a connecting rod. Victory was impossible, but there was only one way De Palma would accept defeat, and that was on his own terms. He got out of the car and, with the help of his mechanic, Rupert Jeffkins, began pushing it toward the finish line. The crowd went crazy; eighty thousand spectators cheered him on. By the time De Palma reached the pits, exhaustion overcame him, and the National streaked by to take the checkered flag. Ralph De Palma was the first to congratulate Joe Dawson on his victory. He himself finished eleventh.

Three months later, De Palma and the Grey Ghost were in Illinois for the Elgin road races, where he won both the Elgin National Trophy and the free-for-all, the latter at a record-breaking 68.9 mph. (Bergdoll was second in his Benz.) De Palma then traveled to Milwaukee for the Vanderbilt Cup on October 2, followed by the Grand Prize on the fifth. De Palma won the Vanderbilt easily (Wishart's Mercedes was third), but the Grand Prize was catastrophic.

Even before the starting flag the atmosphere was ominous because, during practice, the twenty-four-year-old David Bruce-Brown, driving a new Fiat, had crashed to his death. De Palma very nearly died in the race itself. It was his fault, he insisted. During the closing laps, as he was attempting to overtake Caleb Bragg in the leading Fiat along the Fond du Lac straight, he edged too close. The Mercedes

Vanderbilt Cup, Santa Monica, 1914. De Palma knew a non-stop run was the only chance his aging Grey Ghost Mercedes had in a field of brand-new race cars. By mid-race 11 of the 15 starters had retired. Only Oldfield was left to challenge. Driving with patient consistency — his fastest lap 6 minutes 20 seconds, his slowest 6:42 — De Palma swung wide (top), looked back and saw a way to trick Oldfield into a pit stop. Jubilant revenge was his (above) as he crossed the finish line, the winner at 75.49 mph to the runner-up's 75.06. Barney tried to convince reporters that a broken piston ring had lost him the race. Few were fooled. "Victory Due to Headwork" was one newspaper headline.

nicked the Fiat's left rear wheel, then plunged off the road. "Boys, don't forget Caleb Bragg wasn't to blame," De Palma gasped to reporters before the ambulance took him away. "He gave me all the road." The accident kept De Palma in the hospital for nine weeks and sent the battered Mercedes back to Schroeder's garage in New Jersey. But both car and driver had one more bow to take that year: De Palma's drives on the Mercedes earned him the AAA national championship.

Of all his racing victories, De Palma always said his favorite was the 1914 Vanderbilt Cup in Santa Monica, California. If things had gone as planned, he would have been driving a Mercer; instead he was driving his Grey Ghost Mercedes. That was one of the reasons the win was his favorite. Another was the man he beat. A third was the way he did it.

After leaving the hospital in Milwaukee shortly before Christmas, 1912, De Palma had accepted the offer of the Mercer Automobile Company to be the captain of its racing team. The Mercer, produced in Trenton, New Jersey, was a rising star in American motor sport, a vigorous challenger to the Indianapolis-built Stutz. The cars for 1913 were new and, though De Palma's first season with the team produced some fine wins, much of it was spent correcting faults, making adjustments and preparing for 1914, which promised to be Mercer's year. Then, a month before the new season opened in Santa Monica, Mercer decided that having America's two most famous drivers on its team was a good idea. The company signed up Barney Oldfield, who once again unretired. De Palma was infuriated. For one thing, he intensely disliked Oldfield; for another, there was a principle involved: as captain of the team he had not been informed beforehand, and Oldfield's arrival meant that one of his team members would be displaced. So De Palma quit the team instead.

With the Vanderbilt now about three weeks away, De Palma contacted his old patron, Schroeder, and asked if he could have the Grey Ghost Mercedes back. Schroeder financed the repairs and an overhaul and shipped the car to California.

The stage was set. Oldfield would be driving the Mercer that De Palma had spent the previous season

developing into a winner. De Palma's car was essentially vintage 1908—"the old grey Mercedes," reporters called it. "My *ancient schöne rennwagen*" was De Palma's more affectionate term. "If he gets that old boat fixed," Barney Oldfield laughed during practice, "I'll run him clean off the course." De Palma disagreed. He knew the Mercer well. But he also knew the Mercedes, they had been through a lot together, and he was convinced the car had one race left.

The Santa Monica course, lined with palm and eucalyptus trees, measured 8.4 miles per lap, with thirty-five laps to be run for a total of 294 miles. The pace was blistering from the beginning. By the halfway point, eleven of the fifteen starters had retired. A Mason and a Stutz fought for third place, several laps back, while De Palma and Oldfield were battling it out up front. Oldfield stopped once for a new tire, once more to refuel. De Palma was in the lead. On the thirtieth lap, swinging wide at the Nevada Avenue corner, he glanced back and noticed that the Mercer's tires were beginning to shred. So close to the finish, he knew Oldfield would never stop unless . . .

As the two cars came barreling down the straight toward the pits, De Palma "risked the highest revs of the entire race . . . and the old Mercedes howled," as he said later. But he pulled far enough ahead of Oldfield so that when he signaled his crew he would be coming in for a pit stop on the next round, Oldfield could not fail to notice it. Then De Palma let the Mercer pass him. As Oldfield made a pit stop on the next lap, the Mercedes sailed by. In a rage, Oldfield roared out of the pits and tried to catch up. A nonstop run in any major race of that era was virtually unheard of, but the Grey Ghost's driver was sure the Mercedes wouldn't fail him and it didn't. De Palma crossed the finish line two hundred yards ahead of Oldfield. "This," said De Palma years later, "was the high spot, the top-most thrill in nearly thirty thousand miles of racing."

The Grey Ghost was not the only venerable Mercedes still competing. In England the Mercedes colors were being flown by Gordon Watney, an enterprising speed merchant who set himself up in

(Above) In 1907, when Brooklands Track opened in Weybridge, a pair of 1906 Grand Prix Mercedes — one driven by British Mercedes agent J.E. Hutton, the other by Dario Resta — finished one-two in the day's feature event. The Resta car was owned by sportsman F.R. Fry, who enjoyed wagering and lost his bet that day. But Resta — Italian-born though raised in England from age two — had his day and was back in Fry's good graces the next year, when he drove the same car to world records of 88.8 and 95.5 mph for the 10-lap standing and half-mile flying starts. Fry was so pleased he later bought one of the 1908 Grand Prix Mercedes for Resta to drive. (Top) A second 1908 Grand Prix Mercedes was bought by Gordon Watney, who streamlined its tail, did a 109-mph flying mile in 1911 and sold the car to Lord Vernon.

Major L.G. Hornsted at Brooklands, 1911. His first Benz developed only 27.3 bhp but was streamlined even more radically than the Watney Mercedes, so Cupid managed to lap the track at 95 mph. He tried a 1908 GP Benz next, then ordered the Big Benz.

business in Weybridge, a short distance from Brooklands, and specialized in buying up old Mercedes to race himself or for aristocratic sportsmen anxious to do likewise. His stable included Jenatzy's 1903 Gordon Bennett winner and one of the 1908 Grand Prix cars which set a 109-mph Brooklands lap record in February, 1911. In August that year, Watney challenged the Maharajah of Tikari to a 100-pound match race. The Maharajah's Renault was driven for him by Eric Loder. Lord Vernon drove Watney's Mercedes and won easily, also winning a handicap event from a Benz the same day.

The losing Benz had been driven by the Mannheim company's representative in Britain, Major L. G. Hornsted—Cupid to his friends. The car was the first of three in which he would compete. The second was a 1908 grand prix model in which he

lapped Brooklands at 103.76 mph in February 1912. At the end of that season, Hornsted went to Mannheim to ask for more horsepower. Aware of the Blitzen's performance in the States, he requested a similar 200-hp car built to his specifications; it was known simply as the Big Benz. That it had as much torque as the Blitzen was indicated by Cupid's comment that wheelspin resulted "if you even looked at the accelerator too sharply." In December 1913 Hornsted took the standing kilometer at 73.57 mph, and in January a flying mile at 124.10. The Big Benz was the fastest car at Brooklands, and Hornsted drove it there at every opportunity.

He took it to Ostend, Belgium, in July 1914 and won three races. But no one paid much attention. The French Grand Prix, held on July 4, produced even more thunderous headlines than the Big Benz.

Cupid Hornsted at Brooklands, 1913. In addition to proving that his Big Benz was the fastest car at the track, Hornsted was delighted to give "a fine demonstration of the Benz steering" by taking his hands off the wheel at 90 mph on the banking.

CHAPTER FIVE

THE STAR AND
THE LAUREL

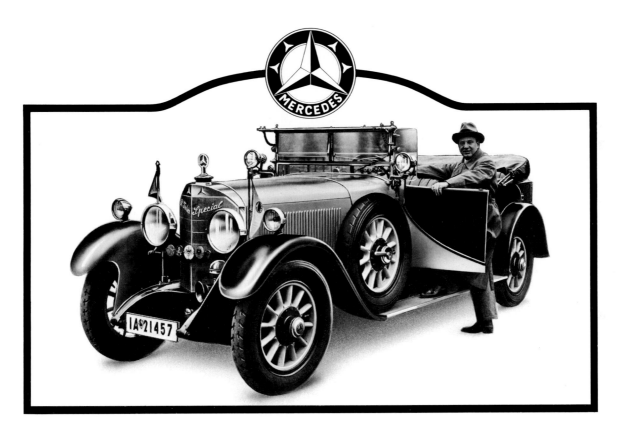

1 9 1 4 — 1 9 2 6

To every thing there is a season,
and a time to every purpose
under the Heaven.
ECCLESIASTES

The French Grand Prix, reinstated in 1912, was won that year and the next by the formidable new twin-cam Peugeots. The driver both times was the dashing Georges Boillot, who looked as if he had leaped from the pages of a Dumas novel. That this daring musketeer would win again in 1914 was almost a foregone conclusion.

In Mannheim, Benz & Cie. was not interested. The American successes with the grand prix cars and the exploits of the Blitzen and the Big Benz were all promoting their products nicely. The company, which had invested heavily in expanding its commercial and passenger vehicle production and in diesel and aircaft engine development, had no money left for racing. Since Victor Hémery was interested only in the latter, he left Benz to join a French firm similarly inclined, taking two other Benz drivers, René Hanriot and Franz Heim, with him. Not surprisingly, the new Lorraine-Dietrichs they raced in the French Grand Prix were virtual copies of the grand prix Benz.

In Untertürkheim, Daimler-Motoren-Gesellschaft appeared similarly uninterested. The company sat out 1912, and the word in sporting circles was that DMG was content to live on the reputation Mercedes had already earned. In 1913 the company did make an effort by building several six-cylinder

Paul Daimler (1869-1945). He began his career helping his father at age 14; at age 38 he replaced Wilhelm Maybach as chief engineer of Daimler-Motoren-Gesellschaft.

cars for the French Grand Prix, but their entry was disallowed because it had been made not by a manufacturer but by the Belgian distributor, Théodor Pilette. DMG must have known this might happen. The cars were run instead in a subsequent event at Le

Paul Daimler-designed six-cylinder race car for the 1913 Grand Prix at Le Mans, photographed at the factory with Théodor Pilette behind the wheel, his friend, fellow Belgian Léon Elskamp, beside him.

Grand Prix de France, Le Mans, 1913. The Mercedes team included one 1908 GP-type chassis with tuned four-cylinder production engine driven by Elskamp (top) and three new six-cylinder aircraft-engined cars for Pilette, Salzer and Lautenschlager (above). Retention of chain drive, Pilette's preference, was thought "most curious" by the press but the tapered frames, detachable wire wheels and vee radiators were considered "good streamlined fittings." With Peugeot abstaining, the 338-mile contest proved a Delage-Mercedes battle, which Delage won. But all four Mercedes finished (Pilette third, Salzer fourth, Lautenschlager sixth, Elskamp seventh). It had been good practice.

Mans, where they finished third, fourth, sixth and seventh—which was fine with Paul Daimler, because he was practicing for something bigger. All efforts were focused on building cars for the 1914 Grand Prix, which was already being viewed as Mercedes' official return to the sport.

On June 28, 1914, less than a week before the race, Gavrilo Princip, a young Bosnian member of a terrorist organization, assassinated the Austrian Archduke Franz Ferdinand and his wife at Sarajevo, Yugoslavia. Just one more Balkan crisis, some observers thought, another in the long series to which the world was becoming accustomed. But this one would grow into a giant volcano.

Over many decades, an intricate web of alliances had been woven on the Continent. Britain, France and Russia were united in the Triple Entente, Germany, Austria-Hungary, and Italy formed the Triple Alliance. Determined to attack Serbia in the wake of the assassination, Austria asked Kaiser Wilhelm for German support if Russia came to Serbia's aid. Neither of Wilhelm's alternatives was inviting. To say yes to Austria could involve Germany in war; to say no would isolate her on the Continent. The Triple Entente was strong. Italy was the weak partner in the Triple Alliance; Austria-Hungary was the only ally

Germany could rely on, as Austrian diplomats made clear to Wilhelm in the days ahead.

The deliberations of the Habsburgs and the Hohenzollerns had an indirect but significant effect on policy decisions at Daimler headquarters. In January 1912, alarmed by French advances in military aviation—the French army already had over 230 trained pilots, the German fewer than 50—Kaiser Wilhelm offered a substantial award (50,000 goldmarks for first prize, 30,000 for second) for the best aviation engine produced by a German firm. The competing engines were to be tested and the award was to be made on the Emperor's birthday. Twenty-six German companies entered the competition. Benz & Cie. won; DMG was second. The four-cylinder, 115-hp single overhead camshaft engine developed for the grand prix Mercedes was based on the Kaiser's aviation engine contest.

Paul Daimler meant to win the 1914 race. DMG entered a full team of five cars, the maximum allowed any manufacturer. Driving them would be Lautenschlager, the 1908 Grand Prix winner, and four other veterans: Salzer, the Belgian Pilette, the seasoned Parisian Louis Wagner, and Max Sailer, jack of all trades. "I was engineer, driver, team manager, quartermaster in charge of finances and press officer," Sailer related. The son of an Esslingen

The Mercedes six-cylinder 100 hp Kaiserpreis engine established four aviation records in 1913. Victor Stoeffler and crew are shown here following a September flight from Habsheim (Alsace) to Warsaw.

blacksmith, he had apprenticed under Maybach and then spent several years racing Dixis for the Eisenach factory before being rehired by the DMG engineering department. "In those days we tried to save money wherever possible," he said. "We only used a minimum of people"—most of the money going into the cars. Months before the event, the drivers were dispatched to the 23.3-mile circuit outside Lyon to study the roads; an estimated 30,000 miles of testing preceded race day.

Which arrived on July 4. The skies were overcast; there was a cooling breeze. Along the circuit 300,000 spectators awaited the start, most of them confident of a Boillot victory in particular and Gallic dominance in general. Of the thirty-seven cars in the race, a third were French. Fiat was Italy's strongest challenger, Sunbeam and Vauxhall sent teams from Great Britain, Piccard-Pictet was there from Switzerland and Nagant from Belgium. The Fiats, Peugeots and Delages were fitted with four-wheel brakes, which enabled their drivers to keep the accelerator pedal to the floor many yards closer to a corner than could a two-wheel-braked car—an advantage that was thought to be good for at least a minute a lap. But the time needed for development had prevented

Mercedes from adopting such a system. Although front brakes had been fitted experimentally to a touring Mercedes as early as 1902, Paul Daimler decided that rear-wheel brakes, combined with better road-holding and faster acceleration, would be just as effective for this race.

Considerable secrecy surrounded the Mercedes camp. The cars, hoods down, were made available to the photographers, but returned to the garages immediately afterwards. In the pits, the Mercedes supplies were organized: fuel in red containers, oil in yellow, water in white. In addition to the usual stopwatches, there were charts to log in car positions on each of the 20 laps.

The atmosphere was tense, and there was a noticeable lack of the camaraderie usually present at contests of this kind. Boillot was edgy. The Mercedes drivers were taciturn. Only Jules Goux, who had startled Indianapolis spectators the year before by filling up on champagne as well as fuel at pit stops as he won the 500, seemed as relaxed as usual. And the crowd was clearly nationalistic. The French cars were applauded at the starting line; the others got a subdued greeting—if any at all.

The start was set for eight A.M., a more amenable

Mercedes Grand Prix car, 1914. Its clean lines from front to curved pocket tail were likened to "that complete-from-every-point-of-view appearance" of naval war vessels. The exhaust pipe was asbestos-wrapped to avoid burning the mechanic.

hour than the six A.M. of the 1908 race. Starting intervals had been halved to thirty seconds, and the cars were dispatched in pairs rather than singly. Only ten and a half minutes were required before all the cars were on the road (as opposed to nearly fifty minutes in 1908). "This close starting sounds a fearsome thing," an onlooker commented, "but is actually void of excitement or strenuousness for drivers accustomed to racing."

The starting order, as usual, had been drawn by lot. First off the line were a French Alda and a German Opel, followed by a Nagant and a Vauxhall. Speeds during practice indicated the only contest would be among the Delages, Peugeots, Sunbeams and Mercedes. The first excitement came when Boillot was sent off in Peugeot No. 5. Ninety seconds later Sailer, in the No. 14 car and the first Mercedes, came to the line.

As far as Sailer was concerned, there was only one other car in the race, Boillot's Peugeot, and he took after him with a fury. Ten minutes after the last car had started, the first car completed the initial lap: Boillot, passing the grandstand to loud cheers. A minute and twelve seconds later, Sailer sailed by, hardly noticed; but when the times for the first lap were posted, the Mercedes was revealed to be leading the Peugeot by eighteen seconds. Next were a Delage, a Sunbeam, another Peugeot, and another Mercedes. This confirmed the pre-race assessment of the cars, but Boillot, surprisingly, was not in the lead. On the second lap the Frenchman cut his time by ten seconds, but Sailer shaved twenty. On the third, Boillot was another twenty seconds faster, but the German had sped up a half-minute. On the fourth lap Sailer surged past Boillot and was soon thirty seconds ahead of him on the road, which gave him a full two-minute lead in the race. On lap five he increased his lead by forty-four seconds; on lap six he went out with a broken crankshaft.

Sailer's retirement was a relief to most spectators, who recognized only that their favorite was once again in the lead. But there was no relief for Georges Boillot. Sailer's blistering pace had proven the Mercedes was faster than the Peugeot, and Boillot knew that he could not let up because no matter how fast he

drove, a white Mercedes would be at his heels—car No. 28, Lautenschlager's. Next in order was Jules Goux; behind Goux were the Mercedes of Wagner and Salzer, the last starters in the event. The Delages and Sunbeams had dropped back by now and were out of contention.

Pursued and pursuer raced on. Steadily, lap by lap, Lautenschlager gained on Boillot. "The sweetest music I have ever heard was the sound of this engine," Lautenschlager said afterwards, "although at 3,500 [rpm] the vibration was pure hell." Realizing that his teammate was in trouble, Goux tried to help on the fourteenth lap. Approaching the downhill corner at Les Sept Chemins, he crept close to Lautenschlager, hoping the latter would forget his two-wheel brakes. The ruse didn't work. Lautenschlager let Goux pass him on the braking, and, once past the corner, accelerated ahead again.

CIRCUIT DE LYON

GRAND PRIX
de
L' A. C. F.
4 JUILLET 1914

Photographed at the weighing-in for the 1914 French Grand Prix. (Top) Louis Wagner. This was his first Mercedes race. At 32, the Frenchman was five years younger than Lautenschlager, had driven to European racing stardom for the Darracq team, and in America won the 1906 Vanderbilt and 1908 Grand Prize for Fiat. He was working at a French aviation factory when he was offered the Mercedes drive. (Above) Christian Lautenschlager. After winning the 1908 Grand Prix he had returned to his regular job as chief road tester of Mercedes production cars. No one at the factory was happier when racing was resumed than he. Joining Lautenschlager and Wagner on the Mercedes team were Belgian distributor Pilette, the veteran Salzer and young engineer Max Sailer.

The circuit for the 1914 French Grand Prix was the most difficult since the 1905 Gordon Bennett. Beginning at Les Sept Chemins with its tricky ess and wicked hairpin, the circuit wound its way through 23.3 miles of hilly countryside outside the industrial city of Lyon. Less than 10 miles allowed flat-out driving. The rest required skillful negotiation. Lautenschlager is seen negotiating the ess (top) and the hairpin (above) at Les Sept Chemins.

By the end of the seventeenth lap, the scoreboard revealed that after more than six hours of racing, only fourteen seconds separated the Peugeot and the Mercedes. The eighteenth lap was Lautenschlager's fastest yet, and for the first time since Sailer retired, Boillot lost the lead. By the nineteenth lap, Lautenschlager was over a minute ahead. A hush fell over the crowd. The invincible Boillot was capable of miracles, and the spectators waited for one. Having started five and a half minutes before Lautenschlager, he would be first to cross the finish line. If the Mercedes weakened, if Boillot could just manage one stupendous last lap, there was still a chance.

Boillot never appeared. His Peugeot gave out on the far side of the circuit, the final retirement of a race that saw twenty-six cars fail before the finish. And it was only at the finish that the full impact of the day's events was realized. The race had been the most dramatic and exciting ever seen in Europe, with virtually everyone's eyes on the battle between Lautenschlager and Boillot—but the first Mercedes across the finish line was followed by Wagner and Salzer. The Mercedes team had defeated the entire field of thirty-two cars. It was the first one-two-three finish in grand prix history, and it was greeted in stony silence. "Although it may be a severe blow to French pride," the American *Automobile* reported, "the admission has to be made in Paris that the best cars and the best men won the 1914 Grand Prix at Lyon last Saturday."

"Germany vanquished France, Britain and all other rivals . . . and no amount of explanation or wriggling will dispose of the fact," reported the British *Autocar.* "The German organization has set a new standard from which we have much to learn," it added, noting that the French Grand Prix of 1915 promised to be an even "bigger international competition than that of last week."

But at the moment, Daimler-Motoren-Gesellschaft wanted to celebrate. After zealously hiding the cars before the contest, the company was now ready to raise the hoods and let the world see; automobile magazines on both sides of the Atlantic published lengthy technical articles on their engineering. As for the cars themselves, one remained in France to be displayed in the DMG showroom on the Champs-

The clean sweep in the French Grand Prix: Lautenschlager winning at 65.3 mph, Wagner (No. 40) second at 65.1, Salzer (No. 39) third at 64.6. "A magnificent exhibition of how to . . . keep quite cool, leaving theatricalities to actors," wrote a British journalist of the Mercedes team performance. The race had been run in the shadow of Sarajevo. Twenty-four days later Europe was at war.

Elysées in Paris, another was dispatched across the Channel to the Long Acre emporium of Milnes-Daimler-Mercedes, Ltd. and the rest were returned to the factory. There were celebrations in Stuttgart, and in England Gordon Watney gave a party in Weybridge attended by Hugh Locke King (the founder of Brooklands), Lord Montagu and a legion of British motoring enthusiasts. On July 17 Milnes-Daimler-Mercedes held a banquet at the Trocadero in London.

On July 28 Austria declared war on Serbia. On August 1 Germany and France mobilized. Great Britain declared war on the third. There would be no French Grand Prix in 1915.

But motor sport continued in America. One American who had been in Europe for the grand prix knew the car he wanted to race next. Ralph De Palma, who had driven a Vauxhall at Lyon, wanted one of the Mercedes. Fortunately, he had a new and generous sponsor, the Chicago publisher E. C. Patterson, who had also sponsored Pilette's Mercedes-

Knight entry in the Indianapolis 500 and who now arranged with the factory to buy one of the grand prix cars. It left Germany on July 25, a fortnight before the British blockade of German ports, and arrived in Chicago in time for the big race weekend in mid-August.

"Snatched from the jaws of war," *The Automobile* reported melodramatically, "the German Mercedes which Louis Wagner drove to second place in the French Grand Prix was piloted to victory by Ralph De Palma... in the fifth annual road races at Elgin... winning the Chicago Automobile Club Cup and the Elgin National Trophy." De Palma's performance in the Mercedes had been phenomenally consistent. Each race was 301.83 miles and De Palma broke records in both of them, averaging 73.55 mph in the Elgin National Trophy and 73.91 in the Chicago Automobile Club Cup. (A Mercer and a Stutz, respectively, placed second.)

That weekend De Palma won $4,400 in prize money. Patterson had two trophies and, as one reporter said, "now can boast as loudly as E. J. Schroeder," the New Jersey sportsman who had ear-

In 1914 Ralph De Palma accepted Laurence Pomeroy's invitation to race for Vauxhall in the French Grand Prix. (His number was 18; this photo was flopped.) Forced out early with gearbox problems, De Palma watched the rest of the GP from the sidelines — and knew immediately what car he wanted to take back to America to race.

Elgin Road Races, August 1914: De Palma in the French GP Mercedes. "In a spectacular race meet of epochal results," as J. C. Burton reported in *Motor Age,* De Palma shattered the course record twice and "earned the title of The Invincible."

lier been well rewarded in silver after De Palma's drives in the Grey Ghost Mercedes. Schröeder had imported a Peugeot after the French Grand Prix but when he heard that De Palma was otherwise engaged in the Elgin races, he refused to ship the car from New York and began looking for another top-ranked driver instead. De Palma kept on winning: the first weekend in September he and the new Mercedes took five events, including the 100-mile Labor Day Sweepstakes at the Brighton Beach race course in Brooklyn.

By the start of the 1915 season in late February, Schroeder had found a driver for his Peugeot, the veteran Dario Resta, who won both the Grand Prize and the subsequent Vanderbilt Cup at the site of the Panama-Pacific Exposition in San Francisco. De Palma was on hand with another Mercedes, one of the 1913 six-cylinder machines which had run on the the Le Mans circuit and which DMG had long since written off as an experiment. The car did not perform well in either event.

The 1914 grand prix car was not on the West

Hamlin Track, October 1914. De Palma fit a new radiator shroud to his Mercedes to make the engine run warmer in cool Minnesota. Nonetheless he lost the 100-mile race on the mile dirt track to Tom Alley's Duesenberg, a rare loss for De Palma.

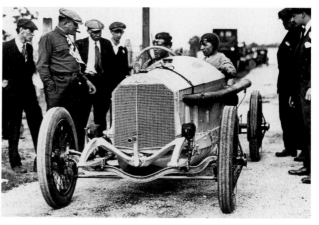

Although De Palma had been AAA National Champion twice and winner of the Dirt Track Championship four times, victory on the bricks at Indianapolis was not his until 1915. And he drove a masterful race to get it. Ironically, three laps from the finish, his Mercedes threw a connecting rod — the same misfortune which had cost him the race in 1912 with the Grey Ghost — but in this case Ralph was able to nurse the car home. "He slowed up perceptibly," *The Automobile* reported, "but gave no evidence of distress other than the usual sound of a missing cylinder." De Palma's winning average was 89.84 mph, to Dario Resta's 88.91 for second place. His victory won him $22,600.

Coast because it was in Detroit, being overhauled and studied at the Packard Motor Car Company. A few months later it would be in Indianapolis for the 500. Though Patterson was the official sponsor, the car now belonged to Packard, whose chief engineer, Jesse Vincent, headed the pit crew. Dario Resta was there with the Peugeot.

At the drop of the flag, Resta charged to the front. De Palma played it carefully. At 175 miles he moved into the lead; at 325 miles Resta overtook him, but only for a lap; on the next lap De Palma took charge, and never relinquished the lead again.

In three successive weeks in July 1916, De Palma and the Mercedes won impressively on the concrete speedway in Minneapolis, on the boards in Omaha and on the dirt track in Kansas City. Those were his last Mercedes drives. After his Kansas City win he joined Packard's engineering staff. The next cars he drove, in non-competitive speed trials, carried a new Packard power plant for which the Mercedes had been the prototype. It served as the basis for America's Liberty aircraft engine.

In England, the grand prix Mercedes on display at the Long Acre showroom had elicited similar interest on the part of a British engineer, who secured it after war was declared and sent it to Rolls-Royce in Derby for study. "It is common knowledge that all Rolls-Royce aero engines built during World War I were based quite closely on this engine," W. O. Bentley said in his memoirs.* The grand prix Mercedes on display in the Champs-Elysées showroom was commandeered by the French military and sent to the motor pool for use as a staff car.

In Germany, following the declaration of war, the factories of Benz & Cie. and Daimler-Motoren-Gesellschaft were ordered to place their production facilities at the disposal of the military. The Benz plants were turned over largely to submarine and aviation engine work, with the workforce increased from 7,700 to more than 12,000. DMG's commitment to the military effort was even greater. Its employment rolls in Untertürkheim increased from

3,765 to 16,000, and in 1916 the company undertook the construction of a new plant in Sindelfingen, a small village about 12 miles south of Stuttgart, for the production of aircraft. Most of the equipment for the new factory had to be delivered by horse-drawn wagon, since all trucks had been consigned to the war effort; another major problem was providing food and housing for the workers—initially only two hundred, but over 5,000 by the end of the war. DMG built nearly 20,000 military aircraft engines, mostly at Untertürkheim, and 3,000 trucks at Marienfelde. Production of staff cars totaled 2,200.

That motor vehicles had potential as military machines was recognized by the armies of all nations. Indeed, the world's first fully documented self-propelled vehicle, the experimental, steam-powered Cugnot tractor of the early 1770s, had been produced for the artillery. But now that the motor vehicle was a practical reality, the question was how to use it, and at first no one was really sure.

Early in the war, in September 1914, General Gallieni's use of Paris taxis to carry troops to the Marne front had shown that standard automobile transport could be put to military advantage. And two years later, in September 1916, the greatest technical invention of the war rolled against Germany. It was British and, to keep its existence secret, early dispatches had given it the name of an innocuous container for holding liquids: it was called a tank. "Mind you, this is far from being exact," a German colonel replied to a war correspondent who asked for a description later that month. "Well, they are about 65 feet long, almost 10 feet high and not much narrower. The most striking feature is propulsion by endless steel lattices. . . . They move slowly, at hardly more than five miles an hour, and that makes them splendid artillery targets." The colonel was unduly optimistic.

Ultimately Germany too would build tanks, though no more than seventy-five, while the British and French armies rolled with six thousand. The force of tradition had weighed heavily in Germany's belated development of such a vehicle. As early as 1904 Paul Daimler had offered both Germany and Austria a four-wheeled armored truck, but neither

*Bentley also acknowledged that, after the war, he patterned the valve gear and cam drive of his first Bentley on the Mercedes.

The Benz factory at Mannheim during World War I. Memoranda from 1915 indicate the company "overworked with orders from the armed forces." Truck production doubled.

army was interested. Both DMG and Benz built some wheeled and tracked platform artillery vehicles during the war, but that was an old idea. Britain developed the tank because Winston Churchill had foreseen its effectiveness, while Kaiser Wilhelm and his general staff were still dreaming of hooves and marching boots, of the splendor and elegance of the cavalry.

In July 1919, a month after the signing of the Treaty of Versailles officially ended the war, the Weimar Republic was proclaimed. The new German democracy was a turmoil of social unrest and rival political factions. With the beginning of reparations payments, the economy went into a tailspin; the value of the mark plummeted from 4.20 to the dollar before the war to 62 to the dollar in May 1921. "Compared with Paris, London or Brussels, the first impression received in Berlin is that the use of automobiles has ceased," the journalist W. F. Bradley wrote in November 1920. "This impression is increased by a more extended tour through Germany." There *were* cars—32,500 of them, according to registration fig-

Benz aviation engine production. By war's end a total of 11,926 units had been built in Mannheim. Daimler produced 20,321 aviation engines.

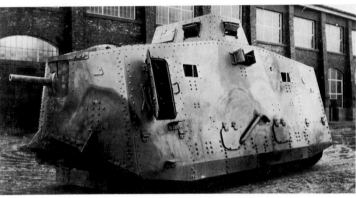

By the fall of 1915 over 55,000 of the nearly 70,000 private motor vehicles in Germany had been conscripted by the military. Supplies to build DMG's new Sindelfingen factory were delivered by horse-drawn wagon. Only automobiles for military staff use were allowed to be produced at both Daimler and Benz. Daimler built the first caterpillar, the Marien-Wagen, in 1916; the following year Benz produced the A7V tank. Benz advertising stressed patriotic themes and the new aviation, while recalling the traditional cavalry as well.

ures, half the number that had been registered in 1914. But Allied blockades had cut off shipments of gasoline and rubber early in the war, and civilian use of automobiles was prohibited; when this embargo was lifted late in 1920 the mark was so low and people's purchasing power was so limited it had little effect. Abandoned cars of the winning armies clogged the market for months; refurbished, they were generally sent to Scandinavia for resale. Fuel, if it could be found, was expensive, and automobiles carried a 15 percent luxury tax.

The end of the war found Daimler-Motoren-Gesellschaft sadly fallen from its prewar prosperity. Before 1914 DMG had established wholly owned branches in a dozen German cities and in London, Moscow, Odessa, Vienna and Zurich; there were strong independent dealerships in many other cities as well. And the company had substantial cash reserves. But the war turned all its carefully laid plans upside down. Almost 49 million marks was spent on expansion for military production, an astounding expense borne by DMG alone, with no help from the government; 24,700 workers were employed at Sindelfingen, Untertürkheim, and Marienfelde. Six thousand of these workers were now laid off at Untertürkheim, and 3,000 at Sindelfingen. The Daimler branches in London and Russia were liquidated. For a while Marienfelde did not operate at all, and Sindelfingen was reduced to building furniture, though automobile body production, DMG's plan for the facility from the beginning, soon began there, if fitfully. Production at Untertürkheim was equally fitful. In 1919 just 621 cars were built there, all of them a single prewar Mercedes-Knight model. Coal shortages shut down the assembly line several times. Daimler workers were terrorized by Communists and other radical agitators, and the factory was struck. The situation became so dangerous that, in late August 1920, the Württemberg government closed the plant for a month, locking out even the executive personnel.

In Mannheim Benz & Cie. thought it had prepared well during the war years, but the company could not have foreseen the devastating shortage of materials that followed the armistice, not to speak of

the near-total collapse of the market for automobiles. Benz struggled back into production in 1919, turning out 988 cars in Mannheim in three models of what was essentially an updated prewar design. Fewer than 800 trucks were built in Gaggenau.

Precisely who at Benz, during this difficult period, first had the idea of joining forces with a strong partner is not known. But in all of Germany there was only one partner Benz would even consider. That spring Karl Jahr of the Rheinische Creditbank, a Benz board member since 1910, made a subtle overture to Daimler. The people in Stuttgart were receptive. Three years earlier, during the war, they had even talked casually among themselves about buying into Benz, with the ultimate goal of merger. Now, in 1919, Jahr and Nallinger from Benz and DMG board member Ernst Berge sat down to talk. They could not agree. Benz wanted to go slowly, reaching first a communion of interests, with both companies remaining independent; DMG wanted an immediate merger under its leadership. That Mannheim would not accept. "It seems that the Benz company is not really ripe," Berge wrote von Kaulla, the DMG chairman. But he was convinced that their rivals soon would be. The merger plan was abandoned, for the moment, on December 10, 1919.

In the face of adverse circumstances, both firms made important technical advances. For DMG this meant supercharging, a technique the company had used in aircraft engine development during the war. As further development in aviation was curtailed by the Versailles Treaty, Paul Daimler now tried supercharging as a palliative in passenger car design. The dismal lubricants of the war years had diminished the performance of Mercedes-Knight engines, but supercharging improved it. Daimler realized, too, that the Mercedes star would not long shine brightly in the Knight; sleeve-valve engine development itself was curtailed and a new series of single overhead cam fours was evolved and then supercharged. The Mercedes was the first car in the world to be offered with a supercharger as standard equipment.

For Benz, advancement meant further work in the diesel field. Prewar development had demonstrated the diesel engine's potential both in terms of purchase price and economy of operation. With Germany poverty-stricken, such advantages were increasingly important, and Friedrich Nallinger directed Prosper L'Orange to step up his experiments. During a patent search L'Orange discovered that Harry Leissner, a Swedish engineer, had devised a diesel concept in 1915 which was an improvement on his own 1909 patent. Eager to develop the idea further, L'Orange was dismayed to learn his own patent had lapsed; Benz & Cie. had neglected to renew it during the war. Fortunately, as Benz lawyers discovered, any patents not used during the war had been automatically renewed, and L'Orange could proceed. The resulting diesel engine design was patented March 18, 1919. By 1922 a contract was signed with a Berlin syndicate for the building of stationary diesel engines in the old Benz works in the Waldhofstrasse. By now Benz & Cie. had decided to concentrate its attention entirely in transportation. The development of lighter diesel units for vehicles followed. A farm tractor was tried first; a diesel tractor was exhibited at the Königsberg Fair the following summer.

In late September 1921, the Berlin Automobile Show marked the official reentry of the German automobile industry into the world marketplace. The show was held in the Kaiserdamm Palace, a huge hall built by the German Association of Automobile Manufacturers and completed just before the outbreak of war. This first postwar show was well attended, attracting a large contingent of foreign purchasers: with the depreciation of German currency, no better automotive buys could be found anywhere (by now the mark was equal to about one American cent). The most expensive Mercedes at the show was $3,300, the most expensive Benz a hundred dollars less.

After the long conflict, old loyalties returned. "The war had severed our connections with our numerous friends abroad, but scarcely was it at an end, when correspondence and enquiries rained upon us from different parts of the world," a DMG brochure published during the summer of 1921 stated. "Our old friends returned to us, even from the countries which had up to that time been our enemies. . . . We rejoice in this." Given the condition of the home market, they had reason to rejoice.

The arrival of the new supercharged cars was greeted on both sides of the Atlantic. "We kept the car hard at work for an hour on the track, to discover if it would develop any signs of distress or overheat-

Mercedes 10/40/65 Sport, one of two new supercharged four-cylinder single-overhead-cam models introduced at the Berlin Automobile Show in 1921. The 10/40/65 was popular with amateur enthusiasts and was driven to many victories by Ernes Merck, the most famous German woman driver of the period.

ing," *Motor Sport* reported after an outing at Brooklands with the supercharged 12/40, "but the longer it ran the more it seemed to enjoy itself, so we eventually turned south for Bournemouth . . . " British Mercedes Ltd. put up a flying lap at Brooklands with a 33/180 at 95.43 mph.

By early 1922, Benz Motors (England) Ltd. had moved from its temporary postwar quarters in St. James's Street to new showrooms on Grafton Street. "Fascinates the most Fastidious," said the London importers of their new Benzes in 1922. The *Auto Motor Journal* agreed: "The accumulated experience of manufacturing high-grade vehicles right from these early days is reflected in the latest models, which have a distinct and unmistakable personality." In 1921 an internal company memo noted that Benz was "quite astounded" that its cars found favor outside Germany so soon after the war. The hard cash those sales brought was badly needed.

But for every bright spot, there was a cloud. Though the French Grand Prix, Europe's premier road race, was revived in 1921, German cars would be barred for several years—a circumstance which bothered Benz less than it did DMG. Racing had become so much a part of the Mercedes image that not competing could jeopardize sales to the sporting clientele which represented a significant percentage of the Mercedes market. Besides, Paul Daimler liked to race, and so did Max Sailer, the engineer-pacesetter of the 1914 Grand Prix.

The question was where and how. Where was answered first: a German car would be accepted in the Targa Florio in Sicily. How was largely a matter of grit. Germans traveling abroad were restricted by red tape and the difficulty of obtaining foreign currency; if they went by car, obtaining fuel and tires added to their problems. Nevertheless Max Sailer decided to drive to Sicily.

A single car was built, Daimler and Sailer creating it out of a prewar 28/95 production chassis which had usually carried a sedan body. The wheelbase was shortened a foot, the radiator was lowered, the engine was given a new carburetor, two seats and flared fenders were fitted.

The Targa Florio was not a contest for the timid. Established in 1906 by Vincenzo Florio, scion of a prominent Sicilian family whose fortunes had been built on lemons, olive oil and Marsala wine and himself a former race driver of modest renown (he had finished third with a Mercedes in the 1904 Brescia-Verona-Brescia), the Targa was unique in motor sport. Scenically the circuit was breathtaking, but this was no race course; some of the roads had hardly changed since the armies of Rome and Carthage had traveled them during the Punic Wars, and others built in the two millennia since seemed to have been laid out for mountain goats, with hairpin turns in the mountains and nowhere to pull off the road because the only shoulder was an abyss. Each 67-mile lap might see climatic conditions ranging from glorious sunshine to dense fog or driving rain. There were four laps for 268 miles. For the prudent, they were a terror; for the daring, a delight. For Max Sailer, they were a delight. Sailer was, as W. F. Bradley said, "the most daring, skilled, and even reckless driver Germany could produce at that time."

The Targa was wild, with few rules. The overall event was a free-for-all open to anything on four wheels; the Coppa Florio, run simultaneously, was for production-based touring cars. Sailer's Mercedes qualified for both. Most entries were Italian: Alfa Romeo, Fiat, Ceirano and Itala entered full factory teams of three cars each. Still, Sailer guessed that his stiffest opposition would be an independent entry, the updated 1914 Grand Prix Fiat driven by Count Giulio Masetti. And he was right.

Simply stating that the race was won at an average of 36.2 mph speaks volumes about the difficulty of the course. That was the speed of Masetti, as bold and headstrong a driver as Sailer; he took the Targa. Sailer was behind him, at 35.9 mph, and took the Coppa. Count Masetti drove brilliantly, but he would not have won if Sailer's black-market tires had not failed him, requiring nine time-consuming stops for changing. Significantly, Masetti returned to the Targa Florio in 1922 behind the wheel of a Mercedes.

Because Sailer's solitary trip had been so successful, DMG decided on a full Sicilian expedition in

1922: seven cars and a crew of 20. Three of the former 1914 grand prix cars were updated with front wheel brakes and entrusted to Masetti and the DMG veterans Lautenschlager and Salzer. The Count had purchased his car, which the factory painted Italian racing red for him (though Masetti's choice of color may have been dictated by a special form of nationalism: Sicilian peasants tended not to throw as many stones at native products). Because he had come so close to winning the year before, Sailer elected to remain with a 28/95, though his car this year had the Stuttgart "speed secret" of supercharging. An unsupercharged 28/95 was provided for Christian Werner, a slim, sad-eyed DMG mechanic and chauffeur who would be making his racing debut. The other two entries were one-and-a-half-liter supercharged sports cars assigned to the veteran Italian driver Fernando Minoia and to DMG mechanic Paul Scheef.

As the sort of careful planning that helped Mercedes win the 1914 Grand Prix was impossible in the Targa, DMG based its hopes of victory on sheer numbers. And victory was the result. Though Sailer was fifteen minutes faster than he had been in 1921, Count Masetti in the grand prix Mercedes won the Targa again, at a record-breaking 39.1 mph.

Meanwhile, at Brooklands in England, lap speeds of better than 100 mph were being recorded by a Benz and a Mercedes—and sometimes by a car that was both. Count Louis Vorow Zborowski, like his father before him, had a fondness for both Mercedes and adventure; his friend S.C.H. "Sammy" Davis described him as "impetuous almost to a fault." At this time the machines in which Zborowski demonstrated his impetuosity were called Chitty-Bang-Bang (the name was derived from a bawdy British rhyme)—cars composed of prewar Mercedes chassis lengthened to allow the insertion of a wartime aircraft engine. Scrap iron served for the body, which was mostly hood. The result looked terrible but drove fast: 108 mph for Chitty I at Brooklands' Easter Meeting in 1921. DMG promoted the Zborowski performance in full-page ads, though without any photos of the beast.

Chitty I had a 300-hp Maybach engine and a spectacular end. A tire left the rim during practice for the Brooklands Autumn Meeting in 1922, the car surged through the timing box at the head of the Railway Straight and catapulted to the soft ground beyond, at which point the front axle took leave of the chassis and landed some 45 yards away. The Count sat safely and sanguine in the cockpit, perturbed only that he now "would have to be content" with his Ballot for upcoming events.

Count Zborowski's Chitties were not the only aircraft-engined colossi. No doubt spurred by the Chitty success, one E. T. Scarisbrick of Greaves Hall, Banks, had C. H. Crowe & Company, a London firm specializing in Mercedes repairs, build

Sicilian fruits of victory, 1921. For Max Sailer and the modified 28/95 Mercedes production car, the Coppa Florio (left). For Count Masetti and his GP Fiat, the Targa cup. For both, the Targa plaque.

In 1903 20-year-old Vincenzo Florio was shanghaied by his brother to a remote island off Sicily to prevent his participation in the Paris-Madrid race. Having come of age in 1904, Vincenzo drove his Mercedes (above) to finish third in a 231-mile race in northern Italy. By 1906 Florio had returned to Sicily to inaugurate the famous race bearing his name. After placing second in the 1909 Targa, he confined his further race efforts to sponsorship. (Top) Max Sailer winning Vincenzo's Coppa Florio in 1921.

Targa Florio, 1922. That the Sicilian roads were wild is graphically demonstrated in the photo above of Count Masetti at speed. Eyewitnesses reported he cornered more gingerly and kicked up less dust and gravel than his competitors. Conversely, Mercedes teammate Max Sailer, according to journalist W.F. Bradley, "drove as if he were at war with his car but meant to bring it to its senses." Masetti won the Targa; Sailer placed sixth overall and first in class. DMG's first major competition since the war was a resounding triumph. Of 42 starters, only 24 finished but among them were six of the seven Mercedes entered, including Werner (center), eighth overall and second in class.

him one, too. Into a Mercedes chassis of approximate 1907 vintage, Crowe fitted a six-cylinder 240-hp Benz aircraft engine taken from a captured World War I plane. Scarisbrick designated his sporting hybrid a Benz-Mercedes.

Zborowski's Chitty II also sported a Benz aircraft engine in its Mercedes chassis, as well as four seats, for both racing and touring the Continent. Chitty III was a Mercedes-Mercedes (28/95 chassis, Unter-türkheim aircraft engine) and could carry luggage. Both cars were good for 108 mph at Brooklands.

And the Blitzen was back. Bob Burman's old car had somehow found its way to England from the States after the Armistice, but it was a really old warrior now, and a considerable handful. More successful were the two new 200-hp cars that Benz & Cie. put together at the factory from parts on hand. Among the parts available was the "Cupid" Hornsted Big Benz chassis, which was streamlined and Blitzenized into "Skinny Joe" (the factory nickname) and sent to Benz Motors (England) Ltd. in 1922 for workouts at Brooklands. The other car, dubbed "the Grandmother" because of its antique appearance, was driven by Franz Hörner, who had learned to race under Hémery and Fritz Erle, in hill

climbs and sprints on the Continent wherever German cars could compete: Italy, Spain, Holland and Russia; Hörner put up 126.6 mph in St. Petersburg. Skinny Joe was not quite as speedy, though at Brooklands Captain John Duff recorded a fastest lap of 114.49 mph in September 1922. And Skinny Joe did not stop as well as it ran; Duff passed the finish line, proceeded up over the banking, smacked a telegraph pole, bounded through a tree and ultimately landed, frightfully battered, on the ground below.

Neither Skinny Joe nor the Grandmother had made serious demands on the Benz budget, and they kept the Benz name in the sporting news, which was all that was expected of them. Expectations were not realized, however, by a sensational new Benz that went racing in 1923: the Tropfenwagen, or teardrop car. A decade later, it would have been avant-garde; in its own time, the car seemed fit for Buck Rogers— and this from Benz & Cie., which had traditionally viewed motor sport with a production-car focus, and had planned the Tropfenwagen as the standard-bearer for a new line of rear-engine passenger cars.

Inspired by the streamlined Tropfen-Auto displayed by the German aviation pioneer Edmund Rumpler at the 1921 Berlin Automobile Show, the

Brooklands, 1921. Count Zborowski first raced Chitty I with a makeshift four-seater body and an exhaust made out of a drain pipe — and lapped at 108.15 mph. "Refining" the car with a ducktail body, plus streamlined radiator shroud and oil tank, increased Chitty I's lap speed to over 113 mph.

TIME REMEMBERED

THE ART OF DAIMLER, MERCEDES AND BENZ

1 8 8 6 – 1 9 8 6

All men dream: but not equally.
Those who dream by night
in the dusty recesses of their minds
wake in the day to find that it was vanity:
but the dreamers of the day are dangerous men,
for they may act their dream
with open eyes, to make it possible.
—T.E. LAWRENCE,
SEVEN PILLARS OF WISDOM

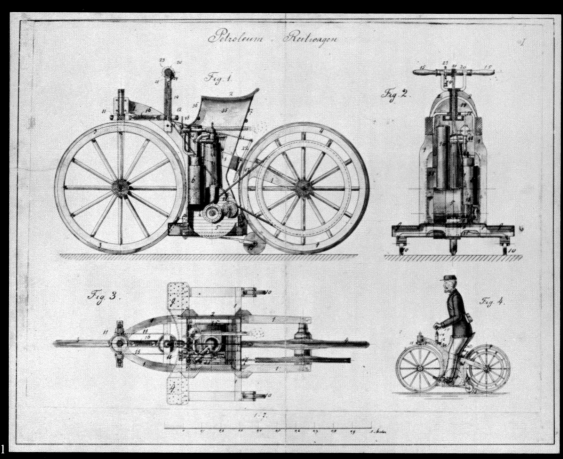

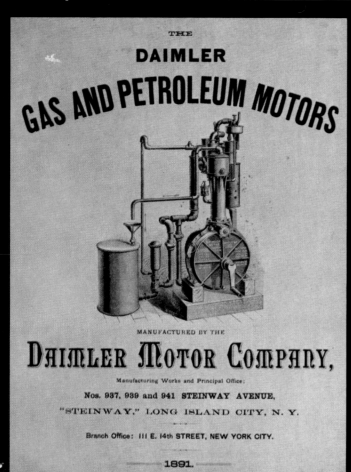

1) Drawings, probably by Wilhelm Maybach, for the 1885 Daimler, the world's first motorcycle. The term *"petroleum reitwagen"* indicates Daimler's view of the vehicle as a motorized horse, not a bicycle. **2)** Cover of catalog published by William Steinway in 1891 illustrating all Daimler products to date. Though engines and motorboats were emphasized, Steinway's inclusion of automobiles for sale was a first for America. **3)** Catalog page from 1896. Engine sales kept Daimler in business until the automobile idea caught on. **4)** Mercedes catalog cover, 1911. **5)** English brochure, 1922. **6)** Special edition of the Daimler company publication celebrating Christian Werner's win in the 1924 Targa Florio.

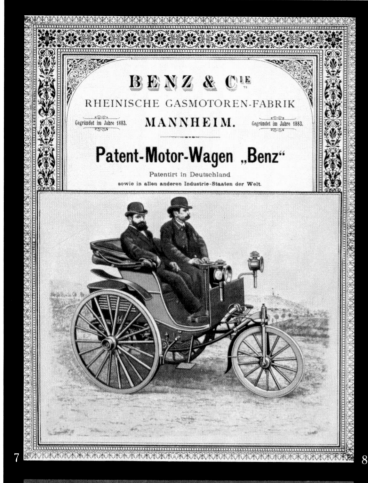

7

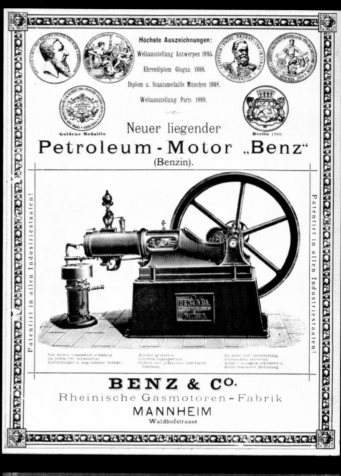

8

9

10

11

12

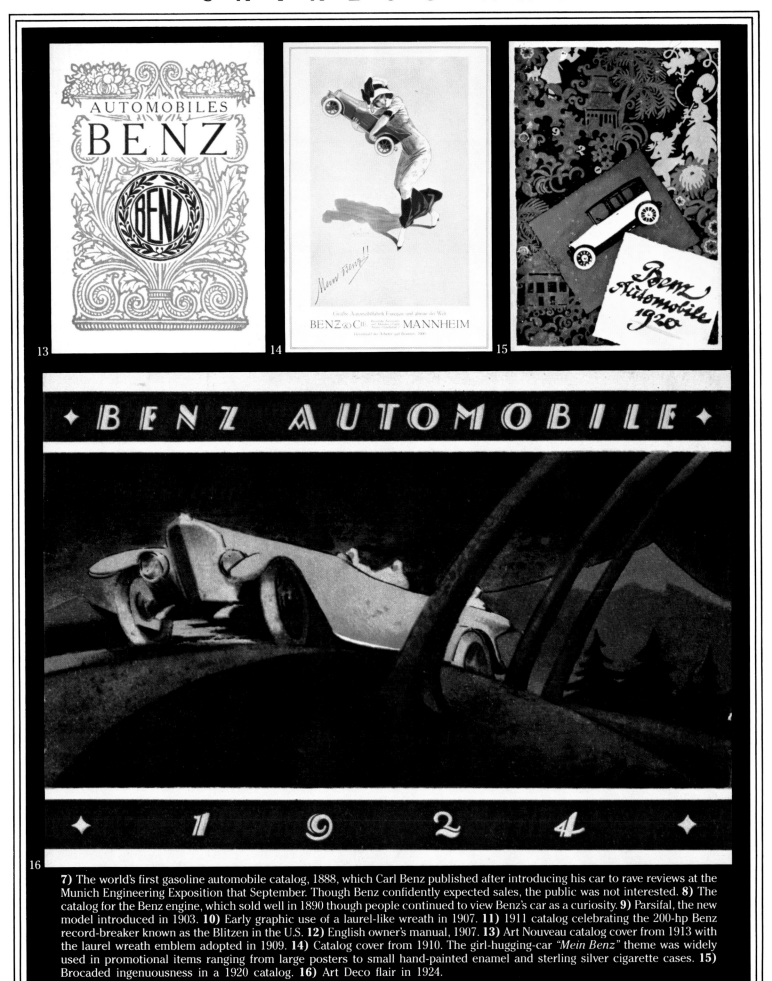

7) The world's first gasoline automobile catalog, 1888, which Carl Benz published after introducing his car to rave reviews at the Munich Engineering Exposition that September. Though Benz confidently expected sales, the public was not interested. 8) The catalog for the Benz engine, which sold well in 1890 though people continued to view Benz's car as a curiosity. 9) Parsifal, the new model introduced in 1903. 10) Early graphic use of a laurel-like wreath in 1907. 11) 1911 catalog celebrating the 200-hp Benz record-breaker known as the Blitzen in the U.S. 12) English owner's manual, 1907. 13) Art Nouveau catalog cover from 1913 with the laurel wreath emblem adopted in 1909. 14) Catalog cover from 1910. The girl-hugging-car *"Mein Benz"* theme was widely used in promotional items ranging from large posters to small hand-painted enamel and sterling silver cigarette cases. 15) Brocaded ingenuousness in a 1920 catalog. 16) Art Deco flair in 1924.

24

25

17) Spanish catalog, 1928. **18)** French catalog, c. 1929. Although Daimler used the accents in Mercédès Jellinek's name only briefly, some foreign branches did so for several decades. The 4.6-liter Nürburg was the company's first eight-cylinder road car. Named after the racing circuit on which the prototype was tested for 20,000 kilometers, it was introduced at the Paris Salon in 1928. **19)** The six-cylinder Mannheim, named for the city in which it was built, made its debut with the Stuttgart six in late 1926, soon after the merger. This German catalog illustrates the 1928 3.5-liter model which succeeded the original 3.1. **20)** Spanish catalog for the 2.6-liter Stuttgart 260, which followed the Stuttgart 200 in 1929 and was the company's best-selling model. More than 3,600 were produced in a half decade. **21)** 1929 catalog for the supercharged six-cylinder, 7.1-liter SSK, the most famous Mercedes of the period and the most limited in production; just 31 were built. **22)** 1936 catalog for the 170H. Just over 1,500 of these rear-engined four-cylinder cars were sold in four years, compared with over 65,000 of its front-engined version. **23)** Catalog for the six-cylinder 320, successor to the 290 in 1937. **24)** 1934 catalog drawing for the 130, the rear-engined Mercedes that anticipated the VW Beetle in concept, though not in commercial success. **25)** Catalog drawing for the 290, with all-round independent suspension, introduced at the Berlin Automobile Show, February 1933.

BENZWERKE GAGGENÄU

26

EFS1

MERCEDES-BENZ
DIESEL 2³⁄₄-TONNER
TYP Lo 2750

27

MERCEDES-BENZ-

DIESEL

1,1 TONNER · TYP L 1100

28

MERCEDES-BENZ DIESEL 2³⁄₄-TONNER
TYP Lo 2750

29

ÜNİVERSAL UNIMOG TRAKTÖRÜ

30

MERCEDES-BENZ
145-PS-DIESEL-OMNIBUS

TYP
O-6600

31

32   33   34

35   36

26) 1919 catalog cover. Benz built 797 trucks that year. 27) 1933 catalog cover. Daimler-Benz production was 3,520 trucks that year. 28) and 29) Diesel trucks produced into the war years: the 1.1-ton pickup introduced in 1927, the 2¾-tonner of the early thirties. 30) Unimog, the vehicle that helped rebuild Germany after the war. This catalog was for the model produced from 1949-1954. 31) Bus catalog for the model produced from 1949-1954. 32) A Mercedes and a Daimler-engined Zeppelin. Henri Rudaux painted this poster in 1910, several months after Count Ferdinand von Zeppelin and his backers inaugurated a passenger airline. Orville Wright had been a guest on a test flight in 1909. 33) Behr Mann's fanciful poster of 1912. 34) Elegance in an Ernst Schreiber poster, c. 1914. 35) Poster from the same period promoting the company's showrooms and agencies in the world's major cities, including Cairo. 36) Mercedes and biplane in 1914, painted by Ludwig Hohlwein (1874-1949), the most famous German poster artist of his era. Self-taught, Hohlwein broke away from Art Nouveau extravagance and developed a style characterized by vivid color, sharp contrast and dramatically flat patterns.

37

38

39

40

37) Benz poster from 1914, promoting the luxury of the car and the company as the oldest automobile builder in the world, which didn't make Daimler happy. **38)** Lehmann Steglitz poster from 1914 for Benz cars and airplane engines. **39)** 1914 variation on the piquant *"Mein Benz"* theme. **40)** Prince Heinrich of Prussia, Kaiser Wilhelm's brother and ardent Benz enthusiast. This 1914 illustration is from the Berlin *Motor* magazine series. The Benz depicted was well known in the capital city since Prince Heinrich routinely parked it in front of the main stairs to the Bleichröder-Palais on his frequent visits to the Automobile Club of Germany. **41)** 1928 poster by Cucuel Offelsmeyer. **42)** An early post-merger poster, 1926, using both emblems. **43)** Offelsmeyer's late twenties poster for the "last word" in sporting cars. **44)** Walter Müller's Type S poster from 1928. **45)** Yet another Offelsmeyer rendering of the Type S, 1928.

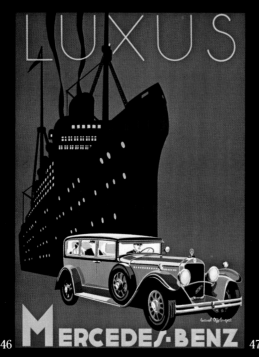

46) Offelsmeyer poster for the Nürburg, c. 1929. **47)** 1929 poster by "Henry" celebrating the company's decade of providing buses to the Post Office, which traditionally carried both passengers and the mail in Germany. **48)** Presenting the company's typical clientele in a poster of the late twenties. **49)** Extolling the ultimate in 1931: the Grosser. **50)** A 50th anniversary poster, 1936, depicting Carl and Bertha Benz in the 1893 Victoria and the then victorious Mercedes-Benz grand prix car. **51)** Magazine cover from 1955: Mercédès Jellinek painted by Lilo Rasch-Nägele. **52)** The Gi Neuert design for a 1985 exhibition celebrating the origin of the name. Young Mercédès Jellinek dominating the montage amid the three-pointed star, Gottlieb Daimler on a pedestal, the first Mercedes car, and Emil Jellinek's Villa Mercedes and Mercedes yachts.

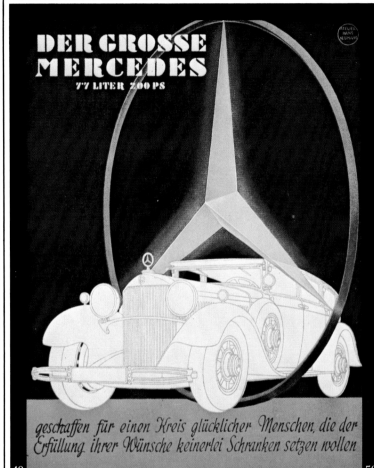

49

50

51

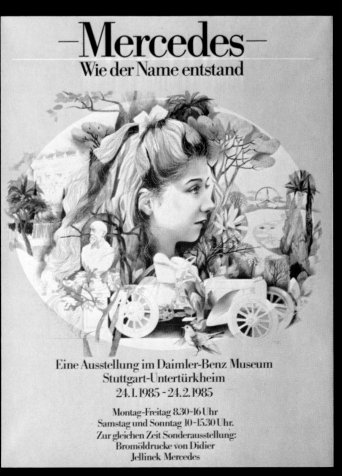

52

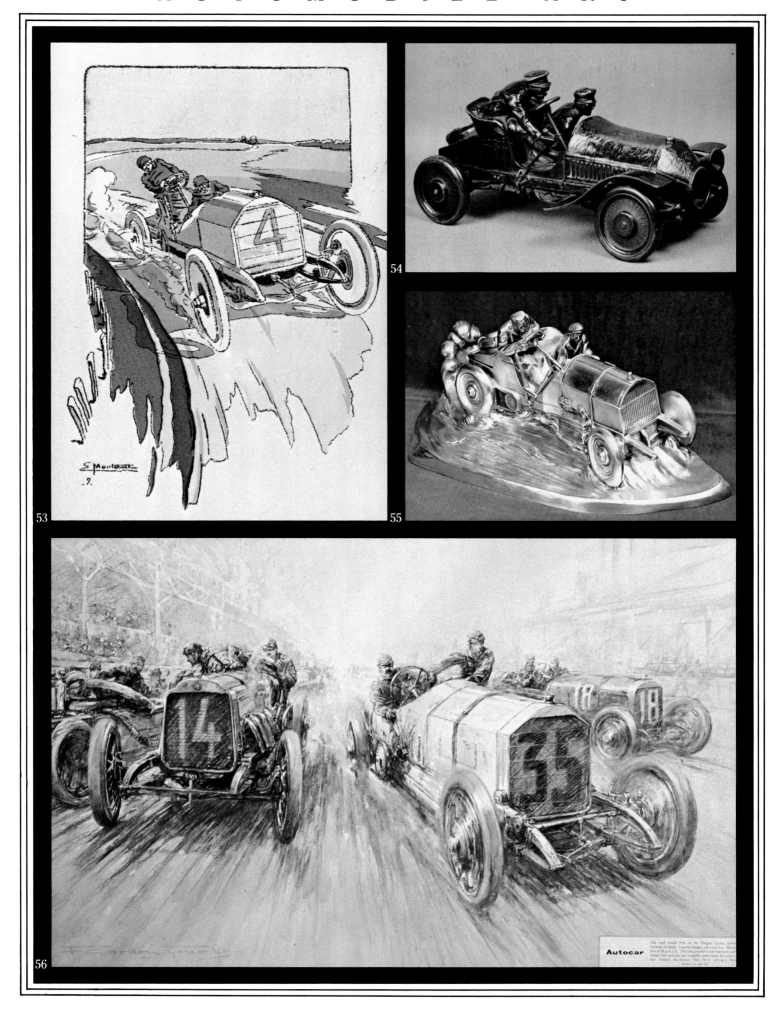

53

54

55

56

Autocar

57

58

53) The French artist Edouard Montaut (1874-1909) is regarded as the father of automotive art and the inventor of the technique for visually defining speed. This lithograph shows Jenatzy driving to victory in the 1903 Gordon Bennett. **54)** Shown at speed in this three-inch bronze, signed Löder, is Baron de Ċaters, who raced his Mercedes at 75 mph at Ostende in 1903. **55)** Another small Mercedes bronze, c. 1905. **56)** F. Gordon Crosby (1885-1943) was England's most celebrated automotive artist of the between-wars years and resident race chronicler for *The Autocar.* Here Crosby depicted the 1908 French Grand Prix, with Lautenschlager's winning Mercedes flanked by Jenatzy's Mors and Moore-Brabazon's No. 18 Austin. **57)** and **58)** Peter Helck (1893-   ) ranks among the foremost American illustrators of the 20th century and is America's most beloved automotive artist. Barney Oldfield and the Blitzen Benz are shown here on the board track at Playa del Rey (with De Palma's Fiat and Robertson's Simplex) and on a fairgrounds dirt track, both in 1910.

59

60

Peter Helck painted his first automobile in 1901, at the age of eight, and in 1906 attended his first automobile race, the Vanderbilt Cup on Long Island. The "you are there" feeling in these four Helck paintings reflects the enthusiasm of an artist who was on hand during racing's early thundering years. **59)** August 21, 1909: Oldfield's grand prix Benz dices with De Palma's Fiat and Zengle's Chadwick in the Indianapolis Speedway inaugural. Barney was the winner. **60)** July 7, 1908: Lautenschlager leads the Nazzaro Fiat at Eu bridge en route to victory in the French Grand Prix. **61)** May 31, 1915: De Palma's ex-French GP Mercedes is the easy winner over Resta's No. 3 Peugeot in the Indianapolis 500. **62)** May 30, 1912: A gallant defeat in the 500 as De Palma and his mechanic push the Grey Ghost to the finish line.

61

62

63

64

65

66

67

68

Facing page: Mercedes champions painted by Peter Helck. **63)** February 26, 1914: De Palma's favorite victory, as he and the Grey Ghost outsmart Oldfield on the Mercer in the Vanderbilt Cup at Santa Monica. **64)** July 23, 1938: Rudi Caracciola, *"Der Regenmeister,"* demonstrates his uncanny skill on a rain-soaked Nürburgring during practice for the German Grand Prix. **65)** April 27, 1924: Christian Werner leads André Dubonnet's Hispano-Suiza as he cuts a close corner en route to victory in Sicily's Targa Florio. **66)** May 1, 1955: Stirling Moss, with navigator Denis Jenkinson and the 300SLR, leading a Ferrari and the entire field on his way to winning the fastest Mille Miglia in history. This page: Walter Gotschke (1912-   ), Czechoslovakian-born artist whose bold impressionistic style established him as the most spectacular automotive artist of the postwar era. **67)** Werner battling the abominable roads of the Targa Florio, 1924. **68)** March 1901, on the Promenade des Anglais in Nice: Emil Jellinek (pince-nez, pointing finger) and his daughter Mercédès (in the driver's seat) following the sensational competition debut of the first Mercedes.

69

70

71

72

A poster for the 1931 Masaryk Grand Prix began his art career, and for two decades from the late thirties Walter Gotschke was art director for Daimler-Benz. His intimate knowledge of his subject and his proximity to the motor sport scene are vividly embodied in these four paintings. **69)** September 16, 1928: Caracciola's SSK starts a record-breaking ascent of Semmering. **70)** July 25, 1937: Scene at Nürburgring, the cars lining up for the start of the German GP, the drivers in casual conversation, Baby Caracciola in center foreground. **71)** July 5, 1937: Rosemeyer's Auto Union and Caracciola's Mercedes W125 head into a corner at Roosevelt Raceway during the Vanderbilt Cup. **72)** May 30, 1937: Hasse's Auto Union is leading, but Lang soon roared past to win Avus at 162.61 mph. No race would be won at a faster speed until Monza in 1957.

Sr El celebre incidente en la III Carrera Panamericana. Un buitre voló contra el coche de Karl Kling, rompió el parabrisas e hirió al acompañante Klenk

Facing page: W196 and the 1955 season painted by Gotschke. **73)** A cool Juan Fangio driving to victory on January 16 in the blisteringly hot Grand Prix of Argentina. **74)** May 24: Stirling Moss at speed in the European GP at Monaco. **75)** At Spa, June 5: Moss leading Eugenio Castellotti's Lancia toward Malmédy in the Belgian GP. **76)** The track temperature was 131° as Moss stopped at trackside in the Argentine GP. This page: **77)** Leslie Saalburg (1902-1975) was, with Lawrence Fellows, America's foremost fashion illustrator of the thirties and forties. He also produced paintings (unsigned) for Ford and Lincoln. Car portraiture in period settings distinguished much of his postwar automotive art. This painting of a 1909 Mercedes was commissioned by the car's owner, Henry Austin Clark, Jr. **78)** Winning an art contest sponsored by *Speed* (the magazine of the British Racing Drivers' Club) in the mid-thirties launched the career of Roy Nockolds (1911-1980), who became one of England's best-known motoring artists. Action scenes were his specialty. Here Lautenschlager is shown after overtaking Boillot's Peugeot in the 1914 French Grand Prix. **79)** German artist Hans Liska (1907-1983) produced several hand-captioned art albums for Daimler-Benz during the fifties. This dramatic sketch shows the famous crash of a buzzard through the windshield of the Kling-Klenk 300SL during the 1952 Carrera Panamericana.

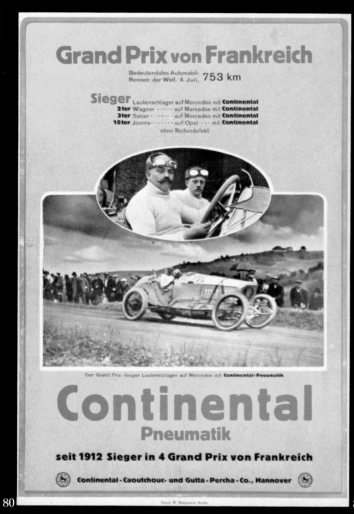

80) The Continental tire company celebrated its victory in the French Grand Prix with this 1914 poster. **81)** and **82)** The popularity of the Indianapolis-winning Mercedes is indicated in the representational race cars promoting the 1915 and 1916 board track races in Brooklyn. Peter Helck was a struggling young freelance artist when he painted these program covers. **83)** Barcelona GP, 1935: Fagioli and Caracciola finished one-two. **84)** Tunis GP, 1936. **85)** Poster that celebrated Avus 1937 and graphically captured Lang's 162.61 mph winning average. **86)** German GP, 1937: a one-two finish. **87)** Same finish, Masaryk GP. **88)** A clean sweep at Tripoli, 1939. **89)** Yet another clean sweep, 1938 French GP. **90)** Victory in Italy, 1938. **91)** through **94)** These four posters, and No. 89, were illustrated and designed by Walter Gotschke.

86

87

88

89

90

91

92

93

94

Nach harter Zerreißprobe

DOPPELSIEG

im 24 Stunden-Rennen von Le Mans

1. Lang-Rieß
2. Helfrich-Niedermayr

Auf Mercedes-Benz Typ 300 SL

Neuer absoluter Streckenrekord · 3733 km 780 m in 24 Stunden gefahren

95

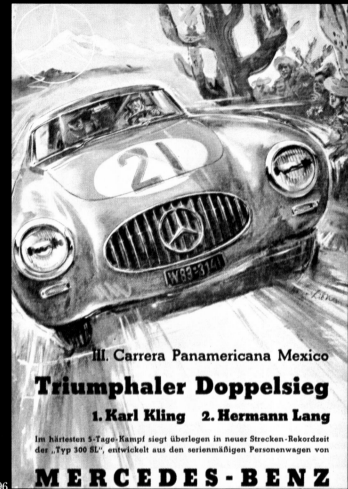

III. Carrera Panamericana Mexico

Triumphaler Doppelsieg

1. Karl Kling   2. Hermann Lang

Im härtesten 5-Tage-Kampf siegt überlegen in neuer Strecken-Rekordzeit der „Typ 300 SL", entwickelt aus den serienmäßigen Personenwagen von

MERCEDES-BENZ

96

Überlegener Sieg

im Großen Jubiläumspreis vom Nürburgring
für Sportwagen

1. Hermann Lang, 2. Karl Kling, 3. Fritz Riess, 4. Theo Helfrich
alle auf Mercedes-Benz Typ 300 SL

Lang fährt die schnellste Runde mit 131,5 km/std und neuen Streckenrekord

MERCEDES-BENZ

97

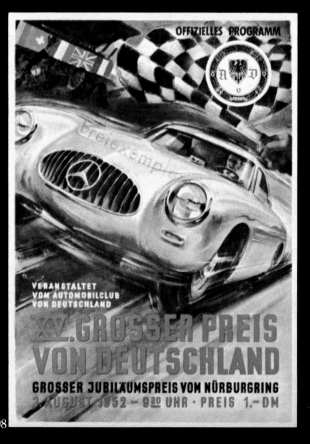

OFFIZIELLES PROGRAMM

VERANSTALTET
VOM AUTOMOBILCLUB
VON DEUTSCHLAND

XV. GROSSER PREIS VON DEUTSCHLAND

GROSSER JUBILÄUMSPREIS VOM NÜRBURGRING
1. AUGUST 1952 · 9.30 UHR · PREIS 1.—DM

98

99

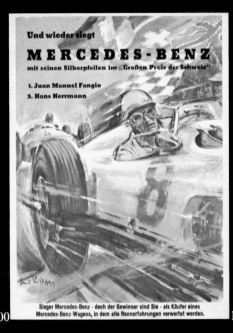

100

101

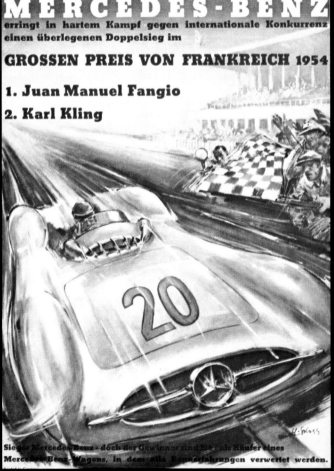

102

103

Though his production-car artwork for Daimler-Benz was exquisite, Hans Liska was at his best full throttle. A specialist in speed, his race posters portrayed the swashbuckling drama and compelling urgency of competition, as these nine examples from the fifties indicate. **95)** At night at Le Mans, 1952. The Mercedes driven to victory by Hermann Lang and Fritz Riess is signaled from the pits while lying second to Pierre Levegh's No. 8 Talbot. **96)** Desert heat and the hot pace in the Carrera Panamericana, 1952. **97)** The view from the driver's seat of one of the four 300SL's that romped to a commanding victory in the sports car race preceding the 1952 Grand Prix of Germany. **98)** The official program for that same race day. **99)** A triple victory for the 300SL in the Prix de Berne for sports cars, 1952. **100)** Fangio winning the 1954 Grand Prix of Switzerland. **101)** Fangio leading teammate Hans Herrmann in the 1954 Italian Grand Prix. **102)** Again, Fangio the victor in the 1954 French Grand Prix. **103)** A clean sweep of the 1954 Grand Prix of Berlin.

Dreifacher Sieg der Rennsportwagen (300 SLR)

Tourist Trophy Irland 1955

1. Stirling Moss / J. Fitch
2. Juan M. Fangio / K. Kling
3. Graf B. v. Trips / A. Simon

104

Dinuovo una vittoria in Argentina

Gran Premio di Buenos Aires 1955

1. Jl campione del mondo J. M. Fangio
2. Stirling Moss
4. Karl Kling

105

Überlegener Mercedes-Benz-Sieg

XXII. MILLE MIGLIA 1955

Rennsportwagen (300 SLR)   1. Stirling Moss/Jenkinson
                           2. Weltmeister J. M. Fangio

Seriensportwagen (300 SL) 1. Fitch/Gesell
                           2. Gendebien/Bascher
                           3. Casella

Dieselklasse (180 D)   1. Retter/Larrcher
                           2. Reinhard/Wiesnewski
                           3. Masera/Cardinar

106

MERCEDES-BENZ

Victory
in
Monte Carlo

The result of the most difficult European Rallye 1960:

1st	Schock/Moll	Stuttgart
2nd	Böhringer/Socher	Stuttgart
3rd	Ott/Mahle	Stuttgart
5th	Tak/Swaab	Netherlands

all on Mercedes-Benz 220 SE

Daimler-Benz AG Stuttgart-Untertuerkheim

107

108   109   110

111   112

Facing page: **104), 105), 106)** Making a point in posters—three of a series celebrating an all-conquering season of motor sport.
107) 1960 poster with Walter Schock alongside the 220SE in which he led a three-car Mercedes sweep in the Monte Carlo Rally.
This page: Mercedes advertising of the twenties. **108), 109), 110)** *"Als andere noch,"* the "comparatively speaking" campaign of
1929, contrasted the Mercedes with such other memorable firsts as Eiffel's tower, Edison's talking machine and the electric
trolley. **111)** This 1925 New York Automobile Salon catalog ad typified the romanticized high style of American prestige
automobile advertising in that era. The car itself played a supporting role (an approach pioneered by the Calkins & Holden
agency for Pierce-Arrow two decades before), but the message that the owner of a Mercedes was "wrapped in luxury" was
unmistakable. **112)** This Zurich agency ad, also from 1925 and painted by Swiss illustrator Eric de Coulon, suggested none too
subtly that a supercharged Mercedes was the perfect car for the Alps.

Im vornehmen Stil seiner äußeren Gestaltung, im erlesenen Ge-
schmack seiner Ausstattung, in der vollendeten Harmonie von
Leistung und Fahreigenschaften ist das Zweisitzer-A-Cabriolet
des „Typ 170 S" ein Meisterstück der Automobilbaukunst.

MERCEDES-BENZ

113

114

Pavlova Danced, Caruso Sang and Mercedes Was Winning Races

MERCEDES-BENZ *Type 190 SL*

The Sports Car you've waited for

The Mercedes-Benz model 190 SL successfully and skillfully combines the characteristics of a high-performance sports car with the comfort of a touring car, and offers the sporting driver those qualities of acceleration, road holding, manoeuvrability and exciting top speed which make driving a pleasure and every road a challenge. At the same time through generous provision for luggage as well as a third optional seat, this model may be used for practical everyday transportation, city driving, and family touring. Provided with a 125 HP o.h.c. motor capable of turning continuously at 6,000 rpm, giving a top speed of 118 m.p.h., brilliant acceleration throughout, and with typical Mercedes-Benz superior road holding, the 190 SL represents an extremely desirable choice for those interested in the smaller sports car.
Here is a product truly worthy of the Mercedes racing and sporting traditions, embodying at the same time the practical comfort for which the standard sedans are famous.

115

116 **MERCEDES-BENZ** 117

The Mercedes-Benz 450SL. Spoil yourself.

118

What Mercedes-Benz has learned from 74 years of cheating the wind.

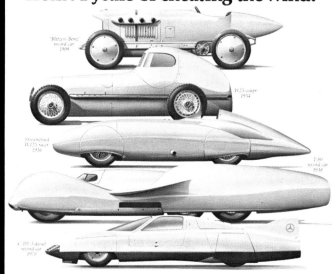

"Blitzen Benz" record car 1909

W25 coupe 1934

Streamlined W125 racer 1936

T80 record car 1938

C 111-3 diesel record car 1979

119

Stamp collecting, started soon after the systematic use of postage stamps was pioneered in Great Britain in 1840, gained further impetus in 1893 when the U.S. issued what is generally regarded as the first major commemorative to celebrate the Columbian Exposition. All nations have since issued commemoratives, largely with collectors in mind. Because of its unique status in world automobile history, Daimler-Benz has often been featured on German postage stamps, as illustrated by the various issues shown here, including celebrations of the firm's 50th and 75th anniversaries. The set of four stamps commemorating the 50th anniversary of Avus was circulated by the Berlin post office, which issues its own stamps. Other nations have frequently featured Daimler-Benz cars. Monaco is the most famous issuer of automobile stamps, a tradition begun in 1950 after the accession of Prince Rainier, an ardent auto enthusiast. French-speaking African countries, such as Mali, Chad and the Congo, avidly follow transportation themes as well. Stamps are big business for many small nations, their sale representing nearly 100 percent of the government's revenue, with less than five percent of the stamps issued for postal use. The stamps at the top of this page are properly termed "labels" in philately, as they are issued by companies, not governments. The DMG issues date from 1914, the Mercedes typewriter stamps from the twenties.

Brooklands, 1922: Count Zborowski driving Major R.F. Cooper's Benz, the former Burman Blitzen streamlined with new body panels and pointed tail. Its best lap was 106.88 mph, not fast enough to interest Zborowski, who also found the car more treacherous and less comfortable than his Chitty.

new Benz was planned as a collaboration with Rumpler until Mannheim engineers discovered structural weaknesses and decided to begin from scratch. Max Wagner, a Benz engineer since 1910, was in charge, assisted by Hans Nibel. The specifications included independent rear suspension with inboard rear brakes. Three of the cars were ready for the Grand Prix of Europe held at Monza, Italy, in September 1923. Their drivers were Franz Hörner and Willy Walb from the factory and the Italian

Fernando Minoia, who had driven a Mercedes in the previous year's Targa Florio. Walb's engine gave out, but the other two cars finished, Minoia in fourth. The Tropfenwagen was judged the outstanding new car in the race, and a gold medal was awarded to Max Wagner. Next came a sport version, which enjoyed a good record in sprints and hill climbs; a few were sold, including one to Benito Mussolini. But the Tropfenwagen would soon be consigned to history.

By 1923 the German economy was in chaos. In

Like Daimler, Benz began racing after the war with new versions of its prewar race cars or racing versions of its new production cars. Among the former were two Blitzen-like Benzes; among the latter was a neatly streamlined Benz 10/30 Sport racer (above) in which Franz Hörner won the first race held at Avus in September 1921.

January French troops marched into the Ruhr Basin to take over factories and railroads in order to enforce reparations payments. The mark fell so low as to be meaningless. A new Benz cost 25 million marks. The first Benz diesel tractor was sold at the end of the Königsberg Fair to a landowner from East Prussia for 165 million marks. Workers in Mannheim and Untertürkheim stuffed their wages into large satchels—not that a week's wages bought much. Sending a letter from Germany to the United States cost more than a billion marks. Food was the most precious commodity; aristocrats exchanged their Persian rugs and Rembrandts for it; the middle classes and pensioners spent their savings for it. The Weimar Republic seemed about to fall apart.

At Monza that September, the failure of a Mercedes to compete led to rumors that Daimler-Motoren-Gesellschaft was boycotting the race to protest the French occupation of the Ruhr. But politics was probably less the reason than money; with inflation out of control in Germany, the company could no longer afford to compete. They had, after all, just spent a small fortune at Indianapolis.

To race in the 1923 Indianapolis 500 had been a pragmatic decision. The new two-liter formula for this race was the same as that prevailing in continental grand prix competition; new race cars built for Indianapolis could do double duty in Europe. And putting in an appearance at Indianapolis was the first step in what would be a concerted export drive in the States.

But the 1923 Indianapolis 500 was not exactly the success the company had anticipated. For one thing, in the midst of planning for the race, Paul Daimler left DMG to join Horch; his successor arrived only as final preparations were being made. For another, the Indianapolis cars were considerably lighter than the Mercedes to which the drivers, Lautenschlager, Sailer and Werner, had become accustomed. For still another, the brick track was an entirely new experience for road racers. And it rained, which made the surface slick.

"The Germans showed an unfamiliarity with American race practice in many ways," *Motor Age* reported afterwards. "They did not at any time seem to get the exact hang of driving on the track that is partly straightaway and partly banked." On the four-

Following its promising debut in the 1923 European Grand Prix, the Benz Tropfenwagen — which weighed just 1650 pounds — was refined in detail for further events and made even lighter with the drilling of holes in the wheel rims.

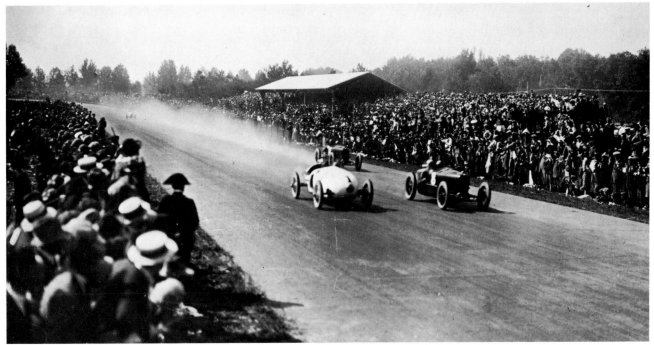

Conceived in 1921, the first prototype completed in 1922 and first raced in the European Grand Prix at Monza in 1923, the Benz Tropfenwagen was both ambitious and portentous. RH, for *Rennwagen Heckmotor* (rear-engined race car), was its official designation. The car bristled with ingenuity, though most observers passed over the swing axle rear suspension and inboard-mounted rear brakes to gawk at the Tropfenwagen's radiator, mounted above and behind the engine. This location, and the sport model's winged fenders, were but two of many aviation-derived features of the car. By 1923 standards the driver sat low in the Tropfenwagen, the mechanic's seat slightly staggered to the rear. Exigencies doomed the RH Benz; the ideas it propounded were reborn a decade later.

In 1923, with inflation out of control, Daimler began printing its own banknotes to pay workers. The 1922 Targa-winning car was pictured on one series.

The catastrophic inflation ended the following year when the worthless currency was replaced by a new, stable mark backed by 30 percent gold. An Allied commission headed by the Chicago financier Charles G. Dawes devised a plan of international loans and a schedule of reparations payments that would allow for economic reconstruction. The French left the Ruhr, and Franco-German relations were improved by the treaties of Locarno. Germany was admitted to the League of Nations. The future began to look brighter.

In 1923 nearly 15 million cars and trucks were registered throughout the world, 83.8 percent of them in the United States. Every other car in the world was a Model T Ford. In Great Britain, where Herbert Austin was building his little Austin Sevens, and France, where André Citroën had introduced American mass-production methods, more than 500,000 and 300,000 vehicles, respectively, were registered. In Germany registrations totaled just 126,092. Only one German in 280 owned an automotive vehicle—but 86 German companies were building 144 different models. The luxury tax on German cars had been lowered to 7½ percent, but the import tax had been lowered as well, and more and more foreign automobiles, mostly American and

teenth lap, Lautenschlager hit an oil slick and then a wall and was out. The two remaining cars completed the two hundred laps. Sailer's eighth place was the best finish of a foreign country; Christian Werner was eleventh. Two Sailers had driven that Mercedes. Max was relieved by his nephew Karl after he had been thrown from the car in a curve. "Never again," said the man who loved racing over the primitive roads of Sicily; the American oval made him dizzy. Despite these setbacks Richard Schilling, the president of the American Mercedes Company in New York, thought the effort was a good warm-up for 1924; but that was not to be.

In October the Communists staged an uprising in Hamburg. In November, in a beer hall in Munich, the thirty-four-year-old leader of an obscure right-wing extremist party led an attempt to seize the city government. Adolf Hitler failed, was arrested, tried and sent to Landsberg Prison.

The Weimar Republic survived the crisis of 1923.

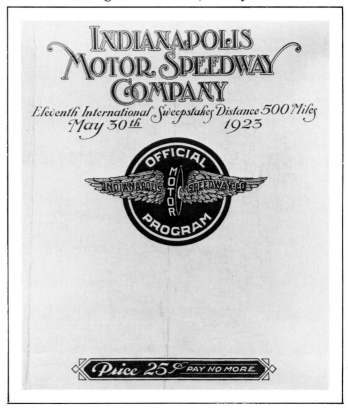

Indianapolis 500, 1923, from the top: Lautenschlager, Werner, Sailer the younger. It was not a good day. Reported the New York *Times:* "The Mercedes crew had tough going . . . Karl Sailer was blown out of his car by backfire at the pits and thrown to the bricks, and their cars began to go to pieces in the last 100 miles." Lautenschlager confirmed the diaster: "I was covered in oil from head to foot and I could hardly see . . . Suddenly I was thrown out, and came down God knows where." Actually most of the teams had problems on the slick course, only three cars of the 24 starters surviving the 500 miles completely unscathed. Sailer's eighth place won Mercedes $1500.

French, were seen on German roads: three foreign cars for every German one in 1924. That year Opel of Rüsselsheim began producing a small Citroën look-alike, painted green and called the Laubfrosch (Tree Toad), but the company found mass production difficult. Thanks to inflation, buying an automobile was very low on the average German's list of priorities. German auto makers began to fail at an alarming rate.

By 1923 pride of commercial sovereignty made no sense to Benz & Cie. and Daimler-Motoren-Gesellschaft, which that year built just 1,382 and 1,020 cars respectively. Paul Daimler had resigned from DMG because he wanted to build an eight-cylinder luxury car, a plan the board vetoed; Daimler took his idea to Horch, which produced the car, and when times got better, it competed with the Mercedes. But in 1923 no one knew when times would get better. DMG was in a serious quandary, as various attempts at diversification now indicated. Marienfelde began building Mercedes bicycles and Unter-türkheim produced typewriters, both products complete with three-pointed star. (The typewriter, however, was called the DMG. Before the war DMG had sold the rights to use the Mercedes name to another typewriter company—and to a shoe factory, the only times the Mercedes name was ever used on a product not manufactured by the company.) The bicycle was produced until 1925, the DMG typewriter until 1927. DMG considered producing a motorcycle, but decided against it. Since Gottlieb Daimler had built the world's first, it would have been appropriate to pick up where the company's founder had left off, but historical niceties took second place when the future itself was in peril.

For its part, in addition to falling sales, Benz & Cie. had to contend with the machinations of Jakob Schapiro, a former small-time Berlin automobile dealer who had maneuvered himself into a position of power in the German auto industry. His keen eye had been fixed on Benz since 1919, when he took over Schebera, a Berlin coach-building house that had done business with Mannheim in the past. The ruinous German economy helped his tactics. He bought Benz chassis for Schebera and cars for his dealership on credit and delayed paying Mannheim

as long as possible; the runaway inflation then saw to it that once Benz got the money it cost Schapiro little and was worth virtually nothing. But Mannheim had no choice but to sell to him. With the factory on half-time and production at its lowest point since 1909, no customer could be turned away.

Meanwhile Schapiro was buying Benz stock. Before the company knew what had happened, he presented his 40 percent ownership as a *fait accompli*. In 1923 he became a member of the board. His idea now was nothing less than a conglomerate of German automobile firms with himself at its head; Benz was merely a cog in the gears of his design. The company directors were aghast—and alone they were helpless. Benz & Cie. really needed a strong partner now.

But Schapiro was not the only German business magnate with dreams of automotive empire. The industrialist Hugo Stinnes and Jakob Goldschmidt, of the Darmstadter and Nationalbank, also had visions of consortiums. So did Emil Georg von Stauss of the Deutsche Bank, a member of the Daimler-Motoren-Gesellschaft board. Von Stauss's idea was a General Motors-like confederation of Daimler, Benz, BMW and Opel.

In February 1924 von Stauss presented Daimler and Benz with a proposal outlining the necessity and advantages of a consolidation (the word "merger" was carefully avoided at this point). An "Agreement of Mutual Interest" was signed by the boards of directors of both firms on May 1. Poignantly, among the first matters agreed upon was the guarantee of financial security for the rest of their lives to Carl and Bertha Benz. More pragmatically, a union of the sales, promotion and service departments and a realignment of the respective product lines were planned. Duplicating or overlapping models were eliminated. DMG would phase out the Knight-engined cars; Benz would discontinue the experimental Tropfenwagen. Though there was a sharing of members on both management committees and boards of directors, for the moment the companies retained their identities. The agreement was valid until the year 2000. Von Stauss was sure that, despite their rivalry, the two companies could hammer out a merger by then.

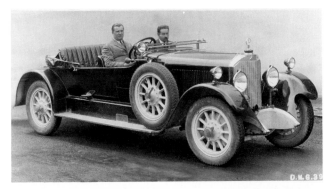

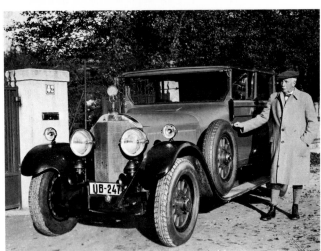

Mercedes, Benz and Mercedes-Benz owners. (Top, left) A young and comparatively svelte Alfred Neubauer with his Mercedes 15/70/100 Sport, 1926. (Top, right) Crown Prince Wilhelm in a Mercedes-Benz 24/100/140 Touring, 1927. (Center, left) Weimar president Paul von Hindenburg alongside his Mercedes 12/55 Limousine, 1926. (Center, right) Richard Strauss alongside his Mercedes 15/70/100 Limousine, 1924. (Above, right) Count Arnim Muskau at home with his Benz 11/40 Touring, c. 1924. (Above, left) Barney Oldfield with Ty Cobb and his Benz 14/30 Sport, 1919. Barney was in the tire business by now. Ty won the batting title with a .384 average for the Detroit Tigers that year.

On April 27, 1924, just a few days before the DMG-Benz agreement was signed, Mercedes again won the Targa Florio. The man most responsible was Paul Daimler's successor at DMG: a brilliant and temperamental engineer who had succeeded Daimler once before, when in 1906 the latter had left the Austrian Daimler company to return to Stuttgart. Though he probably would have taken the post anyway, the new chief engineer's acceptance was made easier by the fact that he needed a job. During a company directors' meeting in Vienna, when discussion turned to cutting his budget, he threw a table lighter at one of the board members and quit. His name was Ferdinand Porsche. And he brought one of his Austro-Daimler race drivers to Stuttgart with him. *His* name was Alfred Neubauer.

Porsche's arrival at DMG coincided with final preparations for the Indianapolis 500 in 1923, a venture from which the team returned complaining about the poor showing; Lautenschlager commented that the prize money got stuck somewhere in the inlet manifold. Porsche spent the next nine months working out technical problems and decided the wild roads of Sicily offered a better chance of success than did a return to Indianapolis.

There were 37 cars in the 1924 Targa Florio, Alfa Romeos, Peugeots and Fiats among them—most of them considerably bigger and more powerful than the three-car team of two-liter supercharged Mercedes which, one reporter commented, crackled "in a most spiteful manner." Only 17 cars completed the event, but three of them were Mercedes, which finished 1-2-3 in the concurrent production-car Coppa Florio. In the Targa, the main event, the tall and wiry Christian Werner won impressively at a 40.5-mph average, posting the fastest lap and also a record for the race. He enjoyed the advantage of youth over his teammate Lautenschlager, who finished ninth: Werner was in his early thirties, Lautenschlager in his late forties. The tag man of the team, who finished thirteenth, shared Werner's youth though not his smooth technique; his fiancée subsequently told him that he drove like "a night watchman." Fortunately Alfred Neubauer would soon discover another aspect of motor sport where it was easier for him to excel.

As for Ferdinand Porsche, the 1924 Targa Florio made him a hero at DMG. Since his arrival he had been regarded warily; his insistence upon being addressed as Dr. Porsche (it was an honorary title from the University of Vienna) was thought rather grandiose by the down-to-earth Swabian personnel. But after the Targa Daimler people didn't care what Porsche called himself. The University of Stuttgart helped out by awarding him another honorary doctorate and he was invited to sign his name in the local "Golden Book," the highest honor the city of Stuttgart could bestow.

Hard times, other products ... the three-pointed star on the DMG typewriter, 1924-1927. Furniture and bicycles were built for a while, too.

Racing in Sicily, 1924. The sun was hot and so was the pace as Christian Werner won the Targa Florio and the concurrent Coppa and established the Targa's fastest lap at 45.29 mph. Race observers compared Werner's smooth cornering style to Count Masetti's.

The Targa was followed by victories in smaller events: Solitude, Eifelrennen, Klausen Pass. For the Semmering hill climb on September 17, Porsche prepared a special car for Otto Salzer, giving the popular veteran driver the chance to break his own record for the hill, which he had established in 1919 and which still stood. The Targa chassis was used, with an engine based on the 1914 Grand Prix type with a supercharger added. Alas, just before the event, the new unit was "*kaput gegangen*," as Salzer put it, so a supercharger from an available production Mercedes was hurriedly transplanted. Salzer broke his own record by two seconds, but Christian Werner, in a two-liter Targa Mercedes, did even better: he drove the first Semmering ascent under seven minutes.

October 19, 1924, was a bad day. The Italian Grand Prix at Monza had been ill-starred from the beginning. Initially it was scheduled for September 7,

The press commented that Werner's Targa victory had been achieved "in competition with as fine a set of cars and drivers as has ever been gathered together for any Continental race." Fifty thousand German race enthusiasts had traveled to Sicily to cheer him on.

Sieger
der Targa- und Coppa-Florio
1924

WERNER auf MERCEDES
-2 LITER-RENNWAGEN
gewinnt
BEIDE TROPHÄEN IN REKORDZEIT
und fährt die
SCHNELLSTE RUNDE
GEGEN SCHÄRFSTE INTERNATIONALE
KONKURRENZ.

Christian Lautenschlager (above) celebrated his forty-seventh birthday two weeks before the Sicilian races. He finished ninth overall (second in class) in both events and was clearly frustrated with his performance, roaring into the pits, in one observer's words, "howling for everything and wanting that everything at once." Such behavior was rare for Lautenschlager, a disciplined driver who set the standard for the Mercedes team in this pre-Neubauer era. Though he never raced again, Lautenschlager remained in the employ of Mercedes. In January 1954, at the age of 76, he died in his sleep in the cottage that had been a gift to him from the company.

Alfred Neubauer as Targa Florio race driver. In the Sascha (top) he finished nineteenth in 1922. In the Mercedes (above, with Ferdinand Porsche) he finished thirteenth in 1924. During World War I, Austrian army officer Neubauer had been assigned to the motor pool in the Austrian Daimler company. When peace came he remained with the firm, now serving under chief engineer Porsche. In 1922 company director Count Alexandre "Sascha" Kolowrat commissioned Porsche to design a small car; the Targa race entry of the 1½-liter double-overhead-cam Sascha was for publicity purposes. The Sascha project died when Porsche joined DMG in 1923, bringing Neubauer with him.

(Top) Otto Salzer was in charge of racing the Indianapolis Mercedes which returned to Germany. Here he is seen in the Werner car, bulbously rebodied, which he drove to victory in a hill climb near Prague in April 1924. (Above) Semmering, September 1924. Competing in Targa Florio-type Mercedes were (from the left) Werner, Salzer and Neubauer. The hill climb in this scenic resort region of Austria had been an annual fixture on the European motor sport calendar since 1899, with victory almost invariably captured by DMG. Werner took the honors this year, in a 6-minute 55.6-second climb that was a new Semmering record. Salzer was second. Neubauer lagged behind in fifth.

The supercharged two-liter double-overhead-cam straight-eight Grand Prix Mercedes designed by Porsche and first raced in the Italian Grand Prix at Monza in September 1924. New Mercedes team member Count Zborowski is seen at the wheel, with his longtime mechanic Len Martin.

and Porsche and his crew had arrived at Monza on the second with a brand-new two-liter supercharged grand prix car, the first eight-cylinder car DMG had ever built. A few practice laps proved the car was not ready, and Porsche returned the team to the factory; Fiat also had technical difficulties and withdrew. With two major contenders absent, the Italian organizers postponed the event to mid-October. Mercedes returned to the starting line, Fiat did not. The principal competition was Alfa Romeo, fresh from victory in the French Grand Prix.

The Stuttgart cars were to be driven by Werner, Count Masetti, Neubauer and Count Zborowski. For Louis Zborowski this was a dream come true. His Chitty-Bang-Bangs had been wonderful fun at Brooklands, but here at last he was being given the chance to prove himself more than just a gentleman driver. He had been accepted as a member of the Mercedes factory team.

Max Sailer directed the race effort. He appeared worried during practice, and with good reason: the cars were still not raceworthy. On the eve of the race, Sailer told Zborowski his car had a clutch problem and would have to be withdrawn. The Count insisted

1924 Italian GP. From the left: Zborowski, Werner, Masetti, Neubauer. On Lap 43, a broken fuel line retired Count Masetti. On Lap 44, a crash cost Count Zborowski his life. Mercedes immediately flagged in the remaining cars.

on racing, and Sailer at last relented. At the starting line, putting on the cuff links his father had worn the day of his fatal crash in 1903, Zborowski offhandedly remarked to a friend, "I must not do my fond Papa's trick today, must I?" On the forty-fourth lap he skidded on some oil, crashed, and was killed instantly. When Sailer received the news, he flagged the remaining Mercedes off the track. Alfa Romeo won, and also took the next three places.

At the 1925 Berlin Automobile Show, Mercedes and Benz cars shared the same stand for the first time. By now, 75 years before their "Agreement of Mutual Interest" was to expire, it was apparent to both companies that full merger was in their best interests. Von Stauss kept a watchful eye on Stinnes and Goldschmidt, particularly on Goldschmidt, who believed he could acquire the Marienfelde and Gaggenau factories because of losses DMG had sustained in investing in an ill-advised auto accessory venture. As for Schapiro, no one was sure what he would do next. "If he says no to the merger," Ernst Berge wrote von Stauss in 1924, "the entire deal will have to be pushed back until the Benz company is nearly bankrupt, which with Schapiro's help should happen in a couple of years."

Schapiro had actually favored the idea of the merger, believing it would guarantee him a major influence in Daimler as well as in Benz. But behind the scenes von Stauss was maneuvering to insure that this would not happen. When Schapiro found out what von Stauss was doing, he attempted to block the merger, but he was too late. And the Deutsche Bank's extension of credit to Benz and DMG thwarted the hopes of Stinnes and Goldschmidt. By pooling all possible stock, Schapiro's share in the merged companies was held to 16 percent; in a few years he was no longer a factor in the German auto industry.

It is astonishing that Daimler and Benz were able to work out their differences with such comparative ease. But the sheer necessity of survival was a powerful reason for the merger. And Stuttgart and Mannheim remained spirited rivals, with little love lost between them. But a major ingredient—the glue that held them together—was the man Karl Jahr of Benz, with the blessing of von Kaulla of DMG, appointed to iron things out: Wilhelm Kissel, a 38-year-old Benz executive. Cool, detached, a tireless worker, Kissel had to be both diplomat and tactician. He played both roles well. Helping him coordinate the merger of the various Daimler and Benz factories was Wilhelm Haspel, a young man in his twenties whom Kissel had found in the business office of DMG, where he worked days while he studied at night for an engineering degree. He was, in other words, both engineer and accountant. Together Kissel and

Principal protagonists in the merger: Karl Jahr (left), head of the Rheinische Creditbank, a Benz board member since 1910; Emil Georg von Stauss (center) of the Berliner Institut, the Deutsche Bank and a Daimler board member since 1920; Wilhelm Kissel (right), Benz engineer/administrator since 1904. Jahr first broached the subject, von Strauss made the first proposal, Kissel made the merger work.

Announcing the merger of the two oldest and largest automobile companies in Germany. This early ad used both the Mercedes and the Benz symbols and was widely distributed to dealers in mat form for insertion of their own message in local newspapers. The transition from spirited rivalry to friendly partnership was no doubt difficult for many former Mercedes and Benz dealers. The stylized car in this ad was designed not to ruffle the feathers of either during the period of dealership realignment.

Haspel set up the central administrative and book-keeping system of the merged companies.

By May 1925 a workable agreement had been reached. The two companies would have one design department. Two-liter passenger car chassis were to be built in Mannheim, four- and six-liter models in Untertürkheim, trucks under four tons in Gaggenau, trucks over four tons in Marienfelde. All body building was to be centered in Sindelfingen. A proper assembly line was to be set up to replace the previous reliance on handwork. This last was a Daimler suggestion; the Benz contingent at first demurred, believing that quantity production methods made sense only if 1,000 cars a month were produced, a figure that at the time seemed unattainable for German quality car makers.

On June 28, 1926, Wilhelm Kissel took the final brief merger agreement, designating the new company Daimler-Benz Aktiengesellschaft, to a Mannheim notary.

The combination of Daimler and Benz meant that the new firm had an estimable cadre of engineers, among them Porsche, Hans Nibel, and Friedrich Nallinger's 24-year-old son. Doubtless Fritz Nallinger got his job because of nepotism, but he kept it because of his talent: it was Porsche who requested his services in Untertürkheim as chief experimental engineer. Young Nallinger had to be good; like most of the people at Daimler, Porsche regarded any Mannheim ideas as suspect. Nallinger was one of the first Benz men to move to Mercedes before the final merger. Immediately after it Wilhelm Haspel, just turned 29, was sent to administer the Sindelfingen factory.

And Wilhelm Kissel moved from Mannheim to Stuttgart-Untertürkheim, the new headquarters of the Daimler-Benz AG. Though DMG had top billing, the managing director of the merged firm was from Benz. Neither brass band nor open arms greeted his arrival in Stuttgart. The most modest car on the company lot picked him up at the station, and when he arrived at the administration building he found that his new office had room for a desk, a chair and a filing cabinet. But having managed the merger Kissel had little difficulty managing to win over the DMG people, and he chose never to move out of that tiny office.

The new boards of the two companies had about equal numbers of Benz and Daimler people. There was an interesting new addition: Franz Josef Popp, the managing director of BMW. Von Stauss still had plans to move BMW into the Daimler-Benz group. Prior to the merger a "friendship" contract had been negotiated between DMG and BMW, which then manufactured only motorcycles and aviation engines. Almost immediately there were arguments; BMW wanted Daimler to give up aircraft engine building, which the company had just resumed; Daimler wanted BMW to keep out of automobile production, which BMW was investigating. But Daimler-Benz continued building aviation engines, and in 1928 BMW began making cars. Nobody talked much about the "friendship" contract.

Meanwhile the Daimler people and the Benz people resigned themselves to the fact that they had best become friends.

Of all the decisions made during the complicated merger process, perhaps the easiest was choosing the symbol for the combined companies' products. That decision practically made itself. In the early twenties, Mercedes placed its three-pointed star within a circle. Mannheim's emblem was the word "Benz" circled by a laurel wreath. The new insignia would be a three-pointed star wreathed with laurel, the word "Mercedes" at the top, the word "Benz" below. The circle was complete.

CHAPTER SIX

INTERMEZZO AND SUPERCHARGERS

1 9 2 7 – 1 9 3 1

If you can look into the seeds of time,
And say which grain will grow and
which will not, Speak.
—WILLIAM SHAKESPEARE,
MACBETH

It was called the Jazz Age, the generation of Flaming Youth, the era of ballyhoo. It had no common denominator anywhere, except perhaps an aversion to tedium. Now, with her economy stabilized, Germany could begin to roar with the twenties, and Germans could throw themselves into the decade when the chaperone, the calling card, and the social note became passé and virtue was hard put to prove it was superior to sin. Hedonism flourished in prosperity. Living for the moment was as much a part of the German *Zeitgeist* as bathtub gin and the speakeasy were in America.

It was an era of fads and rages, from crossword puzzles to Mah-Jongg, from nudism to occultism. Fashion underwent a revolution. From the nearly 20 yards of cloth needed to clothe a woman in 1913, a mere seven were required in the mid-twenties; whereas in 1918 a short-haired female was assumed to be a Bolshevik, six years later bobbed hair became the look of the New Woman. Men tossed aside their heavy suits and waistcoats and took up sporting attire. Knickerbockers were a favorite of the fashionable male; even Thomas Mann wore them. Mass tourism marched alongside mass entertainment. People listened to a new gadget called a radio and went to movies that talked. Germany produced more films in this era than all the other European countries combined.

The first cars called Mercedes-Benz were produced in these years. Contemporary writers sometimes referred to the most imposing of them as Wagnerian or Faustian, but those analogies came from Germany's past, and these cars were very much a part of the German present. They were also among the most significant automobiles ever made anywhere.

From his offices in Stuttgart, Wilhelm Kissel carefully charted the Daimler-Benz AG course. From a total of 864 Mercedes and 1,305 Benzes built in 1926, production rose to 7,918 Mercedes-Benz automobiles in 1927. The diesel program moved forward as well. A diesel tractor had been introduced at the Königsberg Fair in 1923. At the Amsterdam exhibition in February 1924, Benz displayed a five-ton diesel truck which *Motorwagen* declared the most important vehicle, technically, at the show. Before the merger DMG had had its own diesel engine in the works, and now there was rivalry among Benz and Mercedes engineers over which unit would be developed. The Benz version won: it was simpler, lighter and cheaper to build, and used 32 percent less fuel than a gasoline-powered truck; the cost reduction was 86 percent. The Mercedes-Benz diesel truck was put into production in 1927 and the next year won the prestigious Dewar Trophy of the Royal Automobile Club in England for the "most meritorious perform-

Weimar's dying years personified by Marlene Dietrich's Lola-Lola in the 1930 film *The Blue Angel,* based on Heinrich Mann's *Professor Unrath* and directed by Josef von Sternberg.

MERCEDES-BENZ-Dieselmotoren

mit patentierter Vorkammer

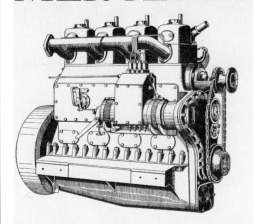

als Zwei-Zylinder	20-30 PS
Vier-Zylinder	40-60 PS
Sechs-Zylinder	70-100 PS

bei 600—1000 minutlichen Umdrehungen

für ortsfeste, fahrbare und Schiffs-Anlagen!

Prospekte und Angebote durch den Vertreter für das deutsche Bodenseegebiet:

Ober-Ingenieur **Franz Meyer** Technisches Büro **Stuttgart**

Kriegsbergstraße 38   Fernruf 221 44/45

10329

cedes Benz Strahsenschlepper Typ O.E.

Economic conditions in Germany after World War I provided the impetus for Daimler and Benz experimentation in diesel engines. First on the market with a tractor, Benz began building 100 diesel engines for agricultural and commercial vehicle use, and completed its first experimental five-ton 50 hp diesel truck in 1923. With the merger of the two companies, Daimler diesel development was subordinated to Benz's in the new Mercedes-Benz trucks and tractors. In 1933 the company celebrated the 10th anniversary of the first diesel truck. Two years later production of diesel vehicles had exceeded 10,000 units.

Introduced in October 1926, the six-cylinder, two-liter Stuttgart 200, though not powerful, was robustly built and was widely used as a taxi in the mid- to late twenties. Over 10,000 had been built by 1929, when the model became the Stuttgart 260.

ance" of a commercial vehicle, officially certified as averaging "51 ton-mpg of heavy oil over a road trial of 692 miles."

In the next six years Daimler-Benz produced over 10,000 diesel trucks, most of them in the former Benz factory in Gaggenau. Though the former DMG plant at Marienfelde eventually manufactured commercial vehicles, for the moment it was turned over to repair work. When integration of the Daimler and Benz factories was completed during the next decade, the old Benz factory in Mannheim was given over entirely to commercial vehicles. But during this period, automobile production continued there.

The first two automobiles to carry the Mercedes-Benz trademark, the Stuttgart and the Mannheim, were named after the cities where they were built. The engineering development of both had been completed before the merger. Introduced in October 1926, the cars replaced the former Benzes in the new company's line.

The old guard gave way to the new in competition as well. Lautenschlager and Salzer retired to factory posts, and newcomers moved into the driver's seat in motor sport.

One of them was a mountain of a man of almost Herculean strength. Otto Merz, it was said, could lift a Mercedes onto a jack unaided and drive nails into a table with his bare hands; witnesses attested they had seen Merz perform both these feats and then grin broadly. S.C.H. "Sammy" Davis likened him to

Flat radiators and ten-spoke pressed steel wheels characterized the early Stuttgart and Mannheim. The latter is seen here. Mannheim production totaled 3,854 in late 1928 when its 3-liter engine was replaced by a 3.5-liter unit.

Krähberg Hill Climb, October 1923, the last event of the season for weekend racer Rudi Caracciola. His was the fastest of all the cars. His Mercedes wins that year came to an even dozen. At 22, his racing career was launched.

a friendly fairy-tale giant. Born in Esslingen in 1889, Merz had followed a typical path into the ranks of Mercedes drivers. He joined Daimler-Motoren-Gesellschaft as a mechanic in 1906, and then served in the same capacity for Willy Pöge, the race driver, and for the Austrian industrialist Theodor Dreher. Then he graduated into the service of royalty; he was a chauffeur in the procession at Sarajevo the day Franz Ferdinand was assassinated and was wounded himself, though whether he was actually driving the Archduke's car is uncertain. He became a Mercedes race driver in the early twenties.

Less typical was the rise to stardom of the man who more than any other would be associated with Mercedes motor sport. Rudolf Caracciola was born in

1901, the son of a successful innkeeper in the town of Remagen on the Rhine, and got his early experience on motorcycles. In 1923 he passed a DMG driving test under Christian Werner's watchful eye and was sent to the Mercedes agency in Dresden as an automobile salesman and occasional race driver. Very quickly his driving became more than occasional.

Otto Merz and Rudi Caracciola both began racing Mercedes in 1923, Merz for the factory, Caracciola on any Saturday there was a race within driving distance and he could borrow a car from the Dresden dealership. In July 1926, just a few weeks after the merger, both men won their first races for Daimler-Benz.

The Grand Prix of Germany at Avus and the

After winning the Rumanian Touring Race and the All-Russian Reliability Drive in 1923, Otto Merz was rewarded with a permanent place on the Mercedes team. He is seen here en route to a record-breaking climb at Solitude in 1924.

Grand Prix of Europe in San Sebastian, Spain, were being run on successive weekends. With Daimler-Benz AG just a few days old and two races on the immediate calendar, it had been decided to contest only one officially. Although the Avus event, on the eleventh, would be Germany's first grand prix, the factory opted for the Spanish race on the eighteenth; a good showing there would help export sales. And a good showing Otto Merz provided, leading a one-two-three sweep of the touring car class.

Aware of the company's decision, Caracciola had driven to Stuttgart to plead for a factory car for Avus. After two hours of talking he got half of what he wanted: Max Sailer would give him a car, but he had to enter it under his own name. The factory did not want to risk its reputation with a 25-year-old weekend racer. As Rudi later remembered, "If things went wrong, I carried the can as far as the outside world was concerned." A young factory man, Eugen Salzer, offered to ride along as his mechanic.

The Avus course, a road leading southwest from Berlin toward Potsdam, was the progenitor of the autobahn. Planning for it had begun under the Kaiser, but completion was delayed by the war; the road was opened in the early twenties. It had two parallel straights totaling 12.3 miles, with a narrow turn to the south and a wider, steeply banked one at the north end. Officially named *Automobil-Verkehrs-und-Ubungs-Strasse* (Automobile Traffic and Practice Highway), the road almost immediately became known by its initials. The car Rudi Caracciola was to drive over it was one of the eight-cylinder vehicles which had proven so disappointing to the factory at its baptismal outing at the Italian Grand Prix the previous October. Another such car was handled by its owner, Adolf Rosenberger, a Pforzheim businessman and a talented amateur driver.

Although the factory was not officially represented, Ferdinand Porsche and Max Sailer showed up in the pits. The race was frenetic for organizers and participants, and thrilling for the 200,000 spectators. At the two o'clock starting flag, the sun shone, though not favorably on Caracciola, whose car stalled in the middle of the track, directly in front of the grandstand. Salzer got out and pushed the big Mercedes back to life, and Caracciola began playing catch-up from dead last in the 44-car field.

Then it began to rain, in torrents, and cars began careening off the course, one of them crashing into a scorer's stand located precariously close to the road. Salzer shouted to Caracciola he was afraid it was Rosenberger, who was leading the race at the time; a stop at the pits for oil and fuel confirmed this. Porsche and Sailer fretted; Mercedes' hopes had been halved.

The first race entered by Daimler-Benz AG was the touring car contest accompanying the Grand Prix of Europe at San Sebastian on July 18, 1926. The trio of new K Mercedes ran away with the event, led by winner Merz (center), with Caracciola (right) placing second, former Benz man Willy Walb (left) third.

The first Grand Prix of Gemany, Avus, July 11, 1926. Caracciola is shown with mechanic Eugen Salzer before the start and parading the course after his victory at an 83.95 mph average. The nearly three-hour race had been marked by torrential rains and numerous accidents, one of them Adolf Rosenberger's on a sister Mercedes. The tank of ether Rosenberger had used to facilitate starting began to leak mid-race and, in leaning out of the cockpit for fresh air, Rosenberger slid on the wet pavement and crashed into a roadside scoring stand. A timer was killed. Not until 1931 would another race be held at Avus.

On the eleventh of the twenty laps, Caracciola pulled into the pits again, with a spark plug cutting out. Under race regulations only drivers could make repairs. Caracciola got out, pulled the first plug and tossed it to Porsche, who checked it with a magnifying glass and tossed it back: it was all right, as was the second, the third, the fourth . . . until the eighth turned out to be the bad one. It was replaced as Salzer clicked his stopwatch. Too much time lost, he told Caracciola as they took off again. Caracciola was sure they could not make it up. He had no idea where he was in the standings, nor who was ahead or behind. He drove on—it was "like running alone in fog, without knowing the direction," he remembered later, but "sense of duty is the only compass."

By the thirteenth lap the rain stopped. Caracciola was exhausted, but that "only compass" and excited signals from Max Sailer in the pits urged him on. On the twentieth lap, when he crossed the finish line after nearly three hours and a total of 243 racing miles, Caracciola was only relieved that it was all over. His legs nearly buckled under him as he got out of the car, his wet coveralls stuck to his body. He had no idea he had just won the first Grand Prix of Germany.

His first reaction was to laugh. But then they put an enormous wreath around his neck as the flag was raised and the German anthem played. His winning average was 83.95 mph and his purse was 17,000 marks—a fine day's pay for a young automobile salesman whose salary was a hundred marks a month, plus 1½ percent commission on every car sold. That evening Caracciola became engaged to the pretty daughter of a Berlin businessman. Her name was Charlotte; everyone called her Charly. The next day, with newspaper headlines shouting his victory, Rudi Caracciola was a hero all over Germany.

The next day at the factory Alfred Neubauer began to ponder another aspect of Avus: when he crossed the finish line, Caracciola did not know he had won. A driver on the racetrack was the "world's loneliest human being," Neubauer thought; surely better races would be run if the driver knew where he was, how fast he was going, how fast he should be going, how much farther he had to go. Officially, Neubauer retired from driving because, as he told Count Masetti, he "lost his speed." That was part of the reason, though his wife's observation that he drove like a night watchman was true too. Neubauer knew that he was not, in his own words, "destined to be a great racing driver," but destiny had another role for him: he became the greatest racing manager in the history of motor sport.

In retrospect, one cannot imagine him as anything else. Biographies insist that at twenty he was the

Comrades in arms, c.1924, before the merger. From the left: rising Mercedes star Caracciola; Benz racer Kappler; Mercedes veteran Otto Salzer; Adolf Rosenberger, who drove both Mercedes and Benzes; Mercedes strong man Merz.

"slimmest and trimmest officer in the Austrian army," and official results confirm that the man who fell in love with automobiles in 1898 at the age of seven when he saw his first car (a Benz) puffing through Neutitschein, the North Moravian village where he was born, actually *was* a racing driver and once even finished as high as fifth. No matter; the Neubauer who has gone down in history is the Neubauer who was born to direct a racing team. That Neubauer first appeared on September 12, 1926, at a race in the wooded countryside near Solitude Castle, just outside Stuttgart.

Three Mercedes were at the starting line. Alfred Neubauer had arranged everything. Crews had been assigned to each car. Signal boards with coded numbers and letters, and small flags in different colors, each providing specific information that could be flashed to the drivers as they sped by, were in readiness. A sign language had been developed so the drivers could communicate with the pits: circling the air with the right index finger asked the number of laps remaining, a finger pointed forward asked how far ahead the car in front was, a thumb backward the converse for the car behind.

As the race was about to begin, Neubauer took his position at trackside, a black and red flag in his hand. An official rushed over and asked what he was doing there. He was the Mercedes team manager, Neubauer replied, and he was there to signal his drivers. The race official was incredulous, but Neubauer was a big man, which settled the argument before it began. He could stay there, the official said, but if a car hit him it would be his own fault. For the next few hours, Neubauer stayed there waving his flags, holding his signboard aloft and answering his driver's signals. No car hit him. The Mercedes team finished one-two-three, Otto Merz in front.

In the years to come Neubauer developed race strategy to a fine art. Though he was the prototype of a racing manager, there was no one else quite like him. He had a voice like a bullhorn and a vast 280-pound physique to match. His suits hung loosely around him as if afraid to get too close; people liked to say his trousers were cut from old zeppelins. He could let loose torrents of invective or behave like an amiable

teddy bear. An uncompromising disciplinarian, he had a warm heart and a wry wit. At races, wearing a necklace of stopwatches, growling orders as he stalked back and forth, the king of the pits became as famous in motor sport as any car or driver. He had, of course, been lucky. In launching a new idea in motor racing, he had the support of the man at Daimler-Benz AG whose approval counted most: Wilhelm Kissel. Responsible for directing a huge company that produced engines and vehicles for air, land and water, Kissel might easily have given up race cars. But he was part enthusiast and all pragmatist: racing was good publicity.

Kissel's support of Neubauer's efforts was pivotal in Mercedes competition history, but his directive to Ferdinand Porsche to design a fast, prestigious touring car to succeed the Mercedes 28/95 was no less so. Porsche came up with an immortal racing car that mere mortals could buy.

The mythic proportions and performance of the S series Mercedes has in retrospect reduced some formidable automobiles to the status of mere predecessors. Still, the eight-cylinder Grand Prix car started in 27 races in three years and finished in the money 21 times. And the K, which was revised from a six-cylinder model known only as 24/100/140, was good enough in its day for Rudi Caracciola to adopt after his Avus win; he spent the rest of the 1926 season winning races with it, making fastest times of the day and establishing new records at Freiburg, Klausen Pass, and Kipsdorf-Oberbarenburg-Altenberg in Germany, and at the international hill climb in Semmering, Austria. The fact that these cars are remembered now mainly as forerunners is an eloquent comment on the automobiles that followed.

The K* (for *kurz*, or short, because the wheelbase was shorter than that of its parent 24/100/140), was joined by the S, for sport, in 1927. The S was as close to a racing car as could be built without really building one, and it was introduced on a brand-new race track on June 19.

---

*The K was the touring car Otto Merz drove in San Sebastian in July 1926, in pursuit of export sales. With a factory guarantee of 90 mph, it could be honestly advertised as the fastest standard model of its type in the world.

The Mercedes-Benz K, introduced in 1926, was derived from the six-cylinder 6.2-liter 24/100/140 model essentially by truncating the wheelbase from 147.5 to 133.9 inches. The K designated *"kurz"* (for "short"), though it might also have referred to *"kompressor."* The flexible exhaust pipes boldly jutting from the right side of the hood were a Mercedes feature subsequently adopted by a number of other factories building supercharged cars, Duesenberg among them. Because the chassis alone weighed 1½ tons the K was a handful to drive, though one British road tester complained only about the heaviness of the clutch after lapping Brooklands at high speed. Others lamented the inadequacy of the brakes, a common failing of high-performance cars of the era (Ettore Bugatti, in a celebrated remark, said that he made his cars "to go, not to stop"). The K would "go" 90 mph, and Caracciola managed to stop his adequately after winning six races and hill climbs during the summer of 1926. Fewer than 250 Type K's were built through 1930. They included factory-bodied versions (facing page, top) and numerous custom-built examples by French (Saoutchik, facing page, below; Million-Guiet, this page, above) and Italian (Castagna, facing page, center and this page, top) coachbuilders.

Lining up for the start of the Nürburgring inaugural race on June 19, 1927 were Caracciola (No. 1) and Rosenberger (No. 2) on the new Type S, von Mosch (No. 3) on his own Type K. They finished in that order; Rudi won at 62.7 mph.

The setting was splendid, in the Eifel Mountains just west of the Rhine near the town of Adenau, and overlooked by medieval Nürburg Castle. The Nürburgring had been built because the German automobile industry, emerging from postwar austerity, needed a test track and major race circuit to demonstrate its wares in international races. And the Eifel area had had neither industry nor tourism; building the track there provided short-term employment and the long-term promise of visitors whenever a motor sport event was held. Visitors arrived by the tens of thousands that inaugural June day.

The Nürburgring circuit totaled 17.563 miles. Adjoining the common start-finish line and pit area were two loops, the *Südschleife* (South Loop) of 4.814 miles and the *Nordschleife* (North Loop) of 14.17 miles. They ran through magnificent pine forests, swooping up and down hills and diving around 174 corners. The circuit was an exacting and exhilarating test of man and machine. Ten laps of both loops

On July 17 three S Mercedes were at the Nürburgring for the German Grand Prix. Werner is seen here en route to second place, less than three minutes behind winner Merz.

were run in the inaugural; the winner was Caracciola with the new Mercedes S. Right behind him was Adolf Rosenberger with another S.

A month later on July 17 the S returned to the Nürburgring for the German Grand Prix. This time there were three cars, driven by Otto Merz, Christian Werner and Willy Walb (a former Benz engineer-driver). Neubauer, learning new tricks with each event, had the car hoods painted with broad colored stripes so the drivers could be readily identified from the pits. The cars finished one-two-three: Merz, Werner, Walb.

Meanwhile Caracciola, by now under contract as a factory driver, was taking an S everywhere. He was all-round winner of a five-day race tournament at Baden-Baden in July. On August 6 and 7 he campaigned the S in the international record days at Freiburg; a week later he captured the kilometer flat race and the hill-climb record at Klausen Pass, taking two class marks. He closed the season in September, winning the President Hindenburg Trophy at the Dreiecks race in Germany and scoring best time of the day at Oostmalle in Antwerp, Belgium. Adolf Rosenberger added to the S's laurels that month with a winning ascent of Semmering.

"Winner of several International races, designed and built especially for the sport element," announced the full-page Mercedes-Benz ads in New York newspapers, in January 1928. "The Model S . . . Now on Display." Given the car's performance in the short four months since its debut more crowing might have been expected from Park Avenue, but the importers may have opted for understatement in the year when Lindbergh had flown the Atlantic, Babe Ruth hit 60 home runs, Calvin Coolidge stated that he did not choose to run, and Henry Ford shut down the assembly line on the Model T. Sometimes understatement does say more—and besides, even better was to come.

In 1928 Ilya Ehrenburg, a Soviet reporter roving through Europe, commented that Stuttgart was the most culturally rich city on the Continent. The town had modern architecture, museums, art galleries, theaters, and a marvelous concert hall. And its automobile factory was producing some of the most glamorous cars in the world, among them the SS and the SSK.

Once again Mercedes was showing the way. The S series cars with their highly polished pointed radiators, small raked windscreens, three great exhaust pipes, and long sweeping hood that was fully half the body became the apotheosis of a sports car, a metaphor for the Roaring Twenties. And they were a symbol of something more: some two decades later the

Klausen Pass in Switzerland virtually belonged to Caracciola, seen here in 1927 storming the 13.3 uphill miles with the S in a sports-car-record-breaking 17.35 minutes and winning the hill climb for the fourth consecutive year.

205

Introduced in 1927, the 6.8-liter Type S was lower (by several inches), lighter (by over 500 pounds) and more powerful (180 bhp vis-a-vis 160) than the Type K. "Silent streams of super-power . . . unbounded flexibility," advertised the Mercedes-Benz company in New York, "comfort to carry you to the ends of the earth." More powerful than any car produced in America, the S could accelerate easily from 5 to 105 mph in top gear, but the comforts provided didn't include luggage space. Owners devised their own (facing page, top) or ordered it on custom-built versions (the English Freestone & Webb body, facing page, below). The four-seater race version (facing page, center) was sold to both professional and gentleman race drivers. Celebrity S purchasers included the Rowe sisters (above), European vaudeville and cabaret stars; Ernes Merck (inset, left), Germany's top woman driver; and Ralph De Palma (inset, right), American ace.

SS was among the handful of automobiles chosen by the Museum of Modern Art in New York City for their excellence as works of art.

Though they measured more than eleven feet between the axles and weighed more than two tons, their drivers did not have to match such heroic proportions. The Baroness von Loen had one. Al Jolson bought one to give to Ruby Keeler and another for himself. André Dubonnet of Paris, Harold Vanderbilt of New York City and Prince Ruspigliosi of Rome purchased S models; SS cars were delivered to the Marquess of Cholmondeley, the Sultan of Johore and the Maharajahs of Bhopal and Alwar. Briggs Cunningham's SS was delivered to him by Caracciola.*

---

*The American sportsman, then in his early twenties, had ordered the car for his honeymoon trip in the fall of 1929 at the London Motor Show, where Caracciola was on hand as a Mercedes celebrity. Cunningham requested that the car be delivered to him in Paris, road-tested and ready for a trek to the south of France; Caracciola said he would see to the testing himself and deliver the car personally. On the appointed day he drove the SS from the factory to the Cunninghams' Paris hotel, complete with a factory mechanic who remained with the car for several weeks until the new owners became accustomed to it. The Cunningham SS was a standard two-door phaeton with seats for four and scant room for suitcases; they had to go on the running-boards, secured by an expanding-gate contrivance. Departures required a bit of logistics. "My wife got in, then I got in," Briggs Cunningham remembers. "Then the luggage was strapped on, the chauffeur vaulted into the driver's seat, and we were off." Before they went back to America the Cunninghams attended a Concours d'Elégance in Cannes, where Mrs. Cunningham won a prize with the SS. When they finally left, their prize-winning car was sent back to Stuttgart to be refurbished and then shipped to their home in Connecticut.

A good many S-series owners acquired their cars to race. The venerable Ralph De Palma drove an S to victory in two events in Atlantic City in 1928. Prince Max zu Schaumburg-Lippe campaigned his SS on the Continent in the late twenties. In England, Earl Howe's SS became an habitué at Shelsley Walsh, where His Lordship won nearly a dozen cups for fastest times of the day—feats that regularly brought him congratulatory letters from Stuttgart.

The SS—the second "S" designated "super" in English-speaking markets—had its race debut in the German Grand Prix at the Nürburgring on July 15, 1928, a scorchingly hot day. Five countries entered cars; the most aggressive challengers to the eleven white Mercedes were seventeen blue Bugattis from Alsace. In the pits Alfred Neubauer waved his flags and worried. He had a lot of automobiles in the race, but he believed that if the Bugattis could be staved off, the victor would probably be one of three drivers: Caracciola, Werner or Merz. After five laps, Caracciola had a commanding lead; Neubauer flagged him to slow down and cool his engine. Merz was lying second, Werner not far behind.

At the end of the ninth lap, Werner pulled into the pits and got out, his arm hanging limp at his side. On one of the Nürburgring's sharp right-hand corners, he had wrung the steering wheel so hard that he wrenched his arm out of its socket. Hastily looking for someone to take over Werner's car, Neubauer spotted

The Grand Prix of Germany at the Nürburgring, July 15, 1928 — a one-two-three triumph for the Mercedes SS. Werner took the winner's flag (above), but shared victory with Caracciola (facing page). Only Merz drove the nearly five-hour race alone, finishing less than two minutes later.

Willy Walb, who had spun out and hit a tree on the second lap; he had just walked several miles in the hot sun from the spot where his mangled Mercedes lay. As Neubauer motioned him into Werner's car, he heard a howl in the background: a mechanic had just popped Werner's arm back into its socket.

When Walb was off, Caracciola came in with one of his rear tires in shreds. Replacing it took two precious minutes, but with Merz in second place Neubauer was not overly worried. Back on the track, Caracciola made up his lost time in two laps, but on the twelfth lap he came in again—and collapsed of heat prostration. Neubauer was aghast. Six laps to go, and a potential winning car was just sitting there; Caracciola should be fine in a couple of laps, but what to do in the meantime? Merz had meanwhile taken over the lead, but Neubauer wanted a one-two finish. Walb was still out on the course, but he was exhausted and far behind some Bugattis.

But two disabled drivers, Neubauer reasoned, might equal one healthy one. He looked at Christian Werner, who shook his head: his shoulder ached. He could do it for a few laps, Neubauer assured him; honor and a prize of 18,000 marks were at stake. "Strap up my shoulder," Werner said, "I'll manage one or two laps." His shoulder strapped with insulating tape produced from the toolboxes, Werner took off and had soon moved in behind Merz as Caracciola was administered to in the pits. Neubauer breathed a little easier; the Mercedes were one-two.

A half-hour later, Werner pulled into the pits. Sponges and cold compresses had brought Caracciola's temperature down; fuzzy but game, he went back on the road, keeping Mercedes in second place behind Merz. The pit crew turned their attention to Werner, strapping up his shoulder again, pouring water over his head, sticking a piece of lemon between his teeth and administering a concoction of black coffee, egg yolk, sugar, a little wine, and a few spices: Neubauer's secret racing elixir, guaranteed to work wonders, so he said, for a few laps. Which was all that remained of the race. Gulping down the potion as Caracciola pulled back into the pits, Werner took over again and fell in behind Merz.

The Mercedes strong man was driving an incredi-ble race. He had been in his car for five hours without relief. The soles of his shoes were scorched, his feet were blistered; physically and mentally, he was battered by the heat. On the final lap, with Werner inching closer, Merz took the Breidscheid corner too fast. The Mercedes screeched across the asphalt as he struggled, successfully, to control it. But in those few seconds, Werner moved into the lead and managed to stay ahead to the finish line.

It was a bitter loss for Otto Merz; there were tears in his eyes at the end. The win was shared by Caracciola and Werner. It was Werner's last big victory. A few months later he fell ill with an ailment the doctors at first could not diagnose, and racing became more difficult for him.

For Neubauer, the 1928 German Grand Prix was a complete victory. Walb had somehow overtaken the Bugattis and crossed the finish line eight minutes after Werner and Merz; Louis Chiron brought in the first of the Bugattis some minutes later. Mercedes had finished another race one-two-three.

Fortunately, not all events were so difficult.

On July 29, two weeks after the German Grand Prix, Caracciola appeared at a hill climb in Gabelbach with a new production car, the SSK—another K for *kurz*, for the wheelbase of this car was a foot and a half shorter than that of the SS. The SSK had the factory's biggest supercharger, aptly nicknamed the "elephant" blower. Caracciola drove it to a new record at Gabelbach; a week later at Freiburg, he won again; the next month at Semmering, he set another record.

Production of the S-series cars was limited. The SSK was the most limited of all: just 31 were built. Most were bought by sportsmen who wanted to race, like August Momberger and Prince zu Leiningen. Carlos Zatuszek, an Austrian who had emigrated to Argentina after the First World War, bought two SSK's. Zatuszek had set himself up in business in Buenos Aires as a mechanic and, with his brother-in-law assisting in the pits, personally campaigned the SSK so successfully in South America that the factory sent him a diamond-encrusted gold pin in appreciation. In Hollywood Zeppo Marx had an SSK,

An unbeatable combination: Caracciola and the SSK, victorious in 26 events in two years. Here Rudi dashes to a new Semmering hill climb record in 1928, averaging 55.7 mph, 3 mph faster than Rosenberger's winning time in an S in 1927.

though he generally used it for motoring on Sunset Boulevard; its single known sporting contest was a match race against a Duesenberg owned by a Hollywood neighbor who managed the business affairs of Clark Gable and Gary Cooper. For that event Zeppo engaged a mechanic to drive.

S and SS cars were built in greater numbers—146 and 111, respectively—but that was an insignificant percentage of the seven to eight thousand Mercedes-Benz cars that by now were rolling out of the factories every year. Yet the S series brought Mercedes its biggest publicity. Wilhelm Kissel had been right when he decided that these money-no-object automobiles

were the best megaphones he could produce to shout the Mercedes name around the world.

Interestingly, although Ferdinand Porsche was later responsible for a number of important vehicles like the Auto Union race car, the prototype of the Volkswagen and the World War II Tiger tank, many people still think of him as the creator of the Mercedes-Benz S-series automobiles.

He was Dr. Porsche to everybody at the factory now, though his only formal education had come from sneaking into evening lectures at the technical university in Vienna while he worked days as a floor

Austrian-born Carlos Zatuszek was a businessman living in South America and a weekend racer who campaigned his SSK with the help of his brother-in-law. His victories were many, this one in the 1931 Argentine Autumn Prize.

211

sweeper and engine oiler at an electric company. To Porsche, engineering was life itself. He could watch a worker turn out hundreds of examples of some small part and then suddenly pick up one of the components, measure it with a micrometer and find it below standard, by a few thousandths of an inch. The hundreds of other components would have to be measured and would invariably be found perfect; somehow Dr. Porsche had spotted the single infinitesimally errant piece.

An awesome temper went with this frightening acuity. From Porsche's Austro-Daimler days in Vienna had come tales of his reaction to a workman's mistake: he would fling his hat on the floor and jump up and down on it. Once after Porsche stormed out the Vienna plant foreman picked the hat up, had it cleaned and reblocked, and gave it back to its owner; it lasted five minutes before Dr. Porsche saw another mistake.

Porsche was no less tolerant of mistakes of his own. The medium-priced Stuttgart 200 had developed a reputation for hard starting in cold weather. Kissel decided to dramatize this defect for his technical director, ordering 15 of the 200's, lined up in a row, to be left out overnight in the dead of winter. In the morning he asked Porsche to join him outside and invited him to start any of the cars. Porsche stomped from one to the next, turning the keys; not an engine

turned over, while Kissel shivered in satisfaction at the end of the line. When the last car's engine failed to start Porsche slammed the door, ripped off his hat, trampled it into the snow and, cursing, stormed off. Whether Kissel picked up the hat has not been recorded, but the Stuttgart 200 soon became an excellent cold-weather starter.

But Porsche and Daimler-Benz were rather like an irresistible force heading for an immovable object, and something was bound to give. The final confrontation revolved around Porsche's desire, nurtured since his Austro-Daimler days, to build a small, inexpensive car. To the Mercedes people, many of whom had grown up with Daimler in Stuttgart or Benz in Mannheim, this was anathema; since the nineteenth century high-quality automobiles had been the stock in trade of both companies, and a cheap Mercedes would be a contradiction in terms. At a board meeting in October 1928, when Porsche was getting the worst of the discussion about economy-car development, he lost his temper and resigned.

Kissel tried to keep him, offering him a cooling-off trip to America to study automotive development there. Porsche regarded that palliative as Gottlieb Daimler, over four decades before, had considered a similar suggestion that he go to Russia; he joined Steyr in Austria instead. A few months later that firm's merger with Austro-Daimler threatened to

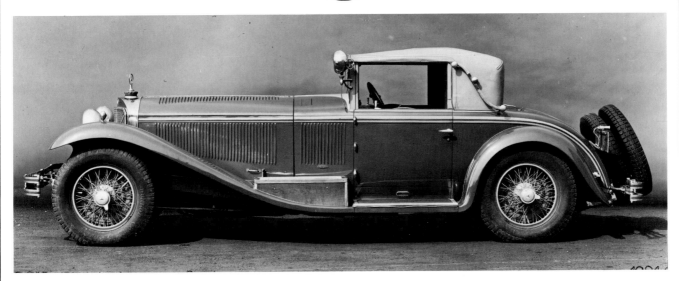

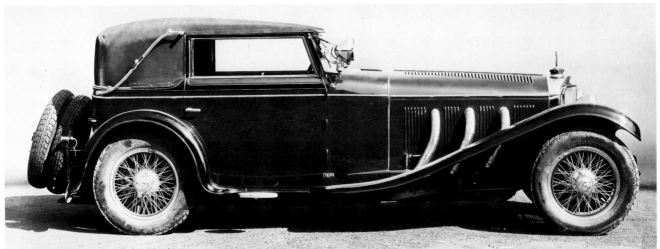

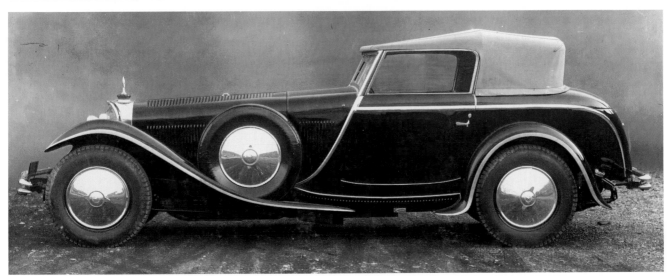

Introduced in 1928, the Mercedes SS was the S with a 7.1-liter, 200 (later 225) bhp engine and a slightly higher radiator. In the S, the hood line barely cleared the engine, which made building graceful yet commodious bodies difficult. Both independent coachbuilders and designers in the Daimler-Benz studios were delighted with the arrival of the type SS. Sedans and coupes as well as open cars were now available from Sindelfingen. These three custom-built cabriolets — from the top, by Castagna of Italy, Keibl of Germany, Saoutchik of France — indicate what a difference 3¼ inches made. An S with its top up was rarely seen; the result was often ungainly. For factory racing purposes, the SS engine was used in the lower-profile S chassis. The catalog cover for the cars sold to the public (facing page) was produced in Germany for the English-speaking markets.

The SSK, also introduced in 1928, had the S radiator, the SS engine and a chassis all its own, abbreviated to a 116.1-inch wheelbase from the 134 inches of the S and SS. Built principally for racing in short-distance events and hill climbs, the SSK was fitted with Mercedes' largest supercharger — the legendary "elephant" blower — and in race tune could deliver over 300 bhp. The SSK chassis price was 29,000 marks (about $6,930), which was 3000 marks more than the S, 2000 less than the SS. Though a few custom-built cabriolets were produced by independent coachbuilders, most of the SSK's sold were the factory-built roadsters, priced at 33,000 marks. Al Jolson, a Mercedes S owner, is seen above outside Paramount Studios in Hollywood in 1930 with the SSK owned by his friend Zeppo Marx. Zeppo was inside with his brothers filming *Animal Crackers*.

bring him back into contact with the board director at whom he had thrown the cigarette lighter half a dozen years before, so he returned to Stuttgart and set himself up as an independent design consultant.

Porsche's successor as technical director of Daimler-Benz AG was Hans Nibel, who had spent the years since the merger in Mannheim directing diesel and truck development. He moved into his new job in Stuttgart in January 1929—and also into Porsche's villa, which he had rented from his predecessor when the latter moved to Austria; Nibel had probably scarcely unpacked before Porsche returned needing his house back. When all the packing and unpacking were over, a good many former Benz men received added responsibilities now that another former Benz man was in charge, men like Max Wagner and Fritz Nallinger, who had begun their careers in Mannheim. But one Daimler man, Dr. Porsche's old Austrian race driver, remained, needless to say, as the company's racing manager.

In 1929 Neubauer allowed Caracciola to pick the races he wanted to enter outside Germany. He may have wondered why when Rudi informed him that the first race he wanted to run was a brand-new one, to be staged that year for the first time in the Principality of Monaco. The very idea of the race was foolish, or so everyone thought except Antony Noghès, the Monegasque sportsman whose idea it was. Every other country in Europe sponsored a big automobile race by now, he reasoned, why not Monaco? The fact that Monaco did not have as much room for a racing circuit as Italy or Belgium was no problem; Noghès, with the backing of Prince Pierre, would simply use the whole principality. But the narrow network of streets made for a race course that looked as if it had been laid out by a serpent.

And this was the unlikely venue where Caracciola wanted to race. Next to the light and lithe grand prix Bugattis, Caracciola's SSK looked like a locomotive. The driver of a Delage said afterwards that his five-speed gearbox was a superfluity; he had never proceeded beyond second on the tight, not-quite-two-mile course. And the winner, William Grover, an Englishman who raced under the pseudonym "Williams," claimed he had reached top gear only in the closing laps when the pressure from behind had eased. The pressure from behind came from Caracciola. He was actually leading at the halfway mark, whipping his shrieking white giant around the course as if it were a soapbox derby racer. But ultimately a long pit stop for fuel (the big cars were thirsty, and in those days gasoline was poured in from cans, not pressure fed) and a time-consuming change of tires (the first two cars to finish went the distance on their original rubber) dropped him back to third. Nevertheless his performance brought as many news column inches as had the winner's; "amazing" was the word reporters most often used. Caracciola's decision to race in Monaco, Alfred Neubauer decided, had not been so foolish after all.

The decision to compete in the International Alpine Trial that summer came from the front office. This reliability event, 1,700 miles up, down, and across the Alps, was entered by both European and American factories, bringing a kaleidoscope of the world's cars to the start at Katschberg. Stuttgart sent a little of everything. Interestingly, the big limited-production S-series cars and several K's were entrusted to factory people who spent most of their time in the engineering office or behind an administrative desk, while the top Mercedes race drivers drove the cars that most company customers purchased: Caracciola and Merz were in Nürburgs, an eight-cylinder model introduced in 1928, and Werner, whose illness still had not been diagnosed, was in a six-cylinder Stuttgart. "Direktor Wenzler in his SSK car was awarded the Alpine Plaque," a journalist reported afterwards. "On the fourth day he had struck a wall on a hairpin bend at a speed of 50 miles per hour. The wall went down but Direktor Wenzler's Mercedes-Benz car went on." The professionals, of course, drove better; Caracciola was first at the finish in Como. When the reliability points were added up, Mercedes won more Alpine Cups than any other factory, a grand total of eight; to Caracciola, Merz, Werner, three K's and two SSK's.

The following week Daimler-Benz was in Ireland for the Tourist Trophy race in Ulster. Inaugurated the year before by the Royal Automobile Club, the TT

The first Grand Prix of Monaco, April 1929. Only a Caracciola would have dared pit the SSK sports car against nimble GP racers on this short 1.98-mile circuit. Rudi, seen here sandwiched between two Bugattis, finished an amazing third.

was a sports car event based on Le Mans regulations, though unlike the 24-hour French race the Irish contest was a six-hour daylight affair on the 13-mile Ards circuit outside Belfast. The inaugural Tourist Trophy in 1928 had been such a success and Great Britain was such an important export market that Neubauer decided to take two drivers, Caracciola and Merz. Both would be racing SS's.

Sixty-five cars started in the TT—a wonderfully odd lot ranging in size from little 750cc Austins to the 7,100cc Mercedes SS's. There were five Bugattis, one driven by the Monaco winner, "Williams"; a full team of Alfa Romeos from Milan and Bentleys from Cricklewood (W. O. Bentley himself was the mechanic in the car Sir Henry "Tim" Birkin drove); a good many Alvises, Rileys, Lagondas, Lea-Francises, Triumphs, Frazer-Nashes and Amilcars, and even a couple of Model A Fords and a Stutz. This variety made for an interesting contest, and so did the handicap regulations based on engine size: if a small

Rudi rounding the station hairpin at Monaco, 1929. "We had chuckled among ourselves when we saw the SSK arrive for the race," said Bugatti driver René Dreyfus, "but what Rudi did with that big car was simply incredible."

car surpassed the average speed set for it, that automatically raised the average for all the other classes. "The big cars had therefore to go for all they were worth," wrote the journalist-driver S.C.H. "Sammy" Davis, who was behind the wheel of a 1089cc Riley, "thus greatly increasing the excitement."

And there was plenty of excitement. Hundreds of flags decorated the grandstand as thousands of spectators made their way to their seats; along the course thousands more settled into the spots they had homesteaded by putting up tents the night before. On race day thousands of others joined them, streaming out from Belfast in the early morning; attendance at the 1929 Tourist Trophy was estimated at half a million.

Caracciola, Merz and Neubauer had not raced in the British Isles before. In pre-race practice on the circuit the German team had been given a spirited welcome and were enjoying themselves immensely. There was no language barrier—the British Mercedes agency did all the necessary interpreting. Charly Caracciola tried to flout regulations by entering the pit area disguised as a man but was discovered and amiably led away, amid cheers and laughter, by a

member of the Irish constabulary. Betting on the race outcome was a new, and legal, twist that Neubauer had not encountered before. The big Bentleys, as a home team, were heavily favored, so a bet for the Mercedes brought long-shot odds; Neubauer put ten pounds on each of his drivers to win and place and even before the starting flag fell was planning for the windfall he was sure his forty-pound investment would bring.

But before the windfall there was rainfall: sometimes in torrents, sometimes a drizzle, sometimes one thing on one section of the course and another on another. Spectators and drivers alike were soaked to the skin. This was the race that established Caracciola forever as *Der Regenmeister* (the Rain Master). Nobody has ever handled a race car in the rain like Caracciola—and the skies opened on the 1929 Tourist Trophy soon after the flag was waved and the drivers sprinted to their cars for the start.

The big battle in the early going was Mercedes versus Bentley—specifically Caracciola versus Glen Kidston in the big six-cylinder Cricklewood car, followed by Tim Birkin with W.O. and the first of the 4½-liter supercharged Bentleys, and then Otto Merz

August 17, 1929: the Tourist Trophy, Belfast, Ireland. The Le Mans sprint to the cars was followed by a fast rolling down of car tops before drivers and their mechanics could proceed with the first of 30 laps of the 13-mile Ards circuit.

Mercedes SS at the Tourist Trophy, 1929. Merz (No. 71) at speed during the race and Caracciola (No. 70) waving to the crowd after winning, then enjoying a beer and appearing bashfully pleased with victory (at the top). Much of the race had been run in the rain, which obscured driver vision — "a feeling of helplessness is inevitable in such circumstances," understated S.C.H. "Sammy" Davis — and led to numerous accidents. Of the 65 cars that started in the TT, 27 crashed or retired; just 22 finished with the time schedule.

in the other Mercedes. To the delight of the crowd, Caracciola and Kidston swung into the New-townards Square virtually abreast, but at the end of the first lap the white Mercedes flashed by the grand-stand at incredible speed. Kidston and Birkin followed, then Merz and the factory Alfas and the rest of the field in bunches, with the little Austins and the Model A Fords puttering along at the back of the pack.

But then the rain began coming down in sheets, and the Tourist Trophy turned into another race altogether. Cars began sliding off the slippery course. Williams fractured the fuel pipe on his Bugatti, a Lea-Francis driver motored straight into the New-townards Town Hall, a Model A narrowly missed a pub in Dundonald, an Alfa skidded wildly at Bal-lystockart Bridge, and many cars slid into sand-banks. The engine of the Stutz caught fire coming into Newtownards and Sammy Davis, driving by on his Riley and thinking the Stutz's extinguisher might not be sufficient to put out the blaze, slowed down and rolled his own extinguisher to the disabled car. The fire was put out, and the Stutz rejoined the race.

Up front, it was still Caracciola versus Kidston, Birkin versus Merz. Approaching the fast curve near Bradshaw's Brae, Kidston swerved on the wet road and his Bentley crashed nose first into a ditch, narrowly missing a pole. Kidston was heard to remark good-naturedly afterwards that he had "never seen a telegraph pole move so quickly before." But the big battle was over. Birkin had fallen back and although the factory Alfas were challenging, the pack of little Austins was Caracciola's biggest concern now; they had been turning laps at better than 60 mph, well above their handicap. When another cloudburst hit, spectators were convinced the rain was in the baby cars' favor since they could slow down without losing position; nobody thought the big cars could possibly hold their speed under such conditions. But Carac-ciola did not let up. With cascades of water pouring off the Mercedes' hood and spiraling in fountains around its wheels, he stormed past the grandstand lap after lap at better than 110 mph, overtaking the Austins so quickly the little cars seemed to be travel-ing backwards. The crowd was mesmerized. So were

the other drivers. "Whenever he passed me at that terrific speed," Tim Birkin said afterwards, "I felt no envy, but only incredulity at his skill, his courage and the endurance of his car. He broke records with ease under a deluge of rain, on a road that was at times almost flooded, and never sacrificed the safety of others to his own ambition."

After his astounding victory—at a 72.82 mph average; the second-place car, an Alfa, finished at 67.54—Rudi Caracciola was asked to say a few words. He spoke only about his admiration for the little Austins and the good spirits of the spectators. Caracciola was an immensely popular winner of the 1929 Tourist Trophy.

But what of Otto Merz, who when last seen had been fighting it out for second with Birkin's Bentley? In the rain near Dundonald Merz had skidded and his car's left fender was damaged, pressing dangerously close to the tire. Ever resourceful, Merz stopped, got out, tore the fender off with his bare hands, tossed it into the back seat, and continued. A race official approached Neubauer soon afterwards and said that Merz's car would have to be disqualified. Why, Neu-bauer wanted to know; the rules stated that all parts of the car had to be carried on the car, and the fender still was. The official replied that not only did all parts have to be on the car, they had to be where they belonged and if they were inadvertently detached, they had to be restored to their proper place with tools carried in the car. Neubauer objected, among other things, that surely the race committee did not expect the cars to carry welding equipment; but the official would not budge. So Neubauer lost his place money on Merz, though Caracciola's victory netted him £250 from the bookmaker.

Back in Stuttgart a week later, Wilhelm Kissel received a letter from the Royal Automobile Club and called Neubauer into his office. "They don't want to see you over there again," Kissel said. "Apparent-ly you described the Irish as swine." Neubauer pro-tested that he hadn't been referring to all the Irish, just the race committee; but he agreed to apologize to the Royal Automobile Club, and the incident was quickly forgotten. Not so soon forgotten was Carac-ciola's victory. The Mercedes showroom in London became a very busy place.

1929 was a year of firsts and records. The *Graf Zeppelin* became the first aircraft ever to fly around the world (21 days, 7 hours); the SS *Bremen* set a transatlantic speed record for passenger liners (4 days, 17 hours, 42 minutes). The first Oscars were awarded, to Emil Jannings and Janet Gaynor. Marlene Dietrich was the Blue Angel in Berlin. Paris had a new luxury hotel, the George V; Atlantic City had a new convention hall on the Boardwalk. Clarence Birdseye introduced frozen food; Daniel Gerber began selling baby food. Alexander Fleming tried penicillin at St. Mary's Hospital in London. On St. Valentine's Day there was a massacre in Chicago. Hoagy Carmichael wrote "Star Dust," and Erich Maria Remarque finished *All Quiet on the Western Front*. And two automobile pioneers died: Carl Benz, age 85, and Wilhelm Maybach, 84.

But 1929 was also the end of an era. On October 24, the Wall Street stock market crashed.

In mid-June 1930, the smallest field ever lined up for the start of the 24-hour race at Le Mans. One of the most exciting days in motor sport followed. Mercedes had sent a small team: one car (an SS), two drivers (Caracciola and Werner), some mechanics and the usual racing manager. Neubauer had convinced Kissel that competing at Le Mans was a good idea. Kissel had agreed, but in the uncertainty surrounding the stock market debacle he told Neubauer to hold expenses to a minimum; the 24-hour race was an unfamiliar one to the Stuttgart factory, and a major effort was neither financially feasible nor necessary. Bentley, on the other hand, was there in force: a works team of Speed Sixes, the Hon. Dorothy Paget's team of blown 4½'s, five cars in all. Victorious in the three previous Le Mans events, Bentley had to win again. But as the challenger, one car against five, Mercedes had to look good.

A pre-race lunch party had been arranged by Charles Faroux, the legendary doyen of French motor sport. Sponsored by the Automobile Club de l'Ouest, it was held in a lovely old hotel by a quiet river near the circuit. The French hosts were joined by the Bentley and Mercedes contingents, and the party started out to be a bore: the French spoke to the French, the British to the British and the Germans to the Germans. But Caracciola had brought along his mascot, a lovable long-haired Dachshund named Moritz, and Moritz proceeded to fall into the river.

The rescue was an international effort. Words of encouragement in three languages were shouted to Moritz as members of the Bentley and Mercedes teams waded out to fetch him. In the process all hands discovered they could speak at least a few words of everyone else's language and the party came to life, continuing for many hours more than had been scheduled. "The ice was broken forever between the lot of us," Sammy Davis wrote later, "even W.O. [Bentley] came out of his shell." Neubauer proved himself the life of the party with some wicked impressions of current celebrities. Moritz, fed from every plate, must have had the best time of all.

In the race itself there were only 18 cars, including the single Mercedes. With only one car, Neubauer told Caracciola and Werner to go for it from the start; the Bentley strategy was to wear the Mercedes out, dogging it from behind. Though the SS was faster, its supercharger was engineered for occasional bursts of speed, not a 24-hour run; if the Bentleys could keep the pressure on, the Mercedes could not possibly survive.

At the start, Caracciola shot into the lead, followed by the Bentleys. A Mercedes-Bentley battle was a crowd-pleaser; tumultuous applause followed the passage of the cars, one after the other, at speeds of better than 115 mph. In one breathtaking moment near Mulsanne, with the noise of his supercharger deafening him to the approach of any rival, Caracciola looked across to see Birkin overtaking him. The Bentley's two outside wheels were on the grass, and the tread of one tire was completely gone. Despite a shout from Caracciola, signals from his pit and the spectators' cries, Birkin was not aware that his tire was shredded until he lurched into a wild skid after Arnage. He hobbled into the pits to be reshod and, as he later said, to "set out on the chase refreshed."

By now, whenever Caracciola tried to slow down, another Bentley came up on his tail, first Sammy

Davis, then, as the skies turned dark, Woolf Barnato. Werner took over from Caracciola, and the big white car continued in the lead past midnight. Occasionally one of the Bentleys would surge ahead momentarily, just to remind the German drivers they could not relax. Finally, at 1:30 A.M., the lights of the Mercedes flickered, and the car pulled into the pits. Its generator had failed; its batteries were exhausted. Three Bentleys retired as well, but the race now belonged to the two still on the course; the Woolf Barnato/Glen Kidston car was the ultimate victor. Caracciola and Werner were among the first to congratulate the winners.

The tables were turned the next month at the Irish Grand Prix near Dublin, where the single factory SSK was joined by the private Mercedes of Lord Howe and Malcolm Campbell. Caracciola won over several Bentleys in a spirited race. "I saw the white bonnet with its silver star," Tim Birkin commented later, "and then Caracciola himself, staring ahead in his white peaked cap, so close in the Mercedes' left-hand drive that I could have touched him. For a second or two we were level, and then he was past, heading for Mountjoy corner, his spray flying up round my eyes." Sadly, Christian Werner was not in Ireland. His illness had finally been diagnosed as throat cancer, and his racing days were almost at an end. He died in 1932.

For Caracciola and the SSK, 1930 brought 10 victories in 10 hill climbs—easy wins that made him the European Mountain Champion. But he always said afterwards that his best times that year were when he was chasing and being chased by the Bentleys.

At the end of 1930 it was obvious that a worldwide depression had set in. No one knew how bad it would be or how long it would last but preparing for the worst was the wisest course, and that meant paring the non-essential. In Stuttgart Kissel deleted racing from Daimler-Benz's 1931 budget.

Caracciola was crestfallen. But Neubauer had an idea to salvage the situation: Rudi would buy a car, at a good price; Kissel would provide all racing ex-

Catalog covers of the late twenties emphasized the famous symbol. "You drive best under this star," declared one. "The German car of highest class and world significance," said the other.

221

Mercedes owners and their cars, 1927-1932. (Facing page) Anna May Wong with her Nürburg (top, right), Jackie Coogan with a Grosser (top, left), Hans Nibel presenting a Nürburg limousine to Pope Pius XI in 1930 (bottom, left), Emil Jannings with his Nürburg (center), Rudi Caracciola with his (bottom, right). (This page) Claire Rommer with her Nürburg (top, left), Richard Tauber with the six-cylinder "special" delivered to him in April 1927 (top, right), famous music hall clown Grock with his Stuttgart 200 in 1932 (above).

Am 4. April ist

Herr

Dr. ing. e. h. Carl Benz

in seinem 85. Lebensjahre aus einem arbeits- und erfolgreichen Leben geschieden.
Seine Erfolge als Erfinder und Konstrukteur des ersten Automobils sind welt-
bekannt. Daneben hat er das Verdienst, ebensolche Pioniertätigkeit auf dem
Gebiete des Motorenbaues geleistet zu haben. Unter seiner Führung wurde die
Firma Benz & Cie. in Mannheim eine der ersten Motoren- und Automobil-
fabriken. Im Jahre 1922 wurde die Abteilung stationärer Motorenbau dieses
Unternehmens selbständige Aktiengesellschaft. Der Entschlafene ist auch weiter-
hin unserem Unternehmen ein wertvoller Berater geblieben. Das Andenken an
ihn wird in uns fortleben.   78929

MANNHEIM, den 5. April 1929

Motoren-Werke Mannheim A.-G.
vorm. Benz Abt. stationärer Motorenbau

In 1925 a motorcade of ancient vehicles was organized in Munich. Leading the parade was the
Benz Patent Motorwagen, driven by its inventor. (Bertha Benz is at the left.) Four years later Carl
Benz's death, at age 84, was announced in the *Mannheimer Tageblatt.*

penses; Caracciola and Daimler-Benz would share
any prize money fifty-fifty. Kissel agreed, so for 1931
the factory had a one-man racing team.

The car that Rudi bought, for approximately
20,000 marks, was an SSKL, the S-series sports car
engineered to its ultimate by Hans Nibel and Max
Wagner. The L, for *leicht* (light), was realized by
copious drilling of chassis members, plates, brackets,
even pedal pads and brake drum fins—some 250
pounds in all. Only six or seven SSKL's—records are
not clear—were built; none survive today.

Alfred Neubauer had, of course, engineered himself into the racing accounts as manager. Kissel had

also agreed to provide truck transport and money for
tires, fuel, the underwriting of all repairs, and the
services of a co-driver (Wilhelm Sebastian) and a
mechanic (Heinrich Zimmer). Charly Caracciola
was the team's timekeeper. And thus they went racing. Nothing better indicates their success than to say
that an account of all their victories would be boring.

The most sensational victory was the first. The
Italian Mille Miglia was run over a thousand miles of
public roads. The course, roughly in the form of a
figure eight, began in Brescia and ran through
Bologna and Siena to Rome, turned north to Per-
ugia, went across the Apennines, up through Rimini

to Bologna again, turned northeast to Ferrara, Treviso and Feltre, and took a final leg back to Brescia via Vicenza and Verona. Inaugurated in 1927, the race had been won each year by Italian cars driven by Italian drivers—understandably, since they were the most familiar with Italian roads. Indeed, given the long odds on success for the native products, other European factory teams had generally viewed the Mille Miglia as too risky to enter. But Caracciola liked long shots, and the Mercedes team—four men, one woman and one car—showed up in Brescia in early April 1931. The Alfa Romeo factory, with its multi-car entry and some 90 mechanics, was bemused.

Settling in at the Albergo Brescia with a map of Italy spread out before him, Neubauer began to feel, in his words, "like Napoleon before the Battle of Waterloo." Alfa Romeo would have no fewer than 17 replenishing depots around the 1,000-mile course. Neubauer's map told him he would need a minimum of four, at Siena, Terni, Bologna and Feltre. But Caracciola and Sebastian would be in the car, and he, Neubauer, and Charly Caracciola would be at the

start—which left one mechanic, Zimmer, with the impossible task of handling all the pit stops. Fortunately Neubauer was able to persuade two former Stuttgart driver-mechanics, Fritz Kühnle and Karlo Kumpf, to join them in Brescia, which left him just one man short. That, at least, was potentially workable. The Mercedes truck dropped off Zimmer, fuel, tools and tires at Feltre, and left Kühnle with the same supplies at Terni. Karlo Kumpf would have to service two of the stops, doing the first at Siena, and then driving on to Bologna, where with any luck he would arrive before Caracciola and Sebastian. And he would need luck: the distance between Siena and Bologna was about 120 miles, the roads would be partially blocked, and all Italy went crazy whenever a Mille Miglia was run. "If you don't make it," Neubauer told Kumpf, "we're sunk." Kumpf assured him he would make it.

The Mille Miglia was not total lunacy for the Mercedes team. Caracciola had tried the race the year before, with Werner as co-driver; they had finished sixth behind four Alfa Romeos and an Italian O.M., a commendable showing for a reconnaissance

Le Mans, June 21-22, 1930. A lone Mercedes SS went against a "pack of relentless Furies," in the words of Tim Birkin, a member of the pack. The SS battle with five Bentleys was a crowd rouser. Barnato's car is seen closing in on Werner as night fell. The Bentley won the battle.

Irish Grand Prix, Phoenix Park, Dublin, July 18, 1930 — round three in the Mercedes-Bentley rivalry. Bentleys numbered five. Lord Howe and Malcolm Campbell, in their privately owned SS Mercedes, joined the factory SSK of Caracciola, shown above with Charly in the pits. At the top, Rudi (No. 3) is leading Howe in the main event, and Howe (wearing No. 41 in an earlier sprint) leads a Lea-Francis. Rudi put up the fastest lap at 91.3 mph and won the 300-mile GP at 86.2 mph. Howe was third, Campbell fifth.

Gordon Crosby drawing of Rudi passing Birkin's Bentley in the 1930 Irish GP. Said Birkin afterwards, "I thought in 1929 that he could never improve on his performance in the rain at Belfast, but today he proved me wrong."

trip. This year Caracciola was at least familiar with the roads, though he had no co-driver: Wilhelm Sebastian, though a first-rate mechanic, was not an experienced man behind the wheel. Caracciola determined to drive the entire race himself, anticipating no problem as long as Kumpf was there when he arrived in Bologna on the return leg from Rome. But first, of

course, the car had to make it to Rome.

On April 12, at 2:00 in the afternoon, the Mille Miglia began in Brescia. With Caracciola off and running, his wife and Neubauer retired to the clubhouse to listen to the race reports over the loudspeaker. The first news came from Mantua: Achille Varzi's Alfa had retired with water pump problems.

The Mercedes trio in the 1930 Irish GP: Howe, Campbell, Caracciola. Lord Howe's SS was the car Rudi had driven in the 1929 TT; Howe purchased it after the race and fitted it with a new body by Hooper, the royal coachbuilders.

That was good. The next came from Bologna: Caracciola was in the lead. That was better. A half-hour passed, then another, then another. Neubauer thought a bottle of Chianti might help. Then Florence reported; Caracciola was still in the lead, a good five minutes ahead of the Alfas of Tazio Nuvolari and Giuseppe Campari. Fantastic! But the next news, from Siena, was not: Campari had taken the lead, and Nuvolari was right behind him.

In Siena, Kumpf had watched the Alfas pass. He was ready with the pit equipment, but where was Caracciola? Kumpf counted four minutes. Then a shrill whine pierced the early evening air, and the big white car appeared. There was no time for lengthy explanations, but as Sebastian and Kumpf refueled and changed the rear tires and Caracciola calmly drank a glass of water, Sebastian explained that the Mercedes exhaust pipe had broken and he had needed 10 minutes to fix it — barehanded, Kumpf realized, when he saw the dirty, blood-stained handkerchief around Sebastian's right hand. With the car on the road again, Kumpf tossed his equipment in the truck and headed for Bologna.

In Brescia, everyone awaited the news from Rome. Finally the loudspeaker said that Tazio Nuvolari was first into the Eternal City, and the Alfa Romeo people went wild. Suddenly Neubauer, straining to hear further news, brightened up: Caracciola was second, he had passed Campari and was gaining on Nuvolari. Neubauer ordered a bottle of Spumante.

Out on the road, Caracciola and Sebastian were weaving their way through the narrow streets of village after village, dodging the occasional horse cart that ventured onto the road. The refueling stop with Fritz Kühnle at Terni went off like clockwork. But shortly after midnight, in the middle of the Apennines, Sebastian, who had dozed off, was awakened by an ominous sound. Caracciola braked, and the mechanic was out of the car before it came to a full stop. The throttle linkage had jammed and the connection to the supercharger was bent. Twenty minutes later Sebastian tossed the tools back into the car and they were off, but three Alfas had passed them in the meantime.

By now, the Mercedes had been on the road 10 hours, and Caracciola was weary. Sebastian offered to help out at the wheel. Caracciola agreed; he would see to the left-hand curves and Sebastian to the right. At a railroad crossing they almost crashed before Caracciola brought the car under control and then almost gave up: he was exhausted, he said, and he would not risk someone else's life. Sebastian, furious, finally persuaded him to continue, after which Caracciola drove like a man possessed; Sebastian clung to his seat and cheered him on.

Kumpf had made it to Bologna with enough time to set up the supply depot. The Mercedes roared in and took on fuel; Caracciola took on a glass of water and a new pair of goggles; then he was off into the night. He had passed a few cars but was still four minutes behind the leaders with 370 miles to go.

Dawn over the Adriatic was obscured by a thick, blinding mist. Ahead three Alfas drove abreast to pierce the mist with as much headlight illumination as possible. Caracciola caught up to them and eased in behind. At a sharp curve that was invisible until the cars were practically upon it two of the Alfas left the road, and Caracciola reacted: his foot down hard on the accelerator, he roared past the third. He was in the lead again.

The last pit stop, at Feltre, was approaching. Neubauer had told Zimmer to hang a blue-and-white Mercedes banner across the road about 300 yards ahead to warn Caracciola he was nearing the depot. Zimmer also put on his whitest shirt and, when he heard the supercharger's whine, began running on the grass alongside, waving his arms. The stop went quickly, and Zimmer said he thought they were leading by about nine minutes. Caracciola had been behind the wheel for 14 hours; his hands were bleeding, his right foot was a mass of blisters. But suddenly he felt fresh again. He had not much farther to go.

But twenty miles from the finish line one of the Mercedes' tires blew. Both Caracciola and Sebastian were out of the car in a flash; victory could not be denied them now. They changed the tire listening for the sound of another car; it never came. Leaving their tools by the side of the road, they sped toward Brescia. At 7:22 A.M. the Mercedes crossed the finish line, the first foreign car to win the Mille Miglia, and the last for 24 years, when another Mercedes broke the Italian grip on that country's greatest race. But that victory comes later in this story.

In the summer of 1931, the German Grand Prix was scheduled for the Nürburgring as usual. The Mercedes team naturally planned to be there; Bugattis, Alfa Romeos, English sportsmen like Tim Birkin and Lord Howe with their own cars, even Red Shafer from America with his Indianapolis special were slated to be on hand. But the bankruptcy of the Darmstadt und Nationalbank on July 13 brought on a panic and the closing of all German banks for two days; when they reopened depositors were advised that only money necessary to meet tax payments would be released. On July 18 thousands of people with tax-demand notes queued up outside German banks to draw out their savings.

On the nineteenth at the Nürburgring, race organizers were worried about attendance; Alfred Neubauer was worried about the new Bugattis. The Mercedes team had been practicing for almost a week. Several SSK's and SSKL's were independently entered, and Kissel had asked Neubauer to look after them as well as Caracciola. After watching Louis Chiron's lap times with the Bugatti, Neubauer

prayed for rain. The blue cars from Alsace were almost one-third lighter than the Mercedes, which meant they could probably run the entire race without a tire change, something the German cars could never manage. So in the evenings the Mercedes drivers rehearsed tire changing with a new quick-lift racing jack while Neubauer clocked them with his stopwatch. Caracciola and Sebastian were the fastest team, seventy seconds for all four wheels, but those seventy seconds could still lose the race. If it rained, however, the Mercedes weight would be an advantage, for they could hold a wet road better than the Bugattis.

Race day dawned muggy and overcast. As the crowds poured into Adenau, Nürburgring officials breathed a sigh of relief: despite the bank closings and the depression, the spectators numbered more than 100,000. Neubauer breathed easier, too: shortly before the start, it began to drizzle. By the time the cars were flagged off, the rain was coming down hard.

At the end of the first lap, Caracciola was ahead. On succeeding laps he began building a healthy lead over Chiron. Neubauer was soaked to the skin and delighted. His quick-change artists had pulled off a pit stop for tires in just 69 seconds, a record, and he had clocked one of Chiron's stops when merely refueling the Bugatti at 59 seconds. But on the twelfth lap,

SSKL: the S series engineered to its ultimate in 1931. The 2680-pound SSK chassis was lightened 250 pounds through judicious drilling everywhere, including the chassis frame — a technique engineer Max Wagner had learned with the Benz Tropfenwagen. The SSKL was capable of 130 mph.

A season of triumph: Caracciola and the SSKL, 1931. (Facing page, bottom) With Alfred Neubauer looking on, co-driver Wilhelm Sebastian gives a wave and Charly Caracciola a goodbye to her husband before the start of the Mille Miglia. Sixteen hours later, Rudi had won the 1000-mile race at a record-breaking 62.7 mph average. (Center) In 1930 Rudi had won the European Mountain Championship with an SSK; in 1931 he did it again with an SSKL. Seen here with mechanic Fritz Kühnle at Klausen, Caracciola won six hill climbs in the championship series, four of them in record-breaking time. (Top) Victory laurels on the winner at the Nürburgring; Rudi won the 311-mile German Grand Prix in just over 4½ hours at a record-breaking 67.4 mph. (This page) On-the-scene artist Gordon Crosby "reporting" the German Grand Prix chase for *The Autocar.* The Bugattis of Louis Chiron and Achille Varzi relentlessly pursued Rudi's SSKL in the closing laps. When it was all over the GP winner was exhausted, his only thought "a bath and bed."

Avursrennen, August 2, 1931. Not since its inaugural in 1926 had the fast Avus track near Berlin been used for a race. Caracciola had won then, and he won again in '31, averaging 115 mph with the SSKL in the 15-lap, 182.5-mile event.

with 10 laps to go, Neubauer looked up to see an ominous patch of blue in the sky. Within two laps, under bright sun, the track had dried, and Chiron picked up speed; it was a roll of the dice now, Neubauer waving his go-faster flag at Caracciola at every lap. With only a few laps to go, Caracciola revved the Mercedes to 4,000 rpm while Sebastian shook his head in protest. Caracciola, shouting that he had no choice, increased his lead. Only on the last lap, with Chiron now behind by better than a minute, did Neubauer give him the go-easy signal. Caracciola slowed to 3,500 rpm; only his tires could lose the race for him now, and they didn't. At the finish line the crowd went crazy. A bad week had ended well. Germany's favorite driver had won the German Grand Prix.

By year's end Caracciola and the SSKL had captured five more races, and Caracciola was the European Mountain Champion for the second consecutive season. Caracciola's winning ways with the SSKL were the best news Wilhelm Kissel had all year. From nearly 8,000 in 1929, Mercedes-Benz car sales had plunged to just over 3,000 by the end of 1931; commercial vehicle sales had dropped from 3,800 to nearly 2,000. Only two of the six Daimler-Benz plants were operating. Red ink was all over the company ledgers. The firm's net loss of 7,500,000 marks in 1930 had been covered by reserves, but the 1931 losses were twice that, only half of it available from reserves or credit accounts. Fifty percent of Caracciola's race winnings was income, but the expenses of running the team during the season had nearly equaled that. Reluctantly, Kissel decided that supporting the team for another year was not feasible. The only competition Daimler-Benz should be engaged in now was the battle against the Depression.

After winning Avusrennen in 1931, Caracciola posed with his Nürburg cabriolet and his friend Louis Chiron in Berlin. In 1932 Rudi joined Louis in racing Alfa Romeos.

CHAPTER SEVEN

GREAT CARS,
DARK CLOUDS

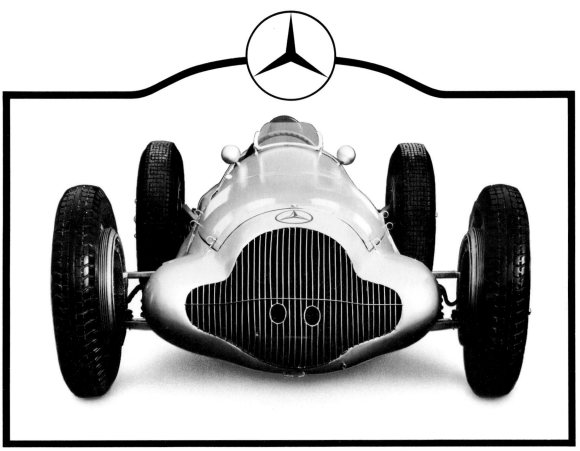

1 9 3 2 – 1 9 3 9

Look upon my works, ye Mighty, and despair!
—PERCY BYSSHE SHELLEY,
OZYMANDIAS

In 1932 Jay Gorney and E.Y. Harburg wrote "Brother, Can You Spare a Dime." There were bread lines all over America, and hunger riots in Minneapolis and Oklahoma City. Twelve and a half million people were unemployed. The average weekly wage had fallen from $28 in 1929 to $17. Many farmers lost everything. Leading American scholars, and writers like John Dos Passos, Sherwood Anderson and Theodore Dreiser, suggested communism might be the answer. Promising the country a New Deal, Franklin Delano Roosevelt was elected president in November.

On Easter Sunday that year, the German painter Käthe Kollwitz wrote in her diary of "people sliding into dark distress," of the "unspeakably difficult general situation . . . the general misery." In Germany there were 6 million unemployed. The Depression had struck just a half-decade after the nation had climbed out of its postwar economic chaos. But the crisis was universal: an estimated 22 percent of the world labor force—30 million people—were jobless. Industrial production in the two largest industrial nations, the United States and Germany, had de-

clined by nearly half.

The automobile industry was devastated. In America, car sales fell from more than 5 million before the stock market crash to just over a million. In Germany, 156,000 cars were sold in 1929, fewer than 52,000 in 1932. On both sides of the Atlantic,

Mercedes-Benz and Berlin Automobile Show posters, 1933. The Depression brought changes to the automobile industry: Daimler-Benz entered the popular-priced field for the first time. On the political front, Germany's "Protektor," Hindenburg, was replaced by a "Führer."

San Francisco bread line, 1932. Never had the world experienced unemployment on such a devastating scale.

the producers of high-quality cars were the hardest hit.

Ironically, some of the most opulent automobiles ever built came on the market during the Depression, cars like the 12- and 16-cylinder super luxury models from Cadillac, Pierce-Arrow, Marmon, Packard and Peerless. They had been planned in the twenties, when it was assumed the good times would go on forever, and even after the crash it was thought the Depression would not last long, so the companies introduced their expensive new models. But the crisis deepened, and the cars found few buyers. Only two of the firms that produced them survived the thirties.

In 1930 Daimler-Benz had introduced its 7.7-liter Grosser, a model designed, according to the sales literature, for those "who always view a maximum achievement as just sufficient for their needs." It had been planned as a top-of-the-line, prestige Mercedes even before Dr. Porsche's departure; now it would be built in small numbers largely for heads of state and movie stars, like young Jackie Coogan, one of the first purchasers. More important for Daimler-Benz was the 170, announced at the Paris Salon in the fall of 1931. It was a remarkably advanced 1.7-liter car with all-independent suspension, central chassis lubrication, four-wheel hydraulic brakes and pressed steel wheels, engineering features the more remarkable because they were offered in a 4,400-mark ($1,000) car. (The usual Mercedes-Benz price range was from 6,000 to 20,000 marks. 60 percent of all automobiles sold in Germany in the twenties cost more than 5,000 marks; by 1932 that percentage dropped to about 12). More than 30,000 Type 170 and the companion Type 200 Mercedes were sold in the next four years.

Not all were affected . . . In Budapest with his Cabriolet D Grosser in the early thirties, the Archduke Josef of Austria, former Hapsburg regent of Hungary, now field marshal.

235

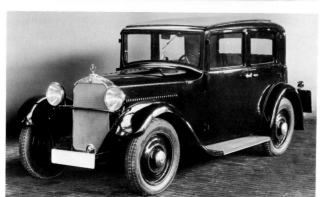

Introduced in 1931, the six-cylinder 170 (top, left) was the first medium-priced Mercedes and Daimler-Benz's best-selling car in the Depression. Though the all-independent suspension, designed by Hans Nibel, was the most widely touted of its advanced engineering features, the new 170 bristled with sophisticated details, including an anti-theft steering wheel lock. By 1933 the *sonnenschein-limousine* (center, left) offered sedan purchasers the quick option of a closed car or "the open sky." Delivery van versions had been introduced the previous year. The four-cylinder 170V with tubular backbone frame (above) followed in 1936 and quickly became the company's new best seller.

The Type 200 Spezial-Roadster (above) was designed at Sindelfingen for the 1933 Berlin Automobile Show. It reflected the Mercedes sporting tradition in this Depression year, and was built as an attention-getting show car only. Meanwhile, behind the scenes, small-car prototypes were being produced. The Type M17 of 1931 (top) carried an air-cooled 1.2-liter 25 hp four-cylinder boxer engine in the rear of a 100-inch wheelbase chassis. The Type M23D of 1933 (center) used a rear-mounted three-cylinder 30 hp diesel engine. Severe vibration problems resulted with the diesel, and twice as many cylinders were tried next. Though the trial runs were many, news of these cars never leaked out.

Wilhelm Kissel's decision to forgo competition in 1932 was no surprise to either Neubauer or Caracciola. The morning after the spectacular win at the German Grand Prix, when both of them were nursing victory-party hangovers, Neubauer had told Rudi, "Next year, dear boy, next year Mercedes is unlikely to race." But to Neubauer's dismay, Caracciola accepted a driving assignment from Alfa Romeo, though he promised to return if competition was renewed. Neubauer's new job at Daimler-Benz was behind a desk in Stuttgart or at automobile shows across the Continent, drumming up business for production cars. He hated it.

Mercedes were raced in 1932 by two drivers of independent means, Manfred von Brauchitsch, the scion of a noted German military family whose first Mercedes, an SS, had been a gift from his uncle, and Hans Stuck, whose family was Bavarian landed gentry and who had purchased an SSK in 1931. In 1932 both drove SSKL's. Though their cars received factory assistance, the evidence suggests both von Brauchitsch and Stuck paid for it. Stuck campaigned in South America, setting a 128-mph record in Bra-

Gridded for the start of the Grand Prix of Monza, 1932: Caracciola in the P3 Alfa Romeo, with race official Renzo Castagneto and Alfa factory personnel looking on. Rudi won three major races with the Alfa in '32 — this one, Eifelrennen and the German GP.

238

Manfred von Brauchitsch. A fortuitous motorcycle accident had washed this young race enthusiast out of military school and the career his family planned for him.

zil, and in Europe, where he won the European Mountain Championship for sports cars, which had gone to Caracciola the two previous years. Von Brauchitsch's most impressive victory was at Avus, where his SSKL appeared with a radically streamlined body designed by Baron Reinhard von König-

Fachsenfeld and built by the Vetter coachworks at Bad Cannstatt. The car was a big surprise to Caracciola, who was at Avus for Alfa; the race turned into a contest between him and von Brauchitsch, the latter winning at 120.7 mph, more than 5 mph faster than Caracciola's average the year before with a standard-bodied SSKL.

Nevertheless Caracciola had a good season with Alfa, winning several important races and the European Mountain Championship for race cars. But at the end of the season Alfa Romeo too decided that racing was a luxury it could do without, and the now-nationalized company turned its competition program over to Enzo Ferrari. Since driving solely for Ferrari did not appeal to Caracciola, he and Louis Chiron formed a two-man independent Alfa team.

Meanwhile, in Stuttgart, Neubauer had accepted a job offer from Auto Union.

Auto Union AG was a new company, dating from the 1928 merger of Audi and DKW. Horch and Wanderer had joined in 1932. For the past two years Wanderer had purchased designs and technical assistance from Ferdinand Porsche's engineering office. In the fall of 1932, with the announcement from Paris of a new grand prix formula for international racing to take effect in 1934, Porsche decided to build a racing car and organized an independent venture for that

Hans Stuck studied agriculture and operated a dairy farm near Munich until he acquired a motorcycle and decided he preferred racing. Seen here at Klausen Pass in 1932 en route to one of 17 victories with his SSKL, Stuck was invited to drive for the Auto Union team in 1934.

Avus, 1932. On the last lap Caracciola's Alfa and von Brauchitsch's Vetter-bodied SSKL (center, left) were head to tail. Coming out of the south curve von Brauchitsch flashed by. A startled Rudi couldn't catch up; the Mercedes crossed the finish line 4.1 seconds ahead of the Alfa. Avus, 1933: Otto Merz before driving the factory-bodied SSKL to Berlin (above) and at the track with von Brauchitsch and Neubauer (top, right). Spectators anxiously awaited the expected duel between the two streamlined SSKL's. It never came. An exhausted Merz crashed on his first practice lap. *"Avus-Flaggen auf Halbmast,"* a Berlin newspaper headlined. *"Der gute Bär"* ("The Good Bear") was dead.

purpose, hoping to convince Auto Union to sponsor it. It was probably Porsche who encouraged the Auto Union managing director, Klaus von Oertzen, to get in touch with his old Daimler-Benz colleague. Neubauer visited the Auto Union offices on November 5, and von Oertzen told him about the future racing plans. Neubauer accepted a provisional contract and went home to write a letter to Wilhelm Kissel.

This was one resignation Kissel would not accept. When he walked into the managing director's office on November 7, Neubauer noticed a portrait of Caracciola hanging behind the desk, in a spot often reserved in German offices for pictures of President Hindenburg (or Kaiser Wilhelm among unreconstructed monarchists). Kissel offered him a raise, and promised Mercedes would race again as soon as it was "economically possible." That was good enough for Neubauer. Kissel took his Auto Union contract and said he would take care of it. (Had he also taken care to hang Caracciola's portrait behind his desk?) But Kissel truly intended that Mercedes would race again.

Early in 1933 Neubauer was given the go-ahead to have an SSKL fitted with a factory-built streamlined body. This car would join von Brauchitsch's Vetter-bodied car at the Avus races in May. Neubauer had hoped to lure Caracciola back with it, but the plan went awry when Caracciola crashed in his Alfa Romeo during practice for the Monaco Grand Prix in April. Otto Merz asked to take his place. Now 44 and a Daimler-Benz production car test driver, the factory's jovial giant wanted one more day in the winner's circle.

The car was completed late. To reach the starting line on time, Merz drove it himself nonstop from Stuttgart to Berlin, at night under a full moon (the car had no headlights). It rained the following afternoon, but the sleepless Merz insisted on practicing and elected not to wait for rain tires to arrive. Neubauer watched as he sped away. Moments later a mechanic rushed to the pits to announce the crash. "He's lying at the side of the road," the mechanic said. "He looks just as if he's asleep." Otto Merz was dead.

Five months earlier, in January, promising nothing less than an immediate solution to all the nation's problems, Adolf Hitler came to power. The aristocratic von Hindenburg detested him as uncouth. Caracciola had told Neubauer of the "profound sense of uneasiness and dread" he felt after meeting the National Socialist leader in Munich in 1931. But in the depths of the Depression, Hitler's resolve to get Germany moving again, his condemnation of the Versailles Treaty, his call upon German pride and his promise of a better life, all had wide appeal. Within a year and a half the political landscape of the nation was transformed. The setting of the Reichstag fire allowed Hitler both to rid himself of political enemies and to suspend the Weimar constitutional freedoms of speech and the press. By 1934, when von Hindenburg died at the age of 87, Hitler was strong enough to add the presidency of Germany to his chancellorship, and to take the title Führer. By then unemployment had been cut in half; soon it would be eliminated altogether. That Hitler was an automobile enthusiast was of particular interest to German auto makers.

In March 1933, in the wave of nationalistic fervor that followed Hitler's rise to power, Kissel decided to commit Daimler-Benz to a full racing program—a decision both patriotic and practical. Among the new government's first acts was the elimination of taxes on new car purchases, followed by the announcement of elaborate plans for autobahn building—a policy with enormous potential for the German automobile industry. And the potential was largely realized. From fewer than 6,000 cars in 1932, Daimler-Benz sales doubled in two years; in three years they passed the 25,000 mark. As Kissel saw it, increased sales made competition, and the publicity that went with it, financially feasible once more. Significantly, too, the government was anxious to support racing.

In 1931, just back from his Mille Miglia victory, Caracciola had shaken Hitler's "limp, nerveless hand" at the Munich Mercedes dealership and then was peppered with the Nazi leader's questions about the Fascist government's interest in Italian motor sport. The prestige it brought his regime was one of the reasons Benito Mussolini favored racing, Alfa

Romeo's efforts specifically; it was also known that Vincenzo Florio had easily convinced him to begin building a new course in Sicily for the Targa Florio. But Hitler was determined to outdo Il Duce's racing efforts.

Early in 1933 the Ministry of Transport offered Daimler-Benz a substantial subsidy for a racing program: a stipend of 450,000 marks a year, with bonuses of 20,000, 10,000 and 5,000 marks for first, second and third place finishes. The offer was made through Jakob Werlin, the Daimler-Benz branch manager in Munich, a personal friend of Hitler since the early 1920s and soon to be his closest advisor on all matters automotive.* Kissel had estimated that at least a million marks—about $300,000—was required to launch a racing effort properly. The government was proposing about half that figure, and by early spring Kissel was informed he would be allowed just half of *that;* the other half would go to Auto Union.

With hat in hand and a sketch of a race car in his pocket, Ferdinand Porsche had visited Hitler and convinced him to support Auto Union as well. Though Porsche's sales pitch was no doubt persuasive, the decision to divide the subsidy as "had King Solomon of yore" (Neubauer's words) was in keeping with Hitler's policy of assigning the same task

---

*Werlin's appointment to the management board of Daimler-Benz in July 1933 was the first clear example of the government's interference in company affairs. It would not be the last.

to two individuals or organizations, in the belief that in competition the stronger would prevail. Both Auto Union and Daimler-Benz were to learn that the government subsidy covered only about 10 percent of the money they needed for racing annually.

But it was government support that encouraged the massive German racing effort. "The Führer has spoken," reported *Mannschaft und Meisterschaft.* "The 1934 grand prix formula shall and must be a measuring stick for German knowledge and German ability. So one thing leads to the other; first the Führer's overpowering energy, then the formula, a great international problem to which Europe's best devote themselves and, finally, action in the design and the construction of new racing cars." Engineers at Daimler-Benz and Auto Union were too busy designing and constructing cars to bother fathoming that bit of propaganda.

The new grand prix formula enacted by the Association Internationale des Automobile Clubs Reconnus (AIACR), the predecessor of today's FIA, specified that cars weigh no more than 750 kilograms (1,653 pounds) without wheels, tires, fuel and water, and be no less than 34 inches wide. This formula was to prevail through the 1936 season. Because there were no restrictions on power plant size, it was tailor-made for Daimler-Benz, whose stock in trade had long been light-alloy, supercharged engines. But though Auto Union was a new company, the man behind its racing effort was one of the

Racing was a weekend hobby for Abruzzi–born Luigi Fagioli until 1930 when he left his family's spaghetti manufacturing business to become a professional race driver. In 1934, at age 36, he joined Mercedes, and is seen here during practice at Avus in late May.

Prototype of the Mercedes W25 Grand Prix car, and posters from the 1934 race season — two from the printing house of Nöcker in Cologne, one by an unknown young artist named Walter Gotschke. Race organizers in Paris had enacted the new Grand Prix formula hoping to lower race car speeds, which were approaching 150 mph and considered too fast. With car weight limited to 1653 pounds, engine size would be reduced to about two liters ... it was thought. "Now the weight limit strikes me as crazy," commented "Casque" (the pseudonym used by Sammy Davis for his sports column in *The Autocar*). Davis groused that the new GP cars would be the size of an MG Midget and perhaps no faster than 120 mph. At the end of the 1934 season, Rudi Caracciola drove the 3.36-liter W25 a record-breaking 197 mph at Gyon.

Eifelrennen, 1934: W25's first race and first victory. Mercedes was faster than Auto Union both on the course and in the pits; Neubauer's crew changed four tires in the time their rivals required for two. Winner von Brauchitsch (above) had but one problem: teammate Fagioli.

all-time great automotive engineers. And he persuaded other Mercedes graduates to help him: Caracciola's mechanic Wilhelm Sebastian prepared the cars, former Mercedes driver Willy Walb managed the team, and SSK/SSKL competitor Hans Stuck was a driver. The Auto Union racing department looked like a Mercedes alumni reunion.

But Porsche's raid did not leave Mercedes bereft. Hans Nibel, who had stepped into Porsche's shoes as Daimler-Benz's chief engineer, had Max Wagner for chassis design, Albert Heess and Otto Schilling for engine development, Fritz Nallinger's experimental department to build and test the cars, and the Unter-türkheim factory manager, Max Sailer, the Targa

driver of yore, to help get the team ready. And of course Daimler-Benz had Neubauer.

The German racing cars which resulted from the Mercedes–Auto Union rivalry were like no others the world had seen. They shared such features as all-round independent suspension, hydraulic brakes and sleek, streamlined bodies. On engines and their placement the two companies diverged. The Mercedes had a double-overhead-cam, supercharged straight-eight mounted in front, the Auto Union a single-overhead-cam, supercharged V16 mounted in the rear. Interestingly, Porsche's Auto Union harked back to the Benz Tropfenwagen, the short-lived technical *tour de force* Nibel and Wagner designed in the

W25 dressed for record breaking at Gyon with new radiator cowl and coupe top, and minus front brakes. Even Caracciola was astounded at its near 200 mph speed. Had the grapes along the road been attached to the car, he joked, they would have been grape juice when he finished.

early twenties,* while Nibel's and Wagner's new Mercedes owed some features to Porsche. For 1934, the Mercedes developed 314 bhp with a 3.36-liter displacement, the Auto Union 295 bhp from 4.36 liters. In the years to come the Auto Union was always ahead on displacement; Mercedes, more skilled at supercharging, usually had greater horsepower. With its engine settling nearly 60 percent of its weight on the rear wheels, the Auto Union put more power on the road, but the imbalance also caused formidable oversteer and a tendency for the tail to break away before a driver could realize it, which made it a very tricky automobile to handle. This was one of the reasons the Mercedes engineers, who had considered a rear engine in their early planning, ultimately decided against it.

The new Auto Union, designated the P-Wagen, was ready in late fall, 1933, several months before the Mercedes. Rivalry started immediately. Because their name was relatively new on the German scene, the Auto Union people were anxious to steal a march on the country's oldest and most famous automotive company, and became a bit overzealous. After private testing on the roads around the Horch works in Zwickau (where the car had been built) and at the Nürburgring, the Auto Union crew took the P-Wagen to Avus in early January and invited the press, which like most German institutions was now under state control. The ensuing newspaper stories infuriated Daimler-Benz. "A large part of the press calls this car *the* German race car as if no other German race car exists," complained an inter-office memo. There was, of course, a kernel of truth in the press reports since the new Mercedes race car was not yet finished. And it was also true that the Auto Union had reached 150 mph at Avus—but that was on the straight and was not, as the press implied, the lap average, which was 124 mph. Stuttgart took further umbrage at the Auto Union denial that it was "out to receive any advance laurels, but that is just what all these articles are." But worst of all to the Mercedes

people was an Auto Union representative's description of them as "pompous fellows."

Whether Daimler-Benz made an official complaint is not known. If so, they would have lodged it with one of two state organizations: the Oberste Nationale Sportbehörde für die Deutsche Kraftfahrt (Highest National Sporting Authority for German Motoring), or ONS, or the National Socialistisches Kraftfahrt Korps (National Socialist Motoring Corps), or NSKK, initials some Germans converted into "Nür Säufer, Keine Kämpfer" ("only drinkers, no fighters"). These organizations took over the traditional roles of the German automobile clubs, with Major Adolf Hühnlein, a Hitler crony from early party days, overseeing both.

In mid-February the Mercedes was taken to Monza, near Milan, for testing. Three months earlier Neubauer had contacted Caracciola, whose thigh was still in a cast from his Monaco crash, and Rudi assured him he would be ready when the car was. But now the Mercedes ace was not available. His wife, Charly, had been killed in a skiing accident in February; Rudi, at home alone, would neither see nor speak to anyone, not even Chiron, his best friend. So Manfred von Brauchitsch drove the new car at Monza. It crashed because of a tire failure, though von Brauchitsch was unhurt. Rebuilt in Stuttgart, the car, with von Brauchitsch, was returned to Monza for further testing in March.

In mid-April Neubauer and an Auto Union representative met with Hühnlein in Berlin to discuss the season's racing and the events each would contest. Neubauer tended to like discipline only when he imposed it, and he was already squirming under the new government's heavy hand. Auto Union had dutifully submitted its roster of drivers for the '34 season: Hans Stuck, August Momberger and Prince zu Leiningen—all former Mercedes drivers and, more important, all Germans. Neubauer had submitted his list, too, and one of his drivers was an Italian, Luigi Fagioli. This was not well received in Berlin. Neubauer, saying that he was after all the team manager, prepared a carefully drafted defense of his choice of the former Alfa Romeo and Maserati ace, citing, in addition to the Italian's outstanding experience and

---

*While he was with Benz & Cie. Willy Walb had raced the Tropfenwagen, as had the businessman-driver Adolf Rosenberger, who was Porsche's financial advisor during this period. Both were ardent proponents of rear-engine design.

skill, Caracciola's questionable status, von Brauchitsch's inexperience, and the fact that winning races required the best drivers available. Moreover, other teams occasionally employed foreigners to advantage and rejecting Fagioli (whom Neubauer apparently had already contacted) might be misconstrued, whereas hiring him would demonstrate Germany's friendship for Italy. Neubauer may have had some help from the diplomatic Kissel in drafting this document; in any case, it worked. Fagioli was allowed on the team, though with the understanding that German drivers would triumph wherever possible, except in Italian events where the Italian driver could run his own race. Now Neubauer had to figure out how to handle Fagioli, who like him was not known to accept discipline well.

By spring Caracciola had pulled himself out of his depression. Whether he was ready physically was another matter. On May 24 he went to Avus to find out. The Mercedes team had been there for several days, both von Brauchitsch and Fagioli driving the cars. When he arrived Caracciola asked if he could take his first practice runs at six the following morning to avoid attention. Neubauer and Nibel agreed. At the appointed hour Caracciola walked slowly to the race car with the help of a cane, but with each lap of the long circuit he increased his speed, until finally he was running faster than either Fagioli or von Brauchitsch.

Rudi was ready, but Nibel decided the cars were not. A fuel system problem demanded attention. At Avus Alfa Romeo finished one-two with an Auto Union in third, and the Mercedes debut was pushed ahead a week to June 3, at the Eifelrennen at the Nürburgring. That twisting course was deemed too arduous for Caracciola's still-weak leg, so only von Brauchitsch and Fagioli would be competing—if any Mercedes were. At the weigh-in the cars were discovered to be one kilogram (2.2 pounds) over the 750-kg limit. They had been weighed at the factory, but the Nürburgring scales were the only ones that mattered, and two brand-new Mercedes race cars sat there, all dressed up in German racing white and no place to go. But Neubauer had an idea: remove the paint. The mechanics worked all night, sanding every

vestige of white from the bodies, and the next morning the two cars, naked in their silvery aluminum, tipped the scales at exactly 750 kg. *

The finish of the Eifelrennen saw the von Brauchitsch Mercedes win at 79.84 mph, with Stuck's Auto Union second at 75.06, and Chiron's Alfa third, four minutes behind. Fagioli could have finished second, but he didn't want to. Infuriated at not being allowed to pass von Brauchitsch, which he could easily have done, Fagioli ultimately stopped his car by the side of the circuit, got out and took a seat in the grandstand. Now Neubauer was sure he had a problem.

The French Grand Prix followed on July 1. Returning there for the first time since the one-two-three finish in 1914, Mercedes was anxious to do well. Instead all three cars retired and Alfa Romeo finished one-two-three, with Chiron in a brilliant victory; the Italian sweep indicated that racing's old guard had plenty of fight.

Next came the German Grand Prix at the Nürburgring on July 15. A crash during practice put von Brauchitsch out for the season. The event itself was a duel up front between Caracciola and Stuck. During the race a suggestion arrived from the Auto Union pits that since Mercedes had won earlier in the year at Nürburgring it would be pleasant if Auto Union could win now. Neubauer, who a few months earlier had fired off a letter to the ONS protesting the truth of a major Auto Union ad praising their car's exploits, was furious; but discretion being preferable to reprisals from higher authority, he simply stalled, saying only that the halfway point was not the time to make such a decision. Some laps later Caracciola's engine gave out and Auto Union won, convincingly and legitimately. But never again was Neubauer requested to lose a race.

Fagioli had been second in the German Grand Prix, but only because he could not catch Stuck. At the Coppa Acerbo in Italy, after Stuck's Auto Union had mechanical problems, Chiron's Alfa caught fire, and Caracciola spun out, Fagioli won; Nuvolari was

---

*Mercedes-Benz race cars remained silver ever after, though later the bare metal was painted that color. The German press nicknamed the cars *Silberpfeile* (Silver Arrows).

second in a Maserati, Antonio Brivio third in a Bugatti. Auto Union was one-two in the Swiss Grand Prix on August 26.

On September 9 the Italian Grand Prix was held at Monza. It was an extraordinarily hot, humid day. Early in the race von Brauchitsch and Fagioli retired with mechanical problems, leaving only Caracciola on the circuit and in the lead when he pulled into the pits, overcome with the heat, his leg aching. The mechanics lifted him out of the car as Neubauer shouted to Fagioli to get in. Luigi did, and won; Stuck's Auto Union was second, an Alfa third. At the San Sebastian Grand Prix on the twenty-third, Fagioli won again; Caracciola placed second, Nuvolari's Maserati was third. At the Czechoslovakian Grand Prix on the thirtieth, Stuck's Auto Union won, with Fagioli's Mercedes second.

Taking stock at the end of the season, Daimler-Benz had reason to be pleased. Four victories was a fine record for any car's maiden year. Except in the early-season events, a German car had outclassed the opposition in every race, though it was unsettling that the German car was sometimes an Auto Union. Fagioli's rebellions were unsettling, too, but after the Eifelrennen and a lecture, he had never again parked himself in the grandstand. Though hot-headed and hard on the machinery, Fagioli was fast, and the team needed him. Neubauer feared, however, that after Caracciola had a winter's rest and was back in form, there might be more problems.

For Neubauer did not doubt that in '35 Rudi would be the Caracciola of old. Late in October 1934, Neubauer had taken a race car and a crew to Hungary for record breaking on the Gyon highway south of Budapest. Since von Brauchitsch was still out and Fagioli was not to be used for German record attempts, Neubauer had selected Ernst Henne, a record-breaking motorcyclist, as his driver. Then Caracciola showed up uninvited one morning, in white coveralls. Neubauer had not wanted to risk his leg, but Rudi insisted and put up 197.35 and 196.78 mph, respectively, for the flying kilometer and mile, the fastest any standard race car had ever been driven on a highway. To Rudi, the experience was exhilarating: "The higher air pressure and the shrill whistling of the wind rushing by, but especially the scenery simply becomes shadowy and races by at an unbelievable speed," he said. Caracciola would indeed be ready for '35.

Looking back on '34, the foreign motor press was staggered by what had happened so quickly in grand prix competition. *Motor Sport* called the new German cars "amazing . . . a big advance on our previous conceptions of motor racing." *The Motor* commented on the cars' "astonishing acceleration . . . a complete surprise." *The Autocar* noted the extraordinary displacement and power of the racers' engines when the rules evolved had supposed "a two-liter . . . to be the largest size that would fit into the weight limit." But the racing world hadn't seen anything yet.

During this period Daimler-Benz had also produced a surprising car for the marketplace. Writing of the 130 in 1934, a technical reporter commented that "obviously it has not been made simply to create a passing sensation, for its builders are . . . the very oldest in the automobile industry, renowned for fast cars and for cars of quality." The 130 was a small car, and not very fast. Its 1.3-liter, four-cylinder engine was mounted in unit with the transmission and differential at the rear axle. It had independent suspension all-around, hydraulic four-wheel brakes, and a tubular chassis. What amazed English reporters was Daimler-Benz's decision not to scale down a larger model but to design an all-new car. What struck *Scientific American* were the "many features that recommend it as a decided advance in the design and construction of automobiles." The subsequent Type 170H (1.7-liter engine, introduced in 1935) was good for 70 mph and 30 mpg, remarkable figures for the mid-thirties and a remarkable performance from a mere 91 cubic inches and 34 horsepower.

Daimler-Benz's interest in small cars was a consequence of the Depression. As the economy began to improve, Kissel noted that the best-selling cars were smaller-engine models that more people could afford. For decades, German motoring had been the province of the upper middle classes and the aristocracy; now Germans from all social classes wanted cars.

In 1929 Germany's only mass producer, Opel, had

The Type 130, introduced at the Berlin Automobile Show in February 1934, was a complete surprise. Not only was it the smallest Mercedes ever (100-inch wheelbase, 50-inch track), but its 1.3-liter (not quite 80-cubic-inch) rear-mounted engine and advanced chassis design were hailed as revolutionary on both sides of the Atlantic. The 1935 *cabriolimousine* is seen at the top; at center is an experimental Type 130 scout car built in 1934. Above is the Type 150 sport-roadster, with its 1.5-liter engine mounted ahead of the rear axle; this location amidships provided better stability in fast curves (a problem with the 130) but eliminated the possibility of more than two passengers.

(Top, right) 1934 Type 150 sports sedan built for Germany's 2000-kilometer reliability trial. Seven of these Mercedes finished in good order, but the German public remained skeptical about rear-engine cars. (Top, left) 1936 Type 170H, its wheelbase 104 inches, like the 150. Though the car was critically well received in the U.S. and available through Mitropa Motors in New York, Americans were no more favorably disposed to rear engines than Germans. (Center) 1938 Type 170VS, the sports edition of Mercedes' front-engined bestseller. (Above) KdF-Wagen, the 1937 prototype (left; a rear window was added before Hitler's unveiling in '38), and as introduced in 1945 as the Volkswagen (right).

built 34,758 cars. That same year nine American companies had production in the six figures (Ford in seven, with more than 1.5 million cars), and no fewer than 20 different American makes were built in greater numbers than the Opel. American motor vehicle production in that banner year, the best the automotive industry had yet known, was over 5.3 million. In Germany the figure was 156,000, less than in France and the United Kingdom, which both surpassed 200,000. The Depression played hob with production figures for several years, of course, although the nations' relative positions remained the same. In 1934, when United States production was still at half the pre-Crash level, Germany's production of 174,566 vehicles surpassed the 1929 peak year and within three years more than doubled. No other nation enjoyed a similar growth in automotive production during this period. And the reason was Hitler.

In his year in the Landsberg prison, Hitler had time not only to write *Mein Kampf* but to read a biography of Henry Ford. Mass production fascinated him. Moreover, he was convinced the automobile could enhance his political prestige; putting every German into a car was a move calculated to earn the nation's gratitude and loyalty. Soon after taking power he eliminated the automobile tax and began building the autobahns; the first autobahn section from Frankfurt to Darmstadt was opened in May 1935. So cars were cheaper, and Germans had splendid new roads to drive them on. Picnic grounds were planned for highways where the distances between towns were great. Antiquated rules of the road were rescinded, and there was even a plan to award badges—in gold, silver and copper—to drivers who "for a certain length of time have not been caught transgressing" the road regulations that remained.

At first the German auto makers welcomed Hitler's enthusiasm. What they did not know was that he was planning to go into business against them. In January 1934, Hitler opened the Berlin Automobile Show, an occasion which allowed him to repeat his familiar speech on the automobile as a great gift to mankind. Shortly afterwards Werlin, his right-hand man in motoring matters, arranged a meeting with Porsche at the Kaiserhof Hotel in Berlin, during

which Hitler talked about and doodled a car for the German people. Among his sketches was one resembling a Porsche experimental car; another bore an unmistakable similarity to the Mercedes 130 he had just seen at the Berlin show. As a car designer, Hitler was a plagiarist, but there is no question that he planned to become Germany's automotive major domo. "No competition," one of his scribbled notes from the meeting reads, "just one Volkswagen."

Unaware, like his fellow auto makers, of the implications of this meeting, Kissel made plans for Daimler-Benz to capture a sizeable share of the burgeoning new German market for cars. The 1934 competition season had augured favorably for the continuing prestige and publicity racing would bring—and Daimler-Benz would of course continue to build the large and powerful supercharged cars for which it had long been famous.

At the Berlin Automobile Show in 1934, the new 500K made its debut alongside the 130. The spiritual descendant of the fabled S series, the new model was a successor of the straight-eight 380 which had been introduced the previous year. The 380 was a good-looking car and, with its massive box frame carrying independent front suspension by parallel wishbones and coil springs (a world's production first) and rear suspension by swing axles, it was well designed. It also weighed more than two tons, and 3.8 liters and 120 bhp had not moved it fast enough. Whence the 5-liter, 160-bhp 500K.

A total of 354 Type 500K's were built in three years (as contrasted with 154 380's in two). The $5,000-range price tag actually bought two cars: a fast, docile tourer with the supercharger disengaged — "At 60 unblown there hardly appears to be movement," *The Autocar* reported, "70 is an amble, and even 80 scarcely noticed"—and a stupendous performer when the blower was cut in and let out "its almost demoniacal howl . . . [as the] rev counter and speedometer needles leap round their dials." *The Autocar*'s road test revealed a 0-60 time of 16.5 seconds, amazing acceleration for the mid-thirties; the top speed of 100 mph was equally impressive. *Motor Sport* summed up its 500K road test by saying that "here is a massive 'unbreakable' car capable of traveling indefinitely at high speed." One British enthusiast, commenting on the 500K as "one of the few cars to raise envy in the hearts of real motorists," was curious that a company whose grand prix cars weighed less than 2,000 pounds should produce a road car weighing more than 5,000, which prompted him to reveries of what a 3,000-pound 500K could accomplish. As it was, the "sheer insolence of its power," as one reporter of the day noted, made it a "master car for the very few." Had the 500K weighed much less, it might have been too much car for anyone but a professional race driver.

Mercedes' 1935 drivers were the same trio as in 1934: Caracciola, Fagioli and von Brauchitsch. The Auto Union managers, encouraged by the ONS acceptance of an Italian on their rival's team the year before, hired an Italian of their own, Achille Varzi. Varzi was as formidable a driver as Fagioli, and both of them were second only to the incredible Tazio Nuvolari in the Italian racing hierarchy. With Varzi's departure from Enzo Ferrari's Alfa Romeo team, Nuvolari was persuaded, supposedly by Mussolini himself, to return to Alfa, a move which provided Italy with its most potent competition to the German cars. Joining Nuvolari on the Alfa team were the stylish French driver René Dreyfus and the Marquis Antonio Brivio, an Italian—both Bugatti veterans and both first-class drivers. Even before the opening race at Monaco on April 22, it promised to be an interesting season.

But the Mercedes racing department had had some anxious moments before it began. Nibel's sudden death of a stroke in November 1934 had plunged the department into gloom; Daimler-Benz's chief engineer has been both well liked and respected, and he would be missed. But the new Mercedes cars, both production and racing, had been completed before he died. The new Daimler-Benz chief engineer was the veteran Max Sailer, he of the French Grand Prix of two decades earlier. His lieutenants were Hans-Gustav Röhr, a brilliant young man who came from Adler and who functioned as chief of passenger car engineering, and Fritz Nallinger, who was moved into the position of chief aircraft and large industrial engine design and development. The grand prix cars

for 1935 had been bored out to 3.99 liters and 430 horsepower.

The Mercedes armada was ready for Monaco— and the word "armada" suggests how Daimler-Benz went racing during this period. For Alfred Neubauer, who only four years before had sat in a hotel room in Brescia with a map of Italy on his lap, trying to figure out how to deploy one truck and three mechanics around four Mille Miglia supply depots, it was a heady experience. Now he had 20 mechanics and at least a half-dozen trucks, one of them a complete traveling workshop with lathes, welding equipment, drill presses and testing rigs. There were log books to record the vital signs of each car, and each car's chief mechanic had a notebook of his own in which to enter relevant data. The cars were warmed up and tested by mechanics before a race, and after 500 racing miles would be torn down and rebuilt before they reappeared at a starting line. While one team of cars was at a race, another full set was back at the factory being prepared for the next event. Two engines were built for each car. Tire pressures were adjusted according to thermometer readings of the road temperature, and tire tread wear was painstakingly checked by special gauges. The racing fuel was a carefully formulated mixture, and after oil was drained from a car's sump, a portion was retained for post-race analysis. White-smocked technicians gave a laboratory look to the pits, and the entire venture had the aura of a scientific expedition.

Neubauer's job was to translate all this science into victory. For 1935, remembering the Fagioli problem the year before, he devised two basic rules: all drivers would make the fastest start possible without straining their engines, and whichever driver first gained a one-minute lead over his teammates would earn the right to victory. That seemed simple enough, and it worked at the Grand Prix of Monaco, chiefly because von Brauchitsch had a gear problem on the first lap and retired and Caracciola retired in the closing laps with a broken valve, which left Fagioli to win. Dreyfus and Brivio were second and third in Alfas; Auto Union did not compete.

The policy worked well, too, at the Grand Prix of Tripoli on May 12. Auto Union was there, and this

Introduced at the 1934 Berlin Automobile Show, the 500K was offered in the same body styles as the 380 and a dramatic new one: the Autobahn-Kurier. Only a handful were produced. In America, Packard's 1106 Sport Coupe, which bore a striking resemblance to the Mercedes, also found few buyers, and Chrysler's Airflow, which many found bizarre, was a marketing disaster. Though offbeat enough to generate sales only among the adventurous, aerodynamic styling did attract attention at auto shows, so Mercedes returned in 1935 with an even more streamlined Autobahn-Kurier (facing page, center and below). And the Berlin coachbuilders Erdmann & Rossi exhibited a flamboyant variation which attracted the attention of King Ghazi of Iraq. The 500K (facing page, top) was delivered to him later that year.

race demonstrated what soon became a verity in motor sport: if both German teams were on hand, the only question generally was which would win. In this case, it was Caracciola's Mercedes helped by Neubauer's typically astute race strategy. Going full bore, Varzi's Auto Union had led for most of the race. In the closing laps, Neubauer signaled his ace to speed up, which Caracciola did; but Varzi, with no more speed left, could not do likewise. The winning average was a sensational 123.03 mph. Fagioli followed Varzi home third; Nuvolari was fourth for Alfa Romeo.

At the Avus meeting on May 26, Stuck's Auto Union took the first heat, Caracciola the second, Fagioli the final. At the Eifelrennen on June 16, it was Mercedes–Auto Union; Caracciola was the winner and one of Auto Union's junior drivers was second. This was Bernd Rosemeyer, of whom considerably more would be heard in future.

These two events were warm-ups for the French Grand Prix at Montlhéry on June 23. Auto Union, which had brought its new 5.9-liter, 500-hp car to Avus, was having problems with it. The French organizers added to them by inserting chicanes at three points in the circuit, officially "to reduce speed at certain dangerous bends" but actually to slow down the faster German cars and give the native products a better chance for success. (The Italians later used similar tactics on their home territory.) The French hopes rested in a 3.8-liter Bugatti so new it had been painted only the day before; it appeared at the circuit about midnight. (Another French entry, the government-backed S.E.F.A.C., was not ready on time.) The French press announced the new Alfas as 3.8 liters, but Alfa engineer Vittorio Jano insisted they were 3,450cc. The Maseratis were 3.8—and the Mercedes, of course, were 3.9.

"Revenge Is Sweet" was one headline after the event. "An Easy Victory for Mercedes-Benz" was another. In the previous year's French Grand Prix the Mercedes team had retired en masse; this year it was Auto Union's turn, and Bugatti was never in the running. Nuvolari's Alfa gave Caracciola a run in the early laps, but Rudi took over thereafter, with von Brauchitsch finishing second. On the last lap it

seemed that Fagioli would make it a clean sweep, but his car began misfiring and he lost third to a Maserati.

At the Penya Rhin Grand Prix in Barcelona the following weekend, the finish was Fagioli-Caracciola. At the Belgian Grand Prix on July 14, the finish was something else. Fagioli, in a surly mood, chose to ignore both his engine's rev limits and Neubauer's rules. Early on, Caracciola established a commanding lead over the Alfas of Dreyfus and Chiron as well as his Mercedes teammates, which was supposed to have settled things as far as the finish was concerned. At half distance von Brauchitsch's car was retired after persistent misfiring, and the rest of the race should have seen Caracciola and Fagioli loping around the circuit. Except that Fagioli would have none of it. He had already established a lap record for the course (not once but twice), and now he bore down on Caracciola. In his mirror Caracciola saw him closing in, waving his arms to move over; Caracciola took a look at his tachometer and gulped. But these antics were not lost on Neubauer, who flagged the Italian into the pits. The ensuing argument ended only when Fagioli climbed out of the car, tore off his linen helmet and goggles and stormed away; meanwhile, Chiron and Dreyfus passed by. Desperately, Neubauer shouted for von Brauchitsch who, believing his race was over, was asleep under a tree. Wiping the sleep from his eyes, he got into Fagioli's car and drove faster than he ever had before, breaking Fagioli's lap record, overtaking the Alfas and preserving the Mercedes one-two finish. (Auto Union had not contested the race.)

Mercedes' last two events in 1935 produced a Caracciola-Fagioli finish in the Swiss Grand Prix and a clean sweep (Caracciola-Fagioli-von Brauchitsch) in the Spanish Grand Prix. Which added up to nine important victories in a single season. No other race competitor could approach the Mercedes success in 1935. Though Auto Union won three events in which the Stuttgart cars were not entered, the only nose-to-nose race in which it prevailed was the Italian Grand Prix where, inexplicably, all the Mercedes retired. The only other major race the Mercedes did not win was the single event it would have been politically prudent to win: the German Grand Prix in July. Auto Union did not win that one, either; Tazio Nuvolari did, with an Alfa. This did not please the Third Reich.

Uncertainty is one of the compelling attractions of motor sport, and the last lap of the 1935 German Grand Prix at the Nürburgring provided it in full measure. Nuvolari, whose Alfa was 20 mph slower than either Mercedes or Auto Union, had driven perhaps the most spectacular race of a spectacular career, hounding the German cars from the starting flag, though in the closing laps it appeared victory would not be his. An agonizingly long pit stop had dropped him back to fight for second with Caracciola and Stuck; in first was Manfred von Brauchitsch. Driving skill not yet the equal of Caracciola's or Fagioli's, and sometimes plain bad luck, had kept him out of the winner's circle thus far. But von Brauchitsch was determined to get there this time. He set the lap record, and pressed on; Neubauer did not hold him back. Then, five miles from the finish at the Karussel hairpin, he burst a tire and Nuvolari shot into the lead. Eight German cars followed him across the finish line, von Brauchitsch limping into the pits on three tires and one mangled wheel rim to finish fifth.

Nuvolari's victory was a shock. "At first there was deathly silence," *Motor Sport* reported, "and then the innate sportsmanship of the Germans triumphed over their astonishment. Nuvolari was given a wonderful reception." So was von Brauchitsch. When his number went up on the scoreboard indicating he would be the next in, 250,000 spectators began shouting as loud and clapping as hard as they had for the victorious Nuvolari. Tears streaming down his face, von Brauchitsch was gently led away from his car by his brother. Nuvolari ran to him immediately.

The drama of the race and its poignant aftermath was lost on the representatives of the Third Reich. Korpsführer Hühnlein angrily tore up his victory speech as Nuvolari was crowned with the wreath which, having been made with one of the robust German drivers in mind, was much too big for wiry little Tazio. Finding an Italian flag to raise took some time, though finding a record of the Italian anthem to play was easy: Nuvolari had brought one with him, for good luck, he said. Korpsführer Hühnlein was not amused.

At the end of the season Caracciola was dispatched to Paris to pick up the AIACR's Gold Medal for the most successful racing driver of the year, and then to England for the automobile show at Olympia. One of the grand prix cars had been sent for exhibit at the request of British Mercedes-Benz Ltd., which probably also requested the presence of Caracciola, who had become a popular figure in England following his Tourist Trophy win in 1929. No, Rudi said at a press conference, last season's grand prix cars would not be put up for sale (the usual practice in racing) because their engines, running at 6,000 rpm, required frequent replacements and were complicated to tune, thus making them useful only to the factory; moreover they had cost more than £8,000 (nearly $20,000) apiece to build, so buying a Mercedes 500K was a better idea anyway. Caracciola also delighted his audience with racing stories, sometimes on himself, like the one about the time in the Spanish Grand Prix when he momentarily forgot he was in the grand prix car and not his personal 500K, stepped firmly on the accelerator instead of the brake pedal and shot up to a corner so fast that the cars ahead of him scattered like chickens. Caracciola the racing driver was a better car salesman than he had been during his early "selling" days in Dresden.

In 1936 Mercedes dealers began selling two new cars which had little in common but the three-pointed star on their hoods. One was the 540K, the most fabulous automobile of the age; the other was the 260D, the world's first diesel production car.

The 540K, an evolution of Nibel's 500K, was engineered by Röhr.* Just over 400 were built. The cars were advertised as the fastest standard production automobiles in the world, and with 180 hp on tap, well over 100 mph maximum, and the ability to

---

*In 1937 Röhr died suddenly of a lung infection. He was 42, and had been on his way to a special place in the history of the company. He had been working on a series of front-wheel-drive cars to be powered by horizontally opposed four-, six- and eight-cylinder engines. After his death, certain highly placed members of management had his experimental vehicles scrapped, and the subject of front-wheel drive vanished from the Daimler-Benz agenda.

cruise an autobahn endlessly at 85, there were few to argue. The 540K was massive and solid, though some said it was over-engineered (a dubious criticism at best). But the car especially shone in the body design wrought by Mercedes stylists, who managed to create a car that was sporting as well as elegant and flashy without being gaudy, no easy feat of design. The 540K had sensuous curves and bold lines with daring sweeps of chrome everywhere. It was a car that could not be ignored. Other manufacturers tried to imitate it, but with no real success. The 540K had that indefinable quality called presence.

The new diesel represented another automotive idea altogether. Daimler and Benz engineers had tackled it independently before the merger, and redoubled their efforts thereafter. By the early thirties Max Wagner was eager to get a diesel automobile on the market and planned to introduce one at the 1934 Berlin Automobile Show. By that time the diesel engine was running well on a dynamometer, but when it was installed in a Mannheim chassis severe vibration problems resulted. Wagner sent Nallinger to the Gaggenau factory to find a solution, and Nallinger returned with the idea of building the engine as a 45-hp four rather than an 82-hp six and installing the

result in a Type 230 chassis. This worked, and the car was now ready for production.

Marketing a diesel automobile represented a considerable risk for Daimler-Benz and adverse criticism was expected, as diesel experimentation elsewhere had indicated that for automotive use it was an interesting but impractical idea. But Daimler-Benz envisioned its production diesel largely for taxicab use. In that application the car's higher initial cost would be offset by its operating economy and longevity. Fuel savings were about 55 percent, and the diesel could even be operated satisfactorily on kerosene. As for longevity, Mercedes-Benz diesels soon developed a reputation unmatched by the engines of any other manufacturer, and accumulations of several hundred thousand miles were not uncommon. In the 1970s, a 220D model in service in the United States actually topped one million miles, and made it through the first 909,000 before it needed a new short block!

Because Daimler-Benz had been apprehensive about the acceptance of this new development in passenger automobiles, the company was both surprised and delighted with the road tests reported in the automotive press. No more surprised than the journalists. "To my utter hornswogglement the thing

Advertising the 1935 season: Caracciola won Eifelrennen, Fagioli was victorious at Monaco. Of 11 races entered that year, Mercedes won nine: Rudi six, Luigi the rest. Of the two races not won, Auto Union took one, Alfa Romeo the other.

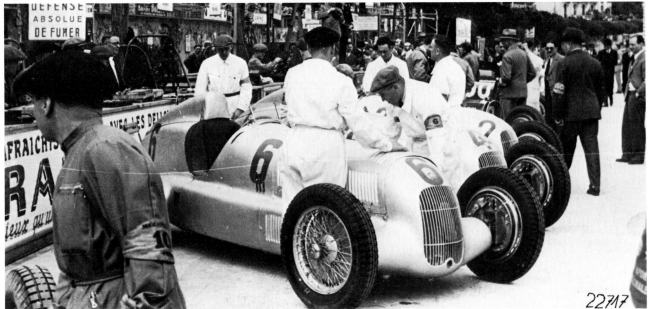

The 1935 Grand Prix season began at Monaco on April 22, with the Caracciola (2), Fagioli (4) and von Brauchitsch (6) cars seen in pit lane before the start (center). During practice all three Mercedes drivers broke the Monaco lap record. The race provided Neubauer some anxious moments as von Brauchitsch and Caracciola retired, but Fagioli saved the day. At 4:00 p.m. on June 16 at the Nürburgring (above), after a hard morning rain, the Eifelrennen saw a battle of the German cars, which Caracciola won for Mercedes, with Rosemeyer second for Auto Union. At the French Grand Prix on June 23, Caracciola (top) was the easy winner. W25's new supercharger inlet filters are prominent in this photo.

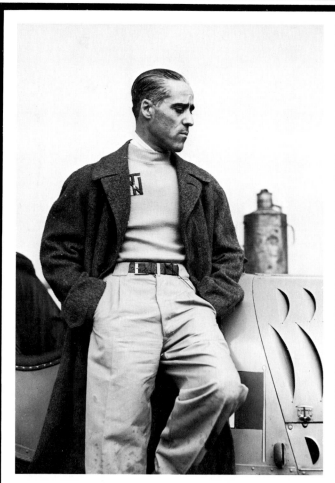

The 1935 German Grand Prix winner didn't resemble the pre-race advertising poster at all. But then no one expected Tazio Nuvolari, driving an outclassed Alfa, to win. The German spectators cheered him as if he were one of their own. No driver in Europe was more beloved than the wiry little phenomenon (he was just five feet five, barely 135 pounds) known as "The Flying Mantuan." In 1936 he captivated New York City after winning the Vanderbilt Trophy (above, the presentation by George Vanderbilt, distant kin to Willie K.). At the banquet that night Mayor Fiorello La Guardia congratulated him in Italian. The yellow jersey that was Tazio's racing "uniform" — complete with tortoise pin, a gift from the poet Gabriele d'Annunzio, an admirer — set him apart from other drivers. So did his racing.

proceeded to tick over like a bloodhound lapping soup," reported David Scott-Moncrieff in *Speed* after testing a Mercedes diesel at the factory. "The cornering . . . has to be seen to be believed, but the thing that really amazed me was the way in which the diesel engine accelerated away from a corner in a manner that would put many petrol engines to shame." By today's standards the early diesels were rough and noisy, especially in starting, but once up to 50 mph, as *The Autocar* reported, the engine was "quiet and smooth, and practically impossible to distinguish from a good petrol unit."

In 1936, the 260D was essentially a marketing experiment. It is safe to say no one ever expected that 50 years later Daimler-Benz would long since have claimed the title of world's largest manufacturer of diesel passenger cars, with a total of more than 3 million built by the time of the 100th anniversary. The 2.6-liter four-cylinder was ancient history by then; current designs included turbocharged six-cylinder models quieter than the gasoline engines of 1936 and capable of propelling their vehicles well in excess of 100 mph.

All in all the 1936 Berlin Automobile Show gave cause for celebration at Daimler-Benz. Not only could the firm mark the Golden Anniversary of Daimler's and Benz's pioneering, not to speak of the launching of the 540K and the 260D, but Wilhelm Kissel and his colleagues could breathe a sigh of relief.

In January 1936, Daimler-Benz had survived a government attempt to take control of its affairs.

Increasingly, the Third Reich was reaching into private industry. In Stuttgart this took the form of two examiners, "specialists of the Reich in business affairs," who arrived to take a look at the books and concluded the firm was being mismanaged. The government charges were given to the Daimler-Benz board in early December 1935, and Kissel immediately called Wilhelm Haspel, the director at Sindelfingen and the man who had been his right hand in coordinating the merger of the two companies nearly 10 years earlier. Haspel had only to glance at the charges to conclude they were theoretical doubletalk. But because of their ominous implications, he prepared a refutation complete with statistics and graphs —176 pages of careful answers to the allegations that so convincingly rebutted the government report that, for the moment, the Third Reich had no choice but to leave the running of Daimler-Benz to Daimler-Benz. Haspel presented his document in mid-January; by the time the automobile show opened the next month he had been appointed a member of the Daimler-Benz board. He was just 38.

Daimler-Benz now looked forward to the opening of the racing season, confident it would see a reprise of 1935. The Mercedes grand prix car was new—a 4.74-liter engine which closed in on 474 hp and was

Wary of public reaction to a diesel automobile, Daimler-Benz produced more than a dozen Type 260D's before the model was introduced in February 1936. As taxi drivers discovered the diesel's advantages, the Mercedes was on its way to becoming Germany's most popular taxicab.

Mercedes-Benz 540K: 1936 Spezial-Roadster (above), 1938 Coupe (center), 1937 Spezial-Roadster (top). A 540K in full touring trim was tested at Brooklands by *The Motor* and with windshield and top up, and supercharger in full cry, did a flying half-mile at 106 mph. The world's fastest standard production model was also among the more formidable. Tipping the scales at 5000+ pounds and stretching 129½ inches between axles (116½ in the short-chassis version), the 540K was not an easy car to park, though at low speeds it was a docile machine capable of "a gliding crawl in absolute silence" (*Motor Sport's* words). Some 500K owners returned their cars to the factory to have the 5.4-liter engine installed. The last 540K chassis was produced in 1939; the last car was delivered during the summer of '42.

W25, 1936: more horsepower in a more compact chassis, a leaf from the SSK (née SS) book. But it failed. Nearly 11 inches shorter in wheelbase, dramatically lower and more elegantly streamlined, the new GP car was also unreliable. It won just two races.

installed in a smaller and shorter car. New to the team this year was Caracciola's friend Chiron. Because of French participation in the League of Nations sanctions against Italy after the invasion of Abyssinia, Chiron, as a Frenchman, would have found it awkward to continue racing an Italian car.

Chiron, having practiced on the 1935 grand prix car before signing his contract, did not like the 1936 car at all. Neither did Fagioli, who liked only winners and winning. Caracciola did manage a victory in the rain-soaked season opener at Monaco on April 13 and the Tunis Grand Prix on May 17, but Fagioli's third at Tripoli on May 10 and Caracciola's second at Barcelona on June 7 were the only other times the car placed well all season. Except for several races when

Nuvolari was able to wring miracles from his Alfa, 1936 belonged as convincingly to Auto Union as 1935 had to Mercedes. Most of all, the year belonged to Bernd Rosemeyer. The car which terrified many who tried to drive it held no perils for him. Since his only previous competition experience had been with motorcycles, he had an advantage: he assumed all competition vehicles with four wheels drove like an Auto Union. Rosemeyer was a phenomenon. He won five races, the championship which Caracciola had gained the year before, and the place in many German hearts which had also been Rudi's.

Two weeks after Rosemeyer won the last grand prix of the season, Neubauer sent a memo to Kissel and the engineering department. It was cheerfully

Redeeming a lackluster summer, October, 1936: V12 engine, GP chassis, full envelope body. "The getaway and acceleration are fantastic," said Caracciola after the record runs. And the dismal GP season? "A small episode," Rudi scoffed. "Next year we shall all be there again."

headed: "Re: Thoughts about our intended records." To mitigate public displeasure and, more to the point, any official criticism resulting from Mercedes' poor showing on the grand prix circuit, Daimler-Benz decided to go record breaking. An engine bench tested at 616 bhp was installed in a 1936 grand prix chassis and enveloped in a highly streamlined body with fully enclosed wheels (a new idea in record breakers). On October 26 car and Caracciola were sent to the autobahn section just south of Frankfurt towards Darmstadt, which was closed for the day. Speeds of 226.4 mph for the kilometer and 228.0 for the mile Class B records were realized before the trials were halted by high winds. Returning on November 11, Caracciola did 10 miles at an average of 207.2 mph, the fastest 10 miles thus far recorded anywhere in the world. "The reason for our attack on the records is to cause a sensation," Neubauer had said in his memo. The company succeeded.

While Caracciola was dashing down the autobahn, back at the factory Daimler-Benz was building 30 prototypes of the people's car Ferdinand Porsche had designed for Hitler. At the Berlin Automobile Show the Führer had read an interminable speech, broadcast by the Ministry for Propaganda and People's Enlightenment into every automobile plant in the nation, which reaffirmed his intention to become Germany's Henry Ford.

In 1936 the United States had over 70 percent of the world's cars. Though German automobile production had increased strikingly in the three previous years, America, with a population just twice that of Germany, had 24 times more cars (24.2 million versus 1.1 million). In America there was one automobile for every 4.5 persons, but only one German in 49 owned a car.* Hitler remained determined to change all that. "The costs of this car will be brought into a tolerable relationship with the income of the broadest masses of our German people," he said in that broadcast, "as we have seen this done so bril-

liantly in America."

Hitler's price tag for his people's car was under 1,000 marks (about $240), less than half the price of America's cheapest cars at the time. But the National Socialist government, despite its promises, had not raised the living standard of the average German worker. Therefore, in order to buy one of America's low-priced three in 1936, an American worker needed to spend 300 percent less of his wages than a German would have had to spend for an automobile, even for one with a price tag under 1,000 marks.

And it was ludicrous to assume that a car selling for $240 could be produced profitably, as Kissel knew even before he set his men to building the 30 prototypes, which cost Daimler-Benz $2,765 each to produce, remarkably cheap for such a short run. Every other German auto maker knew it too, as had Ferdinand Porsche from the project's beginning, when he suggested 1,550 marks as the lowest feasible target price for mass production. Kissel might also have pointed to the Daimler-Benz experience with its small-car program. The Mercedes front-engine 170 models far outsold the rear-engine variations (the final figures were 65,439 versus 1,507). In the mid-thirties the German buying public preferred a conventional automobile with the engine in front. All these realities were irrelevant, however; as one German automobile executive of the period noted, "That was not a government you could fool around with."

By the spring of 1937, Daimler-Benz was completing the people's car prototype program and making final plans for the racing season. 1937 was supposed to have seen a new formula, but the AIACR had difficulty promulgating one agreeable to all manufacturers, so the 750-kg formula was extended a year.

Among the changes in the Daimler-Benz racing organization that Mercedes' dismal 1936 season had brought was the creation of the *Rennabteilung* (racing department), a new entity positioned between Neubauer's fiefdom and the central design office. In charge of it was a 30-year-old engineer, the son of a German father and a British mother and a veteran of five years with the company: Rudolf Uhlenhaut. The

---

*This put Germany behind France and Britain, which had one car per 19 and 21 persons respectively. Italy, with one car for every 103 persons, was even farther behind. Mussolini promoted racing more than automobiles.

executive who felt that Uhlenhaut, then involved in nothing racier than engineering work on the 170V sedan, was the new broom that could help sweep . Mercedes back into the winner's circle should be credited with one of the most inspired decisions in motor sporting history.

Shortly after taking his new post, Uhlenhaut loaded two 1936 grand prix cars on a trailer and took them to the Nürburgring to discover their defects for himself. "After I'd driven for a few miles I realized that a racing car was much the same as a passenger car," he said. "There's not much difference, nothing sensational." He returned to Stuttgart with two worn-out cars and the conviction that an entirely new design was needed to insure success in the 1937 season. After working with Wagner, Nallinger and their associates to design it, his responsibility was the assembly, preparation and testing of the cars before they were released to Neubauer's crew. He would prove himself as uniquely gifted in this work as Neubauer was in his.

Uhlenhaut's disclaimer aside, driving a competition machine is an experience quite unlike driving a sedan. "Naturally, it is a very great advantage to any team," the journalist George Monkhouse commented that year, "to have an engineer-designer who can also drive the car at racing speed without running into things!" Not only did Uhlenhaut not run into things, he was as adept behind the wheel as the professionals. As an engineer who could have been a race driver if he wanted to (he did not), Uhlenhaut was attuned to every nuance of a competition car's performance. Moreover, from the day he arrived, Mercedes drivers, as prone to occasional prima donna tantrums as any others, were reluctant to come forward with minor complaints about their cars lest Uhlenhaut hop in and a few laps later demonstrate that the trouble lay with the driver and not with the car.

But in 1937 Mercedes drivers had little to complain about. The new grand prix car was a great achievement, the *sine qua non* in race car construction for the next generation. Not until the Can-Am sports-racers of the late 1960s would any competition automobile equal the horsepower of the 1937 Mercedes grand prix car. The new 5.66-liter engine was bench tested at 646 bhp, twice the horsepower of the 1934 straight-eight, but it weighed only 41 pounds more—which gives an idea of the enormous progress Daimler-Benz engineers had made in their competition program. Sophisticated chassis and suspension design made for greater stability and improved road holding. The massive power of the engine meant that oversteer could be induced at will. The car was phenomenal, and even Neubauer wanted to experience it. During testing at Monza an armchair was installed behind the driver's seat for him: the team manager had asked for a ride to "observe the suspension," as he said. It was quite a sight, the ample Neubauer perched pontifically atop the car as Caracciola drove—rather briskly, it would seem, because Neubauer required some "reviving" after the run. He thereafter left all at-speed observations to Uhlenhaut.

Caracciola and von Brauchitsch remained with the team for 1937. Fagioli's and Chiron's contracts were not renewed. Auto Union claimed Fagioli; Chiron, who had crashed the year before in an accident Neubauer thought should not have happened, went into semi-retirement. His departure from the team was important for another reason: Caracciola had begun seeing Chiron's mistress, the fabulous Alice Hoffmann. American born, "Baby," as her friends called her, had a Swedish father, a German mother, had lived in France and loved Italy. Neubauer described her as a combination of French charm, German grit, Italian temperament, Swedish sex appeal and American business sense. Neubauer was enthusiastic about the new romance. The ladies in their lives were the personal timekeepers for most race drivers, and Baby Hoffmann was the best timekeeper in Europe.

Elevated to the number three spot on the Mercedes team was Hermann Lang, formerly Fagioli's mechanic and a reserve driver who had shown promise the year before. Another new recruit, via Sussex, Rugby and Cambridge and a fine career as an independent driver, was Richard John Beattie Seaman. Neubauer had been impressed with him during tryouts he held for new drivers, but it took some powerful persuading before the ONS accepted a Briton on the team, and that only with the permission

263

Rudolf Caracciola

Two wins and many retirements in '36, seven victories and finishes in the money in all other races in '37: Mercedes "there again" with the new W125 GP car. The sweeping victory in the Swiss Grand Prix (celebrated in the Mercedes poster at top, center) was led by Caracciola (above), at a 98.59 mph average. The Grand Prix of Monaco (top, right) was a one–two–three romp as well, von Brauchitsch leading the W125 pack. Typical of the occasional non-win was Eifelrennen (the Ludwig Hohlwein poster at top, left, reminiscent of his famous winter Olympics poster of '36), where winner Bernd Rosemeyer's Auto Union was followed across the finish line by Caracciola and von Brauchitsch. Only once all season did a Mercedes not win or follow the winner home — Belgium, where Lang and Kautz finished three–four. (Facing page, top) Avus, 1937. The new 43-degree banking on the north curve, ominously nicknamed the "wall of death," promised even higher speeds for this high-speed track — and since the May event was free formula, Mercedes and Auto Union built special cars for it. Caracciola (seen leading Rosemeyer) won the first heat, von Brauchitsch the second, Lang the finale at 162.61 mph — the world's fastest race. Rosemeyer finished fourth but had the world's fastest lap at 171.74 mph. (Center) Record car in which Caracciola took the Class B speed mark for the mile away from Auto Union at 268.496 mph, January, 1938. (Below) Bernd Rosemeyer, his October '37 Frankfurt Speed Week car, and the monument erected at the spot where he was killed attempting to regain the Class B record for Auto Union.

264

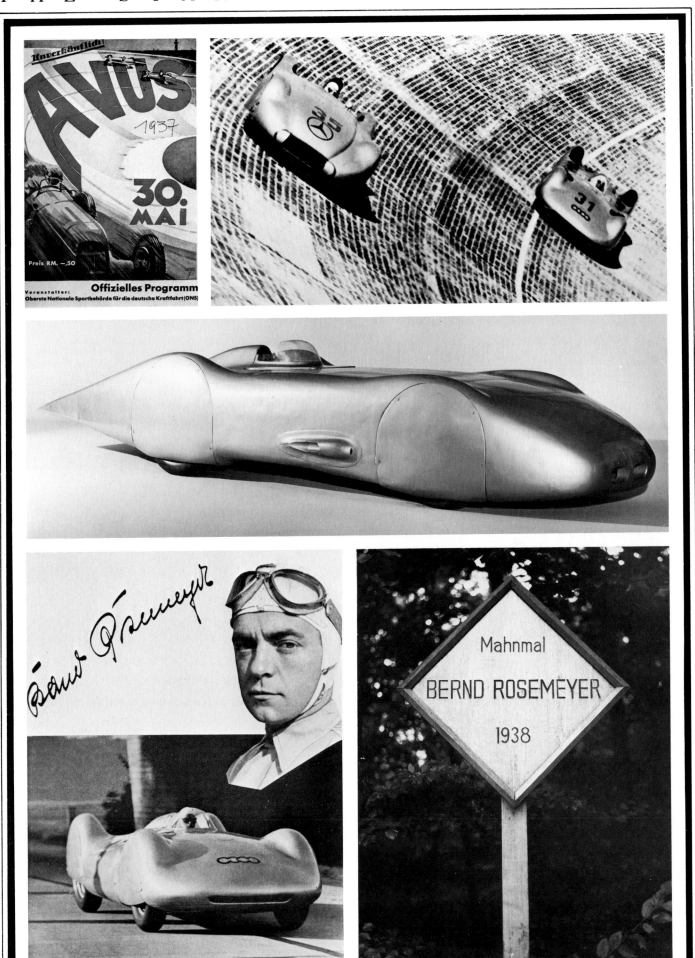

of Hitler himself. "Prominent personages" in Britain were said to favor Seaman's joining Mercedes in order to forge a friendly link between the two nations. *Der Englander* became Seaman's nickname.

It was a fabulous year of racing. At the season opener on May 9 in Tripoli, Caracciola and Seaman had trouble with sand in their superchargers, but Lang carried the day. Earlier he had had a problem of his own: failing the medical examination because of high blood pressure. The German teams' permanent medical officer signed an affidavit attesting to Lang's fitness and the examining Italian doctor finally waved Lang through, admonishing him to cut down on his smoking. Lang did not smoke. Nervous before his first major race, he was cheerfully kidded about it in the pits, but once the race started he put the jitters and the kidding aside and won at a convincing 134.4 mph. Even more convincing was his win at Avus later that month at 162.61 mph, a speed which would not be recorded at the Indianapolis 500 until the mid-1960s.

Except for the Belgian Grand Prix, won by Auto Union's reserve driver Rudi Hasse, only the incredible Rosemeyer could beat the Mercedes in 1937, and among the four races in which he did it was the Vanderbilt Trophy in New York.

Because the Vanderbilt and the Belgian Grand Prix were on consecutive weekends, Daimler-Benz divided its team between them, sending Lang and von Brauchitsch to Spa (Lang drove the fastest lap but finished third behind the Hasse and Stuck Auto Unions; von Brauchitsch retired) and Caracciola and Seaman to New York. Joining them for the transatlantic trip were Neubauer and Uhlenhaut, which may have been less an indication of the importance of the race than of export market considerations and the fact that the two men wanted a trip to America anyway. Three days before the *Bremen* sailed, Caracciola had married Alice Hoffmann—and Baby came along. It was a gala crossing.

Since the early twenties, when most board tracks had fallen down or been torn down and road races were but a memory, the only major American automobile race each year was the 500-mile classic at Indianapolis. The revival of the Vanderbilt Cup at Roosevelt Raceway on Long Island was an attempt to lure European cars and drivers to the States. The first race in 1936 was won by Tazio Nuvolari, who became the darling of the New York press; his victory brought favorable publicity to Alfa Romeo, and probably encouraged the German entry in 1937.

As soon as they arrived in New York, Caracciola and Seaman began practicing and Neubauer and Uhlenhaut began taking notes and watching the Indianapolis cars they would be competing against. There were a number of Alfas on hand as well—and Nuvolari, eager to repeat his victory. When practice was over and calculations had been made, Neubauer was alarmed: all the drivers would be able to complete the 300-mile race without refueling except Dick Seaman. His car's fuel tank was not quite as large as Caracciola's, and Neubauer, hoping his calculations were wrong, estimated Seaman would be caught a half-gallon short. By mid-distance Caracciola's supercharger had problems, and he retired; Nuvolari's engine gave out, and so did he. In the closing laps the race was between Rosemeyer and Seaman, with Seaman steadily closing in on the flying Auto Union; but Neubauer's calculations were correct. On the penultimate lap Seaman had to stop for fuel, 41 seconds were lost, and the Vanderbilt was deprived of a photo finish. Rex Mays, in an Alfa, followed five minutes later in third place. The first Indianapolis car to finish was Bill Cummings in the Burd Piston Ring Special.

It had been a good race, though attendance was just 75,000, about a third of that at a European grand prix. On the Continent motor racing was second only to cycling in spectator interest. In America the Vanderbilt had to vie with a wide variety of more popular sports in 1937. The year produced such headline events as Joe Louis winning the heavyweight boxing championship at 23, War Admiral's sweep of the Triple Crown, the *Ranger's* successful defense of the America's Cup, Don Budge leading the United States tennis team to the Davis Cup, and Joe DiMaggio's fabulous exploits with the Yankees. With such competition in the sports pages the excitement of the Vanderbilt Trophy motor race faded quickly away, not to be repeated.

On July 25, 350,000 spectators crowded the

Nürburgring for the German Grand Prix. Five Mercedes and five Auto Unions were to race against 16 Alfas, Maseratis and Bugattis. Korpsführer Hühnlein had again prepared a victory speech, but the lecture he gave the German drivers after practice was more memorable. Decorum in the pits was his subject, specifically that race drivers should be concentrating on the race, not nuzzling their wives or sweethearts before the start. "There's a principle involved," he fumed. "German men and women do not kiss in public." Neubauer knew there would be trouble when he spied his drivers and the Auto Union team snickering and plotting together after this reprimand. As the field massed for the start and Hühnlein took his seat in the grandstand, every driver of a German car vaulted from his seat, ran back to the pits and grabbed his lady in a long, passionate embrace. The crowd, assuming this mass display of affection was part of the ceremonies, cheered wildly. It is not known whether Neubauer was later advised to have a talk with his drivers, but if he was he would have had trouble keeping a straight face. Neubauer was famous among insiders for his impersonation of the Führer, which he routinely performed at victory dinners.

The 1937 German Grand Prix was part drama, part tragedy. At quarter distance, Ernst von Delius lost control of his Auto Union and slithered across Seaman's path. Seaman survived the crash with a broken nose and thumb; von Delius died of his injuries the next day. After the accident Caracciola, von Brauchitsch and Lang held the first three places. Nuvolari was fourth, driving a magnificent race in an outclassed Alfa Romeo. But Rosemeyer, catching up from eighth place after a wheel collapsed, was driving like a man possessed. He left the road momentarily at Wehrseifen but with the help of some spectators was quickly back on the course, with part of a haystack stuck on the back of the car; then he passed Nuvolari. Lang meanwhile had a tire fail and dropped out of contention, which put Rosemeyer in third, but he could catch up no further, crossing the finish line behind Caracciola and von Brauchitsch. To give an idea of how fast the race had been, Caracciola's winning 82.7 mph average was nearly a mile an hour faster than Rosemeyer's victory pace of the preceding year and a full 2 mph faster than von Brauchitsch's *lap* record of 1935. At the presentation stand, Hühnlein

Rudi Caracciola, in the widely distributed "matinee idol" portrait; at ease, and more like himself, with Moritz; and with Alice, on the terrace of their Lugano home. The Caracciolas' surprise wedding was witnessed by Rudi's friends, the Wilhelm Haspels. Neubauer was delighted with the marriage; he now had a new "assistant" in the pits. Baby's meticulously kept lap charts were the only ones he trusted thereafter, and she was probably the only person during that era who could call him a "lovable teddy bear" and get away with it. Solicitous of Rudi, she marveled at his skill. "The harder the race," she said, "the more calm and collected he seemed to become. He made it all look so easy."

read his victory speech as Caracciola was handed the huge "Goddess of Victory" trophy and Rosemeyer stuck a lighted cigarette in the figure's mouth.

Next, on August 8, was the Monaco Grand Prix, transferred from its usual spring date in an effort to popularize the principality during a slack season. This time the displeasure was all Neubauer's. From early on the race belonged to Mercedes; the Auto Unions had technical problems and all the French and Italian cars were far behind, so the only question was which Mercedes would win. Von Brauchitsch, whose last victory had been in 1934, was determined it would be his, and in defiance of team orders he proceeded to race with Caracciola. Pit stops resulted in the lead changing between them; a lengthy stop for Caracciola was followed by a spirited chase in which he broke the existing lap record by more than 12 seconds. The two cars were wheel to wheel coming to the corner past the pits, when Neubauer was furiously waving his flag ordering von Brauchitsch to let Caracciola pass. Von Brauchitsch responded by driving faster. Caracciola's final pit stop settled the issue. Von Brauchitsch's winning average on the serpentine course was 63.25 mph. Mercedes finished one-two-three; the team reserve driver, Christian Kautz, was third.

There was another clean sweep in the Swiss Grand Prix (Caracciola-Lang-von Brauchitsch), and one-two victories in the Italian Grand Prix (Caracciola-Lang) and the Czechoslovakian Grand Prix (Caracciola-von Brauchitsch). Rosemeyer was third in each of the latter races. The Mercedes crew had noted more than casually that behind the wheel of one of the Auto Unions at Bern was none other than Nuvolari, trying out the car; but the implications of that were submerged by the success of the rest of the season. The final score was seven Mercedes victories, and Caracciola was once again the European champion.

Three weeks after the last 1937 grand prix, in late October, a German Record Week was held on the Frankfurt-Darmstadt-Heidelberg autobahn. Rosemeyer won that one. A Mercedes record car was on hand, but Caracciola could not come close to Rosemeyer's speed without the front end tending to "aviate," as one onlooker said. With a new nose and

175 pounds of lead ballast, the Mercedes returned to the autobahn and Rudi did 248 mph. But Rosemeyer did 252.

It was back to the drawing board in Stuttgart, as a few strings were pulled in Berlin to allow for a new attempt with a revised car that January, before the opening of the Berlin Automobile Show—maneuvers that did not pass unnoticed in the Auto Union camp. On the twenty-seventh the Mercedes crew—Caracciola, von Brauchitsch as standby, Neubauer as organizer and swarms of mechanics—returned to the autobahn, setting up headquarters in a hotel in Frankfurt. Checking with the weather bureau at the Frankfurt airport, Neubauer learned that conditions for an attempt would be ideal early the next morning but that significant winds were expected by 9 A.M. Neubauer telephoned the factory with that news and asked if the car would be ready in time. The car could be on the way to them no earlier than 2:00 A.M., he was told. It arrived shortly before seven. Just past eight, after giving Baby a kiss and his dachshund Moritz a pat on the head, Caracciola got in and regained the record for Mercedes at 268 mph.

"She revs up too quickly," Rudi said afterwards, observing that with a higher axle ratio the car could do 280 easily. "Fine," Neubauer replied, "we'll call it a day." He sent the car to the workshop in Frankfurt for the axle change, saying they would "try again tomorrow." Trying again was deemed necessary because among the first people pushing through the crowd to congratulate Caracciola after his run was Rosemeyer, who smiled and said, "My turn now." An Auto Union was rolled onto the autobahn. Aware of the crosswind that had greeted him at the far end of the run, Caracciola suggested that his rival wait until the next day. Rosemeyer said not to worry, he was one of the "lucky ones." The Mercedes crew returned to Frankfurt, but even Neubauer could not concentrate on breakfast; they went back to the autobahn to watch Rosemeyer. He did a practice run at 268 mph. Shortly before noon, he made the record attempt. A crosswind caught his car, it crashed, and Rosemeyer was dead. Neubauer, Caracciola and von Brauchitsch sat silently for a long time, "unmoving, like statues," in Rudi's words. Record breaking was over for the moment.

The following month Hitler opened the Berlin Automobile Show. "The national spirit is so strong in Germany," *Motor Sport* reported, "that other interests have to take second place." Fourteen German automakers were exhibited in the main hall. Non-German products were few: Italy had three exhibits, Britain, Austria, France and the United States one each. In his opening speech in 1937 Hitler had announced Germany's plan to be self-sufficient in fuel and rubber within two years, and this year a special hall was devoted to exhibits of progress made thus far with synthetic materials. Not on hand was Hitler's long-awaited people's car, though there was a relief model of the enormous factory near Fallersleben where Hitler planned to build it.

A few weeks after the 1938 Berlin show, Germany marched into Austria. In April Hitler engineered a plebiscite indicating that 99.75 percent of the Austrian people wished to be part of the Third Reich. A demand for "self-determination" for the Sudetenland followed, but not before Hitler laid the cornerstone for his people's car factory on May 26. For this occasion several thousand construction workers had been given the day off to attend the ceremony, the bricklayers in white with black top hats, the carpenters in black velvet suits. Uniforms were everywhere and Ferdinand Porsche was conspicuous in a trench coat and no hat. And it was here that Hitler formally named his automobile. It would be called the Kraft durch Freude (Strength through Joy) car, he said, or KdF-Wagen.* Porsche was horrified. How could the car be exported with a name like that?

"An act of such gigantic proportions as to be without parallel in the entire history of mankind," said one fawning local reporter about the Fallersleben factory, which was to be the largest automobile plant in the world. Since private industry was incapable of producing a 990-mark car, Hitler would do it himself. Of course, he would have help: the capital needed to get into production would be provided by the German people themselves through a scheme by which a worker diverted five marks of his weekly wages (more if he could afford it) into a KdF-Wagen savings fund. After investing 750 marks in this pay-before-you-get-it plan, the potential KdF-Wagen owner would be given an order number with delivery promised whenever the car was ready. Despite Hitler's statement that his car would "provide the broadest masses of our people with joy" and would not compete with private industry, every German auto maker felt threatened, especially during this period when protestation woud have been both futile and unwise.*

For the moment, however, Kissel could reflect on the good year 1937 had been. Mercedes-Benz passenger car production had exceeded 25,000, the highest output to date; commercial vehicle production was up to 12,367, and the company was building aviation engines for the government. Lucrative government contracts for aircraft engines had been among the inducements offered Daimler-Benz and other auto makers to encourage their participation in motor sport: go racing, the government said in effect, and we'll give you substantial contracts in other areas so that you can continue racing. Now a Daimler-Benz aircraft engine was being planned for use in a new Mercedes-Benz car . . . to break the land speed record.

Auto Union driver Hans Stuck was the catalyst in this project, and Porsche was the designer of the car. The peculiar circumstances were these. The land speed record at the time, 301.13 mph, was held by Sir Malcolm Campbell. He had set it with his Rolls-Royce aircraft-engine Bluebird on the Bonneville salt flats in Utah in the fall of 1935. Stuck wanted to break the record. Since Hitler was fond of records— "that suits our propaganda," he was quoted as saying —Stuck was convinced he could get government permission. Porsche, who by now had disassociated himself from Auto Union, was excited at the prospect, but said he would need at least 3,000 hp for the

---

*Kraft durch Freude was the organization through which the Third Reich controlled all German leisure activities, from chess playing and bird-watching to participant sports, entertainment and vacation travel.

*Eventually the factory area near Fallersleben became known as Wolfsburg and the name of the KdF-Wagen was changed to Volkswagen. But all that, of course, is someone else's story.

BERN 20./21. AUGUST 1938

V. GROSSER PREIS DER SCHWEIZ
Vᵉ GRAND PRIX DE SUISSE

OFFIZIELLES PROGRAMM MIT STARTLISTE FR. 1.—
VERLAG: DIENAG AKTIENGESELLSCHAFT · ZÜRICH

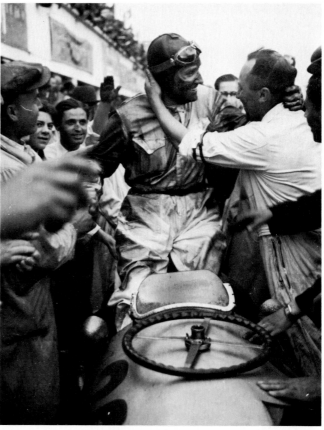

A new formula, the new three-liter V12 W154, and a smashing race season, 1938. At the Nürburgring, pleased after practice (facing page, below) were von Brauchitsch, Seaman, Lang and Caracciola; Neubauer usually smiled only after victories, which he did the next day when Seaman (facing page, top, left) won the German Grand Prix. Two weeks before von Brauchitsch (this page, top) had won the French GP, with Caracciola and Lang following. And the Swiss GP was another one–two–three Mercedes parade finish: Caracciola, Seaman (seen during practice, above) and von Brauchitsch. Mercedes won six races in 1938, three of them clean sweeps. Only late in the season did Nuvolari snatch two victories for Auto Union, including the finale at Donington. Lang broke his windshield, Seaman lost a lap after an oil skid, von Brauchitsch drove with a badly blistered hand — and the three of them followed Tazio across the finish line. At the banquet, Nuvolari jokingly apologized for his victory but said Mercedes had "won quite enough" already but might win more if they "built some new cars." Even Neubauer practically fell off his chair laughing.

job, 500 hp more than the British-government-owned Rolls-Royce unit in the Bluebird. So far as was officially known, no German aircraft engine was even 1,000 hp strong, but Daimler-Benz had recently completed the design of a V12 unit which promised 1,300 hp. Since the government aviation procurement director was an old friend of Stuck, he had little difficulty in arranging for the loan of two of these units. As for the Porsche-designed car to be built around them, Stuck naturally approached his employer first, but Auto Union could not afford the nearly one million marks (about $300,000) required for the project. Stuck next tried Daimler-Benz. Kissel was skeptical, recalling Porsche's acrimonious exit from the company in the late twenties; but Porsche himself was delighted with the idea, since he still regarded Daimler-Benz with esteem, looked on his period with the company as "one of the most interesting" in his career, and thought of his former engineering colleagues as friends he would enjoy working with again. Neubauer liked the project for another reason: Stuck had no peer in sprints and hill climbs, and that sort of short-distance expertise was perfect for a land speed record man. Kissel finally approved, for a typically pragmatic reason: "If we say no, then Stuck takes our two engines and goes to another firm to have the car built."

And so the car was built at Daimler-Benz with the assumption that when it was ready it would be taken to Utah, where the Bonneville salt flats were generally agreed to be the world's best site for land speed record attempts. But by 1938, when the car was nearing completion, Hitler's plans for Czechoslovakia were making the world nervous, and Korpsführer Hühnlein had stoutly declared that a "German world record must obviously be achieved on German soil." A section of the autobahn would be built south of Dessau for the purpose. That a narrow highway could not possibly provide the optimal conditions of Bonneville's salt flats was irrelevant. *

Meanwhile the 1938 grand prix season began. The new formula offered constructors a choice of supercharged or unsupercharged engines (up to 3 liters for the former, 4½ for the latter) with a sliding scale of minimum weight from 400 to 850 kilograms proportionate to engine size. The new Mercedes engine was a supercharged 3.0-liter V12, and the car was lower, longer and sleeker than its predecessor. The new Auto Union was a V12 too, with the engine located amidships. The car looked more conventional, but it was still tricky to handle, and Auto Union had lost the one man who could handle it best when the brilliant Rosemeyer died.

The first race on the calendar was on April 10 at Pau, a pretty French town near the Spanish border where a round-the-houses circuit for a grand prix had been established in 1933. Mercedes had never bothered with the event before and doubtless regretted afterwards that it went this time. But since the new Mercedes was ready and the new Auto Union was not, the decision was made to use Pau as a tryout for the season ahead. Two drivers, Caracciola and Lang, were sent. Lang's car misbehaved during practice and was scratched; the other car completed the event, with Caracciola and Lang sharing the driving, and was beaten by a French Delahaye driven by the French René Dreyfus. Dreyfus had driven a clever race, aware that his "overgrown toy," as he described the Delahaye, was better suited than the Mercedes to the twisty Pau course, and also that he could complete the race nonstop, which the Mercedes could not. Daimler-Benz, as chagrined as the French had been after the Mercedes victory surprises in the 1908 and 1914 French Grand Prix, chose to emphasize that the fastest lap at Pau, a course record, had been put up by Lang after the refueling pit stop when he desperately tried to catch the Delahaye.

Pau was a disappointment in Stuttgart. And anyone at Daimler-Benz with a good memory and service dating back to the turn of the century, veterans like Christian Lautenschlager, for example, might have warned management about Emil Jellinek's excursion

---

*Daimler-Benz also planned an excursion to the Indianapolis 500 in 1938, a logical follow-up of its Vanderbilt run the year before. Neubauer booked space for the cars on a ship leaving Bremerhaven on May 11, but by the end of April the trip was canceled, largely because of a technical misunderstanding about specifications for running at Indianapolis. The political situation and Hühnlein may have contributed to the cancellation, too. In 1939 Neubauer again referred to 500 participation as "desired," but that was as far as that year's plans went.

to Pau in 1901 to try the very first Mercedes ever built. That too had ended dismally—but was followed by smashing victories during Nice Week. The rest of 1938 was equally smashing for Mercedes.

The Grand Prix of Tripoli, on May 15, was the next Mercedes contest, the cars having performed well on that fast eight-mile circuit in the past. Since 1934, when Libya became an Italian colony under the governorship of Italo Balbo, an Italian Air Force marshal and motoring enthusiast, the Grand Prix of Tripoli had emerged as the glamor event of the racing season, with a white tie reception at the palace following each race. In 1937 Lang, running his first race as a first-string driver, had neglected to bring tails with him (he didn't own any), and after his victory had sat sheepishly in a business suit next to Balbo at the head table. He packed tails this year.

Joining Lang in Tripoli were Caracciola and von Brauchitsch (the Italian organizers allowed only three cars from each entrant this year). Neubauer's suggestion that Seaman's car be painted British racing green and run as an independent was disallowed. Alfa Romeo was running four cars, however; Raymond Sommer entered as a French independent. Apparently the organizers hoped that holding down the number of German cars would produce a better Italian showing, but it did not: the finishing order was Lang-von Brauchitsch-Caracciola. Sommer's "French" Alfa was fourth, followed by two Maseratis and Dreyfus' Delahaye. (Auto Union was not on hand.) Tragically, a Maserati and an Alfa driver were killed in the race; the post-race celebration was canceled.

The French Grand Prix, which the two previous seasons had been run as a sports car event, returned this year as a proper grand prix on July 3 at Rheims. Auto Union competed, but its cars retired after the first lap. Four French cars started, but finished dismally. Three Mercedes were on the starting line and finished one-two-three: von Brauchitsch-Caracciola-Lang. Von Brauchitsch's race average of 101.13 mph was faster than the previous lap record.

Next, on July 24, came the German Grand Prix, where Neubauer could run a full team; Seaman would have his chance at last. But the competition was more formidable now. Auto Union had indeed enticed Nuvolari aboard, and Stuck was back after a brief absence. But in practice the Mercedes consistently recorded better lap times than its German rival and easily outpaced the Alfas and Delahayes. At the starting line, Nuvolari, a favorite at the Nürburgring, was given an ovation, but the only matter troubling Neubauer was Rudi Caracciola: he had a bad case of worms, an ailment prettified as indigestion in the public announcement.

From the standpoint of activity in the pits, this was Neubauer's busiest race of the season. At the end of the first lap the four Mercedes were in the lead, but Lang's car began misfiring and Caracciola began to realize that he should not be driving. On the ninth lap he came in, feeling miserable, and Lang took over his car. Three Mercedes were now in the lead, with Stuck and Nuvolari their only possible challengers; Nuvolari, racing the difficult Auto Union for the first time, had ditched his first car and taken over another. On the sixteenth of 22 laps, the three Stuttgart cars remained comfortably in front.

Then von Brauchitsch, who was leading, came in for refueling, a routine Mercedes mechanics had developed into a fine art, pressure-feeding the fuel at five gallons a second. But this time the tank was overfilled, and when it started up again the car caught fire. Neubauer dragged von Brauchitsch from the cockpit and beat out the flames on his arm as three mechanics with fire extinguishers rushed to the car. Meanwhile Seaman, just 10 seconds behind von Brauchitsch, had pulled in for *his* refueling, which his mechanic performed even though his coveralls caught fire in the process. That blaze was extinguished and Seaman sent back on the track, but von Brauchitsch's car was a mass of foam, its driver clearly shaken. Korpsführer Hühnlein, who had been standing nearby, walked over to von Brauchitsch to say that surely he was not planning to retire from the race. Of course not, von Brauchitsch replied, and Hühnlein departed. "Don't let him drive," von Brauchitsch's mechanic begged Neubauer as the crew began wiping the foam from the car, "he's trembling all over." But Neubauer had been overruled. Von Brauchitsch crashed on the next lap, fortunately without injury,

273

and Seaman went on to a spectacular victory, with Lang second, followed by Stuck and Nuvolari. "God Save the King" was played in Seaman's honor after the German national anthem. Neubauer was summoned back to the pits, where a government official announced he was being held responsible for von Brauchitsch's accident and that an inquiry would follow. Neubauer told him who had sent von Brauchitsch back into the race. There was no inquiry.

Next Mercedes won the Coppa Ciano and the Coppa Acerbo. The Swiss Grand Prix followed on August 21. Winning had become so easy by now that Neubauer almost forgot he was team manager and enjoyed the dice for the lead between Caracciola and Seaman as much as the spectators did. But it rained in Bern, and in the rain the *Regenmeister* was unbeatable. The finish was Caracciola-Seaman-von Brauchitsch.

Neubauer had planned a victory dinner for 70 after the Italian Grand Prix on September 11. He enjoyed planning parties almost as much as he liked managing races and he was equally good at it, arranging the seating so that languages and personalities meshed, planning the menu and selecting the wines. The only problem was that after the Italian Grand Prix there was no victory to celebrate. Mercedes' best was only third place; Nuvolari, by now accustomed to the Auto Union, won convincingly, with Alfa a surprising second. The press was delighted; one reporter commented that the season had become "a little monotonous." Neubauer, in a foul mood, called off the victory dinner.

But there was cause to celebrate something that night: Seaman had become engaged to Erika Popp, the beautiful 18-year-old daughter of BMW's managing director.

By now Seaman was as deeply involved in the Mercedes racing effort and as strong a spokesman for the marque as Caracciola. That summer, when *The Autocar* published an article entitled "When Nations Take to Racing," contending that motor sport had no purpose but the aggrandizement of the countries involved, Seaman wrote a reasoned response. "This letter is not intended as a sales talk," he wrote, "but I can assure you that the suspension and road-holding

of this year's Mercedes racing cars would have been considered utterly incredible four years ago." He further noted that the recently introduced 770K model followed the same "principle of chassis and suspension design as the 1937 Mercedes racing cars." But over and above his loyalty to Mercedes *Der Englander* had become fond of Germany; and now he had fallen in love with a German girl.

He did have some clashes with the German drivers, but age, not nationality, was involved. Caracciola was 37 now and occasionally suffered at the appearance on the scene of talented youngsters like Lang, who was 29, and Seaman, just 25. Von Brauchitsch, four years Caracciola's junior, was something of a snob, regarding Lang's rapid rise from mechanic to world-class driver as an affront and failing to understand why the well-born Seaman had become so friendly with the parvenu. (Youthful exuberance sometimes got the better of Seaman and Lang, who both bristled under Neubauer's rules.) But all differences were forgotten that September night in a small Milan restaurant when the Mercedes team got together to celebrate Seaman's engagement. Baby Caracciola's pet monkey, Anatol, who went to all the races, enlivened the proceedings, and Baby promised to instruct Erika in the art of timekeeping. The party went on until dawn.

The next race on the calendar was the Donington Grand Prix scheduled for October 1. The Mercedes team had had an unsettling trip to England. Paris, where they stopped over, was in turmoil, with trains and highways jammed as people left the city. In London trenches were being dug in Hyde Park, gas masks issued, and sandbags placed in front of Buckingham Palace; children were being evacuated from schools and hospitals emptied. After Hitler's ultimatum to Czechoslovakia, war seemed imminent. "We weren't so very interested in politics," Uhlenhaut later said of the Mercedes racing organization. "We were all rather surprised that it came up." Now, in London in September 1938, politics was coming up all around them.

On the twenty-seventh the Royal Automobile Club gave a luncheon in Seaman's honor. The German drivers, Neubauer and Uhlenhaut attended. It

The Type 80 (top) was designed by Ferdinand Porsche and built by Mercedes for Hans Stuck to break the land speed record at Bonneville, Utah. But the Third Reich decreed the attempt be made on German soil and paved five miles of the median strip on the Dessau autobahn. Run there in February, 1939, was a three-liter car (above) in which Caracciola set a Class D standing start mile record of 127.1 mph. The small grille in front brought fresh air to the carburetors; a rear-mounted chest filled with ice provided cooling for the engine. T80 never made it to Dessau. When war came, the car was parked at the factory; its engine was removed and returned to the aviation department.

was a friendly gathering, if not a spirited one; though the French teams had already been called home, Neubauer told the RAC that, for the moment, he hoped they could remain. Erika Popp arrived from Munich that evening. The next morning Lang came down from his room to say that only military music could be heard on German radio. Seaman and Erika sat quietly on a sofa in the hotel lobby. By noon the orders came to leave. Neubauer quickly organized the loading of the cars onto their transporters and the trip to Harwich. It was harder to say goodbye. Neubauer was close to tears and, as he said of the young British driver he regarded almost as a son, "his eyes were also suspiciously moist." Erika Popp said she would remain with Dick Seaman, "whatever happens."

The next day at a meeting in Munich Hitler was given the Sudetenland, and Neville Chamberlain returned to England with a piece of paper guaranteeing "peace in our time." For the moment, the crisis was over. All the participants returned for the Donington Grand Prix, rescheduled for October 22. Nuvolari put on a dazzling show for Auto Union's second victory of the season, with Lang second and Seaman third. Caracciola, nursing a foot injury received in the Italian Grand Prix, had not been at Donington, but his victories during the season brought him the European championship for the third time.

Two months later, on December 7, Dick Seaman and Erika Popp were married in London.

By February 1939, when the Berlin Automobile Show opened, it was obvious that although Hitler's global plans remained in doubt, one conquest was complete. The German automobile industry had been taken over by the state. In the past six months commercial vehicle production had been brought under government rule, and now passenger-car programs were to be similarly regulated. At the ceremonial opening of the show, Hitler announced that the number of German car types would be "drastically reduced," and indeed he was the only German auto maker to display a new model. The KdF-Wagen held center stage, flanked by huge crimson velvet curtains. Production of the people's car was slated to begin within the year.

"German automobile manufacturers generally ap-prove the step taken by the Government," Edwin P. A. Heinze reported in the American trade magazine *Automotive Industries*. This was nonsense, of course, but the Third Reich propaganda machine was in high gear, and no auto maker dared risk the consequences of anything but willing compliance. In March, Kissel took the opportunity of a written directive from Jakob Werlin ordering a 770K Mercedes for Hitler to complain as much as he dared. The Mercedes letter seems to have been written by Haspel, who four years before had adroitly put a stop to the Third Reich's involvement in Daimler-Benz affairs, and he co-signed it. "Since we must live by the principles of the Führer, we naturally do not have a need to ask or to find out why," the letter noted at one point, and carried on with a litany of carefully phrased remarks about the Third Reich's incompetence in automotive matters. The government incursion into truck production was the chief topic: "As far as we are concerned, the quality is not up to our German standards, certainly not our company standards." A coda complained of parts distribution: "It seems lately that under the Führer's sanction you can represent anything you want to represent without asking how it will affect the company" and expressed the "hope and wish" that "in the future we will be able to send things to the exhibitions that our company may be proud of."

By late March, after the capitulation of Czechoslovakia, Hitler demanded Danzig from Poland. Chamberlain, offended by this breach of the Munich Agreement, pledged that Britain would go to war if Germany attacked Poland; the French endorsed the pledge. One afternoon in Neubauer's office Seaman suggested that Hitler was a congenital liar; Neubauer was grateful that they were alone and that his secretary had "an admirable gift for going deaf when occasion demanded it." In late March, from their new home in Garmisch, a wedding present from Erika's father, Seaman wrote Lord Howe, the president of the British Racing Drivers' Club, for advice about the advisability of his remaining with Mercedes. In late April, after consulting with a cabinet minister as well as members of Parliament and the Admiralty, and despite "the awful possibility of war," Lord

Howe encouraged Seaman to stay with the team because retaining "every individual [German] contact" was the best course. "After all," he advised, "our relations with Germany still continue nominally friendly."

Germany was still nominally friendly with Italy as well, though these nations' rivalry in motor sport provided one of the year's rare moments of comic relief. "There is something rather amusing in the thought of the Italians carefully limiting the race to 1,500cc cars so as to break the run of German victories in their great race, only to receive an entry of two Mercedes-Benz after all," *Motor Sport* reported before the Tripoli Grand Prix. "It would be even more amusing if the Mercedes won..." A 1.5-liter ceiling on entries was as subtle as an avalanche, particularly since Alfa Romeo and Maserati were so competitive in voiturette class racing, and it was known that Germany had no 1.5-liter race cars. The new formula for Tripoli had been announced at Monza during the Italian Grand Prix in September 1938, and since Tripoli came only eight months later, the race organizers naturally assumed that no new German car would be ready in time. Not since 1934 had an Italian car won Italy's glamor race in North Africa (Mercedes had won three times, Auto Union once), so 1938 seemed a sure thing.

But the Daimler-Benz racing engineers decided to give it a try. Sailer's promise of a financial bonus if they succeeded made the months of long days bearable—and the car that resulted was Mercedes' first V8, a jewel of a small, streamlined racer. Though the car was developed in secrecy, news that it was in the works was leaked in February 1939 by Charles Faroux, the *doyen* of French auto journalists, and an Italian reporter appeared at the factory and asked to see the 1,500cc car. A 1.5-liter car was duly dragged out of a workshop for him; he made copious notes and took many pictures. But the car was a Targa Florio Mercedes from 1922, the last time the company had built a 1,500cc competition automobile.

Only two examples of the new car could be built at such short notice. Caracciola and Lang were sent to Tripoli to drive them. "The tough little guy," Lang

called the new model; Rudi found the cars "graceful, like toys." Since there were just two of them against a field of 28 Alfa Romeos and Maseratis, the Mercedes engineers had geared Lang's car for maximum speed and Caracciola's slightly lower, for better acceleration. The idea was to drive the first car hard from the outset, to exhaust the opposition, with the second car ready to take over if the "rabbit" wore itself out. Neither driver liked the plan much, Lang because he preferred to win his third consecutive Tripoli rather than be the pacesetter, Caracciola because he didn't relish a young driver getting the faster car. Neubauer tried to convince them that their chances for success were equal; Sailer finally ended matters by pointing out that more than personal glory was at stake, and only one star mattered that day, the three-pointed one. But a quirk of circumstance helped decide the winner. At the starting line, Lang noticed that there were both signal lights and Marshal Balbo with starting flag in hand, and asked Neubauer which he should go by. Neubauer, having checked with the officials, was able to get word to "use the lights" only to Lang before the start. The lights were faster than Balbo, who Neubauer said was suffering from "faulty ignition" that day, and Lang was off with the green light, stealing a march on Caracciola and all the Italian drivers, whose eyes were dutifully fixed on their host for the post-race party at the palace. Lang's finish was no less spectacular than his start; during the second half of the race he was even able to ease up a little. He crossed the finish line to win at 122.9 mph; Caracciola came in second, nearly a lap behind. The Alfas and Maseratis followed.

The one-two finish at Tripoli, with a pair of cars built in just eight months' time, was Mercedes' most spectacular feat in a successful year. The team won five events in regulation grand prix competition in 1939, to Auto Union's two. Lang competed in ten races and won seven and the European Championship.

But that same year a Mercedes driver was killed, the only member of the Mercedes team to die in six years of grand prix competition. A prize of 100,000 francs had been offered for the fastest lap in the Belgian Grand Prix on June 25. Seaman was going

In 1930 Hermann Lang was a champion motorcyclist for Standard, a job he lost as the Depression set in. Finding other work wasn't easy. Lang drove a locomotive awhile, then was hired in 1933 as a mechanic in Mercedes' race department. "I hear you want to be a race driver," Neubauer said to him in '35. Fearful of losing his job, Lang said no. Try it, replied Neubauer condescendingly, "you can bring your grandmother's underpants and cap along." As Lang remembered, Neubauer was "probably thinking, well, so much for this chicken." Lang tried it. By 1937 he was a full member of Mercedes' race team. In 1938, after his second consecutive Tripoli win, Hitler joined him for a photo session (Werlin stands between). In '39, with five GP victories (Pau, above, among them), Lang was European champion.

MERCEDES-BENZ
RACING SUCCESSES
1938-1939.
ALL VICTORIES WERE GAINED WITH THE
NEW RACING CAR DEVELOPED IN ACCORDANCE
WITH THE RACING FORMULA 1938
1938

GRAND PRIX OF TRIPOLI	1st 2nd 3rd
GRAND PRIX OF FRANCE	1st 2nd 3rd
GRAND PRIX OF GERMANY	1st 2nd
COPPA CIANO – LIVORNO	1st
COPPA ACERBO – PRESCARA	1st
GRAND PRIX OF SWITZERLAND	1st 2nd 3rd

RUDOLF CARACCIOLA BECOMES FOR THE
THIRD TIME EUROPEAN CHAMPION ON
„MERCEDES-BENZ" IN 1938.
1939

GRAND PRIX OF PAU	1st 2nd
INTERNATIONAL EIFEL RACE NÜRBURGRING	1st 3rd 4th
VIENNA HÖHENSTRASSE RACE	1st 3rd
GRAND PRIX OF BELGIUM	1st 3rd
GRAND PRIX OF GERMANY ON THE NÜRBURGRING	1st
GRAND HILL CLIMBING PRIX OF GERMANY GROSSGLOCKNER ROAD	1st
GRAND PRIX OF SWITZERLAND	1st 2nd 3rd

HERMANN LANG EUROPEAN CHAMPION OF 1939.

95375

"We all danced for joy," said Lang after the first factory test drives of W165 (above), the 1½-liter voiturette built for the 1939 Tripoli GP. Mercedes was even happier after the race. Not only had Lang–Caracciola finished one–two against 28 Italian cars but Lang's 122.9 mph average was 13 mph faster than the Maserati that had won the 1500 cc class the year before. Mercedes' point being made, the team returned to the 3-liter W154 GP car for the rest of the season. Caracciola (top right) won the German GP on July 23 as the Graf Zeppelin hovered over the Nürburgring. The following week Sammy Davis reported in *The Autocar* that the army had "taken possession of the circuit as a test ground."

for it when he crashed. In the hospital, before the driver died, Alfred Neubauer for the first time cursed racing and his own part in it; Baby Caracciola never forgot the sight of the Mercedes team manager, weeping uncontrollably, and then steeling himself to make the arrangements to send Seaman home. Erika Seaman cried herself to sleep that night in Baby Caracciola's arms.

The following day Kissel ordered all cars to be cleared from Mercedes showrooms in Germany and replaced with Seaman's portrait. At Dover the ferry carrying his body was met by the British Mercedes manager. The Daimler-Benz board was represented at his funeral by Haspel and Carl Schippert. Neubauer was there with Caracciola, Lang and von Brauchitsch; several members of the Auto Union team were on hand as well, and many of Seaman's former British racing colleagues. Erika Seaman, ashen, was steadied by her father.

Three weeks later, Lillian Beattie-Seaman, Dick's mother, wrote to the Mercedes board expressing her gratitude to the company for the "help and encouragement" given her son and for the years with the team which "were without doubt the happiest of his life."

Among the flowers at Seaman's funeral was a large wreath of Madonna lilies from Hitler. The gesture was widely reported; some thought it was a hopeful

sign that peace might still be possible. Two months later Hitler ordered his army into Poland.

Promoting the Berlin auto show and Hitler's automobile, 1939. Since announcement of the layaway plan, over 330,000 Germans had begun making payments for a KdF-Wagen. Not one car had yet been delivered. Not one would be.

CHAPTER EIGHT

RUIN, REBIRTH AND RENAISSANCE

1 9 4 0 – 1 9 5 4

Hope, like the gleaming taper's light,
Adorns and cheers our way;
And still, as darker grows the night,
Emits a brighter ray.
—OLIVER GOLDSMITH,
THE TRAVELLER

On May 8, 1945—V-E Day—the Allies turned their full attention from Europe to the Orient. But in Stuttgart there were no thoughts of Japan. Daimler-Benz had survived its second world war, outlived 12 years of the National Socialist Regime and reached the age—if one counted from the date of Benz's patent—of 59. But where the company was concerned the world was ready to use the past tense instead of the present, because little more was left of Daimler-Benz than of Germany itself.

What happened in Germany from the beginning of the Nazi movement in the 1920s until the end of World War II has been documented in thousands of books, movies and television shows. What happened to Daimler-Benz during this period is not well known outside Germany. Seen from a distance of 40 or 50 years and from the viewpoint of the broad public of the English-speaking countries, the company's principal pre-war activity—except possibly for building race cars—was providing parade transport for Hitler. Whenever he was photographed in a vehicle,

Hitler's parade car: the Type 770 "Grosser Mercedes." Hitler's war: Intermittent bombing of the Daimler-Benz factory complex at Unterturkheim began in 1941; after two weeks of day and night raids in September 1944, the factory was gone.

it was a Mercedes-Benz. Even today there are char-latans selling tickets to view cars that supposedly belonged to Hitler or to his mistress, Eva Braun, or perhaps to Hermann Göring, the head of the Luft-waffe. To this day, companies that rent vintage vehi-cles to film companies prize their mid-thirties Mercedes as profit centers, for there is always an-other movie maker who wants to sell *his* interpretation of history's greatest calamity.

What happened at Daimler-Benz was on the one hand relatively simple and on the other unbelievably complicated and ironic. Daimler-Benz products were as much a part of the German war effort as GM, Ford and Chrysler products were of the American or Rolls-Royce aircraft engines were of the British. From a German standpoint Daimler-Benz's leading contribution was probably the development and pro-duction of the DB 600 series aircraft engines, those V12, fuel-injected, turbocharged powerplants that were in practically every important Luftwaffe plane, not least the Messerschmitt 109. In addition there was the normal complement of trucks, tanks, and whatever else it took to move a modern army. The aircraft engine program had begun in the mid-1930s when Fritz Nallinger left the vehicle group and took over what was euphemistically called "large engine"

development. That Nallinger and his people did their job well is a matter of history.

The internal workings of Daimler-Benz, and its relationship to the New Order of Germany, were more involved. As Hitler and the National Socialists took control of industry, daily living, and even daily thought processes, it became more difficult to main-tain any sort of independence, especially after the government started actively building up the military establishment in the mid-1930s.

It is a matter of record that Kissel, and some of his colleagues, joined the National Socialist party after the takeover of 1933. Evidence indicates that Kissel may have taken this step in an effort to keep his company as free as possible from government influ-ence, though he could not have realized at the time just how pervasive that influence would soon become. The Daimler-Benz "house Nazi" was Jakob Werlin, who had become friendly with Hitler during the latter's Munich years in the mid-twenties and who later be-came his personal advisor on matters relating to trans-portation. Werlin was the manager of Daimler-Benz's Munich branch, which was important not only be-cause of the sales volume generated in the Bavarian capital, but also because in that position he was responsible for export sales to the Balkan countries.

Untertürkheim, 1945. The German surrender found the country devastated. "Neither pictures nor descriptions can adequately convey the extent," an American reporter wrote. Cities were dead, factories idle, bridges down, rails gone. Rubble was everywhere.

Daimler-Benz engineers were the first to successfully adapt fuel injection to aircraft engines, which they did on the well-known 600 series that powered the (top, left) Messerschmidt ME-109, the (top, right) Heinkel He-111, and (above) the Messerschmidt ME-110, as well as other German planes. The injection systems for the 12-cylinder engines were the forerunners of those used on the 300SL coupes, first produced in series form in 1954 and the first passenger cars to use fuel injection.

In 1933, with the help of pressure from Berlin, Werlin became a member of the Vorstand, and from then on was in the middle of every decision made in Stuttgart. Nevertheless, with one crucial exception, in his business dealings Werlin acted more as a Daimler-Benz man than as a member of the Nazi hierarchy. By 1936 there had been so much anti-Semitic violence in Germany that Wilhelm Haspel could not have been elevated to the Vorstand in that year without some sort of tacit approval from Berlin, and Werlin was the middle man.

The Werlin move viewed as treasonous by the Stuttgarters came in 1942, at the height of the war. A Daimler-Benz truck built for the Army had proven less than successful: overweight and underpowered was the verdict. It was to be replaced by an Opel truck, to be manufactured not only in Opel plants but in the Daimler-Benz Mannheim factory as well.

This was a crushing blow to Kissel, now 56 and worn out from years of overwork, and shattered by the loss of his only son in Russia the previous December. On July 18, several weeks after the order came from Berlin (and Werlin clearly had moved it past his Vorstand colleagues without so much as a discussion) Kissel died of a heart attack.

As far as Daimler-Benz was concerned his successor was obvious: Wilhelm Haspel, who had been viewed as the logical heir to his patron Kissel ever since he had moved from Sindelfingen to Unter-türkheim six years earlier. The problem in Berlin,

however, was Haspel's wife: she was Jewish, and given the institutionalized paranoia of anti-Semitism in 1942, she was fortunate not to be in a concentration camp. But Daimler-Benz with the 44-year-old Haspel at the helm was worth more to the Nazis than Daimler-Benz without him, and his appointment as general director was approved. By then all manufacturing was under the direction of a government war production board, so many regular managerial functions had been given up to Berlin—a fact which underscores Haspel's importance, since business was a matter of following instructions more than anything else. In the same year another member of the Vorstand, Otto Hoppe, was forced out of the company; his wife was Jewish, too, and it seems that one Jewish wife per company was enough.

The Aufsichtsrat, or supervisory board, was also affected by the regime. Emil von Stauss of the Deutsche Bank remained Chairman, as he had been since the merger in 1926, but as war approached and normal economic parameters disappeared, the influence of the Deutsche Bank and the Aufsichtsrat disappeared. As early as the mid-thirties the Nazis had relieved the Aufsichtsrat of its four members who were either Jewish or had Jewish relatives. A worse fate overtook Hermann Köhler, a member of the supervisory board who was director of the Deutsche Bank's Stuttgart branch. In 1943 Köhler was arrested for making remarks critical of the regime, tried, convicted and executed.

(From the left) Jakob Werlin, Wilhelm Kissel, Wilhelm Haspel, Otto Hoppe. Werlin's management board membership began with Hitler's rise to power and ended with Hitler's fall. It was Werlin who ensured the safety of Haspel's Jewish wife when Haspel became general director in 1942. After the war Daimler-Benz repaid him by putting him in charge of the Mercedes agency in Rosenheim, a Bavarian town 150 miles from Stuttgart. Hoppe was interim general director until January 1948.

Untertürkheim, 1947. The Russians had taken everything in Berlin. Communication with the Gaggenau factory in the French zone was a problem for several years. Daimler-Benz began rebuilding first in Untertürkheim, then in Sindelfingen and Mannheim, in the American zone.

Hermann Lang, the 1939 European champion, was an aircraft engine inspector at the factory now. The war had taken him away from racing as he hit his peak. Rudolf Uhlenhaut's talents were transferred to cold-weather army vehicle development in Stuttgart; later he was assigned to manage a satellite aviation engine factory in Czechoslovakia. Racing injuries kept Manfred von Brauchitsch and Auto Union's Hans Stuck from active service; the former was assigned as secretary to a general in Berlin, the latter entertained troops with reminiscences of motor racing. Caracciola, who had applied for Swiss citizenship, retreated to the villa in that country that he had built as a wedding present for Baby. A check arrived every month from Daimler-Benz until the company was ordered to stop; Berlin considered Caracciola a deserter, in spite of his bad leg. Neubauer had been sent to a transport department in Berlin.

The first company plant to be bombed, in April

Untertürkheim, 1948. Repairing U.S. Army vehicles and rebuilding used 170V's with salvaged parts put Daimler-Benz back in business. When permission to build new cars was granted in the spring of 1946, a makeshift assembly line was set up. By 1948 over 6,000 cars had been built.

MERCEDES-BENZ
Typ 170V und Typ 170D

MODELL 1952

in Form und Ausstattung
wesentlich verbessert

Bessere Sichtverhältnisse durch größere Windschutzscheibe
Fondsitzmaße wesentlich günstiger gestaltet
verdeckte Scheibenwischer-Anlage
hypoidverzahnte Hinterachse
neugestaltete Motorhaube mit Spezialverschluß
weitumfassende und durchgehende Stoßstangen
neue Farbkombinationen für Lackierung und Polsterung

Fordern Sie bitte Spezial-Prospekte an — machen Sie eine Probefahrt
Unsere örtlichen Vertretungen werden Sie gern beraten

DAIMLER-BENZ AKTIENGESELLSCHAFT STUTTGART-UNTERTURKHEIM

By 1948 the occupation forces allowed Daimler-Benz to resume diesel production, and a 170D joined the 170V (center, right). By 1951 the company had built 531 Type 170Da touring cars (top, right) for the newly formed German *Bundesgrenzschutz* (federal border guards); many of them were still in police service 20 years later. The 170S, introduced in 1949, was slightly larger and more powerful, with a more modern body — and, at 10,000 marks (about $2400), was considered a "luxury" car in that austere era. Introduced in 1953, the 170SV (above) combined the S body with the V chassis for 8180 marks in what general director Fritz Könecke called the "Mercedes for everybody."

1943, was Mannheim, though it was less than half destroyed. But in September 1944 the United States Eighth Air Force began a two-week series of day-and-night raids. Stuttgart was leveled; the Daimler-Benz factories at Untertürkheim, Sindelfingen and Gaggenau, near Baden-Baden, lay in ruins. Haspel was aware that the war was as good as over, but to suggest that openly could only bring appalling consequences, as in the case of Köhler. Because Nazi spies were everywhere, Haspel quietly organized a few trusted colleagues into a committee. "In anticipation of the total collapse . . . ," he wrote later, "we tried to keep our finances fluid, so that we would have cash . . . to be the basis for survival later."

Yet by V-E Day the prospects for survival were bleak. The company's resources were not only damaged but dispersed. Marienfelde was in divided Berlin. Untertürkheim, Sindelfingen and Mannheim were in the American zone of occupation. Communication with Gaggenau, in the French zone, was a problem. And any facilities in the Russian zone were lost. No wonder that the board of directors of the world's oldest auto company stated that Daimler-Benz simply "ceased to exist" in 1945.

Nevertheless by May 20, less than two weeks after V-E Day, 1,240 Daimler-Benz workers had made

their way back to Untertürkheim. Picks, shovels and bare hands were put to work in a massive clean-up. Once the rubble surrounding the factory had been removed and paths cleared to what remained of the buildings, many machines were discovered intact.

Haspel supervised the work until October, when the American military government removed him from the plant. As the head of a war matériel producer, Haspel had to undergo de-Nazification. So the man who had done everything in his power to keep the Nazis out of "his" company had to run it from home for more than two years until he was officially cleared on January 1, 1948. Ironically, while Haspel stayed home, the man the military government allowed to take his place was Otto Hoppe, whom the Nazis had thrown out because his wife was Jewish.

Within months machines had been put in working order, and Daimler-Benz started to work its way back. In the United States plants were being converted to peacetime production with all possible speed, and the 1946 models that appeared in the fall, though they were little more than 1942 models with a different date, found long lines of buyers. But in Untertürkheim, the first profitable activity was not building new cars, but repairing trucks for the American Army. The three-pointed star was still covered

Cause for celebration in March 1952: the assembly of the 100,000th 170 built since the war. Supplying the home market remained the chief concern, though export plans were on the agenda. Only 253 Mercedes were sold in America that year, but it was a quantum leap from 18 in 1951.

by the ashes of war, and under the ashes was the stain of being Hitler's personal transportation. The idea of Daimler-Benz as a *manufacturer*, much less one of international reputation, even less than that as the builder of the glamor cars of the twenties and thirties, simply did not exist at a time when the Morgenthau Plan, named after the United States Secretary of the Treasury and designed to turn Germany into an agricultural nation, was being given serious consideration in some quarters.

As the winter of 1945 set in, plants had to be shut down because of shortages of coal and electricity. Food shortages were critical too. On the main road from Mannheim, which passed a large displaced-persons camp, there was a sign reading "U.S. Drivers Caution—European Jay Walkers." Only the Allied forces had motor transport: Germans went places on foot, or hitched a ride. When permission was received to recondition prewar vehicles, Haspel used cash to buy used 170V's, then bartered the restored cars for raw materials. Two of them bought a temporary bridge American engineers had built over the Neckar; the wood was used to construct an office building in Untertürkheim.

To Haspel, the number one priority was putting people to work rebuilding production facilities, and then producing what people needed: basic transportation. By the spring of 1946, with permission to build new vehicles granted, Daimler-Benz simply picked up where it had left off before the war, with its best-selling model, the 170V. Most of the first ones were fitted with a box or flatbed because utility vehicles were urgently needed. By the end of 1946, 214 had been built; by the end of 1947, 1,045 had left the line, some of them passenger cars. By now over 20,000 persons were at work at Daimler-Benz, about half the prewar level, and hundreds more were being added almost monthly. "Some 200 apprentices are being coached in the finesse of the trade by former racing mechanics, who have the gray look of undernourishment on their faces and who are dressed in clothes held together by patches," the British *Autocar* reported. "Their attitude, however, still breathes precision, speed, and a pride in their work."

The next big step in the German recovery was the currency reform in the summer of 1948. This enabled West Germany—the Iron Curtain was by now a reality; Winston Churchill first used the term in a speech in Fulton, Missouri, in 1946—to progress from black markets and barter to a stable economy based on standard economic principles. In addition to giving the country an economic base from which to

Untertürkheim, 1953: the house the 170 built. Money made from 170 sales bought raw materials for construction, and by the early fifties Daimler-Benz looked like a proper factory again. Company employees numbered over 35,000, nearly three times the work force in 1945.

develop, and a great deal of Marshall Plan aid, the Allies—basically the Americans—also gave the Germans, for the first time since the war, the feeling that someone cared about them. This came in the form of the Berlin Airlift, which lasted from July 1948 to September 1949, when the Russians blockaded Berlin and the United States Air Force flew a total of 1.5 million tons of supplies into the city on a total of 196,000 flights. Forty years later these amounts may not seem like much, but at the time they were a staggering logistical accomplishment and an even greater emotional boost for the West Germans who saw, for the first time, that someone *did* care about them. The Federal Republic of Germany was born May 23, 1949, in the so-called "temporary" site of Bonn, the small, peaceful city on the Rhine south of Cologne that was Beethoven's birthplace. The former mayor of Cologne, Konrad Adenauer, was West Germany's first chancellor—and later turned out to be one of Daimler-Benz's better customers.

At the Hanover Fair of 1949 the first postwar Mercedes was introduced. There were two models: the 170S and the 170D. They were little more than

updated prewar cars; the D signified that the second model was diesel-powered. In 1950 came the 170Va and the 170Da, which had further improvements but which were still little more than refurbished prewar cars. Fritz Nallinger had taken over as chief engineer at the end of the war, and his—and Haspel's—philosophy was straightforward: build something as quickly as possible so that we can put people to work; we'll worry about technical advances later. "If we had decided to develop totally new cars," an engineer from those immediate postwar days recalled, "it would have taken several years to get them ready, and in the meantime the workers would have had no jobs, and our customers would not have received their cars until much later. So doing what we did was the only logical thing."

By 1950, the German recovery was well under way. At Daimler-Benz automobile production doubled from 17,417 in 1949 to 33,906 in 1950, the highest annual output in the company's history. Truck production was nearly 8,500 units, an increase of more than a third over the previous year. Haspel continued to move the company ahead, rebuilding the plants with modern equipment and streamlining pro-

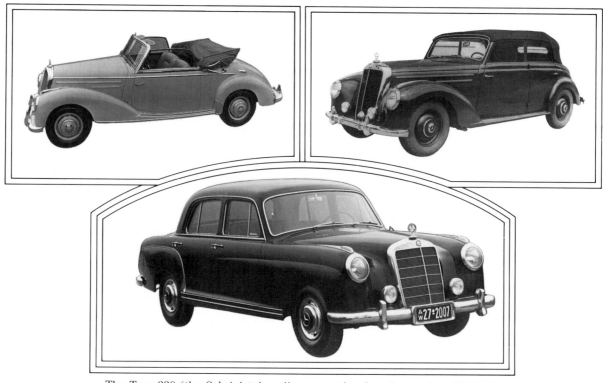

The Type 220 (the Cabriolet A, police car and sedan shown above) had six cylinders and a chassis based on a strengthened 170S. Production began in June 1951; by 1955 nearly 45,000 220's had been sold, one of them to American film actor William Holden.

duction to eliminate overlap and duplication still left from the merger of the companies two decades before. Headquarters, engineering and a new test track (completed in 1956) were centered in Unter-türkheim; manufacture there was confined to engines and transmissions. Passenger car chassis and body assembly, together with the body engineering depart-ment, were in Sindelfingen. Trucks and buses were the products of Mannheim. Once Gaggenau was returned to Daimler-Benz control, Unimog produc-tion moved there. Conceived when the Morgenthau Plan was being considered as Germany's future, the Unimog was a diesel-engined, four-wheel-drive mobile implement carrier that could go anywhere, pull anything and handle farming chores from the planting season to harvesting; about the only attach-ment not provided was one for milking cows.

Haspel ruled Daimler-Benz with a firm hand. Though nothing remained of the Marienfelde plant and it might have been more practical to abandon the site, Haspel chose to rebuild the factory. The com-pany owed it to the employees, he said, and the tragic situation of a divided Berlin could only be helped by Daimler-Benz's remaining there. Stationary diesel engine production began in Marienfelde in 1950.

In April 1951, at the first international West Ger-man automobile show in Frankfurt, two new six-cylinder models were introduced: the 2.2-liter 220 and the three-liter 300, Daimler-Benz's first postwar luxury car. Haspel's directive to body engineer Karl Wilfert and his team had been brief and to the point: the cars' styling was to be modern but the Mercedes radiator grille had to be retained. In an automotive era when "all-new" often meant the elimination of tradition, that decision was pivotal and has not since been violated. A Mercedes remains unmistakably a Mercedes.

"The terrific, new high-performance job that has . . . the European automotive world agog," said the American magazine *Speed Age* of the new 300. Britain's *The Motor* called it "definitely the sensation of the Show and . . . well worthy of this honour." The largest and fastest automobile yet introduced in post-war Germany, the 300 series reigned for more than a decade. At home Chancellor Adenauer was driven in nothing else and became so identified with the model that it was nicknamed the "Adenauerwagen." The 300 was unquestionably *the* prestige car in its native

Variations on the 300 theme: 300S Coupe, 300S Cabriolet, 300 Sedan. In late 1951 the American *Speed Age* commented that Mercedes would henceforth become as well known for "excellent highway automobiles" as for racing cars. Total 300S production was 560; 219 were sold in the U.S.

291

The 220 and 300 were introduced at the Frankfurt Automobile Show in February 1951, the 300S in Paris that November. Commented *The Autocar*: "To have repaired the devastation of war and then to have designed, developed and brought to production these three outstanding new models is a great achievement." More important, Mercedes' traditional clientele returned, encouraged by the rave reviews the new cars received. In America *Road & Track* said of the 300S: "Enthusiasts who regretted the passing of the 540K at the onset of war will hail the arrival of this worthy successor." Among 300 and 300S purchasers in Hollywood were Gary Cooper, Bing Crosby and Yul Brynner.

land. Equally important, it was the model that returned Mercedes to its old international clientele. Purchasers included Frank Lloyd Wright, Gary Cooper, Yul Brynner, Maria Callas and the French comedian Fernandel. The 300 was the car of state for Haile Selassie, Jawaharlal Nehru, the Shah of Iran and King Gustav of Sweden. Even Field Marshal Montgomery, now Viscount Montgomery of Alamein, bought a 300.

"We think very little about racing around here," Alfred Neubauer had written the Caracciolas in January 1947. His job at Untertürkheim was ostensibly the tending of historic cars as they were brought back from the tunnels, abandoned mines and haystacks in which they had been hidden during the war. But Neubauer had made an inventory of the competition equipment on hand as early as that November. And in his determination to take Mercedes racing again, he had a valuable ally: the general director was as determined as he was, In 1948, at the dinner celebrating Neubauer's 25 years with the company, Haspel said the Mercedes sporting tradition was to be carried on.

Neubauer had scoured the countryside in search of prewar race cars. Many of them had been hidden near Dresden in what was now East Germany, but two 1939 three-liter grand prix cars found on a Berlin used car lot were exchanged for one new 170V, and a pair of 1½-liter Tripoli cars in Switzerland were purchased at auction in 1950 by Daimler-Benz's Swiss importer.*

In order to return to motor sport quickly, Haspel had even considered buying Veritas, a small competi-

tion-car factory founded in 1948, and integrating it into the Daimler-Benz organization, but the asking price was too high. The company would go with what it had.

In September 1950 the two grand prix cars bought in Berlin were tried at the Nürburgring. Two of the three first-string Mercedes drivers were there: Caracciola and Lang. After the war von Brauchitsch had made an unsuccessful return to competition and now, beset with personal difficulties, was on his way to a decision for communism and East Germany. His place was taken by Karl Kling, who had driven Mercedes successfully in rallies during the late thirties. After the Nürburgring tryout, a third three-liter prewar car was readied at the factory, and Neubauer prepared to send his drivers to Argentina for the Formula Libre races the following February. But Caracciola, convinced the old cars wouldn't stand a chance, decided not to go, so Neubauer had to replace him. The man he found was a bandy-legged phenomenon named Juan Manuel Fangio, who was driving for Alfa Romeo but would be at liberty for Buenos Aires because the Italian factory had decided not to send a team. Lang and Fangio finished second and third in the Buenos Aires Grand Prix, Kling and Lang in the same order in the Eva Perón Cup. It was all his fault, Fangio insisted afterwards. Thinking he would be driving an Alfa Romeo when the races were planned, he had persuaded his fellow Argentinians to lay out a course with an abundance of curves, which his Alfa could have taken more easily than the larger Mercedes. As it happened, the Ferrari driven by José Froilan Gonzalez won both events.

Although no one admitted it publicly at the time, it was revealed years later that the cars had lost not just because of their extreme age or their size, but because the personnel shortage in Stuttgart kept Uhlenhaut and other veteran racing engineers home designing production cars and the man who went with the vehicles did not know enough about them. He thought the engines were to be tuned like passenger car engines, and as a result they ran in what was, for racing, extremely lean condition.

The Argentine excursion was enough to convince Nallinger to cancel the next event on the Daimler-

*Caracciola had asked Kissel for these cars in 1941, planning to use them (one to race, the other for parts) for his personal return to competition when peace came. With the war on Kissel could not arrange to ship them, and because of Caracciola's bad standing in Berlin dared not put anything in writing. Haspel was aware of his predecessor's promise to Rudi and after Kissel's death informed him of the cars' whereabouts near Dresden. Early in 1945, amidst the chaos of the German collapse, the cars were smuggled to Switzerland. In 1946 Rudi planned to take one of them to America for the Indianapolis 500, but neither his pleading nor Baby's considerable charm could convince Allied control that a German car should be allowed to compete there. The Caracciolas nevertheless traveled to America for the 500, and Rudi was offered a drive in Joel Thorne's Indianapolis car. He crashed during practice and his skull was fractured.

Benz agenda: the Indianapolis 500. A prewar three-liter Mercedes—this one discovered in Czechoslovakia and bought in England by the Californian Tommy Lee—had been entered in 1947 and 1948, driven the first year by Duke Nalon and the second by Chet Miller. Neither had finished the race, probably because of the unfamiliarity of American mechanics with the car's complex engineering. In 1949 Neubauer attended the 500 as a spectator and walked the oval afterwards, taking measurements and photographs and picking up a piece of asphalt to take to Stuttgart for analysis so his team could arrive at the track with the proper tires. But Argentina demonstrated to Daimler-Benz engineers that Caracciola had been right.

With the three-liter Mercedes vetoed for America and impossible in Europe (the prevailing formula allowed 4.5 liters unblown and reduced supercharged cars to 1.5 liters), thoughts turned next to the Tripoli cars in the Swiss Mercedes dealership. Neubauer was sure that with a little further development they could be raced again. In June 1951 he convinced Daimler-Benz. In September a group of engineers attended the German Grand Prix to see the unblown Ferraris and supercharged Alfas battle each other. They came away convinced that even with a lot of work the 12-year-old Tripoli car could not compete. To design brand-new cars required more than a year, which meant they would have just one full season of

competition before the scheduled expiration of the formula in 1953, something that Haspel could not justify economically. Neubauer traveled to Paris to persuade the C.S.I. to extend the formula, but had no luck. In October the new 750cc supercharged 2.5-liter unblown formula was announced, to take effect in 1954. Daimler-Benz began planning for it, but 1954 was three years away.

To Haspel, as to Kissel before him, racing had a single purpose: publicity. Now that his company was back on its feet in Germany and the 300 was proving the war had not dimmed the lustre of the Mercedes image around the world, racing was a new priority. "That's what he said," Uhlenhaut remembered. "He didn't say what. He just said we should do something on the competition side." In June 1951 mention had also been made of sports cars. The cheapest way to get back into racing quickly was to transform a touring car into a competition vehicle, as Mercedes had done once before with the SSK. History was about to repeat itself. "We are just opening a little window on the motor racing scene," Nallinger said. The window was called the 300SL.

Haspel never got to see the 300SL. Shattered by the suicide of his wife and worn down from years of overwork, Haspel suffered a stroke and died in January 1952, just before his fifty-fourth birthday. His replacement was Heinrich Wagner, who became the third head of the company since the merger of 1926,

In 1945, with company approval, Fritz Nallinger (right) headed a group of 150 German scientists and engineers in the development of an aircraft facility for the French. He returned as Daimler-Benz technical director in 1948, the year Rudi Uhlenhaut (left) came back as head of the experimental department.

(Clockwise from top, left) 1951 Unimog, 1953 all-terrain L312, 1949 L3500, 1951 L6600, 1950 L5000. Two months after V–E Day, Daimler-Benz engineers had begun to design the trucks that were vital to rebuilding Germany. Truck production of 2,019 units in 1946 and 2,406 in 1947 was, respectively, ten times and twice the passenger car figures for those years. The Allied Control Commission restricted German vehicle building to two axles, and it was not uncommon to see Daimler-Benz trucks pulling two trailers behind. Powerful diesel engines were designed, both for this exigency and in anticipation of the eventual lifting of the restrictions (which occurred in 1951).

Mechanic Mal Ord adjusting the valves on the prewar Mercedes (top, left) driven by Duke Nalon in the 1947 Indianapolis 500. Though second fastest to qualify (128.032 mph to Bill Holland's 128.756 in the Offenhauser-engined Blue Crown Spark Plug Special), Nalon retired with a blown piston on the 119th lap. The same car failed to finish again in 1948. In 1949 Neubauer (top, right) traveled to the U.S. on a "reconnaissance mission" to see the 500, and Indianapolis was on the Daimler-Benz calendar for 1951. In order to increase speeds in the corners, vertical air-foils were wind-tunnel tested on a model (center, right) and then fitted to a prewar W154 (like the one above) for testing by Karl Kling. Ultimately, Daimler-Benz decided against competing in the 500 with a ten-year-old car.

Monte Carlo Rally, 1952: Kling, Neubauer, Caracciola, Lang and crew after winning the *Prix d'Ensemble.* A total of 328 cars started in the snowbound and gruelling event; only 162 finished.

and who, it turned out, represents little more than a brief interlude in the annals of the firm. Wagner, who had spent most of his career with Opel, had been in charge of the Mannheim factory since 1948. He was not enthusiastic about going racing: indeed, it is doubtful if he was enthusiastic about anything. His first public appearance before the German press was remarkable for his ability to be forthright, if not exactly intelligent, about his role as the principal spokesman and his relationship to the media: "My name is Wagner and I don't read the newspapers," was his opening line. What he said after that has been little noted nor long remembered.

The 300SL, which began life as a stop-gap measure to get the company back into racing and rebuild its image, was in certain respects the most remarkable car ever built by Daimler-Benz. Most cars come into being as the result of a concept, and then as the result of the design, development and construction of the pieces which best fit that concept. The 300SL did not have the benefit of this process, nor indeed of any sort of normal development program. Instead it was simply cobbled together from whatever series production pieces were available, since there was no time and no money available for anything else. The engine, actually too big, too heavy and too underpowered for a

First tested in November 1951, the 300SL was shown to the German press on March 12, 1952, with a demonstration run on the autobahn to Heilbronn. This factory photo was dispatched around the world, and preparation began for the 300SL's race debut in the Mille Miglia in early May.

297

In Brescia, before the start of the Mille Miglia, 1952. Driving the new 300SL's were Caracciola (No. 613), Kling (No. 623) and Lang. Dispatching the 502 competing cars began at 9:01 p.m. Saturday, May 3, and ended at 6:29 the following morning in a streaming rain. Early on, Lang was timed the fastest on the course (at better than 105 mph) but shortly after hit a roadside marker and retired. Caracciola, at 51, drove a careful race in a car not quite as powerful as his teammates', determined to finish the 1,000 miles despite a crippled leg. Kling drove flat out. At the halfway point in Rome, he had an eight-minute lead over Giovanni Bracco's Ferrari. But at the finish line in Brescia, Bracco was the winner, by a narrow margin of 4 minutes 32 seconds. Caracciola finished fourth.

competition sports car, was the same one used in the 300 series of sedans, coupes and cabriolets, and was rated for "civil" purposes, at 115 horsepower. The best the engineers could do, on short notice, was to give it three carburetors, another camshaft and better intake and exhaust manifolds. That brought it up to 175 horsepower, marginal when one considered competing against V12 Ferraris of 4.1- and 4.5-liter displacement and designed from the ground up for competition.

The axles and transmissions were also from the production cars, which in the Daimler-Benz tradition were never accused of being too light. But the *pièce de résistance* was the space-frame chassis and its aluminum body. Although space-frame construction became the norm in competition cars within a few years, this, basically designed by Uhlenhaut, was the first. It was a sensation when compared to the ladder-frame chassis that had previously been the accepted method of supporting running gear, engine, body and driver. Welded together out of a myriad of small tubes, it looked like a sophisticated erector set. To the outside world, the engineering necessity that required tubes to be placed in the area where the door openings would be in each are what gave the 300SL its singular styling. The tubes made it impossible to install doors that could be opened in the "normal" manner, that is, horizontally. A careful review of the international competition regulations revealed that nowhere was it specified *how* the doors opened, as long as they did. So the doors on the 300SL opened vertically, and the driver and passenger in the two-seater coupe clambered in over the high sill. The upper part of the coupe, with both doors open, bore a distant resemblance to a seagull, and the name "Gullwing" was applied to the car almost as soon as the first photograph appeared in the United States. It has been Gullwing ever since in all English-speaking countries, and the term is used in many other countries as well.

The competition coupe made its debut at the Mille Miglia of 1952. The famous Italian 1,000-mile road race (the actual distance varied; it was usually about 990) was started in 1927. Except for Caracciola's win with the SSKL in 1931, it had never been won by a non-Italian car. The race started in Brescia,

went east to the Adriatic, down the coast to a point opposite Rome, turned west to Rome, north at Rome and back up through the Appenines and the Reggio Emilia to Brescia. It was, in its time, the largest one-day spectator sports event in the world.

Kling, Lang and Caracciola were to be the Mercedes team, and except for winning the Monte Carlo Rally team prize in January driving 220 sedans, they had been devoting their energies to practicing in Italy, learning the course, while the engineers were trying to find some more horsepower for the new coupe. The 300SL in early competition form had the astonishingly low drag coefficient of 0.25 and that was also horsepower, so to speak, but Neubauer was not happy, either with the 170-plus horses or with the lack of a five-speed gearbox.

LES 24 HEURES DU MANS 1952
PROGRAMME OFFICIEL
Prix : **200** francs

Le Mans program cover by Geo Ham (1900-1972). Among the greatest illustrators in France, Ham devoted his career to depicting automobiles and airplanes at speed.

Le Mans, 1952. Car No. 22 wore an air brake during practice to test the concept and rattle the competition. Both missions were accomplished. In the race itself, the Helfrich–Niedermayer 300SL (No. 20) finished second, the Lang–Riess No. 21 (above) won. Only 17 of the 57 starters finished, the Kling–Klenk 300SL among the retirees. Spectators cheered the Stuttgart cars' one-two finish, which was heartening to the German team, though Mercedes chose not to exult in the victory on French soil. This pleased no one more than Hermann Lang (top, left) who, at 43, remained as shy as ever and continued to plead with Neubauer not to have "much fuss made over me."

That was too bad, Uhlenhaut explained: the car had to use components from the 300's parts bin for reasons of economy and because the engineers were overburdened with production work and development of the grand prix car. It was either the 300SL as it was, or no 300SL at all. Given Hobson's choice, Neubauer elected to keep quiet about his misgivings and go racing with a car he didn't feel was a winner.

And the 300SL didn't win the Mille Miglia. Lang's race was over 25 miles from the start when he took a curve too fast, hit a kilometer marker and damaged his rear axle. Kling finished second; Caracciola was fourth in a fine effort.* Kling had led at Rome, traditionally a bad omen. Toward the finish, a routine tire change lengthened into six minutes until a sledgehamer finally loosened a recalcitrant knock-off hub. Giovanni Bracco won one of his three Mille Miglia victories in a V12 Ferrari.

---

*It had been over five years since Caracciola's Indianapolis accident. One leg remained crippled and the recovery from his skull fracture had been slow. Rudi was now 51. His wife considered his fourth place after a thousand racing miles "his greatest victory," a triumph over his own doubts that he could still drive competitively. His next race, at Bern two weeks later, was his last. He suffered his only serious crash in a quarter-century of driving the Stuttgart cars, and smashed his good leg. Though he retired from motor sport, Caracciola remained in Daimler-Benz's employ, demonstrating the company's sports cars at American and British installations throughout Europe. He died in 1959.

Though the Italian performance did not wholly satisfy Neubauer, it was greeted with even less enthusiasm in other quarters. The 300SL seemed capable of greater speed than the Jaguar and Ferrari, and engineers in Coventry and Modena hurried to make a few revisions before Le Mans six weeks hence. In the meantime, the 300SL went to Switzerland and Neubauer stopped fretting. The cars finished the sports car Grand Prix de Berne one-two-three, Kling-Lang-Riess. Fritz Riess, a 29-year-old industrialist, a fine driver and, as Neubauer said, "an excellent customer of our firm who already has bought 16 cars," was new to the team. Though the Berne race was insignificant, a mere curtain-raiser to the Swiss Grand Prix, the 300SL performed well.

One month later, 120 miles west of Paris, Le Mans awoke from its provincial tranquility as 300,000 spectators began jamming the Sarthe circuit. During practice the Ferraris appeared faster than they had at the Mille Miglia, and the C-Type Jaguars certainly looked different. Their bodies were truncated at the tail and streamlined in front, the latter effect achieved by sloping the radiator and relocating the header tanks, which revealed severe cooling problems that necessitated some last-minute body revisions. Further down pit row, Briggs Cunningham had

Nürburgring, 1952. Four new 300SL roadsters were tried out in a sports car race. Drivers Lang (above), Kling, Riess and Helfrich finished in that order. Given a driver's tryout afterwards, John Fitch suggested that the 300SL race next in Mexico.

arrived from America with his three-car team. And Pierre Levegh, the master mechanic and Le Mans veteran, was on hand with a Talbot he had prepared himself so he could win the 24 Hours his way.

The Mercedes team was the last to appear. Neubauer liked dramatic entrances. As the 300SL's began practicing, it could scarcely be overlooked that one of them sported a "futuristic roof-top air brake" (in *The Motor*'s words) which down the Mulsanne straight was "flipped up into the slipstream with a 'whupp!' and the car slowed as if a giant hand had reached out and grabbed it . . . from 150 to 75 mph in a matter of split seconds" (according to *Road & Track*). The device was merely being tested and was not used in the race, but its appearance unnerved the opposition. Neubauer liked that too.

At four o'clock Saturday afternoon, June 14, the drivers sprinted to their cars (Lang among the slowest, because he never could understand the rush to win a 24-hour race in the first 30 seconds). Riess was sharing his car. The second 300SL was manned by Theo Helfrich and Norbert Niedermayer. In the third were Kling and Hans Klenk, a pairing that was a phonetician's delight. Neubauer's strategy for the full day of racing was to start slow, take it easy, let attrition shrink the field and pick up speed at the end if

necessary. The attrition came quickly. All three Jaguars overheated and were out of the race in the second hour. The Ferraris began retiring with mechanical problems. At midnight a Gordini led but by dawn it was out with brake failure. Levegh's Talbot took over the lead, followed by two Mercedes (Kling and Klenk had retired with electrical problems). Early Sunday morning Levegh was in front by three laps; mathematically the 300SL's should have increased speed by 3 mph a lap to catch him, but Neubauer kept to his strategy: the two cars continued lapping at the prescribed 98 mph. By noon the Talbot was four laps ahead with four hours to go, though the man behind its wheel was dead tired. For Levegh, winning Le Mans meant winning it alone — driving the entire 24 hours himself. Neubauer didn't think he could make it. He was driving on instinct now, almost robot-like, sometimes hitting grass verges and scraping sandbanks, but he refused to be relieved. An hour and fifteen minutes from the finish, Levegh retired with a broken connecting rod: in his exhaustion, he had missed a shift. Mercedes loped to a one-two finish, with the Lang-Riess car first. A Nash-Healey was third, the Cunningham-Spear Cunningham fourth, a Ferrari fifth.

The French crowd, though disheartened at

Carrera Panamericana, 1952. Publicity photo of the 300SL team car of Kling and Klenk, taken before the race, before the "buzzard bars," before the spectacular victory. Within two years, thanks to Max Hoffman's prodding, the 300SL was a production car.

Carrera Panamericana, 1952. Strategy sessions and road workouts in Mexico began weeks before the event, but even Neubauer couldn't foresee that a bird would almost wreck the team's carefully laid plans. At the depot at Oaxaca, Kling's teammate Klenk (center, right) looks at the shattered windshield; at the finish Kling and Klenk peer through the Gullwing's "buzzard bars" (above) after wining the Carrera at a phenomenal 102.8 mph. Team member John Fitch recalled that before the event Kling (top, left) was "serious and reserved, but positive." Neubauer had stressed that for all three cars to finish the punishing 1,932-mile race was most important. All three cars did. The Mercedes team was exultant (top, right); from the left: Neubauer, Geiger, Fitch, Klenk, Kling, Lang, Grupp.

Levegh's final-hour defeat, accepted the Mercedes victory with grace. Daimler-Benz had worried about the reception German cars would receive on French soil so soon after the war. Diplomatically, the team left Le Mans quietly after the win and saved the celebrating for Stuttgart. A confetti parade welcomed the Mercedes drivers back home.

At the Nürburgring for a sports car race in August, four 300SL's—in roadster form this time—finished one-two-three-four, with Lang the victor. The cars had virtually no competition. Ostensibly that should have ended the season, but one of the Cunningham drivers who had requested a tryout while at Le Mans had come to the Nürburgring for that purpose. Afterward, he suggested the team consider another race. The Carrera Panamericana in Mexico that November was "a perfect chance" for the Mercedes, said John Fitch, who had driven a Chrysler there the year before. Neubauer, though impressed with the American's driving, at first showed no interest in the Mexican race, but on his return home, Fitch found a letter from Neubauer asking for details. A lengthy correspondence ensued. In addition to supplying personal impressions of the five-day race, average speeds and altitude changes over its nearly 2,000-mile course, and meteorological data like rainfall charts and average November weather conditions, Fitch went to the AAA and local travel bureaus for information on what to wear, what medications to bring, what to eat and what not to drink. Neubauer never liked to go anywhere unprepared. Subtly inserted within the reams of material he dispatched to Stuttgart was Fitch's announcement of his availability to drive one of the team cars, if Daimler-Benz was willing. Fitch was signed.

The Carrera began in Tuxtla Gutierrez, 100 miles from the Guatemalan border. Weeks before, the Mercedes team had arrived in Mexico: Lang with his mechanic co-driver Erwin Grupp, Kling and Klenk, and the mechanic Eugen Geiger, who would ride with Fitch. Neubauer drilled his crew like a football team: workouts on the road during the day, blackboard sessions at night until the course was all but committed to memory. The first 331-mile leg started in sand-

dune country and swept up into the mountains and through dense jungle to the ancient Aztec city of Oaxaca. According to Kling, dogs, vultures and Ferraris were Mercedes' principal problems. The entire canine population of Mexico seemed to be on the roads, and the Ferraris were legion (driven by, among others, world champion Alberto Ascari and Mille Miglia winner Bracco from Italy, and Phil Hill and Luigi Chinetti from the United States).

But it was a bird that almost did the Kling car in on the road to Oaxaca. "There was a bang, as if a hand-grenade was going off," Kling remembered. "Quite unconsciously I bellowed 'Haaans!'" Klenk didn't respond: he was unconscious. A vulture had shattered the windscreen, careened off Klenk's forehead and fallen behind the seats — all this while the 300SL was traveling at about 135 mph. Kling managed to keep the car under control and bring it to a halt. Kling revived Klenk, and he said to press on. As the car pulled into the next depot, Günther Molter, Neubauer's assistant and the Mercedes press chief for the expedition, grabbed a bucket of water and a towel and placed them alongside the car so Klenk could clean himself up; the rules forbade him to help further. The bird was removed from the car. In Oaxaca a new windshield was fitted and vertical strips of steel were added to ward off further vulture attacks; these became famous as the Mercedes "buzzard bars."

The rest of the Carrera was comparatively easy for Kling, just the usual desert, wind, mountains, fog, bad roads and countless tire changes. In Parral, at the end of the sixth leg, Bracco, whose Ferrari was leading by 3 minutes 45 seconds, confided that he didn't think his differential would go the distance; and it did not. Kling was driving flat out. Overhead, Neubauer, following in a plane, had no way to slow his driver down. He couldn't even keep up with him; Kling was hitting 160 mph in the final stretches. His winning time for 1,932 miles was 18 hours 51 minutes 19 seconds — an incredible 102.8 mph, smashing the previous year's 88 mph. Lang, who lost one of his Gullwing doors outside Chihuahua, finished second in not quite 19 hours, 30 minutes. Fitch's fourth-place finish was disallowed after race officials reversed an earlier decision that had permitted him to return to the

Parral control for repairs. This was disheartening but not diminishing. Of the 91 cars that had begun the Carrera in Tuxtla Gutierrez, only 39 made it to the finish in Juárez along the Rio Grande—including every one of the Mercedes entered.

The press reaction was fabulous, particularly from Mexico's neighbor to the north. Because American automobiles were competing in the stock car class (won by AAA champion Chuck Stevenson's Lincoln in 21 hours 15.5 minutes; three more Lincolns followed), major United States papers covered the event. And AP and UP stories were picked up by scores of smaller newspapers from coast to coast. A certain nationalism might creep into the headlines— "Lincoln and Mercedes Cop the Mexican Cash" said the headline in one Midwestern daily—but no one could ignore the Stuttgart cars' success. Interestingly, the *Detroit News* reporter referred to the winning 300SL as the "yet unmarketed Mercedes-Benz model." Molter stated the Carrera's significance to Mercedes with eloquent simplicity: "We were nothing in 1945. Now we were somebody again."

Daimler-Benz sat out the 1953 season. The decision was to retire the 300SL so Mercedes engineers could devote all their efforts to the grand prix car for the following season and to the production cars for the marketplace, among them the 300S. In 1953—the year Hugh Hefner founded *Playboy* in America, Ian Fleming introduced 007 in England, and Ben Hogan won the Masters and the U.S. and British Opens— Errol Flynn and Bing Crosby became 300S owners in Hollywood. This new Mercedes, a sportier 300 with a shorter wheelbase, had been introduced at the Paris Salon in October 1951, though Daimler-Benz had not been able to get the car into production until the following July.

Success was taxing. Uhlenhaut was made chief of passenger car development, though this did not excuse him from racing duties. And in passenger cars Mercedes engineers had made the important decision for unit bodies with the 180. It had not been easy. To the non-engineers on the Daimler-Benz board, a Mercedes had to have a chassis to be solidly built, and a car had to be solidly built to be a Mercedes. Nothing less was acceptable. Nallinger won his argument that properly designed unit-body construction meant lower weight without sacrificing rigidity or safety— though for the company's safety, a new 170 series with the traditional chassis was introduced at about the same time. Had customers objected to the 180, with its unit body and "modern" styling, it would have

Type 180D, 1954: the beginning of a new era for Daimler-Benz. The 180's unit-body construction won over the traditionalists by a sales ratio of ten of the new models to one of the older-styled separate-chassis 170's. The gasoline version was introduced in 1953; the diesel soon followed.

been withdrawn from the market. As things worked out, the old 180 faded into obscurity and the company never looked back. The four-cylinder 180 was soon followed by a 180D, with the letter as usual standing for diesel power. The next year, 1954, saw a new six-cylinder 220a that was also of unit-body construction and modern design.

The introduction of the 220a made 1954 a watershed year in the history of the company. For the first time since the war, and on a scale far greater than anything previously envisioned, Daimler-Benz had an integrated passenger car line that ran from its traditional medium-sized base to big cars, and from utilitarian diesels to high-speed sports cars. The 180 and 180D were at the bottom. Then came the 220a and the 220S. The 220 was also represented by limited-edition coupes and convertibles. Then came the six-cylinder 300's, which included a two-door cabriolet and a two-door roadster, a four-door cabriolet and a four-door limousine. On the more sporting side there was the 300SL Gullwing, which made its production-version debut that year, and its little brother, the 190SL.

The line was complete. And it was based on only three engines. Nallinger's team had employed the building-block system to good advantage. Not only

were the cars of excellent materials and workmanship; they were also new, they were attractive, and with the exception of the 180's, they were all capable of exceeding 100 miles an hour on West Germany's rebuilt autobahns—which is the way people usually drove them. There was a line of customers outside the gates in Stuttgart, the German economic miracle was in full bloom, and its outstanding symbol was the three-pointed star.

The first production Mercedes to have its world première in America. Together with the 190SL, the 300SL was introduced at the Seventh Regiment Armory in New York City at the International Motor Sports Show held February 6 through 14, 1954.

306

CHAPTER NINE

THE BASIS
FOR SUCCESS

1 9 5 4 — 1 9 8 5

Only learn to seize good fortune,
For good fortune's always there.
—JOHANN WOLFGANG VON GOETHE,
ERINNERUNG

The first century of Daimler, Benz and Daimler-Benz can be divided in many ways, and one of these is to split the one hundred years into pre- and post-World War II eras. The prewar company, while covered with the glamour that came from exotic sports cars and racing victories, was never, from a business standpoint, a factor in the worldwide automotive picture. Germany invented the automobile but America invented the automobile *business*, and perfected (or so it thought in those halcyon days) the mass production of cars and trucks.

Ford and General Motors, trailed by the other United States companies, were dominant in both passenger cars and commercial vehicles around the world. There were many exceptions to their domination, naturally, as both tariff and non-tariff barriers enabled the manufacturers of various nations to control the automotive markets of their colonial possessions (this was notably true of British and French auto makers, who had the lion's share of markets in their colonies). But Detroit was king in the 1930s, almost regardless of whether the market was Los Angeles, Rio de Janeiro or Johannesburg.

That was 50 years ago. By the time of the hundredth anniversary, Daimler-Benz was generally considered to be the finest manufacturer of mass-produced passenger cars in the world, and was mak-ing more than 500,000 of them annually. In addition, Daimler-Benz was the world's largest manufacturer of heavy trucks (over six tons gross vehicle weight), and had been the holder of this distinction for six years. The growth of the company was so dynamic in the four decades from 1945 until today that almost any statistical comparison verges on the unbelievable. By way of example: in 1954, the watershed year cited in Chapter Eight, Daimler-Benz exported a total of 21,436 passenger cars to all other countries. In 1985, *four times* that many Mercedes-Benz passenger cars were sold in the United States alone. Total Daimler-Benz commercial vehicle sales in export markets in 1954 amounted to 6,925 units. In 1985 more than 5,000 Mercedes-Benz trucks, assembled from parts manufactured in Brazil and Germany and from other parts sourced in the United States, left the Freightliner-owned assembly plant in Hampton, Virginia. The Freightliner Corporation, acquired by Daimler-Benz in 1981, produced more than 16,000 units carrying its own nameplate.

There are various reasons for the success of the oldest resident of a branch of industry that has become increasingly competitive and complicated. Some of them are due to the right persons making the proper decisions at key moments, and others can be attributed to sheer luck—though good fortune usually smiles on those who have helped themselves the most.

From the beginning both Daimler and Benz had preserved their historic vehicles. In 1961, the company's 75th anniversary year, the new Daimler-Benz-Museum opened.

THE CHAIRMEN OF THE DAIMLER-BENZ
SUPERVISORY BOARD

Dr. Emil Georg von Stauss
1926-1942

Hans Rummel
1942-1955

Hermann J. Abs
1955-1970

Franz Heinrich Ulrich
1970-1976

Wilfried Guth
1976-1985

Dr. Alfred Herrhausen
1985-

But the factors in the Daimler-Benz success can be reduced to the workable number of eight. These are, not necessarily in any order of importance:

Quality of Product——Over the long haul, Daimler-Benz products have seldom lacked for quality of manufacture. Robert Braunschweig, for many years the editor-in-chief of the *Swiss Automobile Revue* and the most knowledgeable observer of the European automotive industry, put it succinctly when he said of Daimler-Benz, "They simply didn't know how to make bad cars." Braunschweig was referring to that time in the 1940s and early 1950s when the need for motorization turned practically every European automaker into a commercial success. If it had four wheels on the ground and one to steer with, there was someone out there who would buy it. As a result, some manufacturers didn't worry about quality. Later on, these companies suffered. Cars carrying the three-pointed star had a reputation for quality before the hyphen joined Daimler and Benz, and they have maintained this reputation until the present. Quality at Daimler-Benz has always been thought of as the normal state of affairs, and the responsibility for quality has always been considered a management function. Although it did not start out as a conscious marketing strategy, the extra investment in quality ended up as a major plus, because more and more of the buying public was willing to pay a premium for it.

The Swabian Work Ethic——This could be classified as a sub-topic under quality, but the peculiarities of the region demand that it be treated separately. There are few things more dangerous than generalizations about ethnic or regional groups, since most observations regarding a particular people sooner or later are found to be fallacious. The Swabians, however, seem to be the proverbial exception that proves the rule. To date, at least, no one has been able to challenge the remarkable Swabian attitude toward work. They expect to work, they want to work, and nothing but the best is considered acceptable. And this attitude, through some form of osmosis, has been transmitted from the Swabian base of the company to its various outposts around the globe, and to the various foreign workers who have made their way to Baden-Württemberg to work in the

company's principal plants. Even though more than a dozen languages are spoken on the assembly lines today, there is little doubt that the one carrying the most weight, and the one soon learned, to a greater or lesser degree, by the foreigners, is the Swabian dialect of German. Someone attempting to be humorous once asked if Daimler-Benz was truly a worldwide company, or was it a Swabian company doing business worldwide. There are worse things to be than the latter.

Plant Location——Despite the damage to its factories during World War II, Daimler-Benz was much more fortunate than its competitors. Practically everyone else who built medium-sized or large cars was located in what became East Germany, so the domestic competition disappeared. Once the rubble was swept away, the plants in Untertürkheim and Sindelfingen were found to have usable machinery. Additionally, with the exception of the Gaggenau works, everything else was located in the American Zone of Occupation, where the conditions for economic recovery were the best.

Product Policy——As soon as it could after the war, Daimler-Benz headed for the upper end of the market. Its 2.2-liter cars, introduced in 1951, were considered "big," and its 3.0-liter cars, introduced in the fall of that year, were considered luxurious. By the time the other German and European automakers attempted to challenge Mercedes in this market area, Daimler-Benz products were far too well established. BMW had lost its principal passenger car plant in East Germany. This Munich-based company made an attempt in the early and mid-1950s with its V8-engined 501, 502, 503 and 507 series, but it had little effect. By the 1960s and 1970s, when BMW achieved status in the passenger car field with its medium-sized sedans, Daimler-Benz had so taken over the more profitable upper end of the market that BMW could do no more with its larger "Seven" series than offer token opposition. The Borgward attempt to build a large car in the late 1950s resulted in that company's demise. Even Opel, backed by the power of General Motors, could not build anything that caught the fancy of the German big-car buyer. Large American-made cars, of course, had not been taken seriously in Germany since the 1930's.

The *Wirtschaftswunder*——Or, in English, the German economic miracle, the rapid recovery West Germany made after the war. The Germans needed cars, they needed trucks, buses, and all sorts of motorized equipment. Daimler-Benz was there to fill that need. The fact that there was almost literally a line of customers standing outside the main gate in Untertürkheim, begging to be allowed to leave money in exchange for a vehicle, gave the company more than 25 years of working as fast as it could simply to meet the demand in its domestic market.

The Ownership——Most public companies in the United States operate with one eye on the stock market, and with the chairman, who is usually in office for a period of three to five years, determined to beat the performance of his predecessor. Beat being the operative word, and short-term gains being the goal, many decisions are made with only this in mind. Daimler-Benz has been able to escape this type of management because great blocks of the company stock rest in but a few hands.

To begin with, the Deutsche Bank remained, to a greater or lesser degree, in control, and the chairman of the Daimler-Benz Aufsichtsrat, or supervisory board, has always been a Deutsche Bank man. After Von Stauss, who headed the board from 1926 through 1942, came Hans Rummel, who was chair-

man until 1955. Then came the German financier who wielded great influence in the recovery of German industry — Hermann Abs, who was the chairman from 1955 until mid-1970, and whose influence and guidance went on for a long period after he had given up the gavel. Abs was followed by Franz Ulrich (1970-1976), Wilfried Guth (1976-1985), and the present chairman, Alfred Herrhausen, who assumed office at the 1985 annual meeting. All these men except Von Stauss were also chairmen of the Vorstand, or board of management, of the Deutsche Bank. Whether the Deutsche Bank is the "house" bank of Daimler-Benz or Daimler-Benz is the "house" automaker of the Deutsche Bank is open to discussion, but the relationship has been a good one ever since the bank was instrumental in bringing about the merger of Daimler and Benz in 1926.

The Deutsche Bank controlled, and still controls, slightly more than 25 percent of Daimler-Benz common stock. The number 25 is important because, according to German law, anyone with at least 25 percent of the common stock of a public company has what is known as the "blocking minority." In other words, 52 percent is not enough for control; you need 75 percent. The greatest block of Daimler-Benz stock, however, rested in the hands of the man who had one of Germany's biggest industrial empires before the war and who built another one afterwards:

In Sweden for the sports car races, 1955: Stirling Moss, Juan Fangio and Karl Kling with the 300SL Gullwing. Both the 300SL and 300 SLR won races that day, Kling with the Gullwing.

MERCEDES BENZ

MODEL *190*SL

The Car

The Entire World

Has Waited For...

$3998.

Delivered New York City

MERCEDES-BENZ DISTRIBUTORS INC.
443 PARK AVENUE   **NEW YORK 22, N. Y.**
65 EAST SOUTH WINTER STREET   6465 SUNSET BOULEVARD
CHICAGO, ILLINOIS   LOS ANGELES, CALIFORNIA

A 4 cylinder Overhead camshaft engine that delivers 125 HP* produces astounding performance. Four wheel independent suspension and balance of the light weight car combine to provide roadability and handling ease never experienced before.

Roll up windows and perfect sealing top plus spacious luggage accommodations guarantee luxurious touring. Rich appointments of the interior and built in heating complete *"the car the entire world has waited for."*

*on the clutch at 5500 R.P.M.

The 190SL, the car that U.S. importer Max Hoffman asked Daimler-Benz to build, and one of Maxie's early advertisments for it. More than 25,000 190SL's were produced in the nine years following introduction in 1954. A few lightened versions with plexiglass windshields were sold as competition cars, but prevailing race regulations and the fact that the model was really designed to be a *boulevardier* put a quick end to that. Though overshadowed by the 300SL, the 190SL was well received. "Delightful as the car is at low speeds," wrote John Christy in *Sports Cars Illustrated,* "the upper reaches of the speed range become sheer sensual pleasure." Top speed was 100 + mph.

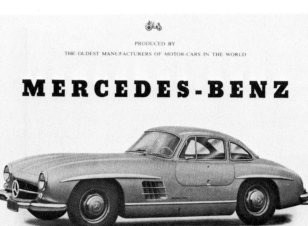

PRODUCED BY
THE OLDEST MANUFACTURERS OF MOTOR-CARS IN THE WORLD

MERCEDES-BENZ

TYPE 300SL SPORTS CAR

The **FIRST, FINEST & FASTEST**
PRODUCTION CAR WITH PETROL
INJECTION TO BE OFFERED
TO THE PUBLIC

Name and address of your nearest distributor available from:
SOLE CONCESSIONAIRES IN THE UNITED KINGDOM

MERCEDES-BENZ (GREAT BRITAIN) LIMITED
58 Camberwell New Road, London, SE5
Telephone: RELiance 5841-5

"Wouldn't it interest you to drive the car which in our opinion is the best performing production model ever offered the public?" the 1955 promotional letter read. "Your nearest Mercedes-Benz dealer will be more than pleased to arrange a demonstration . . . Do contact him — you'll thank us later for the tip." How many of the 1400 Gullwing 300SL purchasers had the opportunity to thank Rudi Caracciola and Juan Fangio for that tip personally is not known. No doubt they would have liked to. The Gullwing became a legend. Pablo Picasso was an owner, as was William Randolph Hearst. Carlo Ponti bought one for Sophia Loren, Porfirio Rubirosa for Zsa Zsa Gabor.

Friedrich Flick. Flick bought the stock at its depressed late 1940s, early 1950s prices, and wound up with 39 percent of the company. Another big investor was the Quandt family. The Quandt brothers, Herbert and Harald, also controlled BMW (eventually holding more than 70 percent of that firm) and amassed slightly over 14 percent of Daimler-Benz. When the Flick, Quandt and Deutsche Bank holdings were added, it meant that approximately 79 percent of the company's shares were in three hands.

All were more interested in long-term growth than in turning a fast deutschmark, and therefore Daimler-Benz was allowed to reinvest and to plan for the long run. To this day, when the stock is in the upper reaches of the stratosphere, the dividends, from an American standpoint, are quite small. To the controlling interests it is not the dividends that are of primary importance; it is the building of equity in the company. There is little question that the guiding hand in all this, especially during the years he had the chair of the supervisory board, was Abs. Under German law banks are allowed to take a far more active role in industry than they are in the United States, and Abs was the man who laid the foundations for the future growth of the star. It was good for his bank, it was good for his country, and it was certainly good for Daimler-Benz.

The Export Markets——Any ambitions to turn Daimler-Benz into a major manufacturer, its management soon realized, would depend on export sales.

The problem was how to get them. In the late 1940s Germans were not particularly welcome in many parts of the world, and new cars were essentially warmed-over prewar models. Yet the company managed to go from this forlorn situation to a point where it now does business in practically every country in the world, to where more than 50 percent of the annual gross sales come from export markets, and to where there are 37 wholly or partially owned subsidiaries among the companies outside Germany that carry the three-pointed star. Additionally, at the close of 1985 there were 16 passenger car and commercial vehicle production plants, and another 31 assembly operations located outside the Federal Republic. Economic downturns in one part of the globe could now be offset by increases in other areas, and Daimler-Benz was truly a worldwide undertaking.

The Sporting Image——Dozens of manufacturers around the world have invested hundreds of millions of dollars in racing in the hope that a victory on Sunday would help them sell more cars on Monday. For the most part, these well-intentioned efforts came to naught. They either sold (or didn't sell) their cars on Monday almost regardless of what happened at the race track. Most of them had no idea how to turn the Sunday victory into a viable sales promotion tool. Others won often, but it didn't help their sales because their production models were not as good as their competition's.

The Daimler-Benz successes in the mid-1950s, on

"A new standard in Grand Prix design," wrote *Motor Sport* editor William Boddy in August 1954 of Mercedes' new W196. The streamliner (facing page) raced first in the French Grand Prix on July 4, the open-wheeled version (above) in the European Grand Prix at the Nürburgring on August 1.

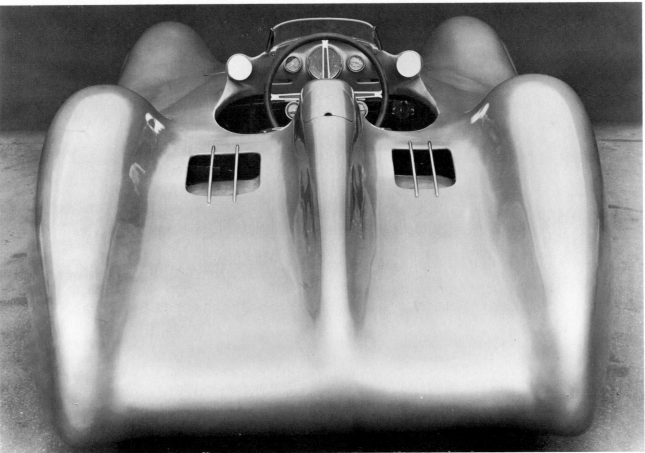

Writing in the mid-fifties with wit and cogency, Laurence Pomeroy compared the BRM Grand Prix car to a "typewriter," the Ferrari to an "abacus," the new Mercedes to "an electronic calculating machine." W196 was a complete surprise, as different from its contemporaries as it was from any Mercedes race car ever before built. The unorthodox is not especially rare in GP car design. But being all new and winning right away is. W196 managed that, with the considerable help of Juan Fangio during its maiden 1954 season. Though both versions were effectively raced, the streamliner was the more aesthetically dramatic. W196 was state of the art; the streamliner was sculpture.

the other hand, fall into a special category, and because they were in this extraordinary time frame, they gave an aura of sportiveness and invincibility to the production cars that continues to this day in many parts of the globe. The victories, with Juan Manuel Fangio winning the world championship in 1954 and 1955, with Stirling Moss winning the Mille Miglia in 1955, and even with the Le Mans and Carrera Panamericana successes of 1952, were doubly impressive. In Germany, the racing success ranked with the World Cup soccer title of 1954 as proof positive to a defeated country that it could once more compete with the best and win—an enormous psychological lift, one that cannot be compared with anything today. To the rest of the world, the fact that Mercedes *cars* won first reinforced the notion that Mercedes cars were *good*, and second impressed on people's subconscious that Mercedes cars were also once more *acceptable*. That romantic figures from other countries, like Fangio from Argentina, Moss from Britain, and John Fitch from the United States, *drove* these cars, emphasized the message: here were foreigners who were good at what they did, and who found German products acceptable.

The fact that Daimler-Benz retired *voluntarily* at the end of the 1955 season, because there were no more worlds to conquer, made this all the more impressive. Whether racing improves the breed has been endlessly debated. Years later, when asked what he learned from his racing cars for his production vehicles, Rudolf Uhlenhaut answered with one word: "Nothing."

But racing did help the image, and that's what sells cars—sold cars then, and sells cars now. Maybe not the second one, but certainly the first.

In the 1950s Abs' man on the scene in Stuttgart was Fritz Könecke, who became the third general director of Daimler-Benz in as many years when Wagner died suddenly, 374 days after the death of Haspel. While Wagner remains little more than a footnote in the history of the company, Könecke was one of those who planned for the future. He was a veteran of the rubber industry when he came to Daimler-Benz, having been with Continental Gummi Werke for many years. He had a master's degree in economics, a doctorate in political science, and the vision of a long-range planner. While Daimler-Benz was rushing to fill its backlog of orders, Könecke and his team started thinking about the future.

Something they could not have foreseen, in fact a project that was already in motion when Könecke took the chair, was the 300SL Gullwing coupe. Absolutes are always dangerous, and when looking at one hundred years of history singling out one of the automobiles built in that century as the most important

French Grand Prix, July 4, 1954 — Mercedes' triumphant return to Formula I competition. In the closing laps Neubauer kept his drivers aware how far ahead of Prince Bira they were. Fangio and Kling finished one–two.

41ᴱ GRAND PRIX
DE L'A.C.F.
REIMS
4 JUILLET 1954

PROGRAMME OFFICIEL   PRIX : 100 FR

French Grand Prix, 1954. Juan Fangio (top, left) had the fastest practice lap at over 200 km/h (a first for a European road circuit), which won the Argentinian 50 bottles of champagne. Hans Herrmann (top, right) set the fastest race lap at 195.463 km/h, a new record for the Reims course. By mid-race Herrmann had retired, but so had most of the works Ferraris, Maseratis and Gordinis. The rest of the race belonged to Fangio and Kling (above), the latter seen nonchalantly scratching his nose as he passed the grandstand. The dice in the closing laps between the two Mercedes drivers livened things up. Behind them, Robert Manzon's Ferrari overtook Bira's Maserati for third.

NÜRBURG RING
ADENAU, GERMANY

89B

IO TRW

European Grand Prix, Nürburgring, August 1, 1954. On race day over 300,000 spectators crowded the 14.25-mile circuit in the Eifel Mountains of the Rhineland. Of Mercedes' four cars, three were open-wheeled versions driven by Fangio (top), Kling and Lang, with Herrmann on a streamliner. Fangio's practice lap of 9 minutes 50.1 seconds broke Lang's course record (9:52.2, established in 1939), and Fangio won the race. Ferraris finished second and third. Herrmann and Lang retired. When Kling pulled in for suspension repair near the end, a crowd of officials and photographers surrounded his car. Neubauer chased them off with his signal flag. Kling finished fourth.

318

Italian Grand Prix, September 5, 1954. Again, Fangio won for Mercedes, although Stirling Moss was a fierce challenger on his Maserati until his oil tank split.

one is risky. But the Gullwing, despite the fact that only 1,400 of the production version were built, stands out as the quintessential Mercedes.

That the Gullwing was produced at all goes to the credit of one of the great automobile salesmen of all time, an Austrian emigré who sold costume jewelry in the old country and cars in the new one: Max Hoffman. The irrepressible Maxie, more than anyone else, was the man who introduced the imported car to postwar America. He was the first to bring the Porsche, Alfa Romeo, BMW and Jaguar, and was the first postwar distributor of Mercedes-Benz. He also was given the opportunity to sell that funny little German car with an air-cooled engine in the back, but after having two of them on his hands for months he thanked Volkswagen for the opportunity and went on about his business. Even legends can be wrong...

Hoffman had seen the Mexico- and Le Mans-winning cars, he wanted them in production form, and he guaranteed Daimler-Benz that he would pay cash and that he could sell 1,000 of them. As if that wasn't enough, Maxie also ordered another car, a

Celebrating the Italian GP victory, from the left: Lang, Neubauer, Fangio, Kling (who broke a radius rod) and Herrmann (who finished fourth). Lang had been on hand for practice but did not race. By year's end he had retired from competition.

319

Swiss Grand Prix, August 22, 1954. The Berne circuit, set amid the pastoral tranquillity of the Bremgarten Forest, was a driver's delight, many of its curves being taken at full throttle. The 4.5-mile course was lapped 66 times in the '54 race, and Fangio (top) led from start to finish. Kling (above) was running with the pack behind the Argentinian until his retirement with ignition failure on the 38th lap. Toward the end, Fangio slowed his lap times by nearly 40 seconds. Behind him, Froilan Gonzales drove aggressively but his red Ferrari could not catch up to the silver Mercedes. Herrmann finished third. Fangio clinched the world driver's championship with this race.

sort of little brother, or better yet, little sister of the 300SL. This one was to be called the 190SL, it was to use the engine from the good but most prosaic 190 sedan, and if it didn't perform as well as its looks suggested, that was OK, too: in America they don't drive so fast. And thus was the 190SL born. Speaking in retrospect more than 30 years afterwards, Uhlenhaut paid homage to Hoffman, saying, "He was the only salesman I knew who could tell engineers what kind of a car he wanted." Research and marketing methods have advanced considerably since Hoffman's day, and Daimler-Benz engineers now work closely with their marketing people. But it is a safe bet that Hoffman's nose for customers would be as sensitive today as it was then.

The production 300SL was, from a styling standpoint, a crowd stopper. It looked like every man's dream of a high-speed sports car; in fact, it looked like it was going 100 miles an hour while it was standing still. Thanks in great measure to the introduction of fuel injection, now used for the first time on a production car, engine power had been increased considerably since 1952 and Mexico; it now stood at 215 hp. This was unfortunately not enough to increase the vehicle's performance over the Mexico entries, since the curb weight of the 300SL was up almost 1,000 pounds over the Mexico race vehicles. But that didn't make much difference. Depending on rear axle ratio, a top speed of almost 150 mph could be achieved . . . or at least that's what it said in the book; few Americans ever had the chance to drive that fast. The car *was* good for 135, however, and in the mid-1950s, there were many roads in the Far West where the adventurous could give themselves a thrill.

The 300SL was one of a kind, and we shall probably not see another.

The 300SL and the 190SL were introduced at New York City's International Motor Sports Show in February 1954. Production was delayed, however, until that summer for the 300 and until the following January for the 190. In the meantime, the W196 grand prix car, a 2½-liter, 280-horsepower straight-eight with fuel injection, desmodromic valve gear and central power takeoff ("rather radical," in Uhlenhaut's typical understatement) was getting ready for its debut in Formula I competition. It was to be built in two versions, a dramatic streamliner for high-speed circuits and an open-wheeled model for twisty courses. As the engineers worked on the final details, Neubauer set about recruiting his team. Karl Kling was all set, but Hermann Lang was tired — a fact apparent both to the team manager and the driver himself. Lang would have retired at 40 if the war had not intervened. Now he was nearly 45. His racing days were coming to an end. "I thought it was time," he said. "If I waited much longer the younger drivers would overtake me and I'd no longer be the fast Hermann Lang, which is how I wanted to be remembered."

Hans Herrmann was taken on. He was from Stuttgart, his driving had attracted Neubauer's attention, and he soon earned the nickname of Mercedes' "racing baker." Now Neubauer needed just one more man: Fangio. That the Argentinian was contentedly driving for Maserati simply made recruiting him all the more interesting. When Fangio drove the Nürburgring in 1953, Neubauer arranged his hotel accommodations (the best in town), sent a doctor when he had an attack of conjunctivitis and then bought him a new pair of goggles that were easier on his eyes, and provided roadside assistance when he spotted Fangio's car in distress on the way back to Stuttgart (that was a bit of luck). Fangio signed on.

The target date for the debut of the new grand prix car was July 4, 1954, which pleased no one at the factory, but the cars could not be made ready sooner. The mid-season start was interesting historically, however, for the July 4 race was the French Grand Prix at Reims, the event that saw the overwhelming Mercedes victory 40 years to the day earlier. "They'll blow up," one veteran race journalist said as the new streamliners were rolled onto the track; "no new design ever wins first time out." Fangio set the fastest practice lap, breaking an average of 200 kilometers an hour for the first time on a European road circuit. But there was a problem. The cars were consuming more fuel than they had during tests at Hockenheim, and extra tanks were necessary to insure that the race could be run nonstop. Uhlenhaut went back to the factory to supervise their construction, and then drove

321

back to Reims. At midnight he and his team were at work installing the new tanks and making final adjustments. At a quarter past one Neubauer and the engineers held their final conference in a street café.

The race was a romp. Herrmann's car retired after he set the fastest lap, but then most of the field also dropped out after a desperate attempt to keep up with Fangio and Kling. Only six of the 21 starters finished. Toward the end, a full lap ahead of Prince Bira's Maserati and Robert Manzon's Ferrari, Fangio and Kling enjoyed themselves in a friendly duel. On the last corner the Argentinian swung wide, Kling came alongside, and they flashed by the grandstand together. On the next lap, with Kling a yard ahead, Fangio caught up as the charging pair passed the grandstand. The crowd loved it; Neubauer was unenthusiastic. Fangio took the checkered flag a second and a half ahead of Kling.

But the British Grand Prix didn't work out as well for the streamliners. It rained and the Ferraris won. The open-wheeled cars had been scheduled for the tight airport circuit at Silverstone, but they were not ready. They were, however, for the next race, the European Grand Prix at the Nürburgring, which Könecke watched from the pits and Fangio won. In the Swiss Grand Prix Fangio led from start to finish. He took the Italian Grand Prix as well.

Although the Argentinian had marched Mercedes to the world championship in 1954, it was apparent to Stuttgart engineers that he was as responsible as the car. Kling's second place in the French Grand Prix and Herrmann's third in the Swiss had been the highest placings of his teammates, and in some races even Fangio's uncanny skill had not been sufficient to defeat the Lancia-Ferraris. That winter the W196 underwent engine and chassis modification. Horsepower was raised to 290 and the roadholding was improved. And Neubauer consulted the little black book he kept on promising drivers and came up with one to add to the team: Stirling Moss.

But Fangio would be number one. This was made clear to Moss. The Argentinian was given precedence over the Englishman in all Formula I races except the British Grand Prix. Moss had no hesitation in accepting these terms because there were other

events where Neubauer would give him free rein. The Daimler-Benz agenda for 1955 included a full sports-racing program. A three-liter version of the 2½-liter straight-eight was installed in a new racing-sports car body, and the vehicle was called the 300SLR.

First up, however, was the Argentine Grand Prix on January 16. The South Americans called Neubauer "Don Alfredo"; Neubauer called the new Mercedes drivers his "embryos"—and he had a problem with them. Moss and Herrmann discovered Buenos Aires night life and broke curfew as diligently as Fangio and Kling observed it; Neubauer threatened to lock them in their rooms. On race day, another problem arose: it was 95° in the shade, and the temperature on the course was 131. Only Fangio could survive it, Neubauer thought; Uhlenhaut wondered about the cars. So did the Ferrari people. The race turned into a swap meet; whichever driver had not collapsed or had been revived was put in whatever car happened still to be running in the torrid temperatures. In the three-hour race the Ferrari that finished second was driven by Froilan Gonzales, Nino Farina, Maurice Trintignant, Gonzales, and Farina again! Another Ferrari finished third in similar fashion. Driving a Mercedes into fourth was Moss, though not in the car with which he started. When that broke down out on the circuit, race officials assumed Moss had as well and assisted him to an ambulance; Moss did not know how to say he was fine in Spanish. But he escaped and returned to the pits to take over for an exhausted Kling, who was driving Herrmann's car. Fangio's victory was grueling. "My cockpit was like a furnace," he said. As far as Uhlenhaut was concerned, the race had proven only that a native Argentinian was better equipped to deal with the weather; it had not proven the Mercedes was superior to the potent Italian cars. The team remained in Buenos Aires for a Formula Libre race two weeks later. The new 300SLR engines were installed in the grand prix chassis for their first competitive testing, which proved something: Fangio and Moss finished one-two.

By February the team had returned to Europe to begin practice for the Mille Miglia. Some 500 cars

Stirling Moss, at age 25, a talented newcomer to Formula I ranks and much in demand at the close of the '54 season. Maserati wanted to retain his services. Enzo Ferrari made him an offer. Then the telegram from Daimler-Benz arrived, and Moss was off to Hockenheim (inset). There, after doing ten laps in a 300SL Gullwing, Moss tried a grand prix car outfitted with a toothy grille designed to protect the radiator from bits of flying paper. Moss put up a lap at 128 mph, which equaled the veteran Kling's best time on the same track. The toothy-grille car never raced (a more attractive solution to the debris problem was found). But Moss did race for Mercedes.

Mercedes 300SLR. Only two Gullwing coupe versions (top) were built. Neither was raced, though one was used as a practice car for the Targa Florio; Rudi Uhlenhaut used the other as his personal transportation. The Mille Miglia team car of Hans Herrmann/Hermann Eger is seen above. The 300 SLR's air brake (center) did more than merely slow the car; as Uhlenhaut explained, in fast corners "it held the tail down and generally enhanced cornering ability." At Le Mans officials asked for another window in the air brake to enhance driver vision to the rear. (Fangio's No. 19 is seen before the addition.) The air brake was used only at Le Mans and in the sports car Grand Prix of Sweden.

entered the 1,000-mile Italian classic in 1955, and one of them made history in what was perhaps the greatest one-man endurance drive since Emil Levassor's solo effort with the Daimler-engined Panhard in 1896. Moss had an advantage over Levassor, his "second brain"—his navigator, *Motor Sport* journalist Denis Jenkinson. Moss and Jenks approached the Mille Miglia as carefully as Daimler-Benz prepared the cars. Trial and error marked their early rehearsals—two practice cars were crashed—but by race day the driver and his navigator had the 1,000 miles in hand. Literally. Jenkinson had transcribed his notes on every nuance of the course onto a sheet of paper 18 feet long, furled in oilskin and inserted in a windowed metal box with rollers top and bottom. The plan was for Jenks to unreel and read the course to Moss as he drove it. Since conversation was impossible in an open cockpit at high speed, they devised hand signals. All corners had been logged and graded.

At 7:22 A.M. on April 30, Moss and Jenkinson settled into their custom-made seats and stormed off in the race they had every intention of winning. It was flat out from the start. When Jenks told Moss that a straight road followed an upcoming crest, Moss took the crest at 170 mph, flew for about 50 yards and sped on. City limits were entered at 150. There was no slowing for railroad crossings. Once Jenkinson noticed they passed an airplane overhead. Moss was

driving at the limit always, over it sometimes, "that awe-inspiring margin that you enter just before you have a crash if you have not the Moss skill," in Jenkinson's words. Jenks lost his glasses at one point, and his breakfast at another, when the G-forces in a turn caused him to vomit. They arrived back at Brescia in 10 hours, 7 minutes, 48 seconds, after averaging 157 kph (nearly 98 mph) for 1,000 miles, a record for the race. They were dirty, grimy and disheveled. Their 300SLR looked as if it had been through a war. But in 1,000 miles of ten-tenths driving, it had required nothing more than refueling and a tire change.

The 1955 Mille Miglia was a complete success. Stuttgart cars took five of the first ten places. Fangio was second, 32 minutes behind Moss, in a 300SLR. Fitch was fifth overall in a 300SL; two other Mercedes took seventh and tenth. And to cap it off, an old superstition had been broken: Moss had led at Rome.

The grand prix cars' first outing in Europe was next, and it was a failure. At Monaco, all three cars retired. Uhlenhaut shrugged his shoulders when reporters asked why. "Gentlemen, unfortunately I cannot tell you," he said. "Only when we take down the engines at the factory will we find the answer." A small unstressed bolt in the valve gear had mysteriously broken in all three cars. That could be easily remedied.

The Eifelrennen on May 29 saw Fangio and Moss

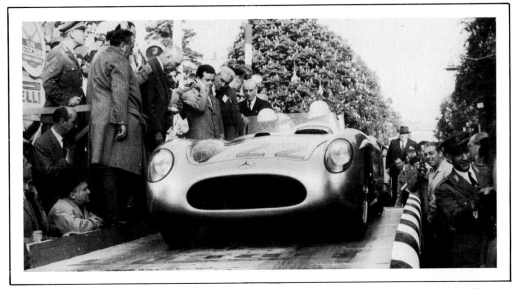

Mille Miglia, 1955. Moss and Jenkinson on the starting ramp in Brescia. Neubauer (standing to the rear) had told Moss to give the 300SLR "plenty of throttle" on the takeoff and not to worry about grounding the car at the end of the ramp.

Mille Miglia, 1955. The start in Brescia: Fangio (center right), Moss/Jenkinson (top right and above). By Rome the Mercedes/Ferrari battle had retired most of the Italian cars, though all four 300SLR's remained, seemingly set to go the distance. Alas, shortly afterwards, a stone pierced Hans Herrmann's fuel tank and Karl Kling retired his 300SLR against a tree. Driving flat out for 1000 miles, Moss was the spectacular winner; Fangio, delayed with a split injection pipe, was second by a half hour, followed 13 minutes later by a Ferrari. In addition to the overall one–two 300SLR finish, Mercedes dominated the unlimited *Gran Turismo* class, John Fitch leading a one–two–three 300SL finish.

finish one-two in SLR's; the Belgian Grand Prix on June 5 resulted in the same finishing order for the Formula I cars. On June 11 came Le Mans . . . and tragedy.

The three Mercedes entered for the race on the Sarthe circuit were virtually the same as the victorious Mille Miglia 300SLR's, with one significant addition: the air brake that had been experimentally tried three years before. Neubauer paired Fangio and Moss in one of the cars, Kling and the Frenchman André Simon in another. For the third Fitch was enlisted to co-drive with Pierre Levegh, the Frenchman who had only narrowly lost the 24 Hours to Mercedes in 1952.

The first two and a half hours saw a great race, with Fangio's SLR and Mike Hawthorn's D-Type Jaguar fighting it out for the lead, with a Ferrari close behind, followed by the SLR's of Kling and Levegh. Then, at 6:30 P.M., in a second, everything changed, and racing was never the same again. After White House corner, on the narrow road in front of pit lane, Hawthorn pulled in to the pits somewhat abruptly; an Austin Healey veered to avoid him as Levegh came down the straight at full speed. The Frenchman's last gesture was an upraised arm to warn Fangio, who was behind him. Then Levegh nicked the side of the Austin Healey, and his car catapulted into the crowd. Levegh was killed instantly; at least 81 spectators died. It was the worst accident in racing history.

In the ensuing panic Neubauer stepped onto the littered road to wave the oncoming cars by. No one was sure what to do next. Uhlenhaut rushed to the race director, Charles Faroux, to ask that the event be stopped. Faroux declined: halting the race would clog the roads and make it difficult to get the injured to hospitals. The race went on. As news of the tragedy spread, telephones on the course were jammed. Finally Fritz Könecke got through to the Mercedes team with the order to withdraw. "The pride of designers and drivers," the official statement read, "must bow to the grief suffered by countless French families in this appalling disaster." The two remaining Mercedes were flagged in at 2:00 A.M. The Fangio-Moss car was in the lead by two laps; the Kling-Simon car was lying third. Inquiries were held afterwards, but no car or driver could truly be blamed; it was simply that narrow straightaway in front of the pits. Ironically, Levegh had mentioned his misgivings —"a feeling of being hemmed in"—to Fitch before the race.

Five days after Le Mans, on June 16, Daimler-Benz announced its decision to retire from grand prix competition at the end of 1955. The rest of the GP season was a romp for Mercedes: Fangio and Moss finished one-two in the Dutch Grand Prix, the cars took the first four places in the British Grand Prix at Aintree (Moss, Fangio, Kling and the Italian Piero Taruffi in his first Mercedes drive), Fangio and Taruffi were one-two in the Italian Grand Prix.

Mille Miglia, 1955. "We clasped each other in delirious joy," said Jenkinson after Moss's victory. Flanking the winning team, from the left, were Mercedes engineers Ludwig Kraus, Rudi Uhlenhaut and Hans Scherenberg.

GRAND PRIX D'EUROPE AUTOMOBILE

MONACO
22 MAI 1955
CHAMPIONNAT DU MONDE DES CONDUCTEURS
XIIIᵉ GRAND PRIX AUTOMOBILE DE MONACO

PROGRAMME OFFICIEL   Prix : 100 Frs

European Grand Prix, Monaco, 1955. Mercedes' problems began during qualifying when Herrmann smacked into a stone balustrade trying too hard to join Fangio (No. 2) and Moss (No. 6) on the starting row. Slight injuries kept him out of the race. Kling was recovering from the Mille Miglia, so André Simon was hurriedly enlisted to drive the third team car. At the start Fangio and Moss beat the No. 30 Ferrari and No. 26 Lancia into the first hairpin, but by half distance Fangio had retired and, just 40 miles from the finish, while leading, Moss followed. Ferrari won.

Belgian Grand Prix, June 5, 1955. It was Fangio and Moss all the way, the Argentinian (No. 10) cool but intent, the Briton (No. 14) displaying his celebrated "armchair" style. Fangio, who had established the fastest lap before retiring at Monaco, took fastest lap honors again, at 121.13 mph, a new record for the Spa-Francorchamps circuit. Fangio finished the 315-mile race in 2 hours 39 minutes 29 seconds. Moss was just eight seconds behind him. Giuseppe Farina followed a minute and a half later with his Ferrari for third. Paul Frère's Ferrari was fourth.

The 300SLR traveled in style. Underneath the hood of this custom-built transporter was a 300SL engine. The vehicle could cruise at 100 mph — complete with cargo.

Before all these events, someone from the factory visited the course to ascertain its safety.

Many races had been canceled in the wake of Le Mans which altered Mercedes' plans for the rest of the sports car season. The team entered the Swedish sports car grand prix on August 2; it was a breeze for Fangio and Moss. And in September, after Uhlenhaut had checked out the Dundrod circuit in Northern Ireland, the Mercedes team traveled there for the 623-mile Tourist Trophy, Neubauer pairing Moss and Fitch, Fangio and Kling and signing up the young German nobleman Wolfgang von Trips to co-drive with Simon. The team finished in that order.

Moss drove spectacularly. During practice he told Fitch he wanted to drive most of the race himself — and that he did, 78 of the 84 laps, with little more than a half-hour breather in over seven hours of driving, most of it in a battle with Hawthorn and his D-Type.

That evening in his hotel room Neubauer wrote down some figures. Since the 300SLR's had initially been entered in only a limited number of competitions, it was thought Daimler-Benz had no hope of winning the world sports car championship. For most of the season Ferrari and Jaguar had a big lead in the point standings. But the sweep of the TT changed that.

Pierre Levegh with his Talbot at Le Mans, 1953. The Frenchman finished 8th that year; a minor accident ended his hopes in 1954. Levegh was determined to win Le Mans. "So happy at this chance," his wife said, after he was offered the Mercedes ride.

Le Mans, 1955. Levegh (top left) was paired with Fitch in No. 20, Kling with Simon in No. 21, Fangio with Moss in No. 19. Like Lang before him, Fangio didn't bother trying to win the race on the sprint to the cars and was halfway back in the 60-car field after the start. By the second lap he had dexterously worked his 300SLR into sixth place, and moved up steadily lap after lap (one of them at a record-breaking 120 mph for the Sarthe circuit). By the second hour he was leading the race, ahead of Mike Hawthorn's Jaguar in the esses (above). Then . . . tragedy.

Le Mans, 1955, seconds after the crash. Warned by Levegh, Fangio had passed through safely.
The battered Austin Healey had spun to a stop. An ashen Kling had just pulled in to the pits.
In the black smoke, Levegh and many spectators were dead.

There was a chance for Mercedes after all, if a 300SLR won the Targa Florio and Ferrari was held to no better than third. Because Italian cars had dominated the Targa since the early thirties, there was a certain bravado in thinking it could be done, but Neubauer never lacked for that. Convincing Daimler-Benz of the wisdom of trying was his next task.

Most management board members were in Frankfurt for the automobile show, and Neubauer hastened there. The news was bad. That morning the board had settled on a sports car race in Venezuela, an important export market, as the team's final event of the season. When he heard that, Neubauer decided to plead his case when everyone was relaxing over coffee after dinner. "As a general rule, I'm all in favor of long meals," he said later, "but this one seemed to go on forever." Neubauer buttonholed Uhlenhaut first, and together they approached Nallinger, who in turn convinced Könecke. The Targa was three weeks away.

Since the job to be done required not only winning the race but holding the Ferraris at bay, Neubauer

Stirling Moss in the pits before the start of the 1955 British Grand Prix on the Aintree circuit
outside Liverpool. The end of the day was memorable twice over. Moss won his first Formula I
race and was the first Englishman to win the British Grand Prix.

Though Italy was on hand with three Ferraris and eight Maseratis, France with three Gordinis and England with three Connaughts, two Vanwalls and a Cooper, the British Grand Prix belonged to the four silver cars from Stuttgart. The order of Mercedes' quadruple victory was Moss–Fangio–Kling–Taruffi. Only a car length separated No. 12 and No. 10 at the finish. In the winner's circle, after the playing of the German and British national anthems, Moss put the victory garland on Fangio's shoulders and announced that the Argentinian could have passed him but chose not to. Then Uhlenhaut, Neubauer and Scherenberg joined the victorious Mercedes quartet for a photo.

Italian Grand Prix, Monza, 1955. Moss had the fastest lap — 134.013 mph — trying to catch up after a pit stop to replace a broken windscreen. But he also blew his engine.

used a safety-in-numbers approach. In addition to the factory cars, he encouraged private Mercedes owners to join in the trip to Sicily. Telegrams were dispatched to round up the professionals: Fangio would drive with Kling, Moss with his fellow Englishman Peter Collins, Fitch with an Irishman, Desmond Titterington. Both Collins and Titterington, Neubauer had noted in his black book, drove very well in the Tourist Trophy. Less than a week later the Mercedes team landed in Sicily: five 300SLR's, more than a dozen private cars, 45 mechanics, seven trucks. Ferrari, leading Mercedes in the point standings by 19-16, had six mechanics, three cars and confidence.

A number of independent drivers, including the Texan Carroll Shelby, had entered their own Ferraris. With the championship now beyond its grasp, Jaguar decided not to enter, but Maserati was there with a dozen cars, all with factory assistance.

The Targa had one stretch that might loosely be called a straight; on the rest of the course, a driver's speed depended largely on his daring. Since the circuit was not closed prior to the race, practice often resembled slapstick comedy. Kling narrowly averted a donkey, Collins avoided a pedestrian but hit a rock, Titterington slid on loose gravel and smacked a bridge, Fitch was almost hit by a gravel truck. Mer-

Fangio en route to winning his fifth Formula I race of the season and his second consecutive world driver's title. His average for the 312-mile Italian GP on the fast Monza circuit was 128.34 mph. Taruffi's Mercedes placed a close second.

cedes mechanics spent their pre-race time banging car bodies back into shape—a day-and-night job. Heavy rains washed out parts of the circuit. But that was no reason to stop the Targa. To conform to sports car championship regulations, this year's event had been raised from eight to 13 laps of the 44.64-mile circuit: a total of 580.32 miles, perhaps 10,000 curves and close to 10 racing hours. On October 16, the 47 cars were sent off individually, 30 seconds apart. The Targa promised to be a wild race, and it was.

Free rein and three driver changes was Neubauer's strategy. The 3.5-liter Ferrari had a 500cc advantage over the SLR, and Neubauer recognized Ferrari driver Eugenio Castellotti as the biggest threat. Castellotti was expected to drive in three-lap shifts; if the Mercedes drivers could handle four laps before being relieved, the team would gain a time advantage. Four laps of that tortuous circuit was asking a lot, but Neubauer flattered his drivers into it. His only other instruction was to go for it — every man for himself.

Moss responded with a first lap of 44 minutes, which broke the old course record by two and a half minutes and was the first time the circuit had been covered at more than 60 mph. Though he was among the last to be flagged off, Moss had passed every car on the road. Fangio was third, Titterington fourth; Castellotti's Ferrari was second. The standings remained thus for the next three laps. Neubauer's heart sank. Castellotti was still in the Ferrari and at the end of the next lap, when he came in for the driver change, he was leading. Where was Moss? He was on the opposite side of the course, at the bottom of an embankment, on top of a rock, spinning his wheels; his car's headlamps were broken, and its body was battered. On his third lap Moss had broken his own record and was trying to do it again when he ran out of road. Several dozen spectators rushed to help. After being removed from the rock, Moss bumped across the field, got back on the course and returned to the pits, losing six minutes; the car was now in fourth. Collins took over as Moss told Neubauer what happened. Rules in the Targa were lax, so Neubauer was less worried about the spectator assistance than about the condition of the car. That it was running at all was a miracle, but how could it last?

Ferrari was leading now, but Fangio was gaining. In the pits an official flagged a Maserati into the Argentinian's path; though he deftly avoided a crash, the incident sent Neubauer into a towering, bellowing rage—"A wounded elephant," in Fitch's metaphor. Fangio kept cool and turned the Mercedes over to Kling in the lead. Meanwhile Collins was driving as quickly as Moss; he had overtaken Titterington and was moving up on the second-place Ferrari. Fitch replaced the Irishman and held fourth position despite the sideswipe of a stone wall he was convinced should have destroyed his rear axle. Collins drove straight up another stone wall. His front wheels spinning in the air, he nonchalantly reversed and was back on the course in a flash. When he turned the car back to Moss at the end of eight laps, Collins had overtaken not only the Ferrari but Kling as well.

Neubauer breathed easier: Mercedes was one-two, with Ferrari a distant third. Moss drove his final laps as adventurously as he had his first. When he crossed the finish line, he was nearly five minutes ahead of Fangio-Kling and nearly ten minutes ahead of the Castellotti-Manzon Ferrari; the Fitch-Titterington car was fourth. Mercedes had won the sports car championship. And how it had been done! "Despite Stirling's efforts and my own to write the machine off," as Collins said. Said Fitch: "The incongruity of the SLR . . . it was built like a tank but as responsive as a jungle cat—a truly fabulous accomplishment in the field of automotive design." Truly fabulous, too, was the SLR record. It had been entered in a half-dozen races, had won five and was leading when withdrawn from the sixth. The car never lost a race. And it had been impossible to break.

A "personal and confidential" letter awaited Neubauer when he returned to the team's villa at sunset. "After prudent consideration," Fritz Nallinger wrote, "the board has decided to withdraw from motor racing for several years." Neubauer was stunned, though wistful. The Targa Florio had been his first race in 1922; it was fitting that it be his last in 1955. He was 64. That evening, he did not tell the team of the decision at the victory celebration.

The official Daimler-Benz announcement followed

Targa Florio, 1955. (At the top) Peter Collins smiling, and driving like a hellion. That the 300SLR he shared with Moss "managed to last right through this race [despite] going over precipices and through walls and shunting other cars" was a source of amazement to Collins. But last it did, and win they did. And Mercedes' second and fourth places in the Targa helped win the company the world sports car championship. (Above) Looking understandably pleased with themselves afterwards were, from the left, Fitch, Titterington, Collins, Moss, Fangio and Kling.

Other venues, other victories. (Top, left) Paul O'Shea began driving a 300SL in 1955, sometimes winning on tracks so small he never got out of third gear. He is seen here leading a Cunningham en route to one of his back-to-back (1956–1957) SCCA national titles. (Top, right) Walter Schock and Rolf Moll en route to winning the 1956 Sestrière Rally — and the world rally championship. (Above) Olivier Gendebien, with navigator Stasse, after a rally win in 1955. Gendebien and his newly-purchased 300SL also won the Stella-Alpine that year and snatched victory from a factory Ferrari in the Dolomite Cup, a performance so impressive Gendebien was hired for the Ferrari team.

six days later when team members gathered in Stuttgart for a reception in their honor. "I didn't know beforehand," Uhlenhaut said, "but I wasn't surprised." Nor was he displeased. For over two years, seven-day weeks had been the norm for his engineers as they juggled both passenger and race car development. "Grossly overworked" was Nallinger's phrase. It was time to channel all energy into vehicles for the marketplace. Production was nearing 50,000 a year —not nearly enough. Customers in Germany were waiting more than two years for their cars.

Among the reasons Neubauer had urged participation in the Targa was the possibility of adding the world constructor's championship for sports cars to the Formula I title, which as things turned out was a successful venture. At the same time, even more laurels were being wrapped around the three-pointed star in 1955. Olivier Gendebien, at the time an up-and-coming young Belgian driver, used a 300SL to win Liège-Rome-Liège, in those days the toughest and fastest of all European rallies. Gendebien also finished seventh overall in a 300SL in the Mille Miglia, taking second place in the grand touring category behind Fitch. Hans Tak, a Dutchman, took another 300SL to the overall victory in the Tulip Rally, his country's event counting for the European championship, and, like Liège-Rome-Liège, a far cry from the timekeeper's nightmare that constitutes rallies on this side of the Atlantic. Werner Engel of Hamburg won the European rally championship, alternating between a 220S and a 300SL in various events. In the United States, 300SL's were successful in Sports Car Club of America events, most notably when driven by Paul O'Shea.

No manufacturer had ever, it seemed, enjoyed such a complete conquest of a single season.

The Daimler-Benz decision to discontinue grand prix racing followed closely on the heels of the tragedy at Le Mans and was announced before the sweep of the season's final three Formula I races. Nallinger's letter to Neubauer had been mailed before the Targa and the victory clinching the sports car championship. The Daimler-Benz directors could not have known beforehand what the season's final result would be. But they must have been confident. Their confidence, as it happened, was not misplaced.

The reception in Stuttgart to honor Mercedes racing engineers and drivers, October 22, 1955. From the left: Fritz Nallinger, Rudi Uhlenhaut, Karl Kling, André Simon, Piero Taruffi, Juan Fangio, Wolfgang von Trips, Werner Engel, Stirling Moss, Olivier Gendebien, rallyist Gilberte Thiron (with bouquet), John Fitch, Hans Herrmann, Peter Collins, Hans Tak.

CHAPTER TEN

QUALITY IN AN EGALITARIAN AGE

1 9 5 5 — 1 9 8 5

The past is but the beginning of a
beginning, and all that is and has been
is but the twilight of the dawn.
—H.G. WELLS,
THE DISCOVERY OF THE FUTURE

By 1955 the company was back on its feet, it had re-established its name through racing, it had a satisfactory waiting line of customers, and two of the industrial powers of West Germany—the Deutsche Bank and Friedrich Flick—were in control of its stock. But despite the worldwide reputation of its vehicles, despite the company's rebirth and the fact that its products were being sold in more than 120 countries, Daimler-Benz in 1955 was still a Swabian undertaking working a six-day week and attempting to do business on a worldwide scale. Passenger car production for 1955 was 63,683; a total of 28,228 commercial vehicles were built; and gross sales amounted to approximately $360 million. In Detroit Daimler-Benz was scarcely noticed, except by some stylists who were attracted to the two new sports cars, the 190SL and the 300SL.

But 30 years later, as the company and the industry it started turn toward their second century,

Daimler-Benz is a worldwide economic force with Swabian undertones. It produced more than 540,000 passenger cars in 1985, plus 210,000 commercial vehicles (in a declining truck market), and gross sales were approximately 60 billion marks, which translates to about $23 billion if you use 2.60 as the exchange rate. Products bearing the three-pointed star are the envy of Detroit, and the American auto industry knows that Mercedes-Benz passenger cars are the standard by which all others are measured.

This rise in the company's fortunes, during which passenger car sales multiplied almost tenfold and gross sales multiplied more than thirtyfold, can be traced to three areas of effort: the German domestic market, the United States, the pacesetter for the entire export effort, and the export drive in the rest of the world.

But the product led everything else. Daimler-Benz is a company whose operations have always been

One era ends, another begins…1958 D'arcy ad for Studebaker-Packard, promoting the 300SL roadster; 1965 Ogilvy & Mather ad for Mercedes-Benz of North America, with an earnest Heinz Hoppe trying to talk Americans into considering a diesel. MBNA had inherited a thousand Mercedes diesels from Studebaker. This approach helped sell them.

(Center, from the left) Heinz Hoppe, the man whose vision made Mercedes-Benz of North America a reality; Karlfried Nordmann, Hoppe's successor in 1971 and MBNA president for a decade; Walter Bodack, MBNA president since 1981 and the man who had shared Hoppe's dream. Bodack secured the new company's headquarters in Fort Lee, New Jersey (top) after Hoppe's phone call from Stuttgart announcing that the negotiations with Studebaker had been successfully concluded. In April 1965 Mercedes moved in. MBNA sold 12,117 cars that year. In 1972 the company moved into its new corporate headquarters (above), 25 miles north of Fort Lee in Montvale, New Jersey. MBNA sales topped 40,000 cars that year. By 1986 more than 85,000 Mercedes were being imported into the United States annually.

ruled by its engineers, and the engineers have designed and built excellent products.

The United States looms large in the last 30 years of Daimler-Benz's history because it was and is the company's great export success, it is today the principal export market in the Daimler financial picture, and most of all because lessons learned in the North American market were carried back to Stuttgart and from there were redistributed around the world as Daimler-Benz pursued its expansionist course.

The first steps in the United States were made by Max Hoffman, one of the great automobile salesmen. He gets the credit for encouraging Daimler-Benz to build the 190SL—strictly a Hoffman creation—and the 300SL, a Hoffman-inspired adaptation of the Mexican road-race-winning coupe. Hoffman was the importer, distributor and seller from 1952 to 1957, introducing the three-pointed star to a rather narrow segment of America. Although Daimler-Benz didn't realize it at the time, this segment, however narrow, was the group that made opinions and set styles for a great percentage of the population. But Hoffman, who at one time or another represented Volkswagen, Porsche, BMW, Jaguar, Alfa Romeo and some other companies in America, was on his way out almost before he was in. His showrooms in New York and Los Angeles sold 253 cars in 1952 and another 421 the following year, but Daimler-Benz needed more than that. And the export department, led by Arnold Wychodil, knew there was a lot of territory between New York and Los Angeles with no representation.

Enter Carl Giese. Giese had been the middle man in one of Daimler-Benz's more satisfying expansion steps, the 1954 deal with Tata, the Indian industrial giant which was to assemble Daimler-Benz trucks in India. Daimler-Benz now had truck plants functioning in Argentina and Brazil. In 1954 the company's export sales of approximately $60 million were the best of any West German automaker (the Volkswagen invasion of America had not yet taken place). Giese went to Wychodil and asked for and received the job of expanding Daimler-Benz operations in the United States.

At this point Giese contacted a former major he had known briefly during the war. In 1954 Heinz Hoppe had a responsible job with Freudenberg and Company, a German rubber goods manufacturer near Heidelberg, but Giese talked him into joining Daimler-Benz. As far as Giese was concerned, Hoppe had two prerequisites for the job: he spoke some English, and he had been to the United States—twice. What Giese did not realize was that he had discovered the man who more than anyone else would blaze the trail for the three-pointed star in the world's greatest auto marketplace and establish Daimler-Benz's export activities as a major arm of the company's business.

But Hoppe was at first unsure whether his good job with Freudenberg should be swapped for something as tenuous as the more-or-less unknown market conditions of the United States. "I said, 'What's my assignment?'" Hoppe said, recalling his interview with Giese. "He said, 'Selling cars.' I said, 'How?' and he said, 'I don't know, we'll find out.'" After a crash course in Stuttgart, Hoppe departed for the United States in the fall of 1954, with Giese's instructions not to contact Hoffman. From the fall of 1954 until the fall of 1964—a decade—Daimler-Benz's success in the United States was in question, but Hoppe stayed with it until he had achieved what he was convinced was the right solution: a wholly owned subsidiary that would enable Daimler-Benz to be represented in the best possible manner—by itself.

The ten years after Hoppe's arrival in the United States were adventurous. First Hoffman was disposed of. Then Giese went looking for a Tata-type connection in America, a connection that would, if possible, also provide Daimler-Benz with an aircraft engine builder as a partner. Eventually contact was made with Curtiss-Wright, and that organization was receptive. But in early 1956 Curtiss-Wright was in the process of taking over Studebaker, one of America's oldest manufacturers, but now rapidly going downhill. Still, Giese thought it was a marriage made in heaven: if each of Studebaker's 2,500 dealers sold two cars per month, that meant 60,000 Mercedes sold in the United States per year! So in May 1957 Daimler-Benz had a new American distributor, Studebaker-Packard, despite Hoppe's misgivings about an affiliation with a company that was headed down instead of up.

And indeed, Daimler-Benz sales were soon in trouble. Studebaker dealers had no idea about how to handle prospects for, or owners of, high-priced cars, shipments from Germany were standing hub-deep in mud, and there were no spare parts. The problem with the arrangement should have been obvious to both sides from the beginning: each expected the other to be its salvation. Curtiss-Wright hoped Daimler would bail out its automobile business, and Daimler-Benz hoped Curtiss-Wright would give it a foothold in the North American market. Giese was finally fired and Günther Wiesenthal, an Austrian, was put in as figurehead president of Daimler-Benz of North America, with Hoppe still the man on the scene trying to keep things together.

Mercedes-Benz Sales, Inc., was formed as a subsidiary of Studebaker-Packard, with Hoppe on the board, in August of 1958. Mercedes-Benz Sales, located at Studebaker in South Bend, Indiana, went about the business of distributing Mercedes-Benz and Auto Union passenger cars. Auto Union, Mercedes' biggest racing rival in the 1930s, had been bought by Daimler-Benz and Stuttgart was trying to figure out how to sell the tiny cars with the two-stroke engines, which to American ears sounded like sewing machines gone mad and which required some oil to be poured in with every tank of gas—not the typical American gas pump jockey's idea of fun. The Auto Union plant in Düsseldorf had been turned over to Daimler-Benz truck production. The Ingolstadt plant, north of Munich, was to continue building DKW's while the Daimler-Benz engineers set about designing something more attractive.

The Auto Union purchase had been initiated by Friedrich Flick, now the biggest stockholder in Daimler-Benz with nearly 40 percent. After Flick came the Deutsche Bank, with approximately 28 percent, and then the Quandt brothers, Herbert and Harald, with close to 14 percent. The Quandts were also the principal stockholders in BMW, which was then struggling to keep its head above water and which had as its best-selling car the 700, a tiny coupe

powered by the two-cylinder engine the company used in its motorcycles. An attempt to merge BMW with Daimler-Benz failed, narrowly, in 1959. A year or two later BMW's engineers produced the 1600, with its excellent four-cylinder engine, and the Bavarians began a climb to respectability and to a point, a decade or so down the road, where BMW would be Daimler-Benz's biggest passenger car rival in its home market.

In the meantime American sales of Mercedes had climbed to the 13,000 level. But Hoppe was worried; he knew neither the organization nor the cars were right. In an age when big V8's and lots of low-end torque were what Americans expected, the funny little Mercedes, with their high-revving fours and sixes, were more a curiosity than anything else, except to a small group of European car fans. Sales were stagnating. The crisis came in the summer of 1964, when Studebaker shut down its South Bend factory and moved operations to Canada. At a Studebaker board meeting Wychodil asked the Americans for a greater effort and was, in effect, turned down. Later that year Byers Burlingame, Studebaker's president, and Harold Churchill, its chairman, went to Stuttgart to discuss the problems—to no avail. In the fall there was another fruitless meeting in New York. In December, at yet another meeting in Stuttgart, Studebaker said it was willing to give up the Mercedes business if Daimler-Benz would buy out the contract.

The sticking point was the price. The sums discussed seem laughable today. Studebaker wanted $5 million. Certain persons at Daimler-Benz wanted to wait until 1965, when Studebaker sales would almost certainly fall below $35 million, entailing the automatic termination of the contract. Hoppe knew that time was of the essence, and that if Daimler took over after a virtual default, he would have to start from scratch again. The Studebaker people were ready to leave for home when, on the last night, Hoppe contacted first Burlingame and then Churchill and talked them both into agreeing to a $3.75 million buyout. Early the next morning at the plant Hoppe button-holed finance man Joachim Zahn and Wychodil and got their agreement. And when Churchill and Bur-

Entering the seventies with Mercedes: the "New Generation" 250 sedan (top, left), 280SE coupe (center, above), 280SE 3.5 convertible (center, below). Introduced in 1963, the Type 600 (above) was produced until 1981. Said Rudolf Uhlenhaut: "We tried to combine a very good boulevard ride in an automobile that could also be driven in a sporty way." In factory tests this limousine topped 120 mph. Introduced in 1968, the sensational 300SEL 6.3 (top, right) could travel over 130 mph and accelerate from zero to 60 in less than seven seconds. European journalist/race car driver Paul Frère said the car was as much fun as a Ferrari. "Merely the Greatest Sedan in the World," said *Road & Track*.

CHAIRMEN OF THE MANAGEMENT BOARD OF DAIMLER-BENZ

Dr. Wilhelm Kissel
(1926-1942)

Dr. Wilhelm Haspel
(1942-1952)

Heinrich Wagner
(1952-1953)

Dr. Fritz Könecke
(1953-1960)

Walter Hitzinger
(1961-1965)

Dr. Joachim Zahn
(1965-1979)

Dr. Gerhard Prinz
(1980-1983)

Prof. Werner Breitschwerdt
(1983-   )

lingame arrived at 11 A.M., it took 10 minutes to settle on the figure of $3.75 million. Later that day Hoppe called New York. "Walter, get an office right away," he said. "We have an agreement. We're in business tomorrow!"

After hanging up the phone, Walter Bodack moved quickly. Bodack, born in Czechoslovakia, had joined Daimler-Benz in Germany in 1953 at the age of 23, was transferred to India a year later, and arrived in New York as office manager and assistant to the vice-president in 1956. After eight years of working with Hoppe, Bodack expected the unexpected. He also shared Hoppe's dream.

A few months later, in April 1965, Mercedes-Benz of North America, the new company, moved in over a shopping center in Fort Lee, New Jersey, just across the Hudson River from Manhattan. Wychodil, even though he was 5,000 miles away, kept the president's title for himself, but Hoppe, with the title of executive vice-president, was the man on the scene. When Studebaker sold out the company had also canceled all of its franchised dealers. This was a legal maneuver and a good one, because it left the newly formed MBNA free to pick the better dealers out of the now defunct Mercedes-Benz Sales network, and over the next few months the desirable dealers canceled by Studebaker were picked up.

And so a new organization was formed, despite considerable resistance from many people in Stuttgart, where the conventional wisdom of the time was to invest as little money as possible in foreign operations, leaving the major portion of the investment—and the risk—to general distributors. Thanks to Hoppe's convictions, Mercedes-Benz of North America became the outstanding exception to this rule.

Building this organization, entirely new except for the dealer body, was an enormous task. Vehicle preparation centers, parts depots, training schools —the bones the organizational flesh would hang on—were established as Mercedes-Benz of North America sought to pattern itself after the traditional field organization of an American manufacturer. Slowly, the company's physical facilities took shape (a corporate headquarters was the *last*

priority).

What makes the success of this first of the wholly owned Daimler-Benz sales subsidiaries all the more surprising is a review of what the company offered for sale in 1965, at the height of the high-horsepower, traffic-light grand prix atmosphere of the sixties. In that first year, the dealers left over after the Studebaker purge had a rag-tag collection of no less than 20 different models for sale, and actually managed to move a total of 12,117 units, 4,080 of which, or 33 percent, were handed over to their new owners in Europe as part of the tourist delivery program. The biggest seller was a four-cylinder diesel, the 190D, which Hoppe had inherited from Studebaker and for which Ogilvy & Mather, the new company's ad agency, had to run a special campaign. If anyone had paid attention to marketing principles they might well have chucked the whole idea, but instead the dealers cleaned up the leftovers from Studebaker-Packard and hoped for better cars in the future. It took a few years, but the better cars came; the 230SL, one of the early mainstays, was succeeded by the 250SL and then the 280SL; a pair of attractive sedans, the 250S and 250SE, came on stream in 1966, and there was even another diesel for that small segment of the American public that did not mind 0-60 times in the two-minute range.

By 1968, with the introduction in Europe of the so-called "New Generation" of medium-sized sedans, an attractive series with modern, classic lines and four- and six-cylinder engines, business began to improve. The engineers were once again leading the way. The product line now made marketing sense, with the "New Generation" providing the lower-priced end. The new 280S, 280SE and 300SEL were the full-size sedans, and the 300SEL 6.3, the 280SL, and the 280SE coupe and convertible and the 600 limousine were the specialty cars. Performance was better, the air-conditioning was finally a reasonable facsimile of American units, the styling was outstanding and the dealer network was getting better. MBNA never looked back. Sales in 1969 were 26,191, or more than double those of 1965, and the rush was on. In 1970, when Wychodil suffered a stroke, Hoppe was called to Stuttgart to take his place on the management board. Thus Hoppe, who had made his name in a foreign country representing a company he barely knew when he joined it, was able to bring his ideas back to the parent corporation and install them in the more important export markets of the world. He had proved that by taking the entrepreneurial risk you could be far more profitable, and he convinced his colleagues on the board to embark on a campaign of establishing subsidiaries wherever possible. In the following years, with Hoppe as the persuasive force, Daimler-Benz bought out the distributors and established sales subsidiaries in Britain, France, Belgium, the Netherlands, Switzerland, Italy and Australia. A dynamic, forceful man who accomplished much through the strength of his personality, Hoppe was one of the principal agents in the process of turning Daimler-Benz into a worldwide company—not only because its cars and trucks were rolling around the globe, but also because it owned real estate on every continent.

In the 1960s, while Daimler-Benz was seeking to establish itself in the United States, Daimler-Benz in Germany was rolling along, riding the wave of the *Wirtschaftswunder,* the economic miracle of the postwar generation, and doing its best to satisfy the line of customers waiting for their new cars. The strength of the company, of its products, and of the favorable market atmosphere was punctuated by the sometimes swift and unexpected changes on the executive floor. Wilhelm Haspel had died suddenly in 1952, and his successor, Heinrich Wagner, died in 1953. Then Dr. Fritz Könecke took over and provided stability from 1954 through 1960; he retired unexpectedly, however, after the tragic death of his young son, who drowned in a swimming mishap. This time the chairmanship was filled by a Flick nominee who lasted from 1961 to 1965: Walter Hitzinger, a gruff, outspoken Austrian who had been the head of the nationalized steel industry in his native country. Hitzinger, who made an impression that was more in the nature of a dent, insisted on being addressed by his colleagues as *Herr Generaldirektor* and was a foreign body in more ways than his nationality. But the company kept on growing, despite him, and when his five-year contract came to an end he was advised it would not be renewed.

His successor, Joachim Zahn, kept the wheel for 14 years, the longest chairmanship since Kissel. Zahn, a tax expert and lawyer from Wuppertal in the Ruhr, came to Daimler-Benz in 1958 as the management board member in charge of finance. Slight of

Continuing the tradition of the luxury sports car. The 230SL (top, left), successor to the 190SL, was introduced in 1963 and was followed by the 250SL (top, right) in 1966 and the 280SL in 1967. The all-new V8-engined 350SL (above, left) was introduced in Europe in 1970, and was followed by the 450SL in 1972. This series turned into an all-time hit.

347

stature, with dueling scars from his student days and voluble in several languages, Zahn was a workaholic who was capable both of walking the tightrope that stretched among the various principal stockholders and of negotiating his way through the other members of the Daimler-Benz management board.

In a country where corporate law gives each member of a board of management an equal vote in all matters, a consensus is much more of a necessity than, for example, in the United States, and after the Hitzinger experience the other members of the Daimler-Benz Vorstand, each of whom had his own kingdom in Stuttgart, was determined he would never be so subjugated again. Hitzinger was the last man to have the title of general director. Zahn was not given the title of chairman but was called the speaker of the board, or, as he often put it, *primus inter pares*, first among equals. Through a mixture of hard work, guile, negotiating skill and judicious exercise of his powers Zahn kept the board and the company moving in the right direction, and in 1971 the supervisory board awarded him the title of chairman. He remained at the head, with the lights burning late in the *Hochhaus* almost every night he was in Stuttgart, until he retired at the beginning of 1980.

Although the buildup of the export markets and the normal corporate expansion at home kept Zahn and the rest of the Vorstand fully occupied, the passenger car business remained the principal jewel in the crown, and as a consequence the development of new Mercedes models drew more attention than anything else that went on either in the Untertürkheim headquarters or in the far reaches of the growing empire. And passenger car development at Daimler-Benz was for many years in the hands of Rudolf Uhlenhaut of racing team fame and Karl Wilfert, the transplanted Viennese. (For that matter Uhlenhaut too was "transplanted": he was born in London, the son of a German banker father and a British mother, and spent his childhood in Britain, Belgium and the Netherlands.)

Both Uhlenhaut and Wilfert served under three chief engineers, Hans Nibel, Fritz Nallinger and Hans Scherenberg. Though they themselves never reached the Vorstand level they more than anyone else shaped the Daimler-Benz passenger car look, behavior and reputation for more than three decades. They were diametric opposites: Uhlenhaut was quiet and introspective, Wilfert witty, urbane, and sharp-tongued. Uhlenhaut came into prominence by the time he was 30, when he had been instrumental in improving the roadholding of the grand prix cars after a disastrous 1936 season in which the Auto Unions showed their tailpipes to Mercedes. Uhlenhaut took two grand prix cars and a few mechanics to the Nürburgring and drove the cars until they broke. Then he came back and recommended the long-travel suspension that made the race cars winners again and gave Mercedes-Benz passenger cars a feature that in years to come would be adopted by practically every other automaker. Uhlenhaut was very matter-of-fact about his rapid rise: "I could drive fast and then I could tell them what to fix," he said, "so they listened to me. In those days Max Wagner, who was the chief of the engineering design department, couldn't drive, and for that matter neither could Kissel." Uhlenhaut even reduced his race-car driving to simple terms: "It's much easier than a passenger car, you know. . . . Brakes are better, the steering's more precise, and since you can see your front wheels you know exactly where you are putting them; it only gets difficult when you are trying to go very fast." For Uhlenhaut, however, it couldn't have been too difficult; when Fangio and Moss were on the racing team it was Uhlenhaut who held the unofficial lap record at the Nürburgring, set in the 300SLR one day during a practice session.

Wilfert, on the other hand, was more of a manager and a thinker. His Sindelfingen crew, which included the brilliant Béla Barényi, the holder of more than 2,500 patents, was the first to design and patent the crushable front end, thus giving birth to the principle of energy management in a crash and taking into consideration, for the first time, the proposition that cars should be built not only to run but to perform well in accidents. Wilfert's 1966 Stapp Conference paper on the basics of automotive safety is a classic. The controlled-crush front end was patented in the early 1950s, more than a decade before anyone heard of

Ralph Nader and before anyone else in the industry had considered accident survivability ("passive" safety, according to Wilfert) when designing a car.

Although conceiving, designing and developing a car is always the work of many people, Uhlenhaut and Wilfert stamped the Mercedes line with their personalities, and in the days when there were no computers to record every facet of a vehicle's road behavior, it was Uhlenhaut's personal judgment that decided what would or would not be done.

The team's most fruitful period where mass-produced models were concerned began with the 230–250–280SL's that were sold from 1963 to 1970 and the 250S–250SE–300SEL sedans that were introduced in the mid-1960s and were later sold, with 4.5-liter engines, through 1971 in Europe and through 1972 in export markets. This line also included the now-classic 300SEL 6.3, which Uhlenhaut created by shoehorning a large V8 made for the 600 limousine into a space originally intended for an inline six and then making this Stuttgart-style hot rod behave as well as any of the other, more civilized cars. They followed this full-size sedan triumph with the medium-size "New Generation" line that carried four-cylinder gas and diesel and six-cylinder gasoline engines. Then came the 350SL, introduced in 1971. Today, at the time of the hundredth anniversary, it is the longest-lived sports car Daimler ever built and a sports touring model of which more examples have been built than all other Daimler, Benz, and Daimler-Benz sports models put together. It has carried eight different engines during its 15 years of existence. A two-seater coupe with hard and soft tops, it has a certain look about it that has touched car lovers all over the world, especially in America.

The final Uhlenhaut-Wilfert project was introduced in the fall of 1972 and was called, internally, the W116. This was a full-sized modern sedan with a new suspension that came with 2.8- and 3.5-liter engines when it was introduced. It was the most advanced passenger car of its time (which lasted through 1980), with engines ranging from the original 2.8-liter up through a 6.9-liter version of the 600 engine. This last also saw the car equipped with a hydropneumatic suspension. The W116 was given, finally, a turbocharged five-cylinder diesel that gave Mercedes-Benz of North America a leg up during the energy-conscious days of the late 1970s. Close to half a million W116s were built, a fitting swan song for Uhlenhaut and Wilfert. When they retired, they left behind ideas that played an important part in the development of the next generation of passenger cars, and most important, a standard to which every Daimler-Benz engineer—for that matter every automotive engineer regardless of his affiliation—aspires.

Mercedes-Benz has not returned to grand prix or world championship long-distance racing since 1955. Yet the magic of the marque's successes until its well-publicized retirement was such that whenever Daimler-Benz participated in *any* competitive event during the last 30 years, the automotive world and the press took ten times more notice than they would have if another company had done the same.

When Karl Kling announced in 1960 that Mercedes would enter a three-car team in the Monte Carlo Rally, the press assumed it would be an all-out effort. Not quite. It was simply a logical next step. In 1959 Kling, who had never been to Africa before, was given permission to follow the 8,680-mile Algiers-Cape of Good Hope Rally as a "tourist" on the "off chance" the company might consider rallying in the future. Kling prepared a 190D diesel, took along a friend, the Stuttgart radio reporter Rainer Günzler—and, chided over drinks in Algiers that a race driver should really be more than a tourist, decided abruptly to enter the rally. To everyone's surprise except his own, Kling won.

This African success encouraged the factory entry in the 1960 Monte Carlo, though management had to be talked into it. The argument was that a rally, unlike a race, emphasized endurance as well as speed, the cars were production models, and the team would generate favorable publicity for the new 220SE. And the Monte (inaugurated in 1911) was among the oldest and most famous of European rallies.

The Mercedes team included one veteran international pair, Walter Schock and Rolf Moll. Schock, born in Stuttgart, was a food importer; Moll was a graduate student in engineering who was writing his

(Top, left) Karl Kling, in ascot, Rainer Günzler, in sneakers, and their 190D at the finish line in Cape Town following the 1959 rally win which set the stage for factory competition in the sixties. (Top, right) Walter Schock and Rolf Moll and their 220SE en route to victory in the 1960 Acropolis Rally. The Parthenon is in the background. (Center) The Mercedes 219 of Ken Fritschy and William Ellis attracting a small audience on one of the remote stretches of the East African Rally in 1960, which Fritschy–Ellis won for the second consecutive year. (Above) Celebrating the 220SE clean sweep of the 1960 Monte Carlo Rally: the second-place Eugen Böhringer–Hermann Socher team is on the left, the third-place Roland Ott–Eberhard Mahle team on the right. Kling stands between the winning Schock–Moll team in the center.

The Gran Premio Standard of Argentina covered 2,765 miles, many of them over the car-breaking mountain roads of the Andes. In 1961 207 cars entered; only 47 finished, among them Walter Schock and Manfred Schiek (top, left), who won in their 220SE, with another 220SE second. In 1962 the Argentine-winning 220SE was driven by Ewy Rosqvist (right) and Ursula Wirth, who placed third in the four-car Mercedes sweep of the event in 1963 (top, right). Feisty Eugen Böhringer won four rallies that year, among them the Liège-Sofia-Liège (center, left), with a 230SL and navigator Klaus Kaiser. Factory rallying ended in 1965. Karl Kling (above, with his 300SE) retired in 1970. The London-to-Sydney enticed Mercedes back into competition in 1977, and 280E's finished one–two (the Fowkes–O'Gorman car at center, right).

thesis between rallies. They had been a team for years, and in 1956, driving a 300SL and 220S, had won the European rally championship. The two other teams, Eugen Böhringer and Hermann Socher, Eberhard Mahle and Roland Ott, were less experienced. And since the entry was made late, there was little time to practice before the mid-January start. "Our team of three cars had three people helping," Böhringer remembered. "Karl Kling, Alex Korff [Baron von Korff, who would follow Kling as head of the sporting department] and one mechanic. Plus six spare tires—the rules allowed two each."

A total of 345 automobiles participated in the 1960 Monte Carlo Rally, departing from eight European cities and wending their way over 2,250 miles of pre-selected roads, most of them snow- and ice-covered, to converge on Monaco. Only half the field survived the distance. With Warsaw as their departure point, all three 220SE's made it. After the 90 qualifying cars were put through the mountain regularity test, and all points were added up, not only had the Schock–Moll 220SE won the Monte outright—the first German car ever to do so—but the Böhringer–Socher and Ott–Mahle 220SE's were second and third. It was the first and to date the only 1-2-3 sweep in the rally's history.

If Kling's solo effort in Africa encouraged the Monte Carlo entry, that result in turn shouted for more, so in 1960 the factory designated Schock–Moll as the number one team, provided a few more mechanics, and set out in pursuit of the European championship. Schock did not disappoint. Among the veteran driver's subsequent victories was the Acropolis, a rally almost as formidable as the Monte. Instead of snow and ice, this event took place in dust and heat often exceeding 100° in the rugged Greek mountains. Evenings brought no cooling breeze, the dust was so thick even fog lights could not pierce it, and the roads were filled with potholes. Arriving in Athens with penalty points in the hundreds was not out of the ordinary; in 1960 Schock brought his 220SE into the Greek capital without any, which was phenomenal. By year's end Schock and Moll had won the championship.

In 1961 Mercedes had three major victories.

Schock, teamed with Manfred Schiek, won the Gran Premio Standard in Argentina, with Hans Herrmann and Rainer Günzler finishing second, also in a 220SE. In the Central African Rally Günzler rejoined his former partner and Kling caught rally officials off guard with his record-smashing time: they were enjoying coffee in an adjacent barracks as he roared to the finish line in Agadès. Another 220SE placed second. And there was yet another one-two Mercedes finish in the East African Rally.

Then it was Eugen Böhringer's turn. Short, slight, balding and pushing 40, Böhringer looked like the antithesis of a rally champion. But his Mr. Peepers mien was deceptive. Captured by the Russians during World War II, he had spent half a decade in Siberian coal mines. He was a tough little man and, though he could barely see over the steering wheel, he dominated the European rally scene for two years: in 1962 with the 220SE and in 1963 with the 300SE and 230SL.

Böhringer was fast, determined, resourceful and reluctant to give up easily. Once in Yugoslavia, advised to detour because the road ahead was blocked by a disabled truck, he went to see for himself. "On both sides of the truck were huge rocks, and the space between was narrower than the Mercedes," Böhringer recalled. "I assessed the situation. To detour would lose time. So I backed up about 200 yards and gunned it. There were no doors left on the car, but we made it through." And he won.

In 1962 Böhringer started in eight championship events, won three outright (the Acropolis, Polish and Liège-Sofia-Liège), scored seven class victories, placed second twice (once in the Monte Carlo), retired in just a single rally—and was the hands-down European champion. In 1963 he was champion again, though unofficially, since internal dissent in the International Automobile Federation meant there was no official award.

The Gran Premio Standard of Argentina belonged to Mercedes during the early sixties, though not to Böhringer in 1962. "The girls won that one," said he cheerfully. "The girls" were Ewy Rosqvist and Ursula Wirth, superb Swedish drivers and beautiful blondes both. Not only did they capture overall

352

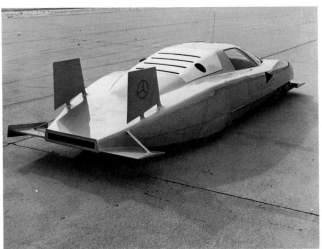

Mercedes' laboratory on wheels. The Wankel-engined ClII was tested in 1969 (top) and refined as the C111-II for the Geneva Automobile Show in March 1970. Its front suspension was subsequently adopted for the S-Class Series 116 sedans, but the Wankel was abandoned. A turbocharged diesel powered the experimental car next, and in April 1978, C111-III (center, left) was driven 199.902 mph for an hour at Nardo, one of nine world records established that day, some bettering previous marks by 40 mph. In April 1979, with a 500 + hp V8 (center, right and above), C111-IV lapped Nardo at better than 250 mph to break a Porsche record, and then went on to establish four more marks.

honors with their 220SE, they did it by winning all six stages—a first in the event's history—in a record-breaking 78.8 mph. (Böhringer lost his engine while fording a stream.) In 1963 Böhringer led a four-car Mercedes sweep in the Argentine—yet another first in the event—and in 1964 he was the leader of a three-car Mercedes sweep. After crossing the finish line in 1964, Böhringer headed right for Buenos Aires airport and a flight to Hong Kong. He had to drive the touring car Grand Prix of Macao next. He won that one, too.

So long as Daimler-Benz remained competitive, rallying was worthwhile for a factory long involved in motor sport, and the publicity was good. But by the mid-sixties the arrival of "homologation specials" from other manufacturers changed the sport. Daimler-Benz did not relish competing against specially built rally cars, nor did the company intend to build any. Better to retire as a winner, and return the sporting department to its role of assistance to independents. Ewy Rosqvist had married Baron von Korff, Böhringer went back to his vineyard in the hills above Stuttgart and, at the age of 60, after three decades of Mercedes racing and rallying, Kling retired.

In 1970 the Beatles disbanded, the Aswan High Dam was completed in Egypt, the Environmental Protection Agency was created in the United States, and Daimler-Benz was receiving checks from enthusiasts all over the world anxious to buy an automobile the company had no intention of producing. Ken Purdy called it the "Wundercar." Mercedes called it the C111.

The desire to build a new sports car had been strong among the engineers and ultimately the board agreed, with the understanding that the project be a laboratory on wheels to test styling and engineering ideas for possible later use. The C111 was Daimler-Benz's first mid-engined car in over 80 years. Its engine was an entirely new one for the company: a rotary-engined Wankel, first, when it was announced in 1969, with three rotors, then with four. The revised car, unveiled at the Geneva Automobile Show in March 1970, was called the C111-11. Its power and performance were breathtaking: 350 horse-power, 0-60 mph in less than 4.8 seconds, with a timed top speed of 187 mph. That's when the letters started coming in. But in addition to its performance, the C111 was appealing because of its looks. For Karl Wilfert and his body engineering team, the project had been a chance to let loose in the creation of the raciest Mercedes since the 300SL and the first Mercedes to utilize fiberglass. Because response to the C111 was so overwhelming, Daimler-Benz management briefly had second thoughts about producing it in a small series—Hoppe said he could have sold a thousand in the United States without even putting a price tag on them—but doubts about the Wankel's long-term reliability in such a high-performance car scuttled the idea. Then the fuel crisis squelched the company's interest in Wankel completely.

The C111 was back in 1976, however, with a new engine. Practical reliability had long been the diesel's forte, but in sporting performance it was generally considered as fast as one's maiden aunt. Daimler-Benz engineers knew that turbocharging could more than double the horsepower of their standard five-cylinder diesel (from 80 bhp to 190) without any reliability loss. The C111-11D was the obvious car in which to try turbocharging, and record breaking was the best way to demonstrate the result. On June 12, 1976, on the Nardo track in Italy, a team composed of Mercedes engineers Hans Liebold, Joachim Kaden, Erich Waxenberger and Guido Moch drove 2½-hour shifts for 60 hours. What could a turbocharged diesel do? This one did 156.867 mph for 5,000 miles, 156.676 mph for 10,000 kilometers, 156.396 mph for 10,000 miles—all absolute world records.

But even better was to come. The horsepower of the turbocharged diesel was raised to 230; wind-tunnel testing developed a new wind-cheating body. The new car was called the C111/111. In late April 1978, the Belgian journalist Paul Frère and Rico Steinemann, a Swiss public relations man, joined Moch at Nardo. They captured nine world records—from 100 kilometers at 196.574 mph to 12 hours at 195.319. Equally significant was a figure never considered in official record lists: in a half-day of flat-out driving, the car had averaged 17.6 mpg.

The C111/111 was the fastest diesel the world had ever seen. And no car had ever been driven so fast on so little fuel.

London to Sydney. No Mercedes had ever traveled so far for victory. Over six and a half weeks of driving, some at 100-plus mph, some in the mountains, some through deserts, some in mud, some dodging kangaroos in the Outback. London-Sydney was the longest marathon in contemporary motoring history. In 1977 Mercedes joined in.

Five new 280E's were independently entered, but they received full factory support, and only one of them didn't make it to Australia. A good many competitors dropped out in the dense rubber-plantation country of Malaysia. Some got lost. But Australia was the worst: heavy rains had brought washouts. Sixty-nine cars started in the London to Sydney, 13 finished within the allotted time. Behind the winning Mercedes team of Britons Andrew Cowan, Colin Malkin and Michael Broad was the 280E of Tom Fowkes and Peter O'Gorman. Two more 280's finished sixth and eighth. The odometer on Cowan's car read 31,760 kilometers (about 19,700 miles) at the finish.

Like the win at Monte Carlo in 1960, the London-Sydney victory in 1977 persuaded Daimler-Benz to go back into competition after an absence of 14 years.

Cowan's subsequent drives for Mercedes were shorter—except for the 18,600-mile Round South America marathon in 1978, a race which Juan Fangio, the Mercedes-Benz president in Argentina, had encouraged Stuttgart to enter. It was a romp for Mercedes: 450SLC's finished first, second and fourth; third and fifth places were taken by 280E's. Cowan was behind the wheel of the winning car.

But dominating in South America was one thing; winning championship rallies was another. The 450SLC was too big and heavy to be a "proper" rally car, and the company remained unwilling to build a special car for this purpose. Still, the cars were competitive, and generally finished well. In the rain-soaked 1979 East African Safari Rally, for example, Hannu Mikkola was second, Cowan fourth, Bjorn Waldegaard sixth. And when the sun shone on the Bandama Rally in the Ivory Coast that year, the Mercedes drivers took revenge on opponents who said they didn't have a prayer in Africa. Only eight of the 59 starters in the 1979 Bandama finished, but among them were all four of the 450SLC's entered — driven by Mikkola, Waldegaard, Cowan and Vic Preston, Jr., in that order. A Toyota was fifth, a Peugeot sixth, Datsuns were seventh and eighth. It was the fastest rally of the year, and the Mercedes performance was unprecedented; never before had any manufacturer enjoyed a quadruple victory in

The 450SEL 6.9 (top, left), late seventies successor to the 300SEL 6.3. The 300TD (top, right), Mercedes' first station wagon, which arrived in 1978. The 500SEL (above, right), introduced in 1979. Daimler-Benz's "Auto 2000" (above, left), the concept car of the early 1980's, which has been tested with gas turbine, V8 gasoline and turbocharged V6 diesel engines.

Africa. And the Bandama was the first world championship rally won by a car with an automatic transmission.

The engine in the 450SLC was used for another car which scored a number of firsts in 1979. The C111 was back. The reason: a try for the record established in 1975 when Mark Donohue drove a 1000-horsepower Porsche 917/30 at 221.027 mph on the 2.66-mile oval at Talladega, Alabama. Although that was not an FIA-recognized mark, Donohue had gone faster than any other man on any circuit. But Mercedes engineers thought they could top his performance.

Turbocharging a diesel had made a record breaker of the C111/11; now the same process would make a world beater of the gasoline engine in the C111/IV. The big V8 was bored out and fitted with two turbochargers for more than 500 bhp at 6200 rpm. Wind-tunnel testing produced a new body shape, with two rear fins and spoilers fore and aft. Again, the 7.8-mile Nardo track was selected for the attempt. On a sunny April 4, 1979, Dr. Hans Liebold, a C111 project engineer, got behind the wheel and after lapping at 250.918 mph to break the Porsche record by more than 30 mph, continued on for a few more. Within a half-hour new world marks were set for the standing-start 10 kilometers (199.140 mph), 10 miles (207.114 mph), 100 kilometers (233.335 mph) and 100 miles (228.196 mph).

The 1980 rally season was less successful, though it ended with another victory in the Bandama. Immediately afterwards Daimler-Benz announced its retirement from rallying.

But the company has continued to participate in quasi-competitive events when the occasion arose. In the summer of 1983 three of the new 16-valve 190's, somewhat modified from their production configuration, ran 50,000 kilometers at Nardo, setting several records en route, including an absolute mark of 153.722 mph for the 50,000 kilometers. Then in May 1984, just before the cars went on sale, a group of 20 former and current grand prix drivers drove as many 190-16's in a one-make race at the opening of the revised, much shortened Nürburgring. It was

nice, just as was the new Ring. But it was a long way from the days in the Eifel Mountains when the snarl of the supercharger echoed through the pine forests as Rudolf Caracciola, Hermann Lang and the rest drove to victory.

Back when the sixties turned into the seventies, while the engineers kept on designing and developing and the Sindelfingen plant was devising new ways to increase production, the waiting lines for new Mercedes grew even longer—partly because of the expanded export market. Hoppe had returned to Stuttgart in the fall of 1970, and early the next year his place in the United States was taken by Karlfried Nordmann, a veteran of the German domestic organization. The momentum built up under Hoppe kept on rolling; the 50,000 mark was passed in 1979 as Mercedes-Benz became a household word in America (if, that is, your household was of the upper-income variety). Two developments played a major role in the expansion of the American market. One was the institution of a near-revolutionary standard-equipment policy. In 1971, a year in which only 20,000 of the millions of cars sold in the United States carried a five-figure price tag and almost half of these were Mercedes, that might have seemed like marketing suicide, but it proved exactly the opposite. Upper-income buyers of high-priced merchandise, MBNA's marketers reasoned, did not want to know that the radio cost X dollars more or that the air-conditioning added Y dollars to the price tag—these features should all be part of the package. Sales boomed. Consequently other manufacturers picked up the idea, offering, like Mercedes, much previously optional equipment as "standard." The other factor spurring MBNA's growth rate in the mid and late 1970s was the five-cylinder diesel, introduced in Europe in 1974 and in North America in 1975. The 3.0-liter power plant was the first to dispel the sluggish diesel image, and the energy-conscious public saw the five-cylinder as an answer to its problems. When the engine was given a turbocharger in the late 1970s and installed in the W116, sales got another boost. For several years in the late 1970s and early 1980s, more than 75 percent of the Mercedes-Benz North American volume consisted of diesel-powered automobiles.

But the updating of the diesel was not the only important change in the Daimler-Benz organization in North America. Nordmann retired early in 1981 and his place was taken by Werner Jessen, the head of the giant Daimler commercial vehicle manufacturing subsidiary in Brazil. Soon after he took over an agreement to purchase Freightliner, an American heavy truck maker, was announced, and Jessen felt he should also be in charge of that activity. Stuttgart disagreed; Jessen insisted—and soon found himself without a job. He left in April, and on July 1 Walter Bodack, Heinz Hoppe's assistant during the turbulent times of the founding of MBNA, became president of the company he had served since its infancy. Freightliner, based in Portland, Oregon, was run separately, and MBNA, Freightliner, and Freightliner Credit Corporation became part of a group headed by Daimler-Benz of North America Holding Company.

In Stuttgart Joachim Zahn's successor was obvious almost from the day he joined the company in early 1974, after leaving Volkswagen. He was Gerhard Prinz, a charismatic figure whose industrial career had been meteoric. From a well-to-do manufacturing family in Solingen, near Cologne, Prinz first earned his law degree, then went to work for a German steel company. He soon became the assistant to Kurt Lotz, chairman of the German subsidiary of Brown, Boveri et Cie, the giant Swiss company. When Lotz went to Volkswagen as chairman Prinz went with him, following a traditional path for many young executives in German industry who serve as assistants to chief executives: if they are good they skip two or three management levels on their way to the top. Prinz was soon head of the NSU-Audi division of Volkswagen, and through this position became a presence in the industry. After Lotz was forced out and Prinz had philosophical differences with his successor, Rudolf Leiding, he knew it was time to leave. Daimler-Benz wasted no time in bringing him aboard as Vorstand member in charge of purchasing, a much more prestigious job in Europe than in the United States and one that gave Prinz freedom of movement.

In that job in 1977 Prinz was the principal force behind the acquisition of Euclid, the Cleveland-based manufacturer of ultra-heavy trucks, and he also spent much of his seemingly limitless energy looking for another suitable American truck manufacturer for Daimler-Benz to acquire. When Zahn retired, although there was some discussion about Edzard Reuter, the Vorstand member for finance, Prinz's appointment as chairman was almost inevitable.

In a company as large as Daimler-Benz it is always difficult to place credit for success or blame for failure on one person, but there is little doubt that Prinz's tenure saw the ship with the three-pointed star on its ensign make a decided change of course. A major factor in this change was a new car model, known internally as W201 and to the buying public as the 190, or Baby Benz. The history of the Baby Benz and how it changed the course of Daimler-Benz's corporate strategy goes back to something basic: oil.

One of the results of the energy crisis of 1973–74 was the United States government's promulgation of fuel consumption standards—part of a new energy-consciousness in a country used to big V8's and cheap gas. These standards, which went under the acronym of CAFE, for corporate average fuel economy, required that all models of any make sold in the United States have an average fuel economy that improved year by year until, in 1985, the fleet average would be 27.5 miles per gallon. This posed little or no problems for most Japanese or European manufacturers, and Detroit's Big Three had enough small cars in their lines to make compliance seem feasible (after an outlay of billions of dollars). But for Daimler-Benz, which made only large and medium-sized cars, it would be impossible, despite the diesel. Ever since 1945, the company's passenger-car business had operated on the unique strategy that it was better to have one car too few than one car too many. Except in North America, where buyers refused to wait and an inventory was necessary, Mercedes customers simply waited—in Germany as long as three years for certain models. Market success was governed by production capacity, and the only passenger car assembly plant, Sindelfingen, was bursting at the seams.

Now, with CAFE, would the company in effect

The 1986 North American edition of the 190E 2.3, with electronic fuel injection and complete equipment. The concept of the 190 series was a challenge that was aggressively met and a gamble that has paid off handsomely. The smaller Mercedes opened an entirely new market.

abandon the market by sending only low-consumption, low-performance diesels to America? That was obviously impossible. So in the winter of 1975–76, the momentous decision was made: Daimler-Benz would develop a completely new small car. Although it would be developed with an eye toward lowering the American fleet average, it would also have to be sold in other parts of the world—which meant that Daimler-Benz not only had to invest in the development of a new vehicle, it also had to spend even more money on expanded production facilities—a second assembly plant. The American regulations were like a pebble dropped in a pond: the ever-widening circle of ripples affected the life of the entire organization.

The decision to go ahead, pushed by Hoppe and the rest of the sales department, was made under Zahn; it culminated, under Prinz, in the introduction of the 190 series in the fall of 1982. The car itself was

built under the aegis of Werner Breitschwerdt, who during its gestation period went from head of body engineering (which includes styling) to chief engineer. And the man who introduced the 190 to the markets of the world was Hans-Jürgen Hinrichs, Hoppe's successor in charge of worldwide sales. The 190 turned out to be the biggest first-year success in the company's history; the several hundred million marks invested in the practically all-new Bremen plant were more than justified, and, as an unlooked-for bonus, the modern, high-performance 190 became a "conquest" car that took the younger segment of the German domestic market away from BMW after the Bavarians had spent 20 years taking it away from Daimler-Benz. At one point in mid-1985, the 190 series was the third best-selling model in Germany in any price category.

But Gerhard Prinz never saw these results. A man

Mercedes in the 100th anniversary year . . . the 300E, with fuel injection, five-speed manual or four-speed automatic, long hood, short deck, wind-cheating body, luxury appointments — a family sedan capable of 140 mph and zero to 55 in 7.5 seconds.

THE MANAGEMENT BOARD OF DAIMLER-BENZ, 1986

Prof. Werner Breitschwerdt

Dr. Manfred Gentz

Hans-Jürgen Hinrichs

Dr. Rudolf Hörnig

Dr. Gerhard Liener

Dr. Werner Niefer

Edzard Reuter

Dr. Peter Sanner

Walter Ulsamer

who sometimes rose before dawn on Sundays to take care of paperwork and who would fly to New York on the morning Concorde and back to Germany the same night, he died in the fall of 1983 alone at home working out on an exercise machine. He was 54, scarcely older than Wilhelm Haspel or Heinrich Wagner. He left behind a company even larger than the one he had taken over, and a gaping hole in a Vorstand that had appeared to be set for at least the next decade. With one exception, Walter Ulsamer, the head of purchasing, the eight-man executive committee was composed of men in their early forties (personnel chief Manfred Gentz) or early to mid-fifties (the rest). Prinz had eliminated the internecine struggles which had from time to time marked the managing board, and the future looked bright. But, though his death stunned the company, Daimler-Benz went back to the business of doing business, and a new chairman was chosen after an unaccustomed controversy among the various members of the supervisory board, headed since 1976 by Wilfried Guth, co-chairman of the Deutsche Bank. The leading candidates for the job were Breitschwerdt and Reuter. The labor members of the board threw their weight behind Reuter, perhaps the leading German industrialist who is also a member of the Socialist Party. The bank backed Breitschwerdt. The bank and Breitschwerdt won, and Daimler-Benz had its eighth chairman in the 57 years since the merger of 1926.

Breitschwerdt, born and raised in Stuttgart and like Gottlieb Daimler a graduate of its technical university, joined the company in 1953 and worked his way up primarily through his performance in the body engineering division at the Sindelfingen assembly plant. He was the first chief engineer to come from this side of the aisle rather than from engine engineering, becoming chief engineer directly from his body engineering post, bypassing the job of chief of passenger car development. Quick-witted, with a sharp tongue and a ready sense of humor, he was working at what he and everyone else believed would be his job until retirement when the chairmanship suddenly opened and he found himself at the age of 56 with the reins of the company in his hands, and seven other men

to help him hold them. These men were Reuter, the finance man; Werner Niefer, in charge of production; Gerhard Liener, in charge of subsidiaries; Walter Ulsamer, purchasing; Richard Osswald, in charge of personnel (soon to retire and be replaced by Manfred Gentz); Rudolf Hörnig, Breitschwerdt's own replacement as chief engineer; and Hans-Jürgen Hinrichs, in charge of sales. Hinrichs had come from Volkswagen at the behest of Prinz, who knew him in Wolfsburg. His career with Mercedes began in the United States, where he became vice-president of Mercedes-Benz of North America in 1976; he took over all North American sales and marketing in 1979. When the search for a successor to Hoppe found no one suitable in Stuttgart, Hinrichs' outstanding performance caused Prinz (and the Deutsche Bank) to reach overseas and bring him in over other candidates senior to him in age and rank. He was the second man from MBNA to head the worldwide distribution organization, and brought to it a remarkable degree of intensity and a thorough background in market research.

The new constellation had barely settled in its orbit when the longest and most destructive strike in the history of the company began in the late spring of 1984. Seven weeks of production were lost over a difference of opinion about working hours in which Daimler-Benz, the most visible company in Germany, was used as a trial horse by the unions. When the strike ended the company continued on its upward course with the introduction of the new midsize series, known as the W124 internally, in the late fall of the year. The series was introduced by a four-door sedan, followed by a station wagon and a coupe which could be fitted with any one of seven engines, three diesel and four gasoline-powered, with displacements ranging from two to three liters. The series was the successor to the W123, which was also built in three body styles from 1976 through (for a few export markets) mid-1985. The W123 was the biggest seller in the company's history: more than 2,600,000 of them were built. The W123 was an excellent car, but its successor was a testimonial to engineering progress. Designed as a four-door family sedan which could be equipped with every item of comfort and convenience known to the industry, the 300E's speed and road behavior were little short of staggering. With the new 3.0-liter, fuel-injected six-cylinder (190 horsepower in non-catalyst European form, 177 horsepower in the United States), the 300E was capable of 140 miles an hour, and there was little doubt that it could better the Nürburgring lap times of the mid-1950s 300SL had anyone been interested in trying.

Under all normal circumstances the new product line would have provided the major news of the year, but other events of 1985 created even bigger headlines as Daimler-Benz made three major acquisitions. The first was the takeover of the remaining 50 percent of the shares of MTU, the jet engine and high-speed diesel engine producer that Daimler-Benz owned jointly with M.A.N., the Munich-based commercial vehicle manufacturer. Next came the acquisition of a majority of the shares of Dornier, the German aircraft manufacturer with a wide variety of interests in high-technology fields, including even a machine to dissolve kidney stones without invading the body. Finally, as the year was drawing to a close and the hundredth anniversary celebrations were around the corner, Daimler-Benz, in a friendly takeover, acquired the majority of the stock of AEG, the German electrical equipment and electronics firm.

All this was a long way from Gottlieb Daimler's greenhouse workshop, or Carl Benz's courtyard where the Patent Motorwagen first ran. A long way—and many millions of vehicles and millions of workers, in Germany and around the globe, and millions of customers, in Germany and around the world. But the principles that Daimler, Benz, and then Daimler-Benz followed on their way to the top remained the same.

Looking to the future as the 100th anniversary approached...Werner Breitschwerdt, chairman of the management board, and an experimental model.

The overriding principle, and what it means to the buyer, the ultimate judge, was perhaps best expressed by a veteran Daimler-Benz engineer, Manfred Lorscheidt, who participated in the preparation of this history but did not live to see it finished.

"An important part of our image is trust," Lorscheidt said. "No single managing director, no single engineer is responsible for this. It has been created by the thousands of people who work for us, by their decency, their integrity, their self-esteem. They created it slowly, step by step, through the years. They have earned it, and when they say 'trust us,' which they do every time a car or truck rolls off the assembly line, it has meaning. It is not just a slogan."

It appears as if Daimler and Benz must have done something right.

INDEX

PHOTO CREDITS

P. 2, Daimler-Benz. P. 11, Daimler-Benz. P. 12, Culver Pictures (2). P. 13, (Top) The Bettmann Archive (3); (Bottom) Picture Collection, NYPL. P. 14, The Bettmann Archive (2). P. 15, (Top, L) Daimler-Benz; (Top, R) The Bettmann Archive; (Middle) Picture Collection, NYPL; (Bottom, L) Culver Pictures; (Bottom, R) The Granger Collection. P. 16, The Granger Collection. P. 17, (Top) Henry Austin Clark, Jr.; (Middle, L) The Science Museum, London; (Middle, R, Bottom) Picture Collection, NYPL. P. 18, Picture Collection, NYPL. P. 19, Daimler-Benz (3). P. 22, Daimler-Benz. P. 23, Daimler-Benz (2). P. 25, Daimler-Benz (3). P. 26, The Bettmann Archive. P. 27, (Top) The Bettmann Archive (2); (Bottom) The Granger Collection. P. 30, Picture Collection, NYPL. P. 31, Daimler-Benz (3). P. 33, Daimler-Benz (3). P. 35, Daimler-Benz. P. 36, Daimler-Benz. P. 37, Daimler-Benz (2). P. 38, Daimler-Benz. P. 39, Daimler-Benz. P. 40, Daimler-Benz. P. 41, (Top, L) Culver Pictures; (Top, R) The Granger Collection; (Bottom) Culver Pictures (3). P. 42, Daimler-Benz (2). P. 44, Daimler-Benz (2). P. 45, Daimler-Benz. P. 46, Daimler-Benz. P. 47, Daimler-Benz (5). P. 50, Bibliothèque Historique de la Ville de Paris (4). P. 51, Daimler-Benz. P. 52, Daimler-Benz. P. 53, Daimler-Benz (4). P. 54, Daimler-Benz (2). P. 55, (Top, L) Daimler-Benz; (Top, R) Ralph Stein; (Middle, R) Daimler-Benz; (Bottom) Ralph Stein. P. 56, Daimler-Benz. P. 57, Daimler-Benz (4). P. 58, Daimler-Benz. P. 60, (Top, L) Culver Pictures; (Top, R) The Granger Collection; (Middle, L) The Granger Collection; (Bottom) Daimler-Benz (3). P. 62, Daimler-Benz. P. 63, Daimler-Benz (2). P. 64, Daimler-Benz (4). P. 65, The Bettmann Archive. P. 66, Bibliothèque Nationale, Paris (4). P. 67, Bibliothèque Nationale, Paris (3). P. 68, Daimler-Benz (4). P. 70, National Automotive History Collection, Detroit Public Library (4). P. 71, Daimler-Benz. P. 72, Daimler-Benz (5). P. 73, Daimler-Benz (4). P. 74, Daimler-Benz (4). P. 75, Ralph Stein. P. 76, Daimler-Benz (3). P. 79, Daimler-Benz. P. 80, © "Editions Gilletta," Nice. P. 81, Daimler-Benz (3). P. 82, © "Editions Gilletta," Nice (2). P. 83, Daimler-Benz. P. 84, Daimler-Benz. P. 85, Daimler-Benz. P. 86, Daimler-Benz (2). P. 87, Daimler-Benz. P. 88, (Top, R) William L. Bailey; Daimler-Benz (3). P. 89, The Bettmann Archive. P. 90, Daimler-Benz (3). P. 91, Daimler-Benz (3). P. 93, Daimler-Benz. P. 94, Daimler-Benz. P. 96, Daimler-Benz. P. 97, Henry Austin Clark, Jr. P. 98, Daimler-Benz (2). P. 99, Daimler-Benz (3). P. 100, (Bottom, L) Wide World Photos; (Bottom, R) Collection Hervé Poulain. P. 101 (Top, L) The Bettmann Archive; Daimler-Benz (2). P. 102, Daimler-Benz. P. 103, (Top, L) Henry Austin Clark, Jr.; (Top, R) Geoffrey Goddard Collection; (Bottom) Daimler-Benz. P. 104, Daimler-Benz. P. 105, Daimler-Benz. P. 106, Daimler-Benz (3). P. 109, Daimler-Benz (3). P. 110, Henry Austin Clark, Jr. (2). P. 111, William L. Bailey (5). P. 112, Daimler-Benz (3). P. 114, (Top, L, Bottom) Henry Austin Clark, Jr.; (Top, R) Courtesy Peter Helck. P. 115, (Top, L) Henry Austin Clark, Jr.; (Top, R) The Bettmann Archive; (Middle) Daimler-Benz; (Bottom) Henry Austin Clark, Jr. P. 116, (L) Daimler-Benz; (R) William L. Bailey. P. 117, Daimler-Benz. P. 118, Daimler-Benz (3). P. 119, (Top, R) Stadtmuseum, München; Daimler-Benz (3). P. 120, Daimler-Benz (3). P. 121, Daimler-Benz. P. 123, (Top) Geoffrey Goddard Collection; Daimler-Benz (3). P. 124, Daimler-Benz (2). P. 125, Daimler-Benz (3). P. 126, (Top) Daimler-Benz (3); (Bottom) Henry Austin Clark, Jr. P. 127, (Top) Henry Austin Clark, Jr.; Daimler-Benz (2). P. 129, The Bettman Archive. P. 130, Daimler-Benz. P. 131, Daimler-Benz. P. 132, Daimler-Benz (4). P. 133, Daimler-Benz. P. 134, Daimler-Benz (2). P. 135, (Bottom, L) Culver Pictures; Daimler-Benz (4). P. 136, William L. Bailey (3). P. 137, Culver Pictures. P. 138, (Top) Daimler-Benz; (Bottom) William L. Bailey. P. 139, Daimler-Benz. P. 141, (Top) Culver Pictures; (Middle) William L. Bailey; (Bottom) Daimler-Benz. P. 142, (Middle, R) William L. Bailey; Daimler-Benz (4). P. 143, Daimler-Benz (2). P. 144, Courtesy Peter Helck (2). P. 145, Courtesy Peter Helck. P. 146, (Bottom) William L. Bailey; Courtesy Peter Helck (3). P. 147, Courtesy Peter Helck. P. 148, (Top) Courtesy Peter Helck; (Middle) Culver Pictures; (Bottom) Indianapolis Motor Speedway Museum. P. 149, Daimler-Benz (2). P. 151, (Top) Courtesy Peter Helck; (Bottom) Culver Pictures. P. 153, (Top) The Bettmann Archive; (Bottom) Daimler-Benz. P. 154, Daimler-Benz (2). P. 155, Daimler-Benz. P. 156, Daimler-Benz (2). P. 157, Daimler-Benz (2). P. 158, Daimler-Benz. P. 159, Daimler-Benz. P. 160, Daimler-Benz. P. 161, Daimler-Benz (2). P. 162, Daimler-Benz (2). P. 163, Daimler-Benz. P. 164, Daimler-Benz. P. 165, William L. Bailey (2). P. 166, (Top, L) Henry Austin Clark, Jr.; (Top, R) Courtesy Peter Helck; (Middle, R) Wide World Photos; (Bottom) Courtesy Peter Helck. P. 168, Daimler-Benz (2). P. 169, Daimler-Benz (4). P. 171, Daimler-Benz. P. 173, Daimler-Benz. P. 174, Daimler-Benz (2). P. 175, Daimler-Benz (2). P. 176, Daimler-Benz. P. 177, Daimler-Benz (2). P. 179, Daimler-Benz (4). P. 180, (Top) Daimler-Benz; (Bottom) Henry Austin Clark, Jr. P. 181, Courtesy Peter Helck (3). P. 183, Daimler-Benz (5). P. 184, Daimler-Benz. P. 185, Daimler-Benz (2). P. 186, Daimler-Benz (2). P. 187, Daimler-Benz (2). P. 188, Daimler-Benz (2). P. 189, Daimler-Benz (2). P. 190, Daimler-Benz (3). P. 191, Daimler-Benz (2). P. 192, Daimler-Benz (3). P. 193, Daimler-Benz. P. 194, Frank Driggs Collection. P. 195, Daimler-Benz (4). P. 196, Daimler-Benz (2). P. 197, (Top) Daimler-Benz; (Bottom) Courtesy Peter Helck. P. 198, Daimler-Benz. P. 199, Daimler-Benz (2). P. 200, Daimler-Benz. P. 202, (Top to Bottom) Daimler-Benz (2); William L. Bailey. P. 203, (Top) Daimler-Benz; (Bottom) William L. Bailey. P. 204, Daimler-Benz (2). P. 205, Geoffrey Goddard Collection. P. 206, Daimler-Benz (3). P. 207, Daimler-Benz (3). P. 208, Daimler-Benz (5). P. 209, Daimler-Benz (2). P. 211, Daimler-Benz (2). P. 212, Daimler-Benz. P. 213, Daimler-Benz (3). P. 214, (Top) Daimler-Benz; (Bottom) The Bettman Archive. P. 216, Daimler-Benz (2). P. 217, Daimler-Benz. P. 218, (Top, L, Middle) Daimler-Benz; (Top, R) Geoffrey Goddard Collection; (Bottom) The Bettmann Archive. P. 221, Daimler-Benz (2). P. 222, Daimler-Benz (5). P. 223, Daimler-Benz (3). P. 224, Daimler-Benz (2). P. 225, Geoffrey Goddard Collection. P. 226, (Middle, R) Geoffrey Goddard Collection; Daimler-Benz (3). P. 227, (Top) Quadrant Picture Library; (Bottom) Daimler-Benz. P. 229, Daimler-Benz. P. 230, Daimler-Benz (3). P. 231, Quadrant Picture Library. P. 232, (Top) Daimler-Benz; (Bottom) Geoffrey Goddard Collection. P. 233, Daimler-Benz. P. 234, (Top) Harris Lewine Collection; Library of Congress (2). P. 235, (Top) Library of Congress; (Bottom) Daimler-Benz. P. 236, Daimler-Benz (5). P. 237, (Top) William L. Bailey; Daimler-Benz (2). P. 238, (Top) William L. Bailey; (Bottom) Harris Lewine Collection. P. 239, Daimler-Benz (2). P. 240, Daimler-Benz (5). P. 242, Daimler-Benz. P. 243, Daimler-Benz (4). P. 244, Daimler-Benz (2). P. 248, (Top, Bottom) Daimler-Benz; (Middle) William L. Bailey. P. 249, (Top, R) William L. Bailey; Daimler-Benz (4). P. 252, Daimler-Benz (3). P. 253, Daimler-Benz (3). P. 256, Daimler-Benz (2). P. 257, Daimler-Benz (3). P. 258, (Top, L, Bottom) The Bettmann Archive; (Top, R) Daimler-Benz. P. 259, Daimler-Benz. P. 260, Daimler-Benz (3). P. 261, Daimler-Benz (2). P. 264, Daimler-Benz (4). P. 265, Daimler-Benz (5). P. 267, Daimler-Benz (3). P. 270, Daimler-Benz (3). P. 271, (Top) Daimler-Benz (2); (Bottom) Courtesy George Monkhouse. P. 275, Daimler-Benz (2). P. 278, Daimler-Benz (4). P. 279, Daimler-Benz (3). P. 280, Daimler-Benz (2). P. 281, Daimler-Benz. P. 282, Daimler-Benz (2). P. 283, Daimler-Benz. P. 284, Daimler-Benz (3). P. 285, Daimler-Benz (4). P. 286, Daimler-Benz (2). P. 287, Daimler-Benz (4). P. 288, Daimler-Benz. P. 289, Daimler-Benz. P. 290, Daimler-Benz (Top, L, Bottom); (Top, R) William L. Bailey. P. 291, Daimler-Benz (3). P. 292, Daimler-Benz (3). P. 294, Daimler-Benz (2). P. 295, Daimler-Benz (5). P. 296, (Top, L) Wide World Photos; Daimler-Benz (3). P. 297, Daimler-Benz (2). P. 298, Daimler-Benz (2). P. 299, Daimler-Benz. P. 300, (Top, L) Daimler-Benz; (Top, R, Bottom) © Klemantaski; (Middle, R) Wide World Photos. P. 301, Daimler-Benz. P. 302, Daimler-Benz. P. 303, Daimler-Benz (4). P. 305, Daimler-Benz. P. 306, Daimler-Benz (2). P. 307, Daimler-Benz. P. 308, Daimler-Benz. P. 309, Daimler-Benz (6). P. 311, Daimler-Benz. P. 312, (Top) Daimler-Benz; (Bottom) L'Art et L'Automobile. P. 313, (Top, L) L'Art et L'Automobile; Daimler-Benz (2). P. 314, Daimler-Benz. P. 315, Daimler-Benz (2). P. 316, Daimler-Benz. P. 317, Daimler-Benz (4). P. 318, (Top) © Klemantaski; (Bottom) Daimler-Benz. P. 319, Daimler-Benz (2). P. 320, (Top) © Klemantaski; (Bottom) Weitmann Archive. P. 323, Daimler-Benz. P. 324, Daimler-Benz (3). P. 325, Daimler-Benz. P. 326, Daimler-Benz (4). P. 327, Daimler-Benz. P. 328, (Top, R) Motor Sport/LAT; Daimler-Benz (2). P. 329, Daimler-Benz (2). P. 330, (Top) Daimler-Benz; (Bottom) © Klemantaski. P. 331, (Top, L) Daimler-Benz; (Top, R) Geoffrey Goddard Collection; (Middle, R) Weitmann Archive; (Bottom) © Klemantaski. P. 332, (Top) Daimler-Benz; (Bottom) © Klemantaski. P. 333, (Top, L) L'Art et L'Automobile; (Top, Inset, Middle, R) Motor Sport/LAT; (Bottom) Daimler-Benz. P. 334, (Top) Motor Sport/LAT; (Bottom) Weitmann Archive. P. 336, Daimler-Benz (3). P. 337, Daimler-Benz (3). P. 338, Daimler-Benz. P. 339, Daimler-Benz. P. 340, Harris Lewine Collection (2). P. 341, (Middle, R) Bachrach; Mercedes-Benz of North America (4). P. 344, Mercedes-Benz of North America (5). P. 345, Daimler-Benz (8). P. 347, Mercedes-Benz of North America (4). P. 350, Daimler-Benz (4). P. 351, Daimler-Benz (5). P. 353, Daimler-Benz (4). P. 355, Daimler-Benz (4). P. 358, Mercedes-Benz of North America (2). P. 359, Daimler-Benz (9). P. 361, Daimler-Benz. (Color section following P. 192) P. 1, Daimler-Benz (2). P. 2, Daimler-Benz. P. 3, Daimler-Benz (3). P. 4, Daimler-Benz (6). P. 5, (Top, L to R) Henry Austin Clark, Jr.; Keith Fletcher Books; Daimler-Benz; (Bottom) Daimler-Benz. P. 6, (Bottom, L) William L. Bailey; Daimler-Benz (6). P. 7, Barrett Clark (2). P. 8, (Top, L) Daimler-Benz; Fred Crismon (3). P. 9, (Top, R) Courtesy Kunstbibliothek, Berlin; Daimler-Benz (4). P. 10, (Top, R, Bottom, R) William L. Bailey; Daimler-Benz (2). P. 11, Daimler-Benz (5). P. 12, Daimler-Benz (3). P. 13, (Top, R) Courtesy Kunstbibliothek, Berlin; Daimler-Benz (3). P. 14, (Top, L) L'Art et L'Automobile; (Bottom) Quadrant Picture Library; (Top, Middle, R) L'Art et L'Automobile. P. 15, © Auto Art/Peter Helck (2). P. 16, © Auto Art/Peter Helck (2). P. 17, © Auto Art/Peter Helck (2). P. 18, © Auto Art/Peter Helck (4). P. 19, Walter Gotschke (2). P. 20, Walter Gotschke (2). P. 21, Walter Gotschke (2). P. 22, Walter Gotschke (4). P. 23, (Top, L) Henry Austin Clark, Jr.; (Top, R) Keith Fletcher Books; (Bottom) Daimler-Benz. P. 24, (Top) William L. Bailey (3); (Bottom) Daimler-Benz (3). P. 25, Daimler-Benz (9). P. 26, Daimler-Benz (4). P. 27, Daimler-Benz (5). P. 28, Daimler-Benz (4). P. 29, (Bottom, L) William L. Bailey; Daimler-Benz (4). P. 30, (Top, R) Courtesy McCaffrey & McCall Advtg.; (Top, L) Daimler-Benz; (Bottom) William L. Bailey. P. 31, (Top, L) Daimler-Benz; Courtesy McCaffrey & McCall Advtg. (3). P. 32, Fred Crismon.